ROSIE'S SECONDARY MARKET PRICE GUIDE
FOR ENESCO'S PRECIOUS MOMENTS® COLLECTION

15th Anniversary Edition

Editor: Rosalie "Rosie" J. Wells

Published by Rosie Wells Enterprises, Inc.
22341 East Wells Road, Canton, IL 61520
Ph. 1-800-445-8745

We thank Precious Moments Incorporated for the use of special line art drawings in this guide and for the use of the Precious Moments® design logo on the front cover. We thank Enesco for their assistance in providing information as well as line drawings. Also thanks goes to our Precious Collectibles® subscribers who contribute yearly to this guide and to Sam Butcher for special art work and his dedication to the Precious Moments® Collection.

Subscribe today to Rosie's magazine, Precious Collectibles®. She has brought Precious Moments® Collectors together since 1983.

Rosie

Sam B

T5-AQT-747

Table of Contents

Hundreds of hours of labor
have gone into this guide...
Oh no! There may be an
error or an omission.
If you find one, please
let us know.

Total Count of Pieces

1978	11
1979	18
1980	40
1981	64
1982	66
1983	60
1984	48
1985	64
1986	80
1987	65
1988	68
1989	48
1990	42
1991	50
1992	52
1993	58
1994	68
1995	95
1996	87
1997	74
Birthday Club figurines and Membership Pieces (through 1996)	39
Membership & Club Figurines, Ornaments, etc. (through 1996)	78
Dolls	24
Century Circle Exclusive Figurines, Ornaments, etc.	7

♪ **Retired Through 1997**

Figurines	87
Ornaments	16
Musicals	9
Bells	1
Dolls	1

♪ **Suspended Through 1996**

Figurines	210
Ornaments	45
Musicals	24
Frames	14
Bells	10
Dolls	11
Containers	7
Plates	5
Candle Climber	2
Night Lite	3
Thimbles	4
Plaque	1

DID YOU KNOW...

... that 1,306 Precious Moments porcelain pieces have been produced by Enesco? This sounds like a lot, doesn't it? But have you ever really stopped to think about the fact that out of those 1,306 pieces, approximately 769 pieces are no longer available? We have! Wow! Included in the 769 pieces which are no longer available are 336 Suspended pieces, 114 Retired pieces, as well as Birthday Club, regular Club, Dated Annuals and Limited Editions. Nearly 59% of all Precious Moments porcelain pieces ever produced are now only available on the secondary market. This is another good reason to stay in tune with what is happening on the secondary market and our guide will help you do just that!

...About the Editor

Precious Moments® have held a special place in Rosie Wells' heart since their creation by Sam Butcher in the late 70's. Even today, Rosie enjoys shopping for Precious Moments collectibles, and her collection has grown with her dedication. Of course, during those first years of Precious Moments collecting, very little information was available for collectors. Early on, Rosie saw the need for a publication that would inform and, at the same time, bring collectors together in friendship. Rosie's goal has always been to "Bring Collectors Together."

The story of Rosie's humble beginnings on her first eight page newsletter to what *Precious Collectibles®* is today, is truly an exciting one to which she gives all the credit to the Lord. Rosie Wells Enterprises, Inc., is housed in a beautiful office building with a scenic view of one of the lakes situated across the road from the Wells' farm. Thirty-seven employees work together to offer readers the best in collecting news through several publications, including *Precious Collectibles®, Collectors' Bulletin™, The Ornament Collector™* magazines and the *Weekly Collectors' Gazette.™*

The cyberage has also come to Rosie Wells Enterprises, Inc. A web site on the World Wide Web has become another way for Rosie to inform collectors about her publications and weekly news on many collectibles.

In addition to this guide for The Enesco Precious Moments® Collection, Rosie Wells Enterprises, Inc., also publishes guides for Applause's Precious Moments® Dolls, Hallmark Keepsake Ornaments, Boyds Bears & Friends™, Hallmark Merry Miniatures and The Enesco Cherished Teddies™ Collection with even more being planned. Prices on new pieces have not increased at the rate as in the 80's when Precious Moments collectibles were the only collectible Enesco boasted of. Rosie Wells Enterprises is now represented by over 110 reps throughout the USA and Canada. The magazines are now on newsstands across the country and on military bases overseas, "Bringing Collectors Together"!

Rosie and her husband Dave have hosted ten conventions across the United States for Precious Moments collectors. They also host the semi-annual Midwest Collectibles Fest held each March and October at the Inland Meeting and Exposition Center in Westmont, Illinois. These shows consist of over 200 collector tables, nearly half of which are older Precious Moments figurines.

Rosie and her staff answer the many questions that come to the office by phone, mail and E-mail. If you have a question or comment, please feel free to call 309/668-2565 for assistance. Write us at 22341 E. Wells Rd., Canton, IL 61520, or E-mail us at Rosie@RosieWells.com. Visit our web site at http://www.RosieWells.com. Enjoy this guide and thank you for purchasing it.

THE PRICES CONTAINED IN THIS GUIDE ARE AVERAGED FROM SALE PRICES ACROSS THE COUNTRY AND SHOULD BE USED ONLY AS A GUIDE TO INSURE YOUR COLLECTION. WE MAKE NO WARRANTY ON THE PRICES CONTAINED IN THIS GUIDE.

What is the Collectibles' Secondary Market?

The term secondary market refers to the buying, selling or trading of collectibles, most generally for a price other than original retail. This secondary market price is usually higher than original retail, but at times can be lower. People involved with the secondary market include those who buy specifically for this purpose (secondary market dealers), those who happen to have a few extra pieces they want to sell or collectors who decide to liquidate their entire collections. Some retailers are also involved in the secondary market.

Factors such as scarcity, age, errors, changes, retirement, suspension, over production and whether or not a piece is dated or a limited edition contribute to the secondary market value.

What about the value of club pieces on the secondary market? The secondary market value of club pieces rose quickly in the early years of the club's existence, especially in 1982-1984. As new members joined the club, hundreds of new collectors sought early club pieces. At present, club pieces increase in value, but not at the rate of the '81-'82 pieces. Many avid collectors today have been club members since the early 1980s and have more than one membership. They may buy several club pieces, making extras readily available for future collectors. Many of the club pieces are very special, and I feel it's of real benefit to join the National Club.

Today's coveted piece still remains the 1981 retired *God Loveth A Cheerful Giver* (E-1378), also known as "Free Puppies." Only a few people bought extra pieces at the time of this piece's retirement. (Many of these buyers were insiders who knew about the retirement announcement before the collectors did.) In 1982 more Ice Cream Cone Boys (E-1374B) were bought up by collectors than any retirement piece to date. As of 1989, the secondary market has just begun to show a demand and a rise in value for this piece. Not all Precious Moments® collectibles increase in value, although not many have decreased.

Of course, as in the past, prices could drop... just like the stock market. We can't always predict the future, but I've never seen anyone selling their collection for less than the original retail. Precious Moments® figurines have been stable on the secondary market since a year or two after they debuted in 1978.

Insuring Your Collection

This guide has been produced to assist you in evaluating your collection's monetary value for insuring, investing, estate planning or reselling. We advise that you record your collection's value and store the records in a safety deposit box, etc., so you have a record of your collection available at a location other than your home in case of fire or other catastrophic damage. Using a video camera to record your collection would be another excellent method of verification when questions might arise filing insurance claims. Insure your collection. It is important to have a detailed inventory. Computer programs using our prices are also available for this purpose. Whatever method you choose, it is very important to give this information to your insurance agent. It is not easy to replace many of the older Precious Moments® figurines. It is even harder when the investment is lost because of lack of insurance. Collectibles usually are not covered with a general homeowner's insurance policy, but require a "rider" policy or "fine arts clause". Check with your agent for all important details and double check to be sure that your insurance agent has copied your list correctly when the policy is written. Insure your collection at replacement value and not retail cost, but keep in mind that some pieces now stay at retail cost for several years. (You also may want to include the amount of state tax you paid.) Use this guide to help direct you to determine the replacement value. There is no need to over-insure, as this just adds to the cost of the policy.

Above all, enjoy your collection. Display your pieces and share the meaning of Precious Moments® with others. This "Loving, Caring and Sharing" has a value which cannot be measured in dollars and cents.

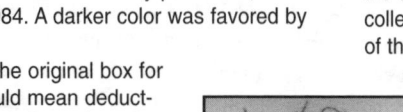

PRECIOUS MOMENTS® POTPOURRI

• Avid Collectors still love to find the "first twenty-one" pieces in a "No Mark." These are E-1372B through E-2013.

• The early figurines were darker in color than today's pieces. In 1982 pieces were produced with a very pale color, then somewhat darker in 1983-1984. A darker color was favored by many collectors.

• At one time not having the original box for "Free Puppies" (E-1378) would mean deducting $50 from the secondary market value of this figurine, but pay the top price if you want the piece, even without the box. In today's current market, not having the box would only bring a reduction of $25 from the secondary value.

• Pieces produced in 1978-1984 and licensed by the Jonathan & David Company have smaller heads than pieces relicensed by the Samuel J. Butcher Company and Precious Moments, Inc. Jonathan & David was co-owned by Precious Moments artist Samuel J. Butcher and his former partner Bill Biel until 1985. J&D closed its doors in late 1988.

• Since 1985, "Sam B." has been embossed on pieces which are licensed through the Samuel J. Butcher Company. Pieces still in production, which were originally licensed through the Jonathan & David Company, are not marked Sam B. and do not have the larger heads. Many of these Jonathan & David pieces have been suspended. E-1381 was

Jonathan & David Logo

Precious Moments® Logo

suspended in 1984, which means it was no longer produced but could be brought back into production at a later date. It was brought back in 1992 as E-1381R, with some changes. (The "R" after the original number signifies a piece that was reissued after suspension.) This reissued piece was licensed under the Samuel J. Butcher Co. and is embossed with "Sam B." It's not unusual to find a current figurine which is missing the Sam B. logo. Precious Moments, Inc. (PMI), is now the licensee of Sam's artwork to Enesco, the licensee.

• Pieces were produced with an embossed mark from mid-1981. There are fewer Triangle marks (the first mark) than any other mark. A newly released piece may have the previous year's mark as its first mark because of production schedules.

• Style/stock numbers did not appear on the bottom of the bases until mid-1982, so No Marks, Triangles and some Hourglass marks do not have a style number. There have been errors on the bottom of the bases, with some being totally blank. Some marks (usually the Fish and the Hourglass marks) are decals. Small stickers imprinted with the words "Sample: Prototype" have also been found on pieces. Sample pieces are given to company sales representatives to display at store events. Earlier, the sales reps were able to purchase these pieces or return them to the company when the shows were over. Many of these samples are in the hands of collectors now. It's my opinion we have underestimated the value of these pieces in the past. Prototypes are from molds which may or may not have been the accepted molds for the collection. Prototypes may deserve a value of $500 up.

• There are figurines still being produced with Jonathan & David as the Licensee (figurines initially produced before 1985).

• The Enesco Precious Moments Collectors' Club began in 1981 with Charter Memberships issued to members joining the first year. The Charter Members continue to receive pieces that are imprinted with "Charter Member." An error was found on some Charter Member pieces produced in 1985; these pieces were marked "1985 Charter Membership" instead of "1981 Charter Membership." This error was corrected later in 1985.

• Sometimes a mold is changed after a piece has been produced and marketed. For example, *Nobody's Perfect* (E-9268), known as the Dunce Boy, was first produced with a smile. The mold was changed to give the piece a frown. The "smile" piece is the errored piece and is "rare" (approximately 5,000 pieces bearing this error were produced; see page 43 for further information).

• Different types of errors have occurred on Precious Moments® figurines; some are more signifi-

cant than others. Generally, the more valuable errors are those which are visible while viewing the piece and not the errors on the bottom of the figurine (unless the error is a double mark). Two highly visible errors collectors have found are the large Columbus piece missing the dog and the spyglass, and *Friendship Hits The Spot* missing the table. A decal error on the base of a piece is usually not significant, although some collectors collect these pieces. For more information about errors, read our publications, *Precious Collectibles®*, *Collectors' Bulletin™* and *Weekly Collectors' Gazette™*.

• Many paint variations occur on pieces now since painting takes place at more than one factory. Usually paint variations do not affect secondary market values unless the variation is markedly different.

• In May 1993 the little boxing girl, *Faith Is A Victory*, was retired. January 1994 found her being shipped to retailers. We received calls by collectors and retailers alerting us of this "eight months later" shipment. When a piece has been retired, look in stores first before buying on the secondary market. At times certain pieces which are retired are very hard to find in stores; these pieces will rise in value more quickly than those easily found. Collectors look for the older marks on retired pieces. Many desired pieces may be found at large swap meets and collectibles shows. (Especially at our Midwest Fest held in the spring and fall in Westmont, Illinois. Hundreds of PMs are there!)

• The 9" Easter Seals pieces: 1,000 were produced in 1988, 1,500 in 1989, and 2,000 in 1990 through 1997. The regular sized Easter Seals pieces are abundant and have been readily available for several years after production. The second year Girl on Crutches piece did not have the Easter Seals logo on it; this error was found on each one of this particular piece. The 1997 Boy in Wheel Chair Easter Seals figurine may be as popular as the 1992 Girl Hand-Signing "I Love You" (527173).

• The 1989 first in series porcelain dated ball ornament is scarce as over 45% of these ornaments were ruined in the kiln. The 1990 dated porcelain Easter egg was also hard to find. The 1990 dated ball ornament was produced in two variations; one with the boy in a yellow shirt and the other with the boy in a blue shirt.

• More and more Precious Moments® accessories are being produced these days. These items are fun for collectors to have, but do not generate much interest on the secondary market.

• In 1995 Goebel introduced hand painted bronze miniature Precious Moments sculptures. Barely an inch tall, the first pieces to debut included seven designs from the "Original 21," plus a limited edition Christmas figurine. Each miniature "cameo" is enhanced with accents to help express its message, and the sculptures are designed to fit into a larger vignette. It's too early to evaluate a secondary market on these pieces.

• Precious Moments® unpainted Jonathan & David pewter is collectible, although the Precious Moments® Company has reissued pewter which is very similar, making it difficult to distinguish between the two. In addition to figurines, Precious Moments Company has produced gold and silver-plated pewter charms, pewter key rings, magnets, spoons and thimbles. Painted pewter debuted in 1989. Chipping has been a problem with these pieces.

• The San Francisco Music Box Company has been licensed to produce music boxes.

• Although not as collectible to date as the figurines, the PMC dolls are very popular. Many doll collectors do not collect figurines.

• Several of the large Columbus pieces that debuted in 1992 were reported to have paint that flaked off, and some were reported with kiln cracks.

• In 1992 the Precious Moments® logo was missing from the base of all fall pieces and the Members' Only pieces. This logo was included on the Spring 1992 pieces with the Vessel marks.

• Debuting in 1993 was the 15 Year Anniversary figurine *15 Happy Years Together: What A Tweet* and the 15 Year Anniversary ornament *15 Years: Tweet Music Together*. The special dealer display dome for the figurine included a commemorative medallion and plaque attached to the dome.

• In June, 1995, the Enesco Corporation invited 35 retailers to an all expense paid weekend at Enesco's Chicago-area location for a mysterious special event. These special retailers became charter members of Enesco's new Century Circle Retailers, an elite group recognized by Enesco as being extraordinarily committed and supportive of the Enesco Precious Moments Collection. Five more retailers were given this status in 1996, making 40 Century Circle retailers nationwide. A new line of limited edition Precious Moments collectibles (LE of 15,000) will be available exclusively at these retailers. The first piece was a figurine, *Love Makes The World Go 'Round,* and the second was an ornament, *Peace on Earth. In God's Beautiful Garden Of Love (261629)* is this year's

Century Circle figurine. Other special event pieces may be available to these retailers this year.

• Precious Moments® artplas ornaments debuted in 1992. However, these have not seen much secondary market activity.

• A special bronze bust of Sam Butcher was commissioned to be created at artCentral in Carthage, Missouri. It was a special tribute to Sam, and collectors donated money for this project. Those making donations had their names engraved on a plaque which is displayed by the bust.

• To debut in the Spring of 1997 at the Precious Moments Chapel will be the Fountain of Angels. This impressive tiered fountain will feature 120 four-foot bronze angels in many different poses. There will also be a laser light show at the Fountain area. A portable ice rink was constructed in the winter of 1995. Over one million Christmas lights twinkled brightly during the holidays at the Chapel in 1996. Each year this display gets bigger and better.

• Visit the Precious Moments Chapel to view some of Sam's modern artwork. The Chapel, with its continually changing exhibits, is very unique and inspirational.

• In 1991 the first Amway Precious Moments Christmas doll, *Jessica*, was a sell-out. *Melissa* was available in 1992 from Amway. The 1993 doll, *Rebecca*, was shown in the Amway catalog as having a yellow dress and plain yellow headband. None were actually produced this way, but were changed to a cream dress and ruffled headband. The 1994 Amway doll was *Maddy*, a blond beauty with a bouquet of flowers, wearing a light blue and pink party dress. *Marissa*, with her dark blond curly hair and brown eyes, debuted in 1995 wearing a long-sleeved pink satin dress accented with lacy white tights and bright pink ribbons tied in her hair, around her neck and at her waist.

• Several collectors have reported at various times having figurines with only half of a Butterfly mark.

• Many times prototypes of figurines are used when Enesco produces the flyers for new introductions. It is not uncommon for changes, such as different colors, different positions and different hair styles to be made to the actual figurine produced. This in no way changes the value of

the figurine.

• 1994 marked the last in the series of dated Precious Moments Easter Eggs. In 1995, Easter figurines debuted with a large cross as a central theme.

• Sam Butcher announced plans to make a Salvation Army Precious Moments figurine to show his appreciation to an organization that helped him in so many ways while he was struggling in the beginning of his career. The figurine will be, of course, a Salvation Army bell ringer, which has always been a long time symbol of this worthy organization.

• New for 1996, a series of baby figurines. *Baby Classics* are reminiscent of those very first Precious Moments, only done with a youthful flair. Instead of a boy and girl sitting on a stump to depict "Love One Another," a baby boy and girl sit on the grass near a tree sprout.

• "Blessed Art Thou Among Women" is artwork which Sam Butcher has been working with to become a new figurine. Hopefully it will be a new introduction to the general line which Enesco plans to introduce, possibly in 1998.

• Sam Butcher has designed Short 'N Sweet figurines not as a collectible, but as an affordable gift item. These figurines are produced by Mr. Butcher's company, Evelyn of Missouri, Inc. The company is named after Sam's mother, Evelyn, who at 4 feet 11 inches tall was definitely "Short 'N Sweet!"

• Roy Rogers and Dale Evans have long been admired by Sam Butcher. To honor them he created a special figurine, naming it "<u>Happy</u> <u>Trails</u>." Only two figurines are in existence. One will be displayed in the Gallery Museum.

• Remember, if you have any collecting questions or comments, you may call us at the office at 309/668-2565. Keeping collectors informed is our specialty!

• An exciting collectibles annual event will be held April 25 - 27, 1997, in Tulsa, Oklahoma. This is the show's fourth year and Sam will again be present to sign figurines for collectors. Plan to attend; Tulsa is beautiful in the spring and only a two hour drive from the Chapel in Carthage, Missouri.

• Use care in cleaning your figurines. Lay a towel in the bottom of your sink to protect them from breakage. We suggest placing a finger over the air hole in the base of the figurine to keep water from going inside (this prevents drips on furniture later). Use a mild soap or Dow Scrubbing Bubbles. Don't use glass cleaner, as we have heard that some Disney porcelain collectibles were damaged by such a cleaner. Lay each piece on its side to dry.

• New factories in Bangkok, Thailand, are producing Precious Moments figurines. Factories in Mexico did not prove to be successful. Other gift and collectible lines by Enesco are produced at the same factories.

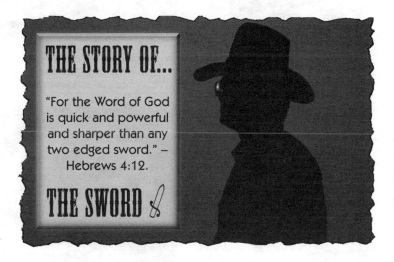

THE STORY OF...

"For the Word of God is quick and powerful and sharper than any two edged sword." – Hebrews 4:12.

THE SWORD

MARKS ⚱ 1997

***S**am has signed many figurines during special visits to stores and conventions. His signature is found on more figurines than possibly any other artists' to date! He meets with collectors often, especially now that he has his own jet!*

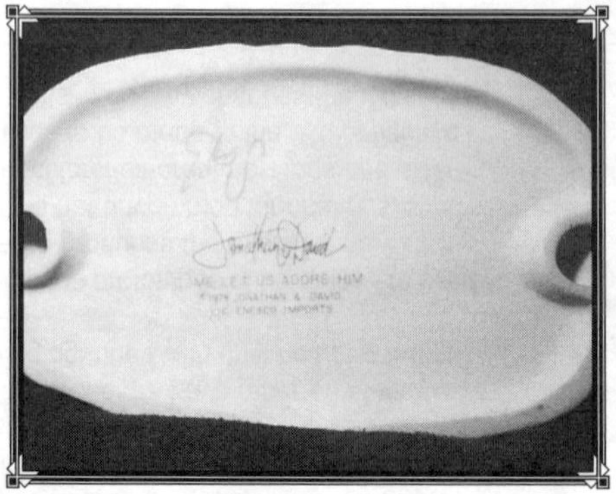

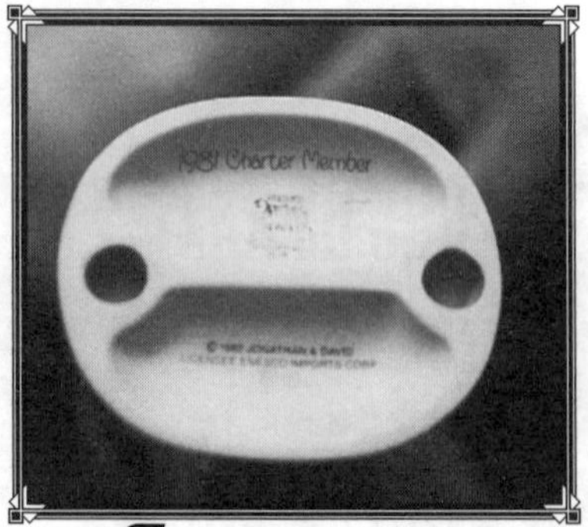

***C**harter Members have "Charter Member" on their present day Membership pieces.*

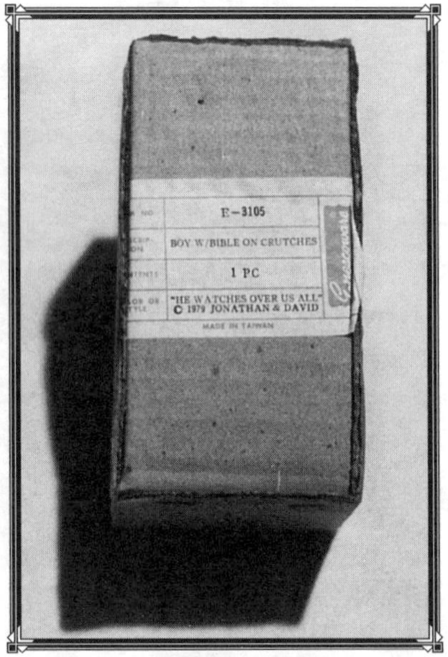

***O**riginal Precious Moments "cardboard" box from the '70s.*

***D**ecal applied backwards on figurine base.*

Love One Another
by
Bill Biel & Sam Butcher
This is plate number 15674
certified to be a true first issue in the
Inspired Thoughts Series
It has been faithfully crafted in fine porcelain and painted by hand to our exacting standards in a collectors' edition limited to fifteen thousand plates

Bill Biel   *Sam Butcher*
Bill Biel   Sam Butcher

©1980 Jonathan & David licensee Enesco Imports Corporation
Elk Grove Village, Illinois, 60007
E-9255

***I**nsignia on back of a plate during early days when Sam and Bill owned Jonathan & David Company together; this business partnership dissolved in 1984-85.*

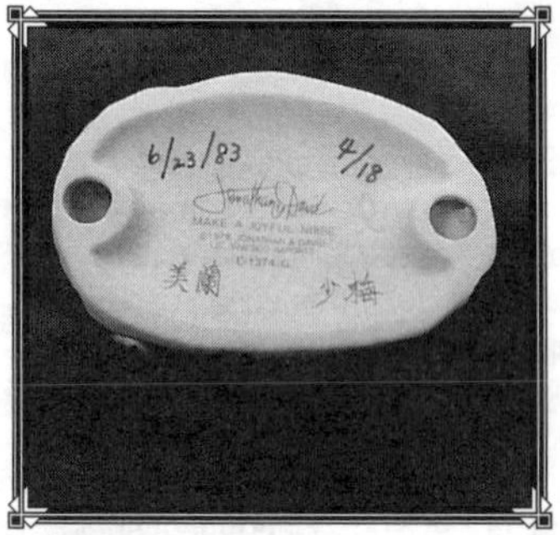

***F**igurine signed by Artisans.*

***D**ecaled Fish Mark*

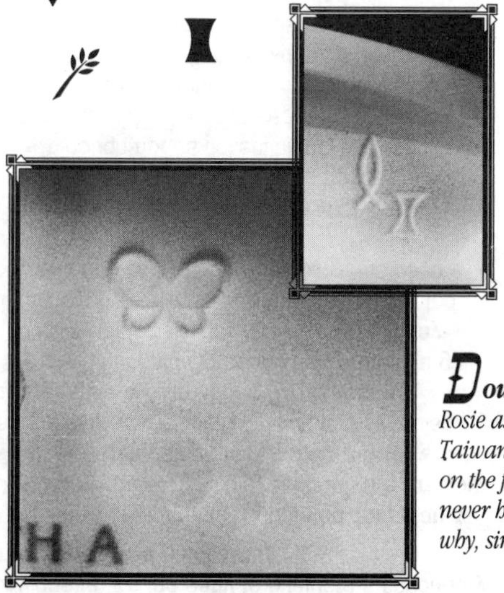

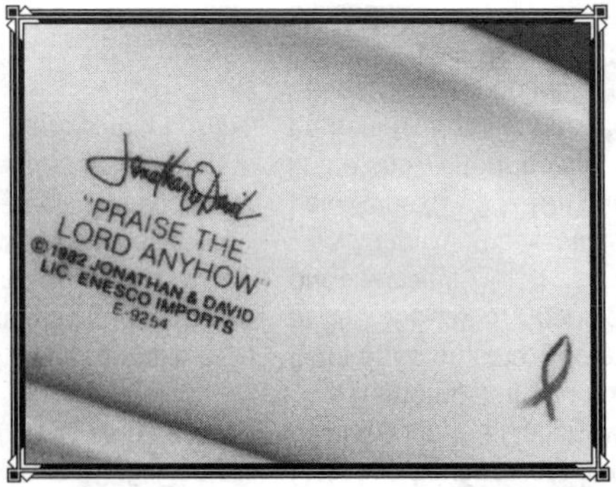

***E**rasable Fish Mark*
These can be easily removed. The Secretary was the first to be found with this mark, and it's my opinion that less than 100 had this mark (mainly found in central Iowa at one location).

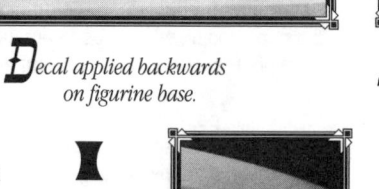

***D**ouble marked figurine*
Rosie asked the project managers in Taiwan how double marks occurred on the figurines. They said they had never heard of this and didn't know why, since the mark is in the mold.

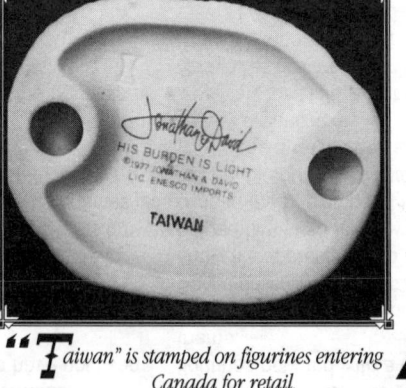

*"**T**aiwan" is stamped on figurines entering Canada for retail.*

SING HALLELUJAH FOR PRECIOUS MOMENTS® COLLECTIBLES

Do you know how our beloved Precious Moments® kids were created? President of Enesco in 1978, Eugene Freedman, was on his way to the Orient and stopped at the Los Angeles Gift Show. There he was shown some of artist Sam Butcher's Precious Moments® drawings featured on cards and posters. Mr. Freedman immediately recognized the potential of Sam's work and felt confident this work could be produced in porcelain. Yasuhei Fujioka, of Japan, would be the master sculptor.

When Mr. Freedman first contacted Sam and his partner Bill Biel about the possibility of producing Sam's artwork in porcelain, Sam was not in favor of the idea. But Mr. Freedman commissioned Yasuhei Fujioka to sculpt a prototype of Sam's art *Love One Another* (boy and girl on stump) and persuaded Sam and Bill to meet with him.

Sam was very protective of his work and wanted to ensure that it stayed in a medium which would glorify the Lord. But after seeing this first sample figurine, Sam fell to his knees, overwhelmed by the realization of the impact these figurines could have in the lives of people. He knew his artistic ability was a gift from God and wanted to use his talent to share the message of God's love. Sam felt this could be accomplished with the porcelain figurines.

We have seen the popularity of Precious Moments® spread across the United States and abroad as people fall in love with Sam's "little kids" and their message of hope and inspiration. Hundreds of local Precious Moments clubs have been formed, allowing collectors to share God's gift of friendship together. These clubs also are involved in sharing with others outside of the club walls as members participate in many volunteer activities, such as Easter Seals fund-raisers, nursing home and children's home visits, the giving of Christmas baskets and gifts for those in need, and much more.

My husband Dave and I have made many wonderful friends as we travelled around the country hosting Precious Moments conventions and shows since 1984. Our goal has always been to "Bring Precious Moments Collectors Together" and we actually thought of our conventions as family reunions.

With a definite leading from the Lord, I started *Precious Collectibles*® magazine as an eight page newsletter in February of 1983 from my kitchen table "down on the farm." This magazine has grown and now reaches collectors across the United States, Canada, Puerto Rico and foreign countries where American servicemen and women are stationed. We publish several magazines and price guides on various collectibles. In 1995, our publications were introduced on many newsstands across the country. 1996 saw us enter the computer age with our very own web page.

Remember, when purchasing Precious Moments, buy what you enjoy. Yes, many pieces escalate in value on the secondary market, but if you buy the pieces that are special to you, you'll never be disappointed if they don't rise in value. If you want to try your hand on the secondary market, remember that not all pieces will be traded easily. Study the information which *Precious Collectibles*® magazine, the *Weekly Collectors' Gazette*™ and this guide offer. Read the classified ads, keep your ears tuned in at club meetings to learn about the pieces collectors are looking for and attend collectible shows. Many times you will find a bargain when purchasing a large collection (if you can afford to do this). You'll be buying hundreds of pieces and, in time, a profit will be made. Keep detailed records and don't forget to pay Uncle Sam his share! As Christians, the Bible tells us to render unto Caesar what is due him and unto God what is due him!

Also remember, *Lay not up for yourselves treasures upon earth, where moth and rust doth corrupt, and where thieves break through and steal: But lay up for yourselves treasures in heaven, where neither moth nor rust doth corrupt, and where thieves do not break through nor steal: For where your treasure is, there will your heart be also.* Matt. 6:19-21, KJV.

Keep everything in perspective. *For what is a man profited, if he shall gain the whole world and lose his own soul?* Matthew 16:26a, KJV.

For God so loved the world, that he gave his only begotten Son, that whosoever believeth in him should not perish, but have everlasting life. John 3:16, KJV.

We want to express our gratitude to the many retailers and book dealers who make this guide available to their customers. We also appreciate our sales representatives and the hundreds of clubs and collectors promoting our publications.

Thank you for purchasing this guide. If there is any way we may be of service to you, please feel free to call or write to us at Rosie Wells Enterprises, Inc., 22341 E. Wells Rd., Canton, Illinois 61520; e-mail Rosie@RosieWells.com; phone 309/668-2212. We'll do our best to help you. Remember to subscribe to *Precious Collectibles*,® our magazine published especially for Precious Moments collectors since 1983. The *Weekly Collectors' Gazette*™ newsletter and *Collectors' Bulletin*™ magazine also will keep you updated on Precious Moments news and ads between issues of *Precious Collectibles*.® Hundreds of older pieces may be found from other collectors through ads in *Precious Collectibles*® and the *Collectors' Bulletin!*™ If you are familiar with the internet and have access to a computer, check out our web site at http://www.RosieWells.com. It changes weekly with information on collectibles. Try advertising on the internet with us!

Rosie

Our 900 collector line offers another way to buy, sell and trade. Leave your ad on line in your own voice ad for less than $5.00! (1½ minute ad for 21 days.) Hot tips which change every Thursday also are available on this line by Rosie! Call 1-900-740-7575; $2 a minute; use a touch-tone phone. You must be 18 years old. Press 1 to hear hot tips, Press 3 to advertise or locate Precious Moments Collectibles, Press 49 to advertise or locate Precious Moments PMC Dolls or press 50 to advertise or locate Precious Moments Applause Dolls.

We want to encourage you to visit the Precious Moments Chapel (off Rt. 44) in Carthage, Missouri. A real blessing awaits you there! Every year you'll find that something new has been added.

Dave, Sam and Rosie

Sam presented Rosie and Dave a plaque in appreciation of *Rosie Wells Enterprises, Inc.,* participation in the Precious Moments Second Annual Licensee Event & Swap N' Sell Show which was held May 31-June 1,1996.

ARROWS ERRORS OMISIONS

"My figurine is different from the one pictured in Enesco's brochure. Do I have an errored piece?"

"The hand on my girl isn't painted. Should I return her to the store where I purchased it?"

"I have two mothers in my Family Thanksgiving set. Is this an error worth keeping?"

These questions and many more come into our office on a regular basis. What constitutes an error worth keeping and which pieces should be returned? What are some errors or changes that an avid collector would seek to add to his or her collection? From the early stages of collecting, changes have occurred on several pieces. I have come to the conclusion, however, that several "errors" didn't reach the market except for sample prototypes which were photographed for Enesco's brochures or for their representatives to show. Some talked-about errors were seen in these photos only.

Sought-After Errors

While a retailer was unpacking a new shipment of figurines, he found a glazed over, unpainted Sugar Town Dog and Cat Sitting on a Bench (529540)! This type of error may sell to a collector for $500 and should be insured for more, but it would definitely be irreplaceable!

Several collectors have reported that the heart with the age numeral from the *Growing In Grace Age 6* is missing. Most pieces with decals are occasionally found missing the decal, but this piece is missing the entire heart!

The Dunce Boy was incorrectly sculpted for the 1982-1983 market. Approxi-mately 5,000 of these pieces were produced smiling. He appeared around Christmas of 1982. *Precious Collectibles*™ was able to get this word to our subscribers before the company announcement was made. This was the "first" real stampede of collectors looking for a **rare** piece! It took only three to four weeks for the retail price ($21) to rise to $400 on the secondary market. When a *Precious Moments*® figurine is hot, it's hot! If you have patience, the price generally drops six months to a year later, but usually not more than 10-15 percent. You may save some money if you wait to purchase it but the price could go up. Even though the Dunce Boy is retired "Smiley" will remain between $400-$500, as he was actually "retired" after 5,000 smiles!

Pretty As A Princess (526053) has been found with one of the points on her crown not painted gold. This error is quite evident and is considered rare.

The patch on the 1981 dated ornament was either missing or not painted within the outline of the patch. Avid collectors eagerly seek this piece.

The Indians' hair on 520772 has been darkened since first issuance. This piece was retired in 1990 and has been one of the most sought after retired pieces. It was not a popular piece due to its original price, poor quality and lack of color in the hair and clothes until after it was retired.

The mold for *May Only Good Things Come Your Way* (524425), has the butterfly on top of the net on the left. The piece shown at left has the butterfly on the right side of the net, upside down.

The Girl Looking at Globe *What The World Needs Now* has been found missing the Bible which should be on the table.

Two more figurines have had smiles changed to frowns: *Faith Takes A Plunge* and *My Days Are Blue Without You*. Both debuted with a smile and have since been changed to a frown or puckered mouth. Because so many were produced these cannot be compared to the 5,000 Smiling Dunce Boys.

Whenever a figurine has more than one piece, it is possible to find a part of the figurine omitted.

I'm Sending My Love Your Way (528609) has been found with a variety of errors. Several reports have been received that the kitten and kite strings are missing and we have also heard reports that the green stripes on the kite are missing.

An interesting error has been found on *Friendship Hits The Spot* (girls at tea party). This piece has been found more than once with the table missing!

Also missing.... *Loving Is Sharing* (E-3110B) has also been found without the dog. This piece has also been found with the boy's lollipop unpainted. Woof!

Other Reported Errors

Figurine sets with errors in duplicated pieces, such as two mothers and no father in the Family Thanksgiving set, is more of a defect than a desired error. This type of error should be returned to your retailer.

Another defect which does not add to the value of a piece is chipped paint. There have been several reports received that the paint on the back of Columbus' hat (the large piece) is chipping or flaking off. The chipped paint decreases the value of this figurine.

Different choices of paint were used on the Ice Cream Cone Boy (E-1374B). Most of the dogs had a black nose but many received a brown nose in 1982 at retirement time. This piece was overproduced for the retirement announcement. It took approximately five years to see its secondary market value climb (on the 1982 mark) to today's price.

Sugar Town's Grandfather figurine is being found with only half of his glasses painted on.

A Reflections Of His Love (522279) has been seen with both a white water reflection and a blue water reflection.

One of the first errors thought to be made was the Sad Boy with the Teddy (E-5200). The original picture shows him with a smile. Collectors, however, have only found him with a little circle mouth.

It's been said the three large camels (E-5624) came without blankets, but has anyone actually found these? If so, I would say only one or two sets, if that many, are all that were produced.

There was a mold shrinkage problem with the Goose Girl figurine. This piece has been found with the goose's bill touching or not touching the girl's face - this doesn't affect the value. Collectors have enjoyed finding the 9" Goose Girl with the touching goose. See page 6 for more details about the shrinkage problem.

The Groom with no hands was changed to have hands. There were so many "no hands" that collectors felt they would never be in demand. Several years later its price is now rising on the secondary market.

The first Chapel piece initially came with "no eyebrows." The Angel by the Cave Chapel exclusive figurine was found with the abbreviation of Matthew misspelled as "Math." instead of the correct "Matt." This was later corrected.

When Boy in Santa's Cap with Dog (E-2805) was retired, on pieces produced for retirement shipments both of the dog's eyes were painted. Previously only one eye had been painted.

Errors with Decals

Any time a figure contains a decal it is possible for it to be accidentally omitted. This also occurs with the inspiration decal. Another problem with decals is that they occasionally are put on "inside out" or "backwards." It appears that these types of errors have occurred more frequently in the last five years than before.

One error I have seen and would love to own is Boy with Slate ornament (E-0535), with "Merry Christmas" upside down on the slate. I am sure there are very few of these errored pieces!

The wrong inscription ("Crowns") appeared on the miniature *Clowns* (12238). Collectors seek this errored piece.

The Five Year Anniversary piece has been found with both bowls for Mrs. Fido and none for the "Mr."

The Lord Is Counting On You (531707) has been found with the decal upside down. This unusual error would increase the insurance value by $100.

There have also been problems with the decal on *Dropping In For The Holidays* (531952). This piece has been found without the "Egg Nog" decal and also with the decal upside down! *Teach Us To Love One Another* (PM161) has been found with the its decal upside down.

Some Heaven Bound ornaments (12416) appeared on the 1987 wreath with decaled words "Heaven Bound" upside down. This mistake adds approximately $50-$75 to the value of that wreath. There is always the possibility of a decal being put on incorrectly or being omitted entirely, such as on the Birthday Club animals. Dates have been omitted from "dated" pieces or have been placed incorrectly on others such as OVEP on *Jesus Is The Only Way* (520756).

Prayer Changes Things (E-5214), Girl and Boy at Table, the title on the Bible was on the figurine upside down. It wasn't an error at the factory, as the original drawing was drawn this way. It was changed. The same error is on the Pilot's book, but the Pilot's book title was not changed, as the book actually would have to be turned to have the title on the correct side.

On the Boy and Girl with the Book (E-2013), there is talk of pieces that had words placed on the pages incorrectly. I have not actually heard of anyone owning one of these. I feel this may have been on sample pieces only. If there are several out there, I feel they are not in the hands of someone who is in touch with other avid collectors or we would know about it.

Errors Occurring on Bases - Marks and Inspirations

We often receive reports from collectors about errors on the underside of their figurines. Quite often people owning these pieces think they have a rarity. In the past, any piece with an "error" on the underside has not done handsprings on the secondary market. Some

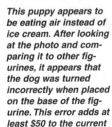
This puppy appears to be eating air instead of ice cream. After looking at the photo and comparing it to other figurines, it appears that the dog was turned incorrectly when placed on the base of the figurine. This error adds at least $50 to the current secondary market value of the figurine.

exceptions are inked marks that come off when rubbed, decaled marks, double incised marks (good ones!), completely "bare" bases, and pieces marked "sample" with nothing else. Another "error" being noted frequently in the last few years is "Missing Marks." It is becoming more common to find that the mark has been omitted from a piece.

Errors with wrong inscriptions have not been highly sought after. Exceptions are "Crowns" instead of *Clowns*. Errors or changes visible to the eye without picking up the piece are the errors that have increased the value of the figurine on the secondary market.

The 1982 membership figurine (E-0202) was produced in 1985 by mistake with an embossed Dove mark. Approximately 700 of these figurines were shipped to Canada. Avid collectors tried to obtain this piece also!

What The World Needs Now with Bible missing from the table.

Inspiration decals may be incorrectly placed or misspelled. A collector wrote that her *Friendship Hits The Spot* figurine is spelled *"Freindship"* on both the box and on the figurine. This type of error is usually worth $25.

All *Merry Christmas Deer* figurines with the Bow and Arrow mark had no *Precious Moments*® logo. There is no secondary market significance.

It's not uncommon to find recently produced figurines with the embossed "Sam B." unintentionally left off. Also, nearly every piece produced since 1985 has been found without a mark.

All figurines shipped to Canada had Taiwan "ink" stamped on the bases due to Canada's import laws.

Errored Boxes, Musicals, Miscellaneous

Line art on boxes is sometimes different than the piece inside or the inscription may be different. Errored boxes have **NO** added value of their own.

The box for the 1982 Bell showed the date on the bell, but none of the bells had the 1982 date on them.

Keep the boxes if you have space to store them. They protect the pieces when storing and shipping and keep the secondary market value MIB. (The prices in this guide are MIB prices - Mint in Box.) Most boxes add from $3 - $5 value to a piece.

The Plates, Bells, Musicals and Dolls have not been produced in as large quantities as the figurines due to less collector demand for these. It seems the larger the piece, the higher the price, the less the demand. The secondary market usually stabilizes almost at the retail level, taking longer for a secondary market increase. This is unusual but true for this collectible. If buying for investment purposes, it is better to buy Club pieces or dated ornaments than to buy one large piece at $175. The Club piece, if popular, may double in price within a year or two, but very seldom has a large piece of $175 doubled to $350 in the same amount of time. I have yet to find any regular sized piece selling for $1,000 as was predicted by some for certain pieces. It may happen in the future, but it has not happened to date, not even for Free Puppies! (Not including the 9" pieces.) It's my opinon a limited edition of 1,500 retailing for $200 up will escalate on the secondary market. However, it takes more time to sell at retail.

Musicals with the wrong music selection have not yet increased on the secondary market.

Call our office with any additional reports of errors or unusual pieces. We would love to receive photos of these pieces to share with our readers.

HATS OFF TO OUR 1996

COLLECTOR OF THE YEAR
MARY LOU HAMOR

It's not how many figurines you own, not how many clubs you've joined... Precious Collectibles' Collector of the Year is one who best exemplifies the Precious Moments theme of loving, caring and sharing.

Mary Lou Hamor attended the very first Precious Collectibles convention in 1984 with her fellow club members Precious Moments With Friends from Covina, California.

Retired from the Armed Forces, Mary Lou is one of the kindest, most gracious, sweetest women I have ever met. She's what I wish I were!!! But I have to stomp my foot sometimes, which Mary Lou would never do!

She travels to the Enesco conventions every year and to the Chapel events. She's guaranteed me she'd travel to another Precious Collectibles convention if we would host another.

Mary Lou should have a Precious Moments designed especially for her... a gramma with li'l ones around her, leaning over, loving, caring and sharing a dish of cookies; or standing in the middle with two friends hugging and smiling.

"Everyone should be like you!" Congratulations, Mary Lou, for being Precious Collectibles' Collector of the Year. You're very special. God must be very pleased in you as God is love and that's what I've seen in you for the past fifteen years."

MOUSE REPORTER OF THE YEAR
CATHY COPELAND

She's done it again!

Cathy's up-to-date, every week reporting has earned her Mouse Reporter of the Year for the second time! The first time was in 1993.

If there's news, Cathy Copeland is on the phone, on a fax, sending smoke signals or jubilantly voicing to us as to what's happening somehow. Her "Mouse Reports" are accurate and just what collectors love to learn!

Many other mice are sending and calling in reports, but Cathy is almost an expected reporter every week with something great.

So to you, Cathy Copeland, Precious Collectibles again salutes you as our Number One Mouse Reporter of the Year for 1996!

Happy 15th Anniversary Precious Collectibles.®

Fifteen happy years of bringing collectors together!

THANKS FOR THE MEMORIES...

Precious Collectibles'® Past Collectors of the Year and Mouse Reporters.

COLLECTORS OF THE YEAR

1996	Mary Lou Hamor
1995	Sharon Barb
1994	Irene Satterwhite
1993	Benny Malin
1991	Don & Bonnie Reed
1990	Cathy Schulz
1989	George & Margaret Welliver
1988	Bob & Marilyn Ohlemacher
1987	Bob & Julie Jackson
1986	Jake & Gloria Toering
1985	Roger Heminger

MOUSE REPORTERS

1996	Cathy Copeland
1995	Ed & Millie Carey & Gwen Stark
1994	Kathy Miller
1993	Cathy Copeland
1988	Bea Butler

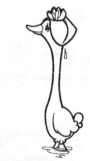

Saturday Night Ho Down

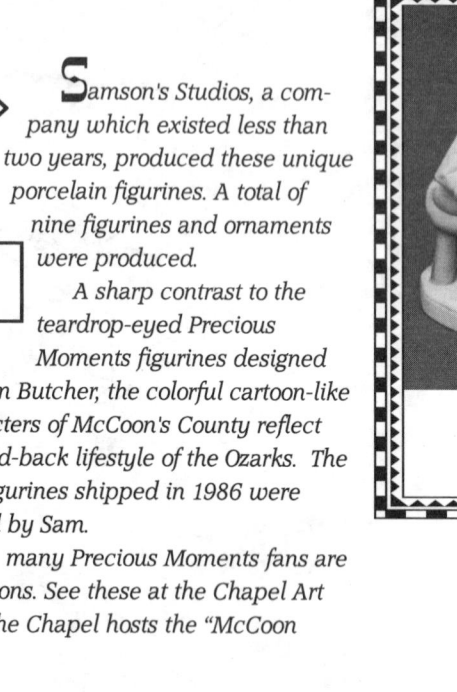

Samson's Studios, a company which existed less than two years, produced these unique porcelain figurines. A total of nine figurines and ornaments were produced.

A sharp contrast to the teardrop-eyed Precious Moments figurines designed by Sam Butcher, the colorful cartoon-like characters of McCoon's County reflect the laid-back lifestyle of the Ozarks. The first figurines shipped in 1986 were signed by Sam.

Because Sam created these figurines, many Precious Moments fans are interested in adding them to their collections. See these at the Chapel Art Gallery with other works of art by Sam. The Chapel hosts the "McCoon County Fair."

Checker Board Square

Mama Sang Tenor

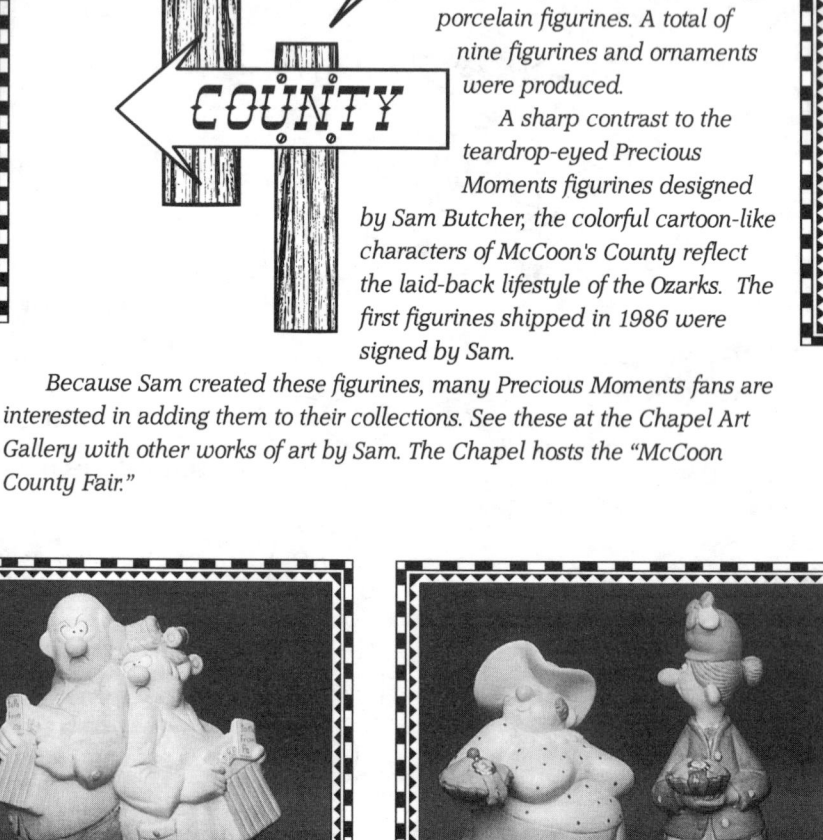

Wishing You A 2 Ton Christmas

McCoon County Fair

Box Social

Mooving on to the

COMMENTS...

1. Precious Moments® Plates were produced in several series but were "slow sellers" and not as collectible as the figurines. Prices in this guide reflect the same lack of demand. Most earlier plates had "no marks." The first dated plate, the 1982 Drummer Boy, was the most popular; the dated 1985 plate was the most scarce. A Mother's Day plate series began in 1994, and in 1996 Enesco began production of very colorful resin plates. Plates do not cause "collectible fever" as do the figurines, probably due to the space required to display them. Plate collectors enjoyed collecting the "shiny glass" plates. These had gray, yellow borders, etc., and retailed for $35-$40 each ($65-75 secondary market value). Bisque plates are enhanced if displayed in an enclosed glass plate frame with light wood edging! The Hamilton Company is owned by Stanhome, as is Enesco, and produces today's "shiny glass" collector plates, selling directly through mail order.

2. Girl with Snowflake Ornament (142662) and others have been found without the decal date on them. It doesn't happen often, but usually when a piece requires a decal, a report comes to our office sooner or later from a collector who found one without the decal. Omitted decals such as dates, words and numerals on the *Birthday Train Series* animals are errors and we recommend adding $50-$75 to the secondary market price for insuring purposes. Decals have been missing from the underside of the bases also. Those decal errors which are visible to the eye rather than under the bases are of more value to the avid collector. "Wrong inscriptions" have been found more often but these errors are not of great importance to the collector compared to visible errors such as missing decals or unpainted figurines. Still, to be properly insured, add $25 to the book price of a figurine found with a "wrong inscription."

3. Several pieces were produced without eyebrows and then later eyebrows were added in the production. The first Chapel piece debuted without eyebrows. Most avid collectors bought this piece in 1989. (Most avid collectors were able to obtain one.) The Chapel piece has been produced as a No Mark, Vessel Mark and G-Clef.

4. Errors found include: one eye not painted, add $100 to value of piece; both eyes not painted, add $200; no white dots in eyes, no added value; different colored clothing or colors of clothing changed from one production to the next and smiles to frowns, value would depend on piece and quantities, etc. Color variations have been noticed on several pieces of *May Your Birthday Be A Blessing* (E-2826), Girl at Table with Dolls, such as black eyes, brown eyes, black nose and brown nose.

The "Baby's First Christmas" ornament came with several variations. Is the one on the left a girl with straight hair or a boy with a bow? This ornament was also produced with curly hair and a bow.

5. The embossed **"SAM B.,"** which has been required on all pieces licensed since 1985 by the Samuel J. Butcher Company, and now Precious Moments Company, has been omitted on many pieces. The embossed marks are placed in the molds. Many figurines are produced from one mold and evidently the embossed **"SAM B."** sometimes is left from that mold. Many molds are produced of the same figurine. Avid collectors who look for errored pieces probably would not pay more for this omission.

6. **TWO MARKS** have been found on the base. While touring the factory, I asked the production managers how this happened and they had no idea! They were very much surprised by this question. Double-marked pieces are rare. Most double-marked pieces had the Fish and Hourglass marks. Other errors have occurred, but less often than these first double-marked pieces. Two different Butterfly marks were found on one piece and a double Flame mark was found. Add at least $100 when insuring these errors.

"Praise The Lord Anyhow" was found with the Flower and Cedar Tree marks, one on top of the other!!

Sometimes collectors get excited about their rare find on new pieces but then learn no error has occurred. The original photos in the Enesco brochures usually are prototype or "sample" pieces and many times a change was made after the sample was produced. An example of this, I feel, was E-5200. The sample had a smile and the original brochure photo had the smile, but actual production consisted of a sad face. The same may be true of E-2013 with the words written across the two pages instead of down each page. Another example is the '97 introduction 260940, *FromThe First Time I Spotted You I Knew We'd Be Friends.* In the brochure, only one monkey is with the leopard. The actual figurine has two monkeys and a paint can. Enesco line cuts used in this guide also differ occasionally from final production.

FRAMES were very slow retail sellers in the late '70s and early '80s. Because they are not as easily available as before, we have seen a slight spark of interest since '93 and continuing through now. I feel they are very special.

Corrected or changed inscriptions (under base) or "visible" writing that changes usually are in the avid collector's collection. Examples include *I Picked a Special Mom* to *I Picked A Very Special Mom* and "he" to "He," "him" to "Him" on pieces E-9261 and E-9262. On the Boy Graduate with Scroll (E-9261), Enesco changed the word "Him" to a capital "H"... *Precious Collectibles™* was first to announce this "error," but was it actually an error? The Holy Bible does not capitalize the word in the King James Version. A similar "error" occurred on Girl Graduate (E-9262) with the word "He" not capitalized in the verse on the scroll. The *Clowns* (12238) debuted with the inscription "Crowns" instead of "Clowns." There was a mistake on the "interpretation" from the Orient. In 1994 a mistake was made on a members' only figurine, Girl with Book (530980). The title was incorrectly printed as *You Fill The Page Of My Life.* The error was corrected to *You Fill The Pages Of My Life.*

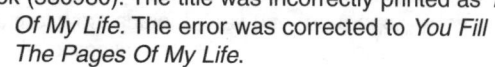
Boy with Teddy (E-1372B) has been used extensively as a "logo" for the collection, along with the Girl with Bunny (E-1372G). The Kids on the Cloud artwork (E-3115) is the official logo for the collection. E-1372G was produced as a 9" Girl. The Boy would be a perfect 9" to match. A 9" version of him is on display at the Chapel Gallery.

Some "Black Eyes" on E-1373B were dark gray, yellowish-brown and, in '82, were so faint that collectors thought they had an error piece without a black eye. (The '82 pieces were all very faint in color until another change was made back to more color in mid '83 and early '84.)

Indeed, the avid collector's "must have" is *God Loveth A Cheerful Giver* (E-1378). Enesco's first retirement announcement in 1981 ended production for this favorite piece. Unlike today's retirement procedures, none were produced after the announcement. Thus, due to the lack of availability, retirement status and being such an adorable piece, this is the most sought after "jewel" of the collection. Most refer to this piece as Free Puppies. She was originally shipped in a cardboard box with white label (see photo of similar box on Errors & Variations picture pages in this guide). This is the only piece that has sold in the past for $50 less without a box. She's special! Several years back she was projected to be the $1000 piece. To date she still can easily be found from $850 to $950 with or without a box!

Angels in Chariot, *Jesus Is Born* (E-2801), has been a very hard piece to find since it has been suspended! Figurines have been found with errors such as the "Holy Bible" decal missing from the Bible. Birthday Club pieces have been found without numerals; add $50-$75 to the value when insuring. Errors of wrong inscriptions on bases have not influenced the secondary market to a great extent except for *Crowns* instead of *Clowns* (12238). Add $25 to the secondary market value of the piece with the wrong inscription. This happens from time to time every year.

Earlier No Mark and Triangle marked pieces licensed by Jonathan & David Co. (such as E-2802) were darker in color than present-day pieces. During 1982 Sam requested lighter pieces. The collectors did not like these "faintly" painted pieces, so in late 1983-1984 the pieces were given more color. The heads on the original J&D pieces were also smaller than the new pieces which have been licensed by the Samuel J. Butcher Co. from 1985 to 1995. The license now is issued to Enesco for the figurines by Precious Moments Incorporated (PMI). Same folks, different name.

15 Collectors have found the word "polish" missing from the bottle on *This Is Your Day To Shine* (E-2822). Again, most pieces with decal print have been found without the "decals." (They're fun to find!) There was no decal on the Bandaged Boy by Sign (E-7159). Add $100 to his secondary market value. Some decals were placed incorrectly on the figurine, such as "OVEP" on the sign on *Jesus Is The Only Way* (520756). The R is P and the decal should be placed closer to the edge... those not are OVEP. In 1994 two figurines were produced with decal errors. *You're As Pretty As A Christmas Tree* (530425) has been found without an inspiration at all, and *Dropping In For The Holidays* (531952) has been found with its "Egg Nog" decal placed upside down. We'll probably hear from someone with a "messy" Egg Nog decal.

Avid collectors enjoy finding variations on figurines. Not only was this little piggy found without the inspiration decal on the front, if you look closely, you'll see that his coins are positioned differently as well.

16 From 1985 to now, the Bride and Groom pieces (E-3114) were changed to have larger heads and other minute changes with Samuel J. Butcher Co. as the licensee and Sam B. embossed on the base. A new figurine, *I Give You My Love Forever True* (129100), introduced for 1995 will make a great wedding topper. Possibly *The Lord Bless You And Keep You* (E-3114) will be suspended... In 1997, new Anniversary figurines were also introduced which "age" with the years.

17 **BELLS** were not as collectible as the figurines in the beginning, thus Enesco later decided to produce only annual dated bells. The collection of bells is outstanding in itself. Most were not marked for several years' production. To date the 1993 bell was the final bell produced in the regular style. The bell for 1994 is totally different and bells were discontinued in 1995.

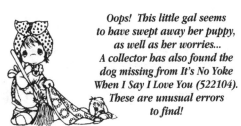

Oops! This little gal seems to have swept away her puppy, as well as her worries... A collector has also found the dog missing from It's No Yoke When I Say I Love You (522104). These are unusual errors to find!

18 Some earlier figurines, such as E-5378, have been found with different license dates on the bases. There is no added value for these errors.

19 **UNPAINTED PIECES** have been found. Approximately three of E-5379 and twelve of the Five-Year piece (12440) have been found unpainted. It has been reported by Enesco that twelve of 12440 were shipped to "who knows where"?! Retailers finding the unpainted 12440 very likely returned these priceless collectibles to Enesco!! We have not heard of any "unpainted" pieces selling on the secondary market to date.

20 The "Follow Me" Angel with Three Kings (E-5641) is an **EXTRA LARGE PIECE** with four figurines on the base. We have found from research that it takes suspension or retirement to cause the secondary market value on such large pieces to increase compared to pieces with lower retail prices. Some examples are the Dealers' Nativity, Mother Sew Dear Doll, Wedding Party figurine, the Five Year Anniversary piece and probably the Fifteen Year Anniversary piece.

21 Most **MUSICALS** resemble a similar figurine. *Silent Knight* (E-5642) was the first that did not.

22 "R" by the style number means the figurine has "returned" from being suspended. E-7156, E-1381, E-9287, 100153 and 100145 are the only figurines to have this status to date. "R" does not mean Retired.

23 When pieces are suspended by the company, they are no longer produced but can be reissued at a later date. If a Jonathan & David piece is suspended, we know that it will have changes if returned. All pieces licensed by the Samuel J. Butcher Co. since 1985 have been produced with larger heads. PMI (Precious Moments, Inc.) is now the licensee, not the Samuel J. Butcher Co. Compare E-1381 with E-1381R *(Jesus Is The Answer),* as well as E-7156 with E-7156R *(I Believe In Miracles).* E-9287R, the girl with lion and lamb, even had a name change, from *Peace On Earth* to *And A Child Shall Lead Them.*

 **DECAL MARKS** on *Love Is Patient* (E-9251) appeared as Hourglass, Fish and Cross marks. Why were decal marks used? No one has the answer. I feel the embossed marks were left from the mold and this was just a way to get the piece marked. ***A similar mark appeared on the Secretary (E-9254) but was called an erasable mark; one could wipe it away very easily*** (see photo, pg. IV).

25 Girl w/Butterfly (E-9258) appeared as the 1991 **EASTER SEALS 9" PIECE** with a Limited Edition of 2,000, retailing for $500. Some of the 1990 Easter Seals pieces remained unordered and by late fall Enesco gave an incentive to retailers; if they purchased another 1990 piece, they would get an identical number for the 1991 Easter Seals Butterfly Girl (to offer as matched numbers). A 9" Easter Seals figurine has been produced each year since. Retailers do not profit from these pieces but hold raffles and sell to collectors at their cost ($500). The collector purchases the piece from the retailer, writes their check to Easter Seals and receives credit for giving. The first Easter Seals piece was the Girl with Bunny and production was limited to 1,000. While visiting the Orient several years ago I saw a "white" Three Kings and the Bride 'n Groom as 9" pieces. Will they be produced later? The President of Enesco, Eugene Freedman, has several 9" pieces similar to the regular line of Easter Seals pieces on display in his office.

 **26** Boy/Girl in Horse Costume (E-9263) was one of the first pieces which alerted collectors that new pieces could come with the prior year's mark. *Precious Collectibles®* was the first to announce that 1983 pieces had 1982's mark! The other pieces which were hard to find that year with the Hourglass mark were *Press On* (E-9265) and *Nobody's Perfect* Dunce Boy (E-9268).

 **27** To date, **THIMBLES** have not been as collectible as the figurines. The only scarce Thimble was the 1985 dated one. Thimbles are "precious" displayed in small shadow boxes. The "Four Seasons" thimbles have been a popular set, too.

28 **IDENTICAL DATED ORNAMENTS** are no longer being produced in consecutive years. This practice is not favorable for a collectible; they're not in demand the second year. In my opinion, color changes should be made if an ornament is produced for two consecutive years.

The production of identical dated ornaments for two consecutive years reduces the demand on the secondary market for several years.

 **29** **DATED ORNAMENTS** began in 1981 with *Let The Heavens Rejoice* (E-5629). The 1988-1991 dated ornaments were not overly abundant due to less production time at the factories (less space, fewer employees, etc.).

30 **BIRTHDAY TRAIN SERIES** - Many pieces have been found without the numerals on the birthday animals. Add $50-$75 on such pieces. The first four pieces are the hardest to find on retailers' shelves, as this is the age group for which most figurines are purchased. When "Jimmy" becomes older, he wants toys and Mom or Gramma will most generally be the one to finish the collection. *Birthday Train Series* pieces with the first marks have risen 50% on the retail market since they were first issued in 1985.

31 Expect **EARLY SPRING PRODUCTIONS** to debut with the previous year's mark. Production time must begin before the new year's pieces debut, thus embossed marks must be put into molds and produced before the new year's delivery. All pieces in the 1996 Spring production debuted with the 1995 Ship mark.

32 It's surprising, but **SPORTS AND OCCUPATIONAL PIECES** must not be selling or be as popular because so many of them are being suspended. The exception to this is the Policeman (12297) and the Navy Boy (526568) which have become more scarce since suspension. Navy Boy's secondary market value is now at $135 and the Policeman is valued at $155, depending on the mark. Several new sports figurines have debuted since 1996.

33 As these pieces debuted later in 1997, they have been listed only with the Sword mark. It is possible that they may debut with the 1996 Heart mark.

34 A new publication that is a sure source of current news including Retirement and Suspension news is *Weekly Collectors' Gazette,*™ direct from Rosie Wells. Also, the Hot Line for Precious Moments® Hot Tips in the U.S. is always a source to keep the collector informed on Retirement and Suspension pieces. For more information see the ads at the back of this publication.

35 Most pieces which were produced for four years or less and then suspended are rising more quickly on the secondary market than pieces produced for more than five years; they are also rising more quickly than some retired pieces. It appears several 1993 retired pieces were still on retailers' shelves in late 1994.

The "Original 21" or the first 21 pieces to appear on retailers' shelves were E-1372B through E-2013. These "No Mark" pieces are considered by many avid collectors as the most desired to own and enjoy.

To God Be The Glory (E-0527), was withheld from the market due to production problems and was suspended in 1985. When it was returned to production the order number was changed to E-2823.

Individual figurines in sets may contain more than one mark (one piece in a set may come with a Triangle mark and another piece may have an Hourglass mark); see E-2386.

Many of the ornaments, because of their small size, are found without a mark (Missing Mark) and an inspiration.

Some pieces may be found without a mark from time to time. Those pieces produced before '81 are considered No Mark because no mark was intended. Earlier Chapel pieces debuted with a No Mark. Now marks are being used. A Missing Mark is considered an error. This means the mark has been left off the mold due to human error. This does not happen very often because of strict quality control. During early productions one mold would be used to produce around 75 pieces. Because of advancements in technology, more pieces can now be produced from a mold. Therefore, there would be fewer earlier pieces with Missing Marks and the replacement value or insurance value would be higher. We are the only source that recognizes the possible insurance value of Missing Mark figurines.

Occasionally, figurines are found with missing or incorrect parts. The large Members' Only Columbus Ship has been found without the dog and spyglass. One collector purchased the 1992 *Friendship Hits The Spot* which was missing the entire table! The Tenth Anniversary figurine has been reported being found with two bowls for Mrs. Fido and none for Mr. Fido and 183873, Growing in Grace Age 10, has been found with only seven bowling pins instead of ten.

"PRECIOUS MOMENTS" BY AVON

Have you seen the Avon "Precious Moments Collection"? In the early 1980s the Avon Company produced a collection of porcelain figurines which were called The Precious Moments Collection. The name of this collection was then changed to Cherished Moments Collection to avoid infringement. Fun to own!

Top Left to Right:

1983	*Come Rain or Shine*	$65
1980	*Ready for an Avon day* (First figurine in the set)	$55

Bottom Left to Right:

1982	*Collector's Corner*	$60
1980	*Which Shade Do You Prefer?* (Third in set)	$75
1980	*Merry Christmas Avon '80*	$65
1980	*The Day I Made President's Club*	$60
1980	*My First Call* (Second in set)	$55

Mini awards were also given to representatives for sales goals in 1982. They were called *Small Treasures* and were created in Japan exclusively for Avon Co.

Not Pictured:

1982:	*Going Avon Calling Award 1982*	$100
	(Rabbit in yellow car, given to reps for Recommendation prize.)	
1985	*We Did It Together* (two rabbits)	$95

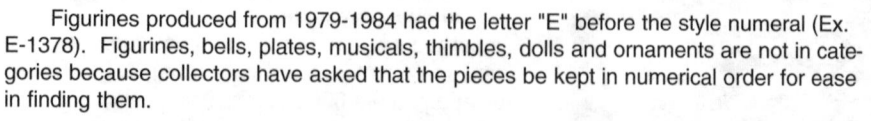

HOW TO USE THIS GUIDE

You will find this guide to *Precious Moments®* collectibles very easy to use. It has been compiled in numerical order.

Figurines produced from 1979-1984 had the letter "E" before the style numeral (Ex. E-1378). Figurines, bells, plates, musicals, thimbles, dolls and ornaments are not in categories because collectors have asked that the pieces be kept in numerical order for ease in finding them.

An alphabetical index by inspiration which includes every porcelain collectible is located at the back of this guide. If you don't know the style number, you probably know the inspirational name of the collectible. This guide also features an alphabetical listing **by description** (© copyrighted index). Here are examples of how it works: Girl with Goose, Girl with Plunger, Boy with Ice Cream Cone. If all else fails, we have line drawings from Enesco to further assist you!

Following this paragraph are the abbreviations for each year's mark which is normally embossed on each porcelain piece. Pieces produced before mid 1981 had no embossed marks and are regarded as "NM" or No Marks. The Triangle was the first actual mark (and the least produced of any mark) placed on the earlier No Mark licensed pieces released after mid 1981 plus new pieces produced during this time. Pieces produced each year thereafter are marked accordingly. The style numbers first appeared on the bases of the figurines in mid 1982. Artwork was licensed by the Jonathan & David Company until 1985, when the Samuel J. Butcher Company started licensing the artwork. Remember, it is not the date on the base, but the embossed mark that determines the year of production and secondary market or insurance value of the collectible.

Marks Appearing on Figurines and Their Abbreviations as They Appear in This Guide:

	Before '81	No Mark (NM)	1991	Vessel (V)
▲	Mid 1981	Triangle (T)	1992	G Clef (GC)
�	1982	Hourglass (HG)	1993	Butterfly (B)
🐟	1983	Fish (F)	1994	Trumpet (TRP)
✝	1984	Cross (C)	1995	Ship (S)
🕊	1985	Dove (D)	1996	Heart (H)
🌿	1986	Olive Branch (OB)	1997	Sword (SRD)
🌲	1987	Cedar Tree (CT)	♦ Special	Diamond
🌼	1988	Flower (FL)	Special	Rosebud
⊕	1989	Bow & Arrow (BA)	⚑ Special	Flag (FLG)
🔥	1990	Flame (FLM)	⚑ Special	Flag w/star (FLG☆)

Error   Missing Mark (MM)

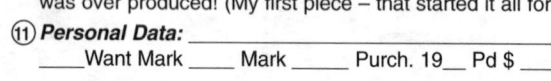

① E-1374B   **Ice Cream Cone Boy** ② ③

One of the "Original 21"
④ *"Praise The Lord Anyhow"*

⑤ **RETIRED 1982 - 15 YEARS AGO**

⑫ ☐

	NM	$120
⑥	T	$100
	HG	$90
Brown Nose	HG	$95
⑦		⑧

⑨ **Comments:** 1976; Original Retail $8.00/$17.00 Dog found with brown nose. Thought I'd found a scarce retired one in '82... Not So. Only produced 3 years but "after retirement" production was over produced! (My first piece – that started it all for me.) ⑩

⑪ **Personal Data:** _____
____Want Mark ____ Mark _____ Purch. 19__ Pd $ _____

1. This is the style/stock number. Numbering for earlier pieces began with "E" -- this is no longer the case. **The style number did not appear on pieces until mid '82.**

2. If nothing is written here, then the item listed is a Figurine. All others such as Ornament, Musical, Doll, Plate, etc., are listed here.

3. Short description of the piece.

4. Inspiration or "name" of the piece.

5. This is the location for noting whether a piece is dated, retired or suspended, followed by the year. **DATED 1984** indicates that the piece was produced only during 1984. **SUSP. 1986** means the piece was suspended in 1986. Suspended pieces are taken from production until further notice. They may or may not return to production. To date, only four figurines have been returned to production from the suspended list (E-7156R, E-1381R, 100145R and 100153R). The "**R**" after the number represents a reissued piece. **RETIRED 1991** means the piece was retired in 1991. A retired piece is no longer in production and will not be reproduced again. **LE 1986** means the piece is a **Limited Edition** and is produced only during 1986. Some Limited Edition pieces are produced for two years, and some have a specified edition size (LE 15,000). Secondary market prices differ according to the mark on the piece. Price information has also been included for "error" pieces. A secondary market value has been entered for each mark.

6. Prices to follow to insure your collection. Pieces are easily found from sellers at these prices.
   "**NE**" after marks means a secondary market price is "**Not Established**" to date. The piece has not sold or research has not found sufficient known sales to establish a secondary market price. Insure at retail unless scarce or rare. **Current** after a mark means the piece is new and is still available at original retail.
   The value listed for each **1997 Sword** mark is the current retail price, effective January 1, 1996. At press time, all of the Spring Introduction pieces had been found with the 1996 Heart mark. If a piece listing the SRD mark is suspended in 1997 before production, we may list this piece with Sword mark and find by mid year the Sword mark was never produced (no significance on secondary market). We will keep you updated in *Precious Collectibles*™ and the 1998 guide.

7. This is the year the original artwork was licensed to Enesco, not the date the figure was produced. Artwork was licensed by the Jonathan & David Co. from 1976 to 1984 and from 1985 on by the Samuel J. Butcher Co. Older pieces still have the J&D name on them in 1996, although most have been suspended or retired.

8. **RETAIL PRICE:** The first amount is the retail price of the figurine when it debuted. The next amount listed is current retail price or final retail price if the piece has been suspended or retired. Over the years some pieces have seen more than one price increase which explains the seemingly large jump on some pieces from original retail to current retail price.

9. **COMMENTS** have been added explaining errors and other variations for each piece. Other information is also included here to explain if the piece is part of series, Limited Edition, etc. Space has been added for your personal comments.

10. **See #36, page XV.** If this is in the comment, it is a reference to an item number and page listed under the "COMMENTS" section which will give greater detail about that particular piece.

11. Space is provided for use for your personal record keeping. List pieces you have, price paid, or which piece (and mark) you want.

12. **Instant Alert** – Do I or do I not have this piece? If this piece is a part of your collection, mark ✓ in the box.

E-0501   Boy Pushing Girl on Sled
"Sharing Our Season Together"

SUSP. 1986 - 11 YEARS AGO	F	$175	D	$130
	C	$140	OB	$130

Comments: 1983; Original Retail $50.00
Also appeared as Musical (E-0519). Very attractive piece.

Personal Data: _____
____Want Mark _____ Mark _____ Purch. 19__ Pd $ _____

E-0502   Boy in Nightcap/Candle
"Jesus Is The Light That Shines"

SUSP. 1986 - 11 YEARS AGO	F	$70	D	$50
	C	$65	OB	$45

Comments: 1983; Original Retail $22.50/$23.00
Very few collectibles honor Jesus as Precious Moments® collectibles do. The only Bible some read.

Personal Data: _____
____Want Mark _____ Mark _____ Purch. 19__ Pd $ _____

E-0503   Girl in Snow Looking at Bird House
"Blessings From My House To Yours"

SUSP. 1986 - 11 YEARS AGO	F	$90	D	$80
	C	$85	OB	$75

Comments: 1983; Original Retail $27.00

Personal Data: _____
____Want Mark _____ Mark _____ Purch. 19__ Pd $ _____

E-0504   Boy Giving Teddy to Poor Boy
"Christmastime Is For Sharing"

RETIRED 1990 - 7 YEARS AGO				
	F	$115	OB	$95	BA	$85
	C	$100	CT	$95	FLM	$75
	D	$95	FL	$85	

Comments: 1983; Original Retail $37.00/$50.00
Same figures on 1983 Dated Plate (E-0505).

Personal Data: _____
____Want Mark _____ Mark _____ Purch. 19__ Pd $ _____

E-0505   *PLATE* - Boy with Teddy
"Christmastime Is For Sharing"

DATED 1983	MM $80	F $60

Comments: 1983; Original Retail $40.00
Second Issue of *Joy of Christmas Series*. Some were not marked as they should have been, thus this guide uses MM for Missing Mark. More MMs were reported in late '95. Plates are not sought after.
See #1, page XI.
Personal Data: _____
____Want Mark _____ Mark _____ Purch. 19__ Pd $ _____

E-0506   Boy with Wreath
"Surrounded With Joy"

RETIRED 1989 - 8 YEARS AGO				
	F	$85	OB	$75	BA	$68
	C	$80	CT	$70	
	D	$75	FL	$70	

Comments: 1983; Original Retail $21.00/$27.50
Not dated as ornament is (E-0513). A similar figurine (531677) of a girl with wreath was produced for sale by the Chapel in '93 and was still available as of late '95. New Chapel pieces continue to debut with No Marks.

Personal Data: _____
____Want Mark _____ Mark _____ Purch. 19__ Pd $ _____

E-0507   Girl Looking into Manger
"God Sent His Son"

SUSP. 1987 - 10 YEARS AGO	F	$95	OB	$85
	C	$90	CT	$78
	D	$85		

Comments: 1983; Original Retail $32.50/$37.00
There were several "manger" pieces in early '80s.
Personal Data: _____
____Want Mark _____ Mark _____ Purch. 19__ Pd $ _____

E-0508   Angels Preparing Manger
"Prepare Ye The Way Of The Lord"

SUSP. 1986 - 11 YEARS AGO	F	$150	D	$135
	C	$140	OB	$135

Comments: 1983; Original Retail $75.00
Six-piece set. Seemed to be a slow seller. Collectors' opinions were "heads too large." Do not see many for sale now. C mark appears more abundant.

Personal Data: _____
____Want Mark _____ Mark _____ Purch. 19__ Pd $ _____

E-0509 Girl Angel Pushing Jesus in Cart
"Bringing God's Blessing To You"

SUSP. 1987 - 10 YEARS AGO

F	$90	D	$80	CT	$70
C	$85	OB	$75		

Comments: 1983; Original Retail $35.00/$38.50
Paper-covered wand and star not remaining in "good condition" on many pieces. Do not see many of these at secondary market shows. Becoming hard to find. Damaged wand definitely de-values piece and will more so with age. It would be nice if Enesco would make wand replacements.

Personal Data: _____

____Want Mark ____ Mark _____ Purch. 19__ Pd $ _____

E-0511 Pig with Hen on Back
"Tubby's First Christmas"

SUSP. 1993 - 4 YEARS AGO

F	$45	CT	$25	V	$25
C	$40	FL	$25	GC	$25
D	$30	BA	$25	B	$25
OB	$30	FLM	$25		

Comments: 1983; Original Retail $12.00/$16.50
Several reports of broken birds from this very fragile piece. Easily found at swap meets recently.

Personal Data: _____

____Want Mark ____ Mark _____ Purch. 19__ Pd $ _____

E-0512 Boy Angel with Red Cross Bag
"It's A Perfect Boy"

SUSP. 1990 - 7 YEARS AGO

F	$70	OB	$55	BA	$55
C	$65	CT	$55	FLM	$55
D	$60	FL	$55		

Comments: 1983; Original Retail $18.50/$27.50
Many added this piece to the original Nativity set. In very little demand for the past few years.

Personal Data: _____

____Want Mark ____ Mark _____ Purch. 19__ Pd $ _____

E-0513 *CHAPEL EXCLUSIVE - ORNAMENT*
Boy with Wreath
"Surround Us With Joy"

DATED 1983   F $68

Comments: 1983; Original Retail $9.00
Date omitted on several - add $50 to secondary market. Similar figurine, E-0506. Chapel piece that debuted in '93 was a little girl in a wreath (531685). ***See #2, page XI.***

Personal Data: _____

____Want Mark ____ Mark _____ Purch. 19__ Pd $ _____

E-0514 *ORNAMENT* – Mother in Chair Sewing
"Mother Sew Dear"

				DECALED C	$85		
F	$30	CT	$20	V	$18.50	S	$18.50
C	$25	FL	$20	GC	$18.50	H	$18.50
D	$25	BA	$20	B	$18.50	SRD	$17
OB	$25	FLM	$20	TRP	$18.50		

Comments: 1983; Original Retail $9.00/$17.00
Similar to figurine E-3106. No space for inspiration on base of ornament. Good candidate for suspension or retirement. Current older pieces secondary market doesn't increase compared to suspended or retired pieces lessening the enthusiasm to pay big bucks.

Personal Data: _____

____Want Mark ____ Mark _____ Purch. 19__ Pd $ _____

E-0515 *ORNAMENT* – Boy in Dad's Duds
"To A Special Dad"

SUSP. 1988 - 9 YEARS AGO   ***INKED C** $75

F	$60	D	$50	CT	$50
C	$52	OB	$50	FL	$50

Comments: 1983; Original Retail $9.00/$12.50
*Found with Inked Cross.

Personal Data: _____

____Want Mark ____ Mark _____ Purch. 19__ Pd $ _____

E-0516 *ORNAMENT* - Grandma in Rocking Chair
"The Purr-fect Grandma"

				DECALED C	$50-$55		
F	$38	CT	$25	V	$18.50	S	$18.50
C	$30	FL	$22.50	GC	$18.50	H	$18.50
D	$25	BA	$18.50	B	$18.50	SRD	$17
OB	$25	FLM	$18.50	TRP	$18.50		

Comments: 1983; Original Retail $9.00/$17.00
Produced for 15 years. Excellent "gift item." Easy to find.

Personal Data: _____

____Want Mark ____ Mark _____ Purch. 19__ Pd $ _____

E-0517 *ORNAMENT* – Grandpa with Newspaper
"The Perfect Grandpa"

SUSP. 1990 - 7 YEARS AGO   **DECALED C** $55

F	$45	OB	$30	BA	$30
C	$38	CT	$30	FLM	$30
D	$35	FL	$30		

Comments: 1983; Original Retail $9.00/$15.00
Remember! Decaled and stamped ink are two different markings!

Personal Data: _____

____Want Mark ____ Mark _____ Purch. 19__ Pd $ _____

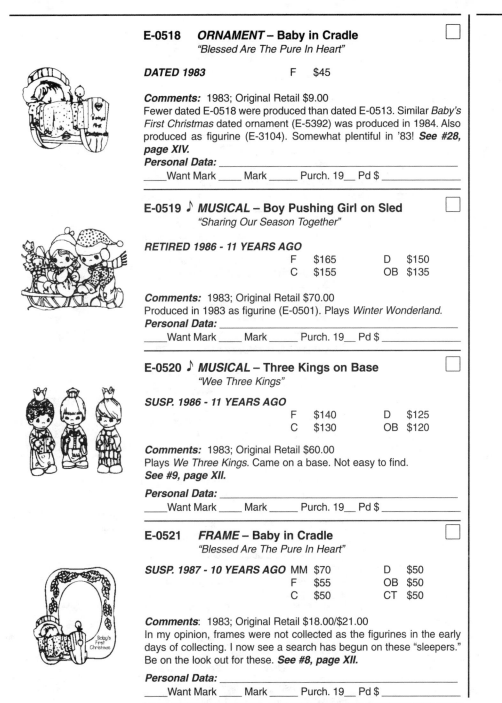

E-0518   *ORNAMENT* – Baby in Cradle
"Blessed Are The Pure In Heart"

DATED 1983　　　　　　　　F　$45

Comments: 1983; Original Retail $9.00
Fewer dated E-0518 were produced than dated E-0513. Similar *Baby's First Christmas* dated ornament (E-5392) was produced in 1984. Also produced as figurine (E-3104). Somewhat plentiful in '83! ***See #28, page XIV.***
Personal Data: _____
____Want Mark ____ Mark _____ Purch. 19__ Pd $ _____

E-0519 ♪ *MUSICAL* – Boy Pushing Girl on Sled
"Sharing Our Season Together"

RETIRED 1986 - 11 YEARS AGO
　　　　　　　　　F　$165　　　D　$150
　　　　　　　　　C　$155　　　OB　$135

Comments: 1983; Original Retail $70.00
Produced in 1983 as figurine (E-0501). Plays *Winter Wonderland.*
Personal Data: _____
____Want Mark ____ Mark _____ Purch. 19__ Pd $ _____

E-0520 ♪ *MUSICAL* – Three Kings on Base
"Wee Three Kings"

SUSP. 1986 - 11 YEARS AGO
　　　　　　　　　F　$140　　　D　$125
　　　　　　　　　C　$130　　　OB　$120

Comments: 1983; Original Retail $60.00
Plays *We Three Kings.* Came on a base. Not easy to find. ***See #9, page XII.***

Personal Data: _____
____Want Mark ____ Mark _____ Purch. 19__ Pd $ _____

E-0521   *FRAME* – Baby in Cradle
"Blessed Are The Pure In Heart"

SUSP. 1987 - 10 YEARS AGO　MM　$70　　　D　$50
　　　　　　　　　　　　　　　F　$55　　　OB　$50
　　　　　　　　　　　　　　　C　$50　　　CT　$50

Comments: 1983; Original Retail $18.00/$21.00
In my opinion, frames were not collected as the figurines in the early days of collecting. I now see a search has begun on these "sleepers." Be on the look out for these. ***See #8, page XII.***
Personal Data: _____
____Want Mark ____ Mark _____ Purch. 19__ Pd $ _____

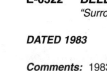

E-0522   *BELL* – Boy with Wreath
"Surrounded With Joy"

DATED 1983　　　　MM　$70　　　　F　$70

Comments: 1983; Original Retail $18.00
If the date is missing from the ribbon add $50 to secondary market value. Anytime a decal is used on a piece, it is not uncommon for a collector to report that it is missing. Attractive bell! Collect them all. The last dated bell with this style (figurine was handle of bell) was produced in '93. A dated '94 bell (different look) was also produced. Prices down from '96! Seem to be more MM sales than F.

Personal Data: _____
____Want Mark ____ Mark _____ Purch. 19__ Pd $ _____

E-0523   Soldier
"Onward Christian Soldiers"

						DECALED F	$130
MM	$125	CT	$40	GC	$40	SRD	$37.50
F	$65	FL	$40	B	$40		
C	$48	BA	$40	TRP	$37.50		
D	$48	FLM	$40	S	$37.50		
OB	$45	V	$40	H	$37.50		

Comments: 1983; Original Retail $24.00/$37.50
Very popular piece. Scarce in 1983. Has been found with MM (an error). RARE! Also found with Decaled F. *Precious Collectibles*® alerted collectors first about "decaled" marks, "erasable" marks, etc., around 1983. Very little demand except for MM and F. Would be a great retirement piece. ***See #24, page XIV.***

Personal Data: _____
____Want Mark ____ Mark _____ Purch. 19__ Pd $ _____

E-0525   Boy and Dog Running Away
"You Can't Run Away From God"

RETIRED 1989 - 8 YEARS AGO		**DECALED** F	$125
HG	$165	D	$90	FL	$85
F	$105	OB	$90	BA	$80
C	$100	CT	$85		

Comments: 1983; Original Retail $28.50/$38.50
Color and dot differences have been found on knapsack; also "no eyebrows" found. Decaled F - exciting to find! ***See #3 & 4, page XI.***

Personal Data: _____
____Want Mark ____ Mark _____ Purch. 19__ Pd $ _____

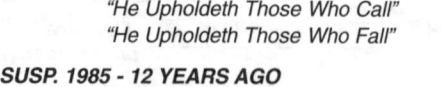

E-0526 Angel Catching Boy on Skates
"He Upholdeth Those Who Call"
"He Upholdeth Those Who Fall"

SUSP. 1985 - 12 YEARS AGO

	DECALED	F	$145
MM	$140	C	$85
F	$90	D	$80

Comments: 1983; Original Retail $28.50/$35.00
Has been found w/MM and Decaled Fish. This piece was originally produced with the name *"He Upholdeth Those Who Call."* It has been changed to *"He Upholdeth Those Who Fall."* To date, we have heard of no one having the changed inspiration, *"Fall."* Do you have *"Fall?"*

Personal Data: _____
____Want Mark ____ Mark _____ Purch. 19__ Pd $ _____

E-0530 Girl with Bird in Hand
"His Eye Is On The Sparrow"

RETIRED 1987 - 10 YEARS AGO

MM	$135	C	$110	OB	$100
F	$130	D	$100	CT	$95

Comments: 1983; Original Retail $28.50/$32.50
Nice piece.

Personal Data: _____
____Want Mark ____ Mark _____ Purch. 19__ Pd $ _____

E-0531 ORNAMENT – Boy Caroling
"O Come All Ye Faithful"

SUSP. 1986 -11 YEARS AGO DECALED F $80

F	$65	D	$50
C	$55	OB	$50

Comments: 1983; Original Retail $9.00/$10.00
Caroler from 1983 Christmas piece E-2353.

Personal Data: _____
____Want Mark ____ Mark _____ Purch. 19__ Pd $ _____

E-0532 ORNAMENT – Angel w/Songbook & Bird
"Let Heaven And Nature Sing"

RETIRED 1986 - 11 YEARS AGO DECALED F $80

F	$55	D	$40
C	$45	OB	$30

Comments: 1983; Original Retail $9.00/$10.00
Price fell from '96 on OB mark. Many sales lower than '96 except F mark!

Personal Data: _____
____Want Mark ____ Mark _____ Purch. 19__ Pd $ _____

E-0533 ORNAMENT – Girl Reading Book to Doll
"Tell Me The Story Of Jesus"

SUSP. 1988 - 9 YEARS AGO

F	$70	OB	$48
C	$65	CT	$48
D	$50	FL	NE

Comments: 1983; Original Retail $9.00/$12.50
One report of a FL mark. Any others? One sold for $65 in '95. The scarcity of suspended ornaments depends upon the time of year the suspension took place.

Personal Data: _____
____Want Mark ____ Mark _____ Purch. 19__ Pd $ _____

E-0534 ORNAMENT – Girl with Kittens
"To Thee With Love"

RETIRED 1989 - 8 YEARS AGO

F	$60	CT	$45
C	$55	FL	$40
D	$55	BA	$30
OB	$50		

Comments: 1983; Original Retail $9.00/$13.50
Most scarce of 1989 retired pieces. Cat faces lacked character on figurine as ornament.

Personal Data: _____
____Want Mark ____ Mark _____ Purch. 19__ Pd $ _____

E-0535 ORNAMENT – Boy with Slate
"Love Is Patient"

SUSP. 1986 - 11 YEARS AGO

F	$70	D	$60
C	$60	OB	$60

Comments: 1983; Original Retail $9.00/$10.00
Becoming very hard to find! One report and photo came to our office of an upside down "Merry Christmas" decal on the slate. (Insure for $135.) (Right Roger?!)

Personal Data: _____
____Want Mark ____ Mark _____ Purch. 19__ Pd $ _____

E-0536 ORNAMENT – Girl with Slate
"Love Is Patient"

SUSP. 1986 - 11 YEARS AGO

F	$80	D	$65
C	$70	OB	$60

Comments: 1983; Original Retail $9.00/$10.00
Not easy to find! Popular!

Personal Data: _____
____Want Mark ____ Mark _____ Purch. 19__ Pd $ _____

E-0537   ORNAMENT – Boy in Nightcap/Candle
"Jesus Is The Light That Shines"

SUSP. 1985 - 12 YEARS AGO

F	$80	C	$80	D	$80

Comments: 1983; Original Retail $9.00/$10.00
Only a three year production on this ornament. Scarce!

Personal Data: _____
____Want Mark ____ Mark _____ Purch. 19__ Pd $ _____

E-0538   PLATE – "Wee Three Kings"

LE 1983 - 14 YEARS OLD

MM	$45	F	$50	OB	$45

Comments: 1983; Original Retail $40.00/$45.00
1983 Limited Edition 15,000. Third issue in Christmas Collection Series. MM means missing mark. Although this was limited to 1983 this has been seen with the OB mark (1986). Most sales found were MM prices which may mean they were more abundant. If plates had been limited to 1,500 as the first 9" Easter Seals pieces I wonder if the plates would have been more popular? Probably!

Personal Data: _____
____Want Mark ____ Mark _____ Purch. 19__ Pd $ _____

E-0539   DOLL – "Katie Lynne"

SUSP. 1988 - 9 YEARS AGO

MM	$185	OB	$180
F	$185	CT	$180
C	$180	FL	$180
D	$180		

Comments: 1983; Original Retail $150.00/$175.00
Interest seems less now than earlier. Porcelain dolls not sought after; price reflects this. It's my opinion one may find this doll at a swap meet for much less than $180 when dealing with seller directly.

Personal Data: _____
____Want Mark ____ Mark _____ Purch. 19__ Pd $ _____

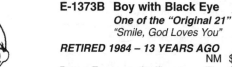
E-1372B through E-2013 were the FIRST TWENTY-ONE pieces to appear on retailers' shelves. These "No Mark" pieces are considered by many avid collectors the most desired to own and enjoy. Those that remain in production and have not come back from suspension still carry the J&D Licensee trade name.

E-1372B   Boy with Teddy
One of the "Original 21"
"Jesus Loves Me"

NM	$120	D	$35	FLM	$28	S	$27.50
T	$125	OB	$30	V	$28	H	$27.50
HG	$55	CT	$30	GC	$28	SRD	$27.50
F	$45	FL	$30	B	$27.50		
C	$40	BA	$30	TRP	$27.50		

Comments: 1977; Original Retail $7.00/$27.50
Next to the Angels on Cloud (E-3115), this piece and E-1372G have become the "logo" figures of the Precious Moments® Collection. A nine inch version of this figurine is on display at the Chapel. Time for retirement! (Fewer T than NM.) **See #10, page XII.**

Personal Data: _____
____Want Mark ____ Mark _____ Purch. 19__ Pd $ _____

E-1372G   Girl with Bunny
One of the "Original 21"
"Jesus Loves Me"

NM	$110	D	$35	FLM	$30	S	$27.50
T	$115	OB	$35	V	$30	H	$27.50
HG	$55	CT	$35	GC	$27.50	SRD	$27.50
F	$45	FL	$30	B	$27.50		
C	$40	BA	$30	TRP	$27.50		

Comments: 1977; Original Retail $7.00/$27.50
Has been found with 1978 license date which is an error. Still has the Jonathan & David trademark as this piece has not been suspended and production has continued on the artwork licensed by J&D. Collectors do not realize there are fewer T than NM for this piece. May find for less if you look. Time for retirement after 22 years! **See #18, page XIII.**

Personal Data: _____
____Want Mark ____ Mark _____ Purch. 19__ Pd $ _____

E-1373B   Boy with Black Eye
One of the "Original 21"
"Smile, God Loves You"

RETIRED 1984 – 13 YEARS AGO

	NM	$115	F	$70
Brown Eye -- no significant	T	$90	C	$55
difference.	HG	$75		

Comments: 1977; Original Retail $7.00/$17.00
1982 pieces have very pale "black eye." This figurine was not as popular just because it's being a part of the first 21. **See #11, page XII.**

Personal Data: _____
____Want Mark ____ Mark _____ Purch. 19__ Pd $ _____

E-1373G Girl with Candle
One of the "Original 21"
"Jesus Is The Light"

RETIRED 1988 - 9 YEARS AGO

NM	$135	F	$60	OB	$55
T	$80	C	$60	CT	$55
HG	$70	D	$60	FL	$55

Comments: 1977; Original Retail $7.00/$21.00
Older marks are more sought after on Original 21 as collectors want to own pieces with the darker colors. When large collections sell, pieces such as this in FL and CT marks could be averaged for less than $35!

Personal Data: _____
____Want Mark ____ Mark _____ Purch. 19__ Pd $ _____

E-1374B Ice Cream Cone Boy
One of the "Original 21"
"Praise The Lord Anyhow"

RETIRED 1982 - 15 YEARS AGO

NM	$120
T	$100
HG	$90
Brown Nose HG	$95

Comments: 1976; Original Retail $8.00/$17.00
Dog found with brown nose. Thought I'd found a scarce retired one in '82... Not So. Only produced 3 years but "after retirement" production was over produced! (My first piece – that started it all for me.)

Personal Data: _____
____Want Mark ____ Mark _____ Purch. 19__ Pd $ _____

Shrinking in the mold during firing has created several variations of the "Goose Girl (E-1374G) above right. There is no significant secondary market value difference as to touching or not touching.

E-1374G Girl with Goose
One of the "Original 21"
"Make A Joyful Noise"

NM	$130	D	$40	FLM	$32.50	S	$32.50
T	$90	OB	$40	V	$32.50	H	$32.50
HG	$60	CT	$35	GC	$32.50	SRD	$32.50
F	$50	FL	$35	B	$32.50		
C	$40	BA	$35	TRP	$32.50		

Comments: 1978; Original Retail $8.00/32.50
Mold shrinkage problems. Goose sometimes touches girl's face. No secondary market difference. Still has J&D on base. **Probably the most popular piece in collection.** Only the old marks are sought after on pieces that have been produced as long as this one. Because of the J & D Licensee name, I thought this would have been retired or suspended and bought back to be a 1374 G.R.

Personal Data: _____
____Want Mark ____ Mark _____ Purch. 19__ Pd $ _____

E-1375A Boy and Girl on Seesaw
One of the "Original 21"
"Love Lifted Me"
RETIRED 1993 - 4 YEARS AGO

NM	$170	D	$75	FLM	$75
T	$120	OB	$75	V	$75
HG	$100	CT	$75	GC	$70
F	$90	FL	$75	B	$50
C	$75	BA	$75		

Comments: 1977; Original Retail $11.00/$37.50
Part of "Original 21." NM very dark in color! Nice! Produced after retirement announcement. NM seems to be the most sought after mark on the secondary market. This piece has been found with a 1978 license date on it; no significant secondary price increase. Price went especially down for B mark from '96.

Personal Data: _____
____Want Mark ____ Mark _____ Purch. 19__ Pd $ _____

E-1375B Boy and Girl Praying
One of the "Original 21"
"Prayer Changes Things"
SUSP. 1984 - 13 YEARS AGO

NM	$225-235	HG	$160	C	$155
T	$170	F	$155		

Comments: 1976; Original Retail $11.00/$22.50
Very hard to find on secondary market for several years. NM is the piece to have! Earlier pieces were more colorful! Price down some from '96. **See #36, page XV.**

Personal Data: _____
____Want Mark ____ Mark _____ Purch. 19__ Pd $ _____

E-1376　Boy and Girl Sitting on Stump
"Love One Another"　　　　　One of the *"Original 21"*

NM	$135	D	$50	FLM	$40	S	$40
T	$100	OB	$50	V	$40	H	$40
HG	$70	CT	$48	GC	$40	SRD	$40
F	$60	FL	$48	B	$40		
C	$60	BA	$45	TRP	$40		

Comments: 1976; Original Retail $10.00/$40.00
Considered ***"First Piece"*** in the Precious Moments art collection. 1978 has been found on some pieces. NM would be the avid collector's choice. The original artwork of this piece was stolen from the Grand Rapids Showroom. Original 21 figurines **still in production** usually do not increase significantly in secondary market value after the T mark. Reported w/no eyebrows. Retail price increased in '96. This piece was changed around 1984-85 with larger eyes for a period of several years.(Still Licensed by Jonathan and David)

Personal Data: _____
____Want Mark ____ Mark _____ Purch. 19__ Pd $ _____

E-1377A　Boy Leading Lamb　One of the *"Original 21"*
"He Leadeth Me"
SUSP. 1984 - 13 YEARS AGO

NM	$137	HG	$100	C	$90
T	$120	F	$90		

Comments: 1977; Original Retail $9.00/$20.00
Not as hard to find with the NM as others in the Original 21 group. NMs are very colorful. Easy to find at listed prices. E-1377A and E-1377B have been found in NMs several times with switched inspirations.

Personal Data: _____
____Want Mark ____ Mark _____ Purch. 19__ Pd $ _____

E-1377B　Boy Helping Lamb　One of the *"Original 21"*
"He Careth For You"
SUSP. 1984 - 13 YEARS AGO

NM	$150	F	$110
T	$125	C	$100
HG	$115		

Comments: 1976; Original Retail $9.00/$20.00
NM becoming hard to find. Popular piece! E-1377B and E-1377A have been found several times with switched inspirations on them in NMs. Incorrect inspirations are not significant for higher insurance or buying/selling price.

Personal Data: _____
____Want Mark ____ Mark _____ Purch. 19__ Pd $ _____

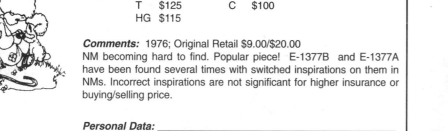

E-1378　Girl with Puppies in Cart　One of the *"Original 21"*
"God Loveth A Cheerful Giver"

RETIRED 1981 - 16 YEARS AGO　　　NM　　　$850-950

Comments: 1977; Original Retail $9.50/ $15.00
First to be retired in 1981 along with E-2011. Also known as Free Puppies. Produced with one air hole first, then two holes. Some puppies' ears darker brown. Errors such as non-painted eyes on puppies have been reported. Most "coveted" piece in collection. Extras were not produced after retirement was announced. The high and low prices will be determined by where one seeks this piece. At one time, not having the original cardboard box would mean to deduct $50 from the secondary market price. Today, deduct $35 from the secondary market price for a no box to insure or resell. Watch for broken necks before purchasing; usually very "clean" breaks occur on this piece and are easily glued back and undetectable. A black light may be used to detect defects. All pieces are "No Marks" and are easily found at prices listed above. **Add $25 to Sec. Mkt. Value if Sam has signed it.**
See #12, page XII.

Personal Data: _____
____Want Mark ____ Mark _____ Purch. 19__ Pd $ _____

E-1379A　Boy with Turtle　One of the *"Original 21"*
"Love Is Kind"

SUSP. 1984 - 13 YEARS AGO

No Hole in Base	NM	$145		
	NM	$140	F	$95
	T	$120	C	$90
	HG	$100		

Comments: 1977; Original Retail $8.00/$19.00
First produced with no hole in base; higher on secondary market. This is a very popular piece! Watch that butterfly when dusting! NMs are becoming harder to locate on these 1300 series of figurines.

Personal Data: _____
____Want Mark ____ Mark _____ Purch. 19__ Pd $ _____

E-1379B　Boy with Report Card　One of the *"Original 21"*
"God Understands"

SUSP. 1984 - 13 YEARS AGO

NM	$140	HG	$105	C	$90
T	$115	F	$90		

Comments: 1978; Original Retail $8.00/$19.00
In 1983 the "eyes" were changed in the molds to be larger. Not as popular as others in the Original 21 group.

Personal Data: _____
____Want Mark ____ Mark _____ Purch. 19__ Pd $ _____

E-1380B Indian Boy *One of the "Original 21"* ☐
"O, How I Love Jesus"

RETIRED 1984 - 13 YEARS AGO

NM	$135	F	$90
T	$120	C	$65
HG	$100		

Comments: 1977; Original Retail $8.00/$19.00
Scarce until late 1982. A collector reported having this with the D mark which was a surprise to me as it was retired in '84. Also heard report of dog having red nose. Add $10 for red nose.

Personal Data: _____
___Want Mark ___ Mark _____ Purch. 19__ Pd $ _____

E-1380G Indian Girl *One of the "Original 21"* ☐

"His Burden Is Light"

RETIRED 1984 - 13 YEARS AGO

NM	$155	F	$100
T	$135	C	$90
HG	$115		

Comments: 1977; Original Retail $8.00/$19.00
Scarce until late 1982. A collector reported having this with the D mark which is surprising, as this piece was retired in '84.

Personal Data: _____
___Want Mark ___ Mark _____ Purch. 19__ Pd $ _____

E-1381 Boy Patching World *One of the "Original 21"* ☐
"Jesus Is The Answer"

SUSP. 1984 - REISSUED IN 1992 AS E-1381R

NM	$185	F	$145
T	$170	C	$135
HG	$150		

Comments: 1977; Original Retail $11.50/$22.50
Reissuing has affected the secondary market somewhat.

Personal Data: _____
___Want Mark ___ Mark _____ Purch. 19__ Pd $ _____

Missing marks (MM) occurring before 1983 are considered more significant than missing marks in recent years. We previously called these No Marks. Many of the older pieces with Missing Marks should have been Triangle marks. Also in 1982, many Hourglass marks were left off pieces. These older MM pieces could be more colorful than later pieces missing their marks.

E-1381R
When this li'l fellow was returned from suspension, several changes from the original were evident: the boy is leaning over the globe more, the ribbon is off the base of the globe and there is a hot water bottle on the top of the globe.

E-1381R Boy Patching World ☐
"Jesus Is The Answer"
RETIRED 1996 - 1 YEAR AGO
RETURNED FROM SUSPENSION 1992

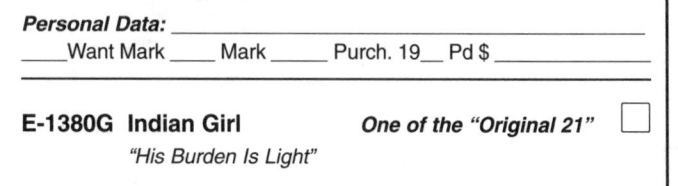

GC	$70	TRP	$60	H	$60
B	$60	S	$60		

Comments: 1977; Original Retail $55.00
This piece was returned from suspension in summer/fall of 1992. Several changes were made to the piece, including: the boy is leaning over the globe more and the ribbon is off the base of the globe. Also, the figurine came back larger with a hot water bottle on the globe. Word had it, with the second production in late '92 or '93, the mold would have a "changed" hot water bottle. No change was seen. E-1381R first debuted with the GC mark. It was reported that it would debut in '93 without a hot water bottle, but this was not the case. This piece has really been a confusing issue – almost as confusing as E-7156R *I Believe In Miracles*. This could be a candidate for suspension or retirement, in my opinion. ***See #22, page XIII.***

Personal Data: _____
___Want Mark ___ Mark _____ Purch. 19__ Pd $ _____

E-2010 Boy Carrying Lamb *One of the "Original 21"* ☐
"We Have Seen His Star"

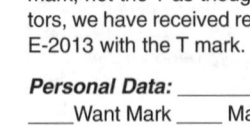

SUSP. 1984 - 13 YEARS AGO

	NM	$120	F	$80
SCARCE!	T	$150	C	$80
	HG	$90		

Comments: 1978; Original Retail $8.00/$19.00
First pieces painted very dark. Most were produced in 1979-1980 through mid 1981, then 1982 on with the HG being the first "embossed" mark, not the T as thought. After researching and asking many collectors, we have received reports of collectors having E-2010, E-2012 and E-2013 with the T mark.

Personal Data: _____
___Want Mark ___ Mark _____ Purch. 19__ Pd $ _____

Happy 15th Anniversary Precious Collectibles®

E-2011   **Boy at Manger**   *One of the "Original 21"*

"Come Let Us Adore Him"

RETIRED 1981 - 16 YEARS AGO

NM $250-275

Comments: 1978; Original Retail $10.00/$14.00
Has not risen on the secondary market compared to "Free Puppies" retired the same year. Price dropped on this piece!!! From $295-315 in '93 to $250-260 in '95 and many sales found to obtain the above secondary market price which has dropped to early '90s value. Prices found for "No Box" were as low as $220! Has been found with one air hole instead of two. For unpainted patch, add $50 to the above value. Several reported sales below $200 in '96.

Personal Data: _____
____Want Mark ____ Mark _____ Purch. 19__ Pd $ _____

E-2012   **Boy/Girl School Play**   *One of the "Original 21"*

"Jesus Is Born"

SUSP. 1984 - 13 YEARS AGO

	NM	$145	F	$105
SCARCE!	T	$175	C	$100
	HG	$130		

Comments: 1978; Original Retail $12.00/$25.00
Once owned a T Mark. More sales found on C than any other recently.

Personal Data: _____
____Want Mark ____ Mark _____ Purch. 19__ Pd $ _____

E-2013   **Boy/Girl with Book**   *One of the "Original 21"*

"Unto Us A Child Is Born"

SUSP. 1984 - 13 YEARS AGO

	NM	$132	F	$110
SCARCE!	T	$155	C	$100
	HG	$115		

A	Is
Child	Born

Correct

Is	A
Born	Child

Incorrect

Comments: 1978; Original Retail $12.00/$25.00
License date appeared on figurine in 1982. Words placed incorrectly on book's pages in 1979 on a limited amount, but only have seen a photo from the company on this. We know of no actual piece with this error in anyone's collection. After researching and asking many collectors, we received a report from one collector who had this piece with a T mark. One collector's piece says "Is Born Is Born" instead of saying "A Child Is Born." Mainly F & C marks readily found on Secondary Market.
See #36, page XV.

Personal Data: _____
____Want Mark ____ Mark _____ Purch. 19__ Pd $ _____

E-2343   ***ORNAMENT* – Angel with Trumpet**

"Joy To The World"

SUSP. 1988 - 9 YEARS AGO

NM	$65	F	$55	OB	$50
T	$60	C	$55	CT	$45
HG	$60	D	$50	FL	$45

Comments: 1981; Original Retail $9.00/$12.50
Featured on J&D Christmas wrapping paper, as was E-0513.

Personal Data: _____
____Want Mark ____ Mark _____ Purch. 19__ Pd $ _____

E-2344   **Candle Climbers**
         Angel with Trumpet, pair

"Joy To The World"

SUSP. 1985 - 12 YEARS AGO

NM	$125	HG	$100	C	$100
T	$105	F	$100	D	$100

Comments: 1981; Original Retail $20.00/$22.50
Candle Climbers are no longer in production; only two styles were produced (E-2344, E-6118). Not easy to find.

Personal Data: _____
____Want Mark ____ Mark _____ Purch. 19__ Pd $ _____

E-2345   **Boy in Pajamas with Teddy**

"May Your Christmas Be Cozy"

SUSP. 1984 - 13 YEARS AGO   HG $90
                                      F $80
                                        C $75

Comments: 1982; Original Retail $23.00/$30.00
Collector wrote to say her piece had an OB mark! Unusual! Only produced for three years. Somewhat scarce!

Personal Data: _____
____Want Mark ____ Mark _____ Purch. 19__ Pd $ _____

E-2346♪   ***MUSICAL* – Angel with Animals Caroling**

"Let Heaven And Nature Sing"

SUSP. 1989 - 8 YEARS AGO

MM	$190	D	$142	BA	$130
HG	$170	OB	$142		
F	$150	CT	$135		
C	$150	FL	$130		

Comments: 1982; Original Retail $50.00/$75.00
Quite limited, especially in 1982; HG mark. Plays *Joy To The World*. Becoming hard to find.

Personal Data: _____
____Want Mark ____ Mark _____ Purch. 19__ Pd $ _____

E-2347 PLATE – Angel with Animals Caroling
"Let Heaven And Nature Sing"

LE 15,000

MM	$50	D	$45
C	$45	OB	$40

Comments: 1982; Original Retail $40.00/$45.00
Second issue of the *Christmas Collection Series*. An edition of 4,000 would have been considered more limited.

Personal Data: _____
____Want Mark ____ Mark _____ Purch. 19__ Pd $ _____

E-2348 Boy by Pot Belly Stove
"May Your Christmas Be Warm"

SUSP. 1988 - 9 YEARS AGO

HG	$145	OB	$115
F	$130	CT	$110
C	$120	FL	$110
D	$115		

Comments: 1982; Original Retail $30.00/$38.50
HG scarce, first production year. HG seems to be the coveted piece. Popular piece! Becoming hard to find.

Personal Data: _____
____Want Mark ____ Mark _____ Purch. 19__ Pd $ _____

E-2349 Girl by Christmas Tree/Doll and Book
"Tell Me The Story Of Jesus"

SUSP. 1985 - 12 YEARS AGO

HG	$120	C	$110
F	$115	D	$105

Comments: 1982; Original Retail $30.00/$33.00
Produced as an Ornament in 1983 (E-0533). Figurine was scarce in 1982; first production year. Very attractive piece! Not easily found.

Personal Data: _____
____Want Mark ____ Mark _____ Purch. 19__ Pd $ _____

E-2350 Boy Ice Skating
"Dropping In For Christmas"

SUSP. 1984 - 13 YEARS AGO

HG	$80	F	$70	C	$65

Comments: 1982; Original Retail $18.00

Personal Data: _____
____Want Mark ____ Mark _____ Purch. 19__ Pd $ _____

E-2351 Two Angels with Candles
"Holy Smokes"

RETIRED 1987 - 10 YEARS AGO

MM	$150	D	$110
HG	$135	OB	$100
F	$125	CT	$100
C	$115		

Comments: 1982; Original Retail $27.00/$33.50
Several found w/MM error.

Personal Data: _____
____Want Mark ____ Mark _____ Purch. 19__ Pd $ _____

E-2352 ♪ MUSICAL – Boy Caroling/Lamp Post
"O Come All Ye Faithful"

SUSP. 1984 - 13 YEARS AGO

MM	$175	F	$130
HG	$145	C	$130

Comments: 1982; Original Retail $45.00/$50.00
Plays *O Come All Ye Faithful.*

Personal Data: _____
____Want Mark ____ Mark _____ Purch. 19__ Pd $ _____

E-2353 Boy Caroling/Lamp Post
"O Come All Ye Faithful"

RETIRED 1986 - 11 YEARS AGO

HG	$100	D	$75
F	$90	OB	$75
C	$85		

Comments: 1982; Original Retail $27.50/$30.00
Attractive piece! HG mark is somewhat hard to find on the secondary market. Seemed to be several more sales on HG reported compared to previous years.

Personal Data: _____
____Want Mark ____ Mark _____ Purch. 19__ Pd $ _____

E-2355 ♪ MUSICAL – Drummer Boy at Manger
"I'll Play My Drum For Him"

SUSP. 1984 - 13 YEARS AGO

HG	$200	C	$185	F	$175

Comments: 1982; Original Retail $45.00/$50.00
Plays *Little Drummer Boy.* Scarce in 1982 as was the figurine E-2356. Scarce because it was only produced 2½ years! Attractive and nice to own!

Personal Data: _____
____Want Mark ____ Mark _____ Purch. 19__ Pd $ _____

E-2356　Drummer Boy at Manger
"I'll Play My Drum For Him"

SUSP. 1985 - 12 YEARS AGO　HG　$125　　　C　$90
　　　　　　　　　　　　　　　F　$100　　　D　$90

Comments:　1982; Original Retail $30.00/$33.00
HG mark is scarce. This is a beautiful piece! Produced for a short period of time. It's my opinion that this is an avid collector's "must have."

Personal Data: _____
____Want Mark ____ Mark _____ Purch. 19__ Pd $ _____

E-2357　*PLATE* – Drummer Boy at Manger
"I'll Play My Drum For Him"

DATED 1982　　　　　　NM　$50-55

Comments:　1982; Original Retail $40.00
First Issue in *Joy Of Christmas Series.* First dated plate. Seek out ads to locate, easily found. NM is correct - plate was not intended to have a mark. Sorry to report... plates are not sought after and prices not going up. Easily found at original retail to $50.

Personal Data: _____
____Want Mark ____ Mark _____ Purch. 19__ Pd $ _____

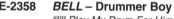

E-2358　*BELL* – Drummer Boy
"I'll Play My Drum For Him"

DATED 1982　　　　　　NM　$60-65

Comments:　1982; Original Retail $17.00
None had the date on them as appeared in the picture on the box. The last dated bell of this style (figurine was handle of bell) was offered in '93. A dated '94 bell (different look) was also produced. Many prices found below last year's average of $70.

Personal Data: _____
____Want Mark ____ Mark _____ Purch. 19__ Pd $ _____

E-2359　*ORNAMENT* – Drummer Boy
"I'll Play My Drum For Him"

DATED 1982　　　　　　HG　$100

Comments:　1982; Original Retail $9.00
Closed Edition. 1982 was printed on the ornament's drum. Several "no dates" were found; add $50 above secondary market price listed. One MM has been reported.

Personal Data: _____
____Want Mark ____ Mark _____ Purch. 19__ Pd $ _____

E-2360　*NATIVITY* – Drummer Boy
"I'll Play My Drum For Him"

HG	$50	CT	$35	GC	$28	SRD $25
F	$45	FL	$30	B	$25	
C	$38	BA	$30	TRP	$25	
D	$35	FLM	$30	S	$25	
OB	$35	V	$28	H	$25	

Comments:　1982; Original Retail $16.00/$25.00
An addition to the Nativity Set. Too similar in size to the ornament and the secondary market was affected for several years because of this. Collectors complaints immediately caused future look alike productions to be changed. Excellent candidate for retirement or suspension.

Personal Data: _____
____Want Mark ____ Mark _____ Purch. 19__ Pd $ _____

E-2361　Girl with Stocking
"Christmas Joy From Head To Toe"

SUSP. 1986 - 11 YEARS AGO
　　　　　　　HG　$90　　　D　$70
　　　　　　　F　$85　　　OB　$70
　　　　　　　C　$75

Comments:　1982; Original Retail $25.00/$27.50
Somewhat scarce with HG mark. Most Christmas pieces were somewhat hard to find compared to 1983-1985 Christmas pieces. We received one report that the dog's nose was not painted. Arf!

Personal Data: _____
____Want Mark ____ Mark _____ Purch. 19__ Pd $ _____

E-2362　*ORNAMENT* – Baby in Stocking
"Baby's First Christmas" written on back

SUSP. 1988 - 9 YEARS AGO
Boy w/Bow - Straight hair w/caption　　MM　$65
Boy in Stocking - Straight hair & no caption　MM　$75
Girl in Stocking - Curly hair & no caption　MM　$45
Girl in Stocking - Curly hair w/caption

MM	$55	D	$35	CT	$30
C	$35	OB	$35	FL	$30

Comments:　1982; Original Retail $9.00/$12.50
First pieces - no print on side. Beginning with March 1983, "Baby's First Christmas" printed on some. There are two different heads, one with straight hair, and one with curly hair. (Picture on box shows with straight hair.) Straight hair looks masculine except for bow. Appeared on earlier piece. *Original ornament looked masculine so it's been called Boy. Curly-haired pieces look feminine. Trading not as evident as back in 80s when the "change" was made and being talked about.

Personal Data: _____
____Want Mark ____ Mark _____ Purch. 19__ Pd $ _____

E-2363 Camel

MM	$60	OB	$40	V	$35	H	$32.50
HG	$55	CT	$40	GC	$35	SRD	$32.50
F	$50	FL	$40	B	$35		
C	$45	BA	$35	TRP	$35		
D	$45	FLM	$35	S	$32.50		

Comments: 1982; Original Retail $20.00/$32.50
The MM was reported in '82.

Personal Data: _____
____Want Mark ____ Mark _____ Purch. 19__ Pd $ _____

E-2364 Goat

SUSP. 1989 - 8 YEARS AGO

MM	$70	C	$50	CT	$45
HG	$65	D	$50	FL	$45
F	$60	OB	$45	BA	$45

Comments: 1982; Original Retail $10.00/$15.00
The first pieces to debut were not marked. Should have had a mark.
The MM was reported in '82.

Personal Data: _____
____Want Mark ____ Mark _____ Purch. 19__ Pd $ _____

E-2365 Boy Angel with Candle
"The First Noel"

SUSP. 1984 - 13 YEARS AGO

MM	$75	F	$65
HG	$70	C	$60

Comments: 1982; Original Retail $16.00/$17.00
MM was an error reported in '82.

Personal Data: _____
____Want Mark ____ Mark _____ Purch. 19__ Pd $ _____

E-2366 Girl Angel in Bonnet Praying
"The First Noel"

SUSP. 1984 - 13 YEARS AGO

MM	$75	F	$65
HG	$70	C	$65

Comments: 1982; Original Retail $16.00/$17.00
MM was an error reported in '82. Sales slowed on this piece…

Personal Data: _____
____Want Mark ____ Mark _____ Purch. 19__ Pd $ _____

E-2367 *ORNAMENT* – Boy Angel with Candle
"The First Noel"

SUSP. 1984 - 13 YEARS AGO

MM	$75	F	$70
HG	$70	C	$70

Comments: 1982; Original Retail $9.00/$10.00
Several MM pieces reported in '82. Sales slow in past years. Do not
over insure.

Personal Data: _____
____Want Mark ____ Mark _____ Purch. 19__ Pd $ _____

E-2368 *ORNAMENT* – Girl Angel/Bonnet Praying
"The First Noel"

RETIRED 1984 - 13 YEARS AGO

HG	$75
F	$65
C	$55

Comments: 1982; Original Retail $9.00/$10.00
C marks easier to find.

Personal Data: _____
____Want Mark ____ Mark _____ Purch. 19__ Pd $ _____

E-2369 *ORNAMENT* – Boy Ice Skating
"Dropping In For Christmas"

RETIRED 1986 - 11 YEARS AGO

MM	$70	C	$50
HG	$65	D	$50
F	$60	OB	$45

Comments: 1982; Original Retail $9.00/$10.00
MM reported in '82. *See #39, page XV.*

Personal Data: _____
____Want Mark ____ Mark _____ Purch. 19__ Pd $ _____

E-2371 *ORNAMENT* – "Unicorn"

RETIRED 1988 - 9 YEARS AGO

MM	$60	D	$50
HG	$55	OB	$50
F	$55	CT	$45
C	$55	FL	$45

Comments: 1982; Original Retail $9.00/$13.00
Tended to be scarce before Retirement. Many "unicorn" collectors
purchased this ornament.

Personal Data: _____
____Want Mark ____ Mark _____ Purch. 19__ Pd $ _____

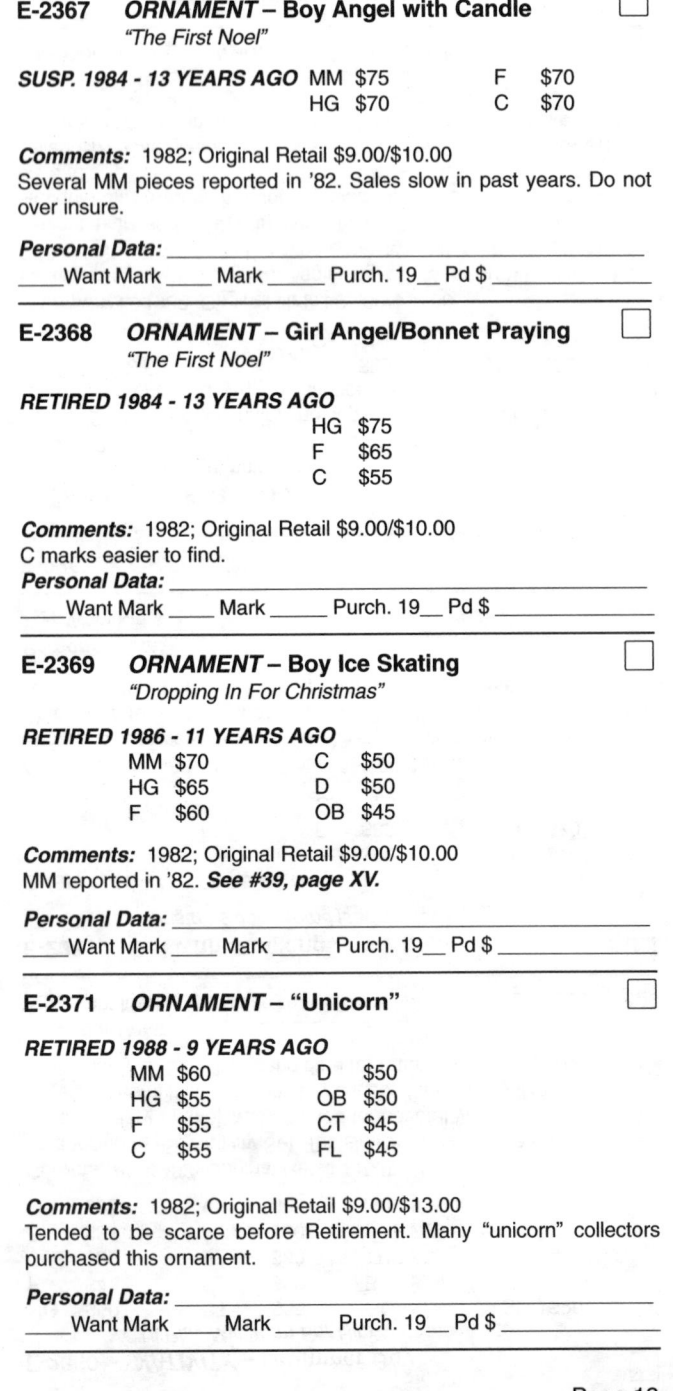

E-2372   ORNAMENT – Boy with Block
"Baby's First Christmas"

SUSP. 1985 - 12 YEARS AGO

	MM	$45	C	$40
Decaled	F	$70	D	$40
	HG	$45		

Comments: 1982; Original Retail $9.00/$10.00
First pieces came with no verse on back side. As of March, 1983 "Baby's First Christmas" was on the back side (same as E-2362 ornament). MM reported in '82. Remember NM and MM have two different meanings.

Personal Data: _____
____Want Mark ____ Mark _____ Purch. 19__ Pd $ _____

E-2374   Girl with Christmas Packages
"Bundles of Joy"

RETIRED 1993 - 4 YEARS AGO

HG	$125	OB	$85	FLM	$75
F	$100	CT	$85	V	$75
C	$95	FL	$85	GC	$75
D	$90	BA	$80	B	$75

Comments: 1982; Original Retail $27.50/$45.00
A similar ornament (525057) debuted in 11/90 as a special offering at Centers only (now called Distinguished Service Retailers).

Personal Data: _____
____Want Mark ____ Mark _____ Purch. 19__ Pd $ _____

E-2375   Girl with Pie
"Dropping Over For Christmas"

RETIRED 1991- 5 YEARS AGO

HG	$135	OB	$90	FLM	$75
F	$110	CT	$90	V	$70
C	$100	FL	$85		
D	$95	BA	$80		

Comments: 1982; Original Retail $30.00/45.00
Was not overly abundant in 1982. There is much demand for the first mark!

Personal Data: _____
____Want Mark ____ Mark _____ Purch. 19__ Pd $ _____

E-2376   ORNAMENT – Girl with Pie
"Dropping Over For Christmas"

RETIRED 1985 - 12 YEARS AGO

HG	$65	F	$55	C	$50	D	$45

Comments: 1982; Original Retail $9.00/$10.00
Personal Data: _____
____Want Mark ____ Mark _____ Purch. 19__ Pd $ _____

E-2377   Girl Knitting Tie for Boy
"Our First Christmas Together"

SUSP. 1985 - 12 YEARS AGO

HG	$110	C	$85
F	$95	D	$80

Comments: 1982; Original Retail $35.00/$37.50
Only produced for four years.

Personal Data: _____
____Want Mark ____ Mark _____ Purch. 19__ Pd $ _____

E-2378   PLATE – Girl Knitting Tie for Boy
"Our First Christmas Together"

SUSP. 1985 - 12 YEARS AGO

MM	$45	D	$35
C	$35		

Comments: 1982; Original Retail $30.00
Open Edition, smaller plate. Plates are not as collectible as figurines. Dated annual plates were produced through 1993. However, in 1994 two additional plates were produced... one for Mother's Day and one to benefit Child Evangelism Fellowship. Annual plates were also produced for Mother's Day in 1995 and 1996.

Personal Data: _____
____Want Mark ____ Mark _____ Purch. 19__ Pd $ _____

E-2381   ORNAMENT – Mouse with Cheese

SUSP. 1984 - 13 YEARS AGO

MM	$135		
HG	$125	F	$110
C	$110		

Comments: 1982; Original Retail $9.00
Scarce before Suspension. MM most sought after. Just try to find this li'l fella. He's scarce! MM reported in early '82.

Personal Data: _____
____Want Mark ____ Mark _____ Purch. 19__ Pd $ _____

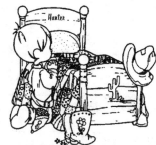

**Now I lay me down to sleep,
I pray the Lord my soul to keep...
Bless my Horse,
my Mom, my Papa and Gramma,
my dog Gus,
my friends Tara,
Linsey and Zak too.**

E-2385   ORNAMENT – Bride & Groom
"Our First Christmas Together"

SUSP. 1991 - 6 YEARS AGO

HG $60	OB $35	FLM $28	
F $45	CT $30	V $35	
C $42	FL $30		
D $40	BA $30		

Comments: 1982; Original Retail $9.00/$15.00

Personal Data: _____
____Want Mark ____ Mark ____ Purch. 19__ Pd $ _____

E-2386   ORNAMENT – Set of 3 Animals

SUSP. 1984 - 13 YEARS AGO

MM $110	F $85
HG $100	C $85

Comments: 1982; Original Retail $25.00/$27.50
Camel, Donkey and Cow. Frequently sets contain different marks on different pieces (ex. HG on one, T on another). ***See #38, page XV.*** MM occurred in '82.

Personal Data: _____
____Want Mark ____ Mark ____ Purch. 19__ Pd $ _____

E-2387   MINI NATIVITY – 3 Houses and Palm Tree – 4 pc. Set

HG $135	CT $100	GC $80	SRD $75
F $120	FL $90	B $80	
C $115	BA $80	TRP $75	
D $110	FLM $80	S $75	
OB $110	V $80	H $75	

Comments: 1982; Original Retail $45.00/$75.00
Very little trading found on this set. May be suspended in my opinion. Very seldom offered by retailers. Do not "over pay" on this set as it is still on the market and easily found.

Personal Data: _____
____Want Mark ____ Mark ____ Purch. 19__ Pd $ _____

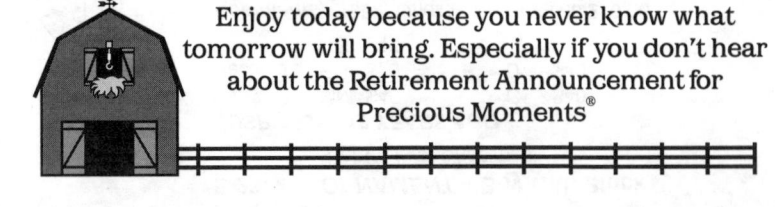

Enjoy today because you never know what tomorrow will bring. Especially if you don't hear about the Retirement Announcement for Precious Moments®

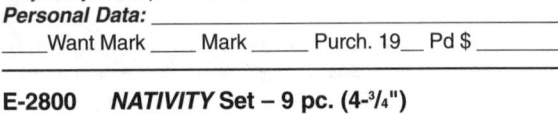

E-2395   MINI NATIVITY – 11 Piece, (3-¹/₂")
"Come Let Us Adore Him"
TURBAN BOY ALONE   HG $90
(Several dozen were replaced by dealers and sold separately from this set. We were the first to learn and report this information to the collectors.)

NM $175	OB $140	V $135	H $130
HG $165	CT $140	GC $130	SRD $130
F $150	FL $140	B $130	
C $150	BA $140	TRP $130	
D $140	FLM $140	S $130	

Comments: 1982; Original Retail $80.00/$130.00
Turban Boy figure replaced Boy Holding Lamb in approximately 5,000 sets. Identical to Ornament E-5630. There are no T marks because of very early 1981 production.

Personal Data: _____
____Want Mark ____ Mark ____ Purch. 19__ Pd $ _____

E-2800   NATIVITY Set – 9 pc. (4-³/₄")
"Come Let Us Adore Him"

NM $225	F $170
T $185	C $165
HG $175	D $160

Comments: 1979; Original Retail $70.00/$90.00
Re-sculpted, changed to #104000 (heads larger). Retailers report popular Christmas gift from husbands to wives. NM good mark to seek out for your collection. ***See #40, page XV.***

Personal Data: _____
____Want Mark ____ Mark ____ Purch. 19__ Pd $ _____

E-2801   Angels in Chariot
"Jesus Is Born"

SUSP. 1984 - 13 YEARS AGO	NM $375	F $320
	T $345	C $300
	HG $325	

Comments: 1979; Original Retail $37.00/$55.00
This piece tends to be scarce. Back in 1979 we thought $37 retail was high. Many collectors didn't purchase this piece for that reason.
See #13, page XII.

Personal Data: _____
____Want Mark ____ Mark ____ Purch. 19__ Pd $ _____

E-2802   Boy Giving Toy Lamb to Jesus
"Christmas Is A Time To Share"

SUSP. 1984 - 13 YEARS AGO	NM $115	F $80
	T $95	C $75
	HG $90	D $70

Comments: 1979; Original Retail $20.00/$27.50
D mark has been reported, but this must have been an oversight at the factory, as this piece was suspended in 1984. ***See #14, page XII.***

Personal Data: _____
____Want Mark ____ Mark ____ Purch. 19__ Pd $ _____

E-2803   Boy Kneeling at Manger/Crown
"Crown Him Lord Of All"

SUSP. 1984 - 13 YEARS AGO NM $120   F $85
                                 T $100   C $80
                                 HG $90   D $90

Comments: 1979; Original Retail $20.00/$27.50
D mark has been reported, but this must have been an oversight at the factory as this piece was suspended in 1984. Plentiful in '80.
See #14, page XII.
Personal Data: _____
____Want Mark ____ Mark _____ Purch. 19__ Pd $ _____

E-2804   Boy on Globe
"Peace On Earth"

SUSP. 1984 - 13 YEARS AGO NM $155   F $135
                                 T $150   C $130
                                 HG $135

Comments: 1979; Original Retail $20.00/$27.50
Somewhat scarce. This figurine saw slight increase from last year.
Personal Data: _____
____Want Mark ____ Mark _____ Purch. 19__ Pd $ _____

E-2805   Boy in Santa Cap/Dog
"Wishing You A Season Filled With Joy"

RETIRED 1985 - 12 YEARS AGO
              NM $130   F $95
              T $120   C $85
              HG $100   D $75

Comments: 1978; Original Retail $20.00/$27.50
Most D marks have two eyes painted on dog; all others have only one eye painted. Two eyes mainly appeared on the pieces produced for retirement in 1985.
Personal Data: _____
____Want Mark ____ Mark _____ Purch. 19__ Pd $ _____

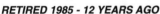

E-2806 ♪ *MUSICAL* – Boy Giving Toy Lamb to Jesus
"Christmas Is A Time To Share"

RETIRED 1984 - 13 YEARS AGO
              NM $185   F $165
              T $180   C $160
              HG $165

Comments: 1980; Original Retail $45.00/$50.00
Plays *Away In A Manger*. <u>Fewer T produced than NM.</u> A few reports of Musicals being defective. All have been quality produced. Fewer collectors of musicals than figurines. This is a popular piece, especially the T and NM. On figurine the box is closer to manger. This is just the difference between line art and actual figurine produced.
Personal Data: _____
____Want Mark ____ Mark _____ Purch. 19__ Pd $ _____

E-2807 ♪ *MUSICAL* – Boy Kneeling Manger/Crown
"Crown Him Lord Of All"

SUSP. 1984 - 13 YEARS AGO NM $140   F $110
                                 T $125   C $100
                                 HG $120

Comments: 1980; Original Retail $45.00/$50.00
Plays *O Come All Ye Faithful*. Most earlier musicals appeared as figurines also. The most sought after musical is the *Silent Knight,* mainly because there was no similar figurine produced.
Personal Data: _____
____Want Mark ____ Mark _____ Purch. 19__ Pd $ _____

E-2808 ♪ *MUSICAL* – Boy and Girl Reading Book
"Unto Us A Child Is Born"

SUSP. 1984 - 13 YEARS AGO
       NM $145   HG $120   C $115
       T $130   F $115

Comments: 1980; Original Retail $45.00/$50.00
Plays *Jesus Loves Me*. Very colorful the first year; not easily found anymore...
Personal Data: _____
____Want Mark ____ Mark _____ Purch. 19__ Pd $ _____

E-2809 ♪ *MUSICAL* – Boy and Girl in School Play
"Jesus Is Born"

SUSP. 1985 - 12 YEARS AGO
       NM $155   HG $145   C $130
       T $145   F $130   D $130

Comments: 1980; Original Retail $45.00/$50.00
Plays *Hark, The Herald Angels Sing*. The T and NM are colorful! Very little trading found, becoming scarcer.
Personal Data: _____
____Want Mark ____ Mark _____ Purch. 19__ Pd $ _____

E-2810 ♪ *MUSICAL* – *NATIVITY*
"Come Let Us Adore Him"

SUSP. 1993 - 4 YEARS AGO

NM	$175	C	$130	FL	$125	GC	$125
T	$160	D	$130	BA	$125	B	$125
HG	$150	OB	$130	FLM	$125		
F	$145	CT	$130	V	$125		

Comments: 1979; Original Retail $60.00/$100
Plays *Joy To The World*. NM and T preferred by collectors of musicals. These marks are coming into much demand. When a piece has been produced for 10-13 years, the secondary market is usually trading the first few marks only. Notice Original Retail went to $100.
Personal Data: _____
____Want Mark ____ Mark _____ Purch. 19__ Pd $ _____

E-2821 Girl with String of Hearts
"You Have Touched So Many Hearts"

SUSP. 1996 - 1 YEAR AGO

F	$70	FL	$42	B	$42	C	$65
BA	$42	TRP	$42	D	$47	FLM	$42
S	$40	OB	$47	V	$42	H	$37.50
CT	$45	GC	$42				

Comments: 1982; Original Retail $25.00/$37.50
Reissued in 1990 for Easter Seals as 9" piece under dome (523283). She was also produced in 1992 with a set of letters to personalize the hearts which did not sell as well because the letters did not adhere to the hearts as planned. Visitors to the Factory in Nagoya have painted their own Girl with Hearts. (The eyes were painted for us. ☺) Mine is purple and yellow! See #523283. Many sales found on this piece; older marks.

Personal Data: _____

____Want Mark ____ Mark _____ Purch. 19__ Pd $ _____

E-2822 Girl Polishing Table
"This Is Your Day To Shine"

RETIRED 1988 - 9 YEARS AGO

C	$120	CT	$95
D	$110	FL	$95
OB	$100		

Comments: 1983; Original Retail $37.50/$40.00
Has been found with the word "Polish" missing from the bottle. Add $50 for this error. Only one report of F mark; seller had it priced at $155 several years ago. Add $100 to the C mark if you have an F mark.
See #15, page XIII.

Personal Data: _____

____Want Mark ____ Mark _____ Purch. 19__ Pd $ _____

E-2823 Boy Holding Empty Frame
"To God Be The Glory"

SUSP. 1987 - 10 YEARS AGO

F	$138	OB	$90
C	$90	CT	$85
D	$90	Decaled C	$235

Comments: 1983; Original Retail $40.00/$45.00
Was to be produced in 1983 but production problems occurred. Style number was originally E-0529 with retail price $23. Sam's favorite piece. Sam designed this piece in his recognition to the Lord for his "gift" of creating Precious Moments®. He acknowledges his works cannot be compared to God's. God receives the glory for Sam's gift. A very unusual and delicate piece. This is a very special piece to have in your collection. Reported with Decaled C; add $100 to the secondary market value if you have a Decaled C. From C to CT prices down slightly.
See #37, page XV.

Personal Data: _____

____Want Mark ____ Mark _____ Purch. 19__ Pd $ _____

E-2824 Girl Dressing in Mom's Clothes
"To A Very Special Mom"

C	$60	FL	$50	GC	$40	H	$40
D	$55	BA	$45	B	$40	SRD	$40
OB	$50	FLM	$40	TRP	$40		
CT	$50	V	$45	S	$40		

Comments: 1983; Original Retail $27.50/$40.00
No air hole in base (air hole is under the hat). Hat added. Several collectors have informed us that their pieces have two holes in the base. Unusual! This is a very attractive piece! Time consuming to produce. May be suspended or retired in the near future.

Personal Data: _____

____Want Mark ____ Mark _____ Purch. 19__ Pd $ _____

E-2825 Girl Fixing Sister's Hair
"To A Very Special Sister"

C	$75	FL	$58	GC	$55	H	$50
D	$60	BA	$58	B	$50	SRD	$50
OB	$60	FLM	$58	TRP	$50		
CT	$58	V	$55	S	$50		

Comments: 1983; Original Retail $37.50/$50.00
Excellent "gift" item. Produced for 14 years, good suspension candidate.

Personal Data: _____

____Want Mark ____ Mark _____ Purch. 19__ Pd $ _____

E-2826 Girl at Table with Dolls
"May Your Birthday Be A Blessing"

SUSP. 1986 - 11 YEARS AGO

F	$125	D	$95
C	$95	OB	$80

Comments: 1983; Original Retail $37.50
Has been found with brown eyes. Cute piece! Only produced for four years; note the difference in prices compared to one produced 8 or 10 years. Supply and demand! Retail would be approx. $40-45 if still in production. C mark most traded for the past 3 years. ***See #4, page XI.***

Personal Data: _____

____Want Mark ____ Mark _____ Purch. 19__ Pd $ _____

E-2827 Girl with Bucket on Head with Cow
"I Get A Kick Out Of You"

SUSP. 1986 - 11 YEARS AGO

F	$200	D	$170
C	$185	OB	$170

Comments: 1983; Original Retail $50.00
Classified as humor category but believe me, when I was a kid it wasn't funny when the ole' cow kicked over the bucket! Becoming more scarce on secondary market as it has been eleven years since it was suspended. Not much trading found in the last year on this piece. This piece has been reported with C mark and the mice on the cows back don't have their eyes painted. Add $50 to the secondary market value for this error.

Personal Data: _____

____Want Mark ____ Mark _____ Purch. 19__ Pd $ _____

E-2828　Girl at Trunk with Wedding Gown
"Precious Memories"

F	$150	FL	$75	B	$70
C	$85	BA	$75	TRP	$70
D	$75	FLM	$75	S	$68
OB	$75	V	$70	H	$65
CT	$75	GC	$70	SRD	$65

Comments: 1983; Original Retail $45.00/$65.00
Very few Fish marks, but have had confirmation from several collectors that they have one or have seen one. Because of the scarcity of F marks be sure to insure at $150. May be able to purchase for a little less. Good candidate for suspension due to retail price for gift giving.

Personal Data: _____
____Want Mark ____ Mark _____ Purch. 19__ Pd $ _____

E-2829　Girl at Mail Box
"I'm Sending You A White Christmas"

C	$90	FL	$65	GC	$55	H	$55
D	$75	BA	$60	B	$55	SRD	$55
OB	$70	FLM	$60	TRP	$55		
CT	$65	V	$60	S	$55		

Comments: 1984; Original Retail $37.50/$55.00
Sam designed this piece to remember his mother wanting to "mail" snowballs to her relatives in Florida when she was a little girl. This piece is displayed separately in a special case at the Chapel with a letter from Sam to his mother upon his graduation from high school. This design appeared on the 1991 crystal ornament. Musical (112402) retired in 1993. Old enough to be suspended or retired. Production costs went up 10% in 1995. Time for a retirement.

Personal Data: _____
____Want Mark ____ Mark _____ Purch. 19__ Pd $ _____

E-2831　Bridesmaid
"No Flower Is As Sweet As You"

C	$40	FL	$28	GC	$25	H	$25
D	$32	BA	$28	B	$25	SRD	$25
OB	$30	FLM	$28	TRP	$25		
CT	$30	V	$28	S	$25		

Comments: 1983; Original Retail $13.00/$25.00
First issue of *Bridal Party Series*. Often purchased by brides for bridesmaids' gifts. Definite gift item.

Personal Data: _____
____Want Mark ____ Mark _____ Purch. 19__ Pd $ _____

Have you heard Sam has designed a special piece with Jesus and the little children? When Sam feels the facial features of Jesus are perfected to what he wants, then this piece will go into production. I foresee it as one of the most popular pieces in this line if it is affordable to everyone besides the avid collector. Also look for a new Salvation Army figurine to help raise money for this organization. Probably will be in Salvation Army uniform with a bell, and perhaps a kettle!

E-2832　Bride with Flower Girl Holding Veil
"God Bless The Bride"

C	$65	FL	$58	GC	$50	H	$50
D	$65	BA	$55	B	$50	SRD	$50
OB	$60	FLM	$55	TRP	$50		
CT	$58	V	$55	S	$50		

Comments: 1983; Original Retail $35.00/$50.00
Most Wedding Party pieces are not being sought after except for first marks as they are abundant and produced for the gift market. A new bride and groom figurine debuted in '95.

Personal Data: _____
____Want Mark ____ Mark _____ Purch. 19__ Pd $ _____

E-2833　Ring Bearer

C	$35	FL	$20	GC	$17.50	H	$17.50
D	$30	BA	$20	B	$17.50	SRD	$17.50
OB	$25	FLM	$20	TRP	$17.50		
CT	$25	V	$20	S	$17.50		

Comments: 1984; Original Retail $11.00/$17.50
Fourth issue of *Bridal Party Series*.

Personal Data: _____
____Want Mark ____ Mark _____ Purch. 19__ Pd $ _____

E-2834　Bridesmaid with Kitten
"Sharing Our Joy Together"

SUSP. 1991 - 6 YEARS AGO

OB	$70	FL	$65	FLM	$50
CT	$65	BA	$55	V	$48

Comments: 1986; Original Retail $31.00/$40.00

Personal Data: _____
____Want Mark ____ Mark _____ Purch. 19__ Pd $ _____

E-2835　Flower Girl

C	$45	FL	$17.50	GC	$17.50	H	$17.50
D	$35	BA	$17.50	B	$17.50	SRD	$17.50
OB	$30	FLM	$17.50	TRP	$17.50		
CT	$25	V	$17.50	S	$17.50		

Comments: 1984; Original Retail $11.00/$17.50
Third issue of *Bridal Party Series*. Small amount of trading reported on this piece. Tends to be true for most all pieces produced seven years or more. Secondary market prices do not rise on more current pieces when in continuous production for more than 5 or 6 years. Wedding pieces are not being traded abundantly. This piece is mainly bought retail for a gift. C mark is scarce.

Personal Data: _____
____Want Mark ____ Mark _____ Purch. 19__ Pd $ _____

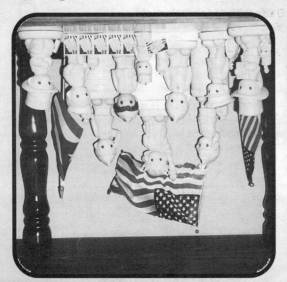

PRECIOUS MOMENTS® COLLECTIONS

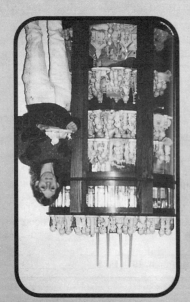

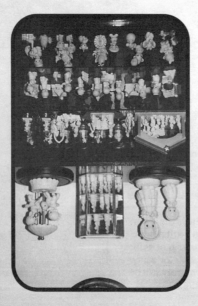

E-2836 Groomsman with Frog
"Best Man"

C $35	FL $30	GC $25	H $25
D $38	BA $30	B $25	SRD $25
OB $35	FLM $30	TRP $25	
CT $35	V $30	S $25	

Comments: 1983; Original Retail $13.50/$25.00
Second issue of *Bridal Party Series*. "First mark" only mark sought after on secondary market for *Bridal Party Series* pieces. C mark down $5 from last year.

Personal Data: _____
____Want Mark ____ Mark _____ Purch. 19__ Pd $ _____

E-2837 Groom

No Hands	OB $50	CT $45-48	
W/Hands	OB $40	FLM $25	TRP $25
	CT $35	V $25	S $25
	FL $28	GC $25	H $25
	BA $28	B $25	SRD $25

Comments: 1986; Original Retail $15.00/$25.00
Sixth issue of *Bridal Party Series*. Groom had no hands on earlier pieces. We called Sam's office first to tell him and he said it would be changed. There were many "no hands" produced. Fewer hands in OB than other marks.

Personal Data: _____
____Want Mark ____ Mark _____ Purch. 19__ Pd $ _____

E-2838 Wedding Party
"This Is The Day Which The Lord Hath Made"

LE 1987 - 10 YEARS OLD	CT	$210

Comments: 1987; Original Retail $175.00/$185.00
1987 Limited Edition, Wedding Party Group. "Large pieces" seldom rise on secondary market as quickly as most lower-priced figurines. Sad to report, but research found selling prices below original retail in 1994 and 1995. A beautiful piece!

Personal Data: _____
____Want Mark ____ Mark _____ Purch. 19__ Pd $ _____

E-2840 Angel Helping Baby Walk
"Baby's First Step"

SUSP. 1988 - 9 YEARS AGO	C	$100	CT	$90
	D	$98	FL	$90
	OB	$90		

Comments: 1982; Original Retail $35.00/$40.00
First issue of *Baby's First Series*. In my opinion this series has become more popular due to the fact that the market was not flooded. Supply and demand!

Personal Data: _____
____Want Mark ____ Mark _____ Purch. 19__ Pd $ _____

E-2841 Baby Posing for Picture
"Baby's First Picture"

RETIRED 1986 - 11 YEARS AGO

C $185	OB $160	
D $165		

Comments: 1983; Original Retail $45.00
Second issue of *Baby's First Series*. C mark seems to be the most traded. Has not reached the $150 mark to date, but the *Baby's First Series* figurines are very popular!

Personal Data: _____
____Want Mark ____ Mark _____ Purch. 19__ Pd $ _____

E-2845 Junior Bridesmaid

OB $32	FLM $27	TRP $22.50
CT $32	V $22.50	S $22.50
FL $27	GC $22.50	H $22.50
BA $27	B $22.50	SRD $22.50

Comments: 1983; Original Retail $12.50/$22.50
Fifth issue in *Bridal Party Series*. Very little trading on this piece. Retail price increased in '96.

Personal Data: _____
____Want Mark ____ Mark _____ Purch. 19__ Pd $ _____

E-2846 Bride

OB $45	FLM $30	TRP $25
CT $40	V $25	S $25
FL $35	GC $25	H $25
BA $35	B $25	SRD $25

Comments: 1983; Original Retail $18.00/$25.00
Seventh issue in *Bridal Party Series*. Some line art provided by Enesco occasionally differs from the figurine later produced. The figurine produced does not include a kitten as shown in line cut.

Personal Data: _____
____Want Mark ____ Mark _____ Purch. 19__ Pd $ _____

E-2847 PLATE – Boy/Girl on Swing
"Love Is Kind"

LE 15,000	MM	$50	C	$40
	F	$45		

Comments: 1983; Original Retail $40.00
Limited to 15,000 pieces. Fourth issue of *Inspired Thoughts Series*. Secondary market demand is very "slow" on plates. May find for much less. An ideal place for your plates is in a plate display case with a ledge; put the matching figurine next to the plate.

Personal Data: _____
____Want Mark ____ Mark _____ Purch. 19__ Pd $ _____

E-2848　*PLATE* – Mother Wrapping Bread
"Loving Thy Neighbor"

LE 15,000
　　　　C　$40

Comments: 1983; Original Retail $40.00
Limited Edition 15,000. First plate with embossed mark.
Fourth (final) issue of *Mother's Love Series*.
Personal Data: _____
____Want Mark ____ Mark _____ Purch. 19__ Pd $ _____

E-2850　*DOLL* – Mother with Needlepoint
"Mother Sew Dear"

RETIRED 1985 - 12 YEARS AGO
　　　　MM $350　　　D　$275
　　　　C　$300

Comments: 1983; Original Retail $350.00
Collectors felt this doll was "overpriced at retail." She was sold to
retailers later for $50 if they would use her in a promotional event as
a door prize, etc.
Personal Data: _____
____Want Mark ____ Mark _____ Purch. 19__ Pd $ _____

E-2851　*DOLL* – 12" Girl Doll
"Kristy"

SUSP. 1989 - 8 YEARS AGO　C　$180　　CT　$170
　　　　　　　　　　　　　　D　$175　　FL　$170
　　　　　　　　　　　　　　OB　$170　　BA　$170

Comments: 1983; Original Retail $150/$170
Dolls have not increased on the secondary market as have the figurines.
Personal Data: _____
____Want Mark ____ Mark _____ Purch. 19__ Pd $ _____

E-2852　Baby Assortment Set (6 styles)
"Baby Figurines"

E-2852A	Boy Standing	E-2852D	Girl Clapping Hands
E-2852B	Girl Standing	E-2852E	Boy Crawling
E-2852C	Boy Sitting	E-2852F	Girl Lying Down

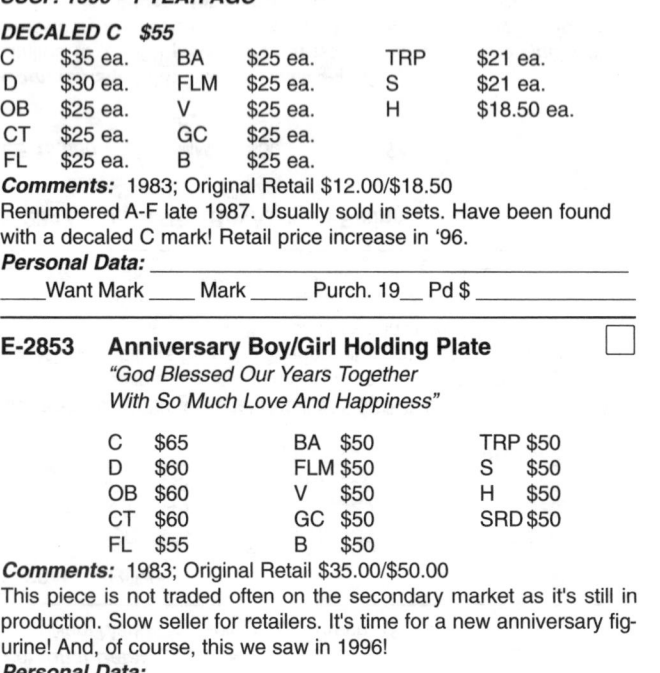

SUSP. 1996 - 1 YEAR AGO

DECALED C $55

C	$35 ea.	BA	$25 ea.	TRP	$21 ea.
D	$30 ea.	FLM	$25 ea.	S	$21 ea.
OB	$25 ea.	V	$25 ea.	H	$18.50 ea.
CT	$25 ea.	GC	$25 ea.		
FL	$25 ea.	B	$25 ea.		

Comments: 1983; Original Retail $12.00/$18.50
Renumbered A-F late 1987. Usually sold in sets. Have been found
with a decaled C mark! Retail price increase in '96.
Personal Data: _____
____Want Mark ____ Mark _____ Purch. 19__ Pd $ _____

E-2853　Anniversary Boy/Girl Holding Plate
"God Blessed Our Years Together
With So Much Love And Happiness"

C	$65	BA	$50	TRP	$50
D	$60	FLM	$50	S	$50
OB	$60	V	$50	H	$50
CT	$60	GC	$50	SRD	$50
FL	$55	B	$50		

Comments: 1983; Original Retail $35.00/$50.00
This piece is not traded often on the secondary market as it's still in
production. Slow seller for retailers. It's time for a new anniversary fig-
urine! And, of course, this we saw in 1996!
Personal Data: _____
____Want Mark ____ Mark _____ Purch. 19__ Pd $ _____

E-2854　1st Anniversary Figurine
"God Blessed Our Year Together
With So Much Love And Happiness"

1st Anniversary Fig. "Years" error
C	$75	D	$72	TRP	$70

1st Anniversary Fig. "Year" correction
C	$65	BA	$50	TRP	$50
D	$55	FLM	$50	S	$50
OB	$55	V	$50	H	$50
CT	$55	GC	$50	SRD	$50
FL	$55	B	$50		

Comments: 1984; Original Retail $35.00/$50.00
Happy Anniversary Series. First figurines changed from "Years" to
"Year." Has been found with TRP having the error "Years." Unusual!
Have you seen one?
Personal Data: _____
____Want Mark ____ Mark _____ Purch. 19__ Pd $ _____

E-2855   5th Anniversary Figurine
"God Blessed Our Years Together
With So Much Love And Happiness"
SUSP. 1996 - 1 YEAR AGO

C	$60	FL	$55	GC	$50	H	$50
D	$60	BA	$55	B	$50		
OB	$55	FLM	$50	TRP	$50		
CT	$55	V	$50	S	$50		

Comments: 1984; Original Retail $35.00/$50.00
Happy Anniversary Series. In my opinion, not many sell. Should be a candidate for suspension.
Personal Data: _____
____Want Mark ____ Mark _____ Purch. 19__ Pd $ _____

E-2856   10th Anniversary Figurine
"God Blessed Our Years Together
With So Much Love And Happiness"
SUSP. 1996 - 1 YEAR AGO

HG	$65	CT	$65	V	$55	S	$50
C	$65	FL	$55	GC	$50	H	$50
D	$65	BA	$55	B	$50		
OB	$65	FLM	$55	TRP	$50		

Comments: 1984; Original Retail $35.00/$50.00
Happy Anniversary Series. This series not sought after on the secondary market.
Personal Data: _____
____Want Mark ____ Mark _____ Purch. 19__ Pd $ _____

E-2857   25th Anniversary Figurine
"God Blessed Our Years Together
With So Much Love And Happiness"

C	$55	FL	$50	GC	$50	H	$50
D	$55	BA	$50	B	$50	SRD	$50
OB	$55	FLM	$50	TRP	$50		
CT	$55	V	$50	S	$50		

Comments: 1984; Original Retail $35.00/$50.00
Happy Anniversary Series. Prices for C mainly for insurance value replacement costs. Very little trading on the anniversary figurines.
Personal Data: _____
____Want Mark ____ Mark _____ Purch. 19__ Pd $ _____

E-2859   40th Anniversary Figurine
"God Blessed Our Years Together
With So Much Love And Happiness"
SUSP. 1996 - 1 YEAR AGO

C	$65	FL	$50	GC	$50	H	$50
D	$60	BA	$50	B	$50		
OB	$55	FLM	$50	TRP	$50		
CT	$50	V	$50	S	$50		

Comments: 1984; Original Retail $35.00/$50.00
Happy Anniversary Series.
Personal Data: _____
____Want Mark ____ Mark _____ Purch. 19__ Pd $ _____

E-2860   50th Anniversary Figurine
"God Blessed Our Years Together
With So Much Love And Happiness"

C	$70	FL	$55	GC	$50	H	$50
D	$65	BA	$55	B	$50	SRD	$50
OB	$60	FLM	$55	TRP	$50		
CT	$60	V	$55	S	$50		

Comments: 1984; Original Retail $35.00/$50.00
Happy Anniversary Series. Not being traded frequently.
Personal Data: _____
____Want Mark ____ Mark _____ Purch. 19__ Pd $ _____

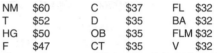

E-3104   Baby in Cradle with Bird
"Blessed Are The Pure In Heart"
SUSP. 1991 - 6 YEARS AGO

NM	$60	C	$37	FL	$32
T	$52	D	$35	BA	$32
HG	$50	OB	$35	FLM	$32
F	$47	CT	$35	V	$32

Comments: 1980; Original Retail $9.00/$19.00
Very plentiful with NM. An original J&D Licensee piece.
Personal Data: _____
____Want Mark ____ Mark _____ Purch. 19__ Pd $ _____

E-3105   Boy with Crutches
"He Watches Over Us All"
SUSP. 1984 - 13 YEARS AGO

NM	$105	HG	$85	D	$65	OB	$60
T	$95	F	$77	C	$60		

Comments: 1979; Original Retail $11.00/$17.00
This was an original J&D licensed figurine.
Personal Data: _____
____Want Mark ____ Mark _____ Purch. 19__ Pd $ _____

E-3106   Mother with Needlepoint
"Mother Sew Dear"

NM	$90	D	$40	FLM	$35	S	$32.50
T	$75	OB	$40	V	$32.50	H	$32.50
HG	$50	CT	$40	GC	$32.50	SRD	$32.50
F	$50	FL	$35	B	$32.50		
C	$40	BA	$35	TRP	$32.50		

Comments: 1979; Original Retail $13.00/$32.50
A plate has been produced with the same figure – *Mother's Love Series.* Doll with the same title was produced in 1984; retail $350. Many felt it was overpriced on retail. Retail price increased in '96. This was an original J&D licensed figurine.
Personal Data: _____
____Want Mark ____ Mark _____ Purch. 19__ Pd $ _____

E-3107 Boy Holding Cat/Dog
"Blessed Are The Peacemakers"

RETIRED 1985 - 12 YEARS AGO

NM	$130	HG	$95	C	$80
T	$110	F	$85	D	$75

Comments: 1979; Original Retail $13.00/$19.00
Becoming much sought after. Original J&D piece.
Personal Data: _____
____Want Mark _____ Mark _____ Purch. 19__ Pd $ _____

E-3108 Girl Rocking Cradle
"The Hand That Rocks The Future"

SUSP. 1984 -13 YEARS AGO

NM	$105	F	$75
T	$90	C	$75
HG	$85	GC	$150

Comments: 1979; Original Retail $13.00/$19.00
This piece was reportedly found with a GC mark in a Gold Crown Hallmark shop in Ohio. The collector who reported this information was aware that this piece had been suspended and said it definitely had a GC (1992) mark on it. This is not unusual – the same has been reported from time to time on other pieces.
Personal Data: _____
____Want Mark _____ Mark _____ Purch. 19__ Pd $ _____

E-3109 Grandma in Rocking Chair
"The Purr-fect Grandma"

NM	$90	D	$45	FLM	$32.50	S	$32.50
T	$85	OB	$40	V	$32.50	H	$32.50
HG	$55	CT	$35	GC	$32.50	SRD	$32.50
F	$50	FL	$35	B	$32.50		
C	$45	BA	$35	TRP	$32.50		

Comments: 1979; Original Retail $13.00/$32.50
NM and T are very colorful. It's time for a new Grandma! Retail price increase in '96.
Personal Data: _____
____Want Mark _____ Mark _____ Purch. 19__ Pd $ _____

E-3110B Boy on Bench/Lollipop
"Loving Is Sharing"

RETIRED 1993 - 4 YEARS AGO

NM	$145	C	$85	FL	$80	V	$75
T	$120	D	$80	BA	$80	GC	$75
HG	$100	OB	$80	FLM	$80	B	$75
F	$85	CT	$80				

Comments: 1979; Original Retail $13.00/$30.00
Not found abundantly after retirement.
Personal Data: _____
____Want Mark _____ Mark _____ Purch. 19__ Pd $ _____

E-3110G Girl on Bench/Lollipop
"Loving Is Sharing"

NM	$110	D	$35	FLM	$32.50	S	$32.50
T	$85	OB	$35	V	$32.50	H	$32.50
HG	$65	CT	$32.50	GC	$32.50	SRD	$32.50
F	$50	FL	$32.50	B	$32.50		
C	$40	BA	$32.50	TRP	$32.50		

Comments: 1979; Original Retail $13.00/$32.50
Because E-3110B was retired, many rushed to get this piece to "match" it. Good candidate for retirement or suspension. Error reported with no decal on book. Collector reported finding this with the dog missing and no evidence of it ever being there. Retail price up $2.50 in '96.
Personal Data: _____
____Want Mark _____ Mark _____ Purch. 19__ Pd $ _____

E-3111 Laundry Girl
"Be Not Weary In Well Doing"

RETIRED 1985 - 12 YEARS AGO

"And Well Doing" Verse Error Error NM $175

NM	$135	F	$95
T	$120	C	$90
HG	$105	D	$85

Comments: 1979; Original Retail $14.00/$19.00
Error on earlier pieces, "Be Not Weary 'and' Well Doing." Not many were produced.
Personal Data: _____
____Want Mark _____ Mark _____ Purch. 19__ Pd $ _____

E-3112 Boy Jogger
"God's Speed"

RETIRED 1983 - 14 YEARS AGO

NM	$115	HG	$80
T	$95	F	$55

Comments: 1979; Original Retail $14.00/$18.00
Seems to be more plentiful than other NM Retired pieces. Much trading reported on F mark as it was plentiful. No tag is found on dog's collar. Remember, line art can be slightly different from actual piece produced. This is due to production decisions made on final piece. When this piece was retired in '83 NMs were still easily found on retailers' shelves.
Personal Data: _____
____Want Mark _____ Mark _____ Purch. 19__ Pd $ _____

E-3113 Tracing in Sand
"Thou Art Mine"

NM	$95-100	OB	$50	GC	$45
T	$80	CT	$50	B	$45
HG	$65	FL	$50	TRP	$40
F	$60	BA	$45	S	$40
C	$55	FLM	$45	H	$40
D	$50	V	$45	SRD	$40

Comments: 1979; Original Retail $16.00/$40.00
Sixteen years in production. Look for Suspension or Retirement of this figurine. It is an original J&D piece. Very special. Be sure to have this one. The turtle has only one eye painted. This is not an error. The position of the turtle does not allow it to be seen easily, therefore no paint was needed. Suspension or Retirement candidate.

Personal Data: _____
____Want Mark ____ Mark _____ Purch. 19__ Pd $ _____

E-3114 Bride and Groom
"The Lord Bless You And Keep You"

NM	$90	OB	$50	GC	$50
T	$80	CT	$50	B	$50
HG	$70	FL	$50	TRP	$50
F	$55	BA	$50	S	$50
C	$55	FLM	$50	H	$50
D	$50	V	$50	SRD	$50

Comments: 1979; Original Retail $16.00/$50.00
Has been a popular wedding gift for cake toppers! Changed from original style around 1985 to larger heads. (The Samuel J. Butcher Company began in 1985.). Retail price increased in '95 and again in '96! Price down $5 in '97. **See #16, page XIII.**

Personal Data: _____
____Want Mark ____ Mark _____ Purch. 19__ Pd $ _____

E-3115 Boy/Girl on Cloud
"But Love Goes On Forever"

NM	$100	OB	$45	GC	$40
T	$80	CT	$45	B	$40
HG	$60	FL	$45	TRP	$40
F	$55	BA	$40	S	$40
C	$50	FLM	$40	H	$40
D	$45	V	$40	SRD	$40

Comments: 1979; Original Retail $16.50/$40.00
Enesco's logo piece for the collection.

Personal Data: _____
____Want Mark ____ Mark _____ Purch. 19__ Pd $ _____

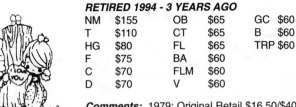

E-3116 Boy Carving Tree
"Thee I Love"

RETIRED 1994 - 3 YEARS AGO

NM	$155	OB	$65	GC	$60
T	$110	CT	$65	B	$60
HG	$80	FL	$65	TRP	$60
F	$75	BA	$60		
C	$70	FLM	$60		
D	$70	V	$60		

Comments: 1979; Original Retail $16.50/$40.00
Originals darkly colored, especially on girl's "red" patch. Long time favorite. NM hard to find! Many original J&D pieces are perfect candidates for suspension in order to relicense popular J&D sellers. NM or T is the avid collector's must.

Personal Data: _____
____Want Mark ____ Mark _____ Purch. 19__ Pd $ _____

E-3117 Boy/Girl Moving with Cart
"Walking By Faith"

NM	$125	OB	$80	GC	$75
T	$110	CT	$80	B	$75
HG	$100	FL	$80	TRP	$75
F	$95	BA	$75	S	$75
C	$80	FLM	$75	H	$75
D	$80	V	$75	SRD	$75

Comments: 1979; Original Retail $35.00/$75.00
"Holy Bible" omitted from Bible on some pieces. Add $75-$100 for that error on any mark. If retired or suspended, I feel NM and T will escalate in price over a three-year period after announcement. Higher priced pieces are generally suspended, not retired. Price down in '97 from '96 by $15!

Personal Data: _____
____Want Mark ____ Mark _____ Purch. 19__ Pd $ _____

E-3118 Girl and Frying Pan
"Eggs Over Easy"

RETIRED 1983 - 14 YEARS AGO

NM	$125	HG	$95
T	$110	F	$90

Comments: 1979; Original Retail $12.00/$15.00
Cute piece!! This is one of the first J&D pieces that did not have an inspirational name. We have heard from several collectors that the egg was missing from their pieces. Add $50 to the secondary market value if the egg is missing. Price remained steady from '96.

Personal Data: _____
____Want Mark ____ Mark _____ Purch. 19__ Pd $ _____

E-3119 Boy/Apple/Books
"It's What's Inside That Counts"

SUSP. 1984 - 13 YEARS AGO

NM	$130	F	$110
T	$125	C	$105
HG	$115		

Comments: 1979; Original Retail $13.00/$19.00
First pieces produced were very dark in color! Especially the apple!
Nice piece to own with NM or T because of their vivid color.

Personal Data: _____
____Want Mark _____ Mark _____ Purch. 19__ Pd $ _____

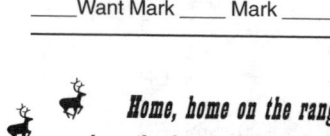

E-3120 Girl with Box of Kittens
"To Thee With Love"

SUSP. 1986 - 11 YEARS AGO

NM	$90	C	$70
T	$80	D	$65
HG	$70	OB	$65
F	$70		

Comments: 1979; Original Retail $13.00/$19.00
We have been told CT mark was produced and have seen ads selling
the CT mark for $80-90.

Personal Data: _____
____Want Mark _____ Mark _____ Purch. 19__ Pd $ _____

E-4720 Boy Graduate
"The Lord Bless You And Keep You"

SUSP. 1987 - 10 YEARS AGO

NM	$50	F	$40	OB	$35
T	$40	C	$35	CT	$35
HG	$40	D	$35		

Comments: 1980; Original Retail $14.00/$22.50
No Marks were abundant. Still remains many collectors' favorite "graduate" compared to current pieces. This piece has been found with a misspelling on the decal, which is located on the bottom of the figurine. "Bless" is spelled B-E-L-E-S-S. This was found with the CT. Add $35-$40 for this error. Notice the present retail for E-4721 Girl Graduate.

Personal Data: _____
____Want Mark _____ Mark _____ Purch. 19__ Pd $ _____

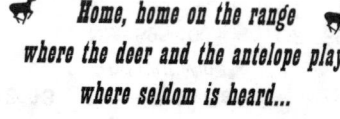

*Home, home on the range
where the deer and the antelope play,
where seldom is heard...*

E-4721 Girl Graduate
"The Lord Bless You And Keep You"

NM	$75	OB	$35	GC	$35
T	$55	CT	$35	B	$35
HG	$50	FL	$35	TRP	$35
F	$45	BA	$35	S	$35
C	$40	FLM	$35	H	$35
D	$35	V	$35	SRD	$35

Comments: 1979; Original Retail $14.00/$35.00
Retail price increased in 1995 and in 1996. Reported with a belt and no belt. Also reported with bird being same color as diploma and others with regular blue bird. Down slightly in '97.

Personal Data: _____
____Want Mark _____ Mark _____ Purch. 19__ Pd $ _____

E-4722 Girl/Piggy Bank
"Love Cannot Break A True Friendship"

SUSP. 1985 - 12 YEARS AGO

NM	$145	F	$115
T	$135	C	$115
HG	$118	D	$95

Comments: 1980; Original Retail $22.50/$27.50
NM becoming more scarce on secondary market. T mark even more so! Most collectors do not realize there are fewer T than other marks. T mark was produced only 6 months! Not easily found!

Personal Data: _____
____Want Mark _____ Mark _____ Purch. 19__ Pd $ _____

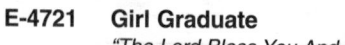

E-4723   Boy Selling Newspapers
"Peace Amid The Storm"

SUSP. 1984 - 13 YEARS AGO

NM	$105	F	$80
T	$90	C	$75
HG	$80		

Comments: 1980; Original Retail $22.50/$27.50
Sample piece had no bird on book as pictured in an earlier brochure.
Remember, often illustrations are not exactly as the figurine!

Personal Data: _____
____Want Mark ____ Mark _____ Purch. 19__ Pd $ _____

E-4724   Boy/Girl/Baby Christening
"Rejoicing With You"

No "E"	NM	$100	HG	$75	
	T	$75	F	$75	
With "E"	HG	$60	FL	$55	TRP $55
	F	$55	BA	$55	S $55
	C	$55	FLM	$55	H $55
	D	$55	V	$55	SRD $55
	OB	$55	GC	$55	
	CT	$55	B	$55	

Comments: 1980; Original Retail $25.00/$55.00
Girl's hand covers "E" of "Bible." Some found with "E" in 1982 -
most with "E" in 1983. Most found before 1983 with "Bibl" which was
correct as the original art had no "E." We have received one report
of this figurine being found with T mark with girl holding Holy "Byble."
This piece has been reported with the "Holy Bible" decal left off. Add
$100 to secondary market value for this find.

Personal Data: _____
____Want Mark ____ Mark _____ Purch. 19__ Pd $ _____

E-4725   Choir Boys
"Peace On Earth"

SUSP. 1984 - 13 YEARS AGO

NM	$105	F	$70
T	$85	C	$70
HG	$75		

Comments: 1980; Original Retail $25.00/$30.00
Appeared late 1981. Produced before marks began in mid 1981. "No
Marks" were plentiful even in 1982 and early 1983. Suspension is
bringing a rise to the secondary market since 1992. Original NM and T
pieces are very colorful!

Personal Data: _____
____Want Mark ____ Mark _____ Purch. 19__ Pd $ _____

E-4726 ♪ MUSICAL – Choir Boys
"Peace On Earth"

SUSP. 1984 - 13 YEARS AGO	NM	$145	F	$115
	T	$125	C	$115
	HG	$120		

Comments: 1980; Original Retail $45.00/$50.00
Plays *Jesus Loves Me.*
Personal Data: _____
____Want Mark ____ Mark _____ Purch. 19__ Pd $ _____

E-5200   Sad Boy/Teddy
"Bear Ye One Another's Burdens"

SUSP. 1984 -13 YEARS AGO	NM	$105	F	$80
	T	$90	C	$75
	HG	$85		

Comments: 1980; Original Retail $20.00/$25.00
Most 5200 series were produced early '81 having a No Mark. Triangle
marks appeared mid '81. Sample piece was smiling! (See Enesco's
1982/1983 brochure.) No report of collectors having a smiling piece.
See #7, page XII.
Personal Data: _____
____Want Mark ____ Mark _____ Purch. 19__ Pd $ _____

E-5201   Boy Helping Friend
"Love Lifted Me"

SUSP. 1984 - 13 YEARS AGO

NM	$110	F	$75
T	$100	C	$75
HG	$80		

Comments: 1980; Original Retail $22.50/$30.00
Personal Data: _____
____Want Mark ____ Mark _____ Purch. 19__ Pd $ _____

E-5202   Lemonade Stand
"Thank You For Coming To My Ade"

SUSP. 1984 - 13 YEARS AGO

NM	$155	F	$110
T	$130	C	$110
HG	$115		

Comments: 1980; Original Retail $22.50/$30.00
Very attractive piece. Almost a must for the avid collector to own!
Seldom seen at Swap Meets…
Personal Data: _____
____Want Mark ____ Mark _____ Purch. 19__ Pd $ _____

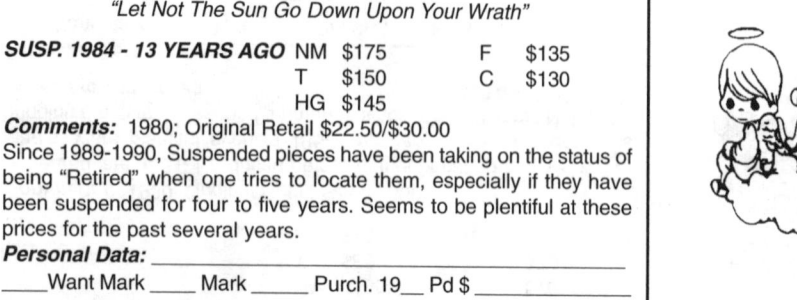

E-5203 Angry Boy and Dog on Stairs
"Let Not The Sun Go Down Upon Your Wrath"

SUSP. 1984 - 13 YEARS AGO

NM	$175	F	$135
T	$150	C	$130
HG	$145		

Comments: 1980; Original Retail $22.50/$30.00
Since 1989-1990, Suspended pieces have been taking on the status of being "Retired" when one tries to locate them, especially if they have been suspended for four to five years. Seems to be plentiful at these prices for the past several years.
Personal Data: _____

____Want Mark ____ Mark _____ Purch. 19__ Pd $ _____

E-5204 ♪ MUSICAL – Girl/Cradle
"The Hand That Rocks The Future"

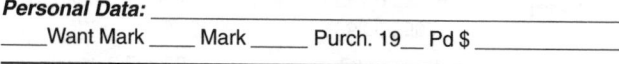
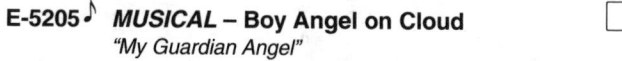

NM	$105	D	$75	FLM	$60	S	$60
T	$90	OB	$75	V	$60	H	$60
HG	$80	CT	$70	GC	$60	SRD	$60
F	$75	FL	$65	B	$60		
C	$75	BA	$65	TRP	$60		

Comments: 1981; Original Retail $30.00/$60.00
Plays *Mozart's Lullaby*. Very little trading taking place on this piece. No doubt because it's been on the shelves for seventeen years. Look for suspension or retirement. **See #21, page XIII.**
Personal Data: _____

____Want Mark ____ Mark _____ Purch. 19__ Pd $ _____

E-5205 ♪ MUSICAL – Boy Angel on Cloud
"My Guardian Angel"

SUSP. 1985 - 12 YEARS AGO

NM	$115	F	$90
T	$105	C	$90
HG	$95	D	$90

Comments: 1980; Original Retail $22.50/$27.50
Plays *Brahm's Lullaby*. Not easy to find. Would be excellent choice to bring back from suspension. **See #21, page XIII.**
Personal Data: _____

____Want Mark ____ Mark _____ Purch. 19__ Pd $ _____

E-5206 ♪ MUSICAL – Girl Angel on Cloud
"My Guardian Angel"

SUSP. 1988 - 9 YEARS AGO

NM	$120	F	$85	OB	$85
T	$95	C	$85	CT	$75
HG	$85	D	$85	FL	$75

Comments: 1980; Original Retail $27.50/$33.00
Plays *Brahm's Lullaby*. Girl's alway $5 higher than Boy.
Personal Data: _____

____Want Mark ____ Mark _____ Purch. 19__ Pd $ _____

E-5207 NIGHT LIGHT – Boy/Girl Angels Cloud
"My Guardian Angel"

SUSP. 1984 - 13 YEARS AGO

NM	$220	F	$145
T	$215	C	$145
HG	$160		

Comments: 1980; Original Retail $30.00/$37.50
This piece without the light was placed under a dome as a special gift to Centers from Enesco in 1982-83 (E-7350) with a plaque on a wooden base. NM and T most sought after. Centers were renamed DSR or Distinguished Service Retailer. More reported sales than in prverious years.

Personal Data: _____

____Want Mark ____ Mark _____ Purch. 19__ Pd $ _____

E-5208 BELL – Boy with Teddy
"Jesus Loves Me"

SUSP. 1985 - 12 YEARS AGO

MM	$55
C	$45
D	$45

Comments: 1980; Original Retail $15.00/$19.00
Most bells from early '80s through 1983 had no marks. Bells not often for sale in ads as in earlier years. Take on a challenge... collect the bisque bells! Probably more MMs than other two marks.
See #17, page XIII.

Personal Data: _____

____Want Mark ____ Mark _____ Purch. 19__ Pd $ _____

E-5209 BELL – Girl with Bunny
"Jesus Loves Me"

SUSP. 1985 - 12 YEARS AGO

MM	$60
C	$50
D	$48

Comments: 1980; Original Retail $15.00/$19.00
Most Bells unmarked. Production cut back on bells compared to early '80s. **See #17, page XIII.**

Personal Data: _____

____Want Mark ____ Mark _____ Purch. 19__ Pd $ _____

E-5210 BELL – Praying Girl
"Prayer Changes Things"

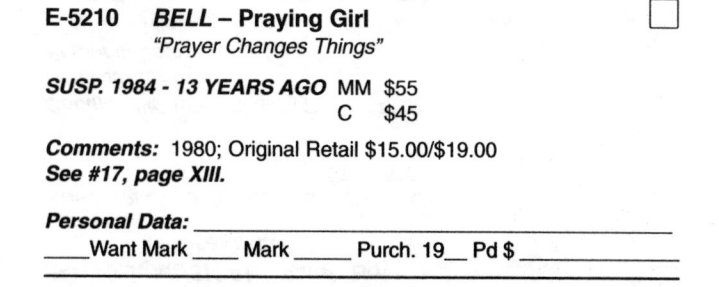

SUSP. 1984 - 13 YEARS AGO

MM	$55
C	$45

Comments: 1980; Original Retail $15.00/$19.00
See #17, page XIII.

Personal Data: _____

____Want Mark ____ Mark _____ Purch. 19__ Pd $ _____

E-5211 BELL – Boy with Report Card
"God Understands"

RETIRED 1984 - 13 YEARS AGO MM $50
C $40

Comments: 1980; Original Retail $15.00/$19.00
Most Bells unmarked. Popular bell as it was Retired, but sales down in '96. *See #17, page XIII.*
Personal Data: _____
____Want Mark ____ Mark _____ Purch. 19__ Pd $ _____

E-5212 Boy in Dad's Duds
"To A Special Dad"

NM	$80	D	$35	BA	$35	TRP	$35
T	$60	OB	$35	FLM	$35	S	$35
HG	$60	CT	$35	V	$35	H	$35
F	$45	CT	$35	GC	$35	SRD	$35
C	$40	FL	$35	B	$35		

Comments: 1980; Original Retail $20.00/$35.00
Similar to ornament in 1983. It would make an excellent piece to Retire or Suspend in '96 as it's been in production 18 years.
Personal Data: _____
____Want Mark ____ Mark _____ Purch. 19__ Pd $ _____

E-5213 Girl with Goose in Lap
"God Is Love"

SUSP. 1989 - 8 YEARS AGO

NM	$120	C	$55	FL	$55
T	$80	D	$55	BA	$50
HG	$70	OB	$55		
F	$65	CT	$55		

Comments: 1980; Original Retail $17.00/$30.00
Mold changed to larger head in 1985. Was a J&D production... now Samuel J. Butcher Co. licensed piece. Girl's face quite chubby on original pieces. Avid collectors should look for this piece with NM, T or HG.
Personal Data: _____
____Want Mark ____ Mark _____ Purch. 19__ Pd $ _____

E-5214 Boy/Girl Praying at Table
"Prayer Changes Things"

SUSP. 1984 - 13 YEARS AGO

NM	$175	F	$100
T	$160	C	$95
HG	$130	D	$95

Comments: 1980; Original Retail $35.00/$37.50
"Holy Bible" written on 1981 and 1982 pieces on back of book; corrected in 1983. First mention of the error appeared in *Precious Collectibles*® magazine.
Personal Data: _____
____Want Mark ____ Mark _____ Purch. 19__ Pd $ _____

E-5215 PLATE – Boy and Girl on Stump
"Love One Another"

LE 1981 - 16 YEARS OLD MM $50
F $38

Comments: 1980; Original Retail $20.00/$40.00
1981 Limited Edition 15,000. First Edition in *Inspired Thoughts Series.* Pretty plate! *See #1, page XI.*
Personal Data: _____
____Want Mark ____ Mark _____ Purch. 19__ Pd $ _____

E-5216 PLATE – Bride and Groom
"The Lord Bless You And Keep You"

SUSP. 1987 - 10 YEARS AGO MM $45 OB $40
C $40 CT $40
D $40

Comments: 1981; Original Retail $30.00/$37.50
Not a lot of trading. Sales drop considerably with no box.
Personal Data: _____
____Want Mark ____ Mark _____ Purch. 19__ Pd $ _____

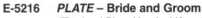

E-5217 PLATE – Mother with Needlepoint
"Mother Sew Dear"

LE 1981 - 16 YEARS OLD MM $45

Comments: 1980; Original Retail $40.00
1981 Limited Edition 15,000. First Edition of *Mother's Love Series.* Plates still not moving on the secondary market. Deals can be found...
Personal Data: _____
____Want Mark ____ Mark _____ Purch. 19__ Pd $ _____

E-5376 Girl Opening Gift
"May Your Christmas Be Blessed"

SUSP. 1986 - 11 YEARS AGO C $80
D $70
OB $65

Comments: 1984; Original Retail $37.50
"Holy Bible" written on 1984 pieces on back of book. Corrected in 1985. Very pretty piece. Not easy to locate from most dealers.
Personal Data: _____
____Want Mark ____ Mark _____ Purch. 19__ Pd $ _____

When you introduce our guide to your retailer and they order for the first time we will give you a one year FREE SUBSCRIPTION to Precious Collectibles® or Collectors' Bulletin™ or 10 weeks of the Weekly Collectors' Gazette™.

E-5377 Girl Giving Cheese to Mouse
"Love Is Kind"

RETIRED 1987 - 10 YEARS AGO

F	$115	OB	$85
C	$100	CT	$75
D	$90		

Comments: 1984; Original Retail $27.50/$30.00
Same inspiration as 1984 Plate, Girl in Swing. Readily available during the retirement announcement time. CT easy to find.

Personal Data: _____
____Want Mark ____ Mark _____ Purch. 19__ Pd $ _____

E-5378 Shepherd Playing Harp
"Joy To The World"

SUSP. 1989 - 8 YEARS AGO

C	$50	CT	$40
D	$45	FL	$40
OB	$45	BA	$35

Comments: 1984; Original Retail $18.00/$25.00
First appeared in 1984 as figurine and ornament but the print first appeared in 1981 on the first tin and on a crewel picture. There is a question as to why the license date should not be 1980 or 1981 as this drawing was used by Enesco at that time. The same question applies also to pieces E-5388, E- 5385 and E-5386 as they had been produced before in a different style of figurine; same piece, so why a different license date? An error, in my opinion. It's been said this was to be a black child. In '94 African-American children debuted.
See #18, page XIII.
Personal Data: _____
____Want Mark ____ Mark _____ Purch. 19__ Pd $ _____

E-5379 Girl Sweeping
"Isn't He Precious"

Unpainted - $500 up/NE

C	$50	FL	$30	GC	$30	H	$30
D	$45	BA	$35	B	$30	SRD	$30
OB	$40	FLM	$35	TRP	$30		
CT	$40	V	$35	S	$30		

Comments: 1984; Original Retail $20.00/$30.00
Three "unpainted" pieces known to have been found in 1988. Appeared on 1983 Christmas card. Part of the Large Nativity Set.
See #19, page XIII.

Personal Data: _____
____Want Mark ____ Mark _____ Purch. 19__ Pd $ _____

E-5380 Shepherd at Manger/Butterfly
"A Monarch Is Born"

SUSP. 1986 - 11 YEARS AGO	C	$90
PRODUCED FOR ONLY 3 YEARS	D	$80
	OB	$75

DARK MONARCH - $300   RARE!
Comments: 1984; Original Retail $33.00
A very vivid orange and black monarch butterfly was found on sample pieces. A change to produce it in pastels disappointed many collectors! I feel there were so many manger pieces that this could have been the reason for suspension. Sometimes these sample pieces get in the hands of Reps to display and they sell them later. Keep a lookout for the "dark" monarch. This piece is probably more scarce than many realize!
Personal Data: _____
____Want Mark ____ Mark _____ Purch. 19__ Pd $ _____

E-5381 Two Shepherds Whispering at Manger
"His Name Is Jesus"

SUSP. 1987 - 10 YEARS AGO	C	$110	OB	$90
	D	$100	CT	$90

Comments: 1984; Original Retail $45.00/$50.00
I feel this is more scarce than collectors realize. One of my favorites!
Personal Data: _____
____Want Mark ____ Mark _____ Purch. 19__ Pd $ _____

E-5382 *NATIVITY – Set of Four   (5")*
"For God So Loved The World"

SUSP. 1986 - 11 YEARS AGO	C	$140
	D	$110
	OB	$115

Comments: 1984; Original Retail $70.00
Has not been as collectible as the original 9-pc. Nativity Set. Many said "heads" were too large.
Personal Data: _____
____Want Mark ____ Mark _____ Purch. 19__ Pd $ _____

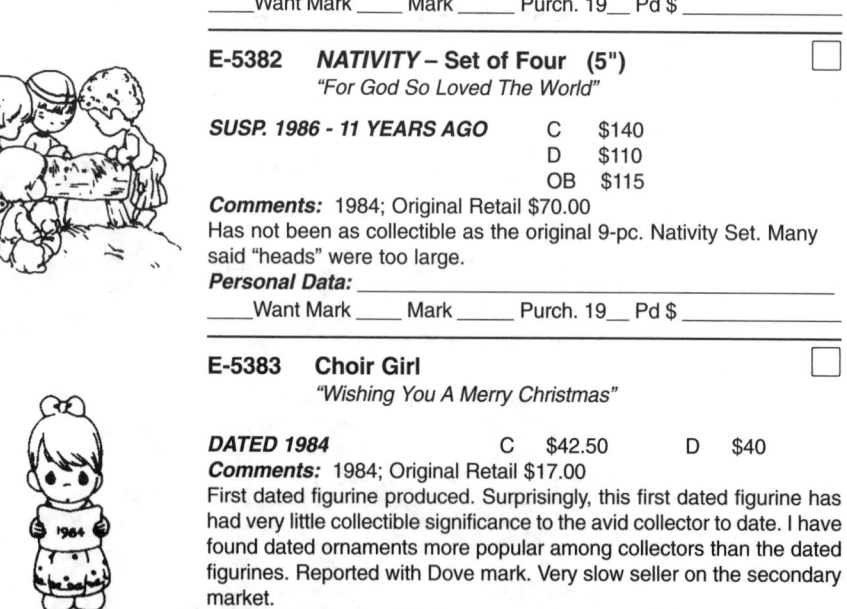

E-5383 Choir Girl
"Wishing You A Merry Christmas"

DATED 1984	C	$42.50	D	$40

Comments: 1984; Original Retail $17.00
First dated figurine produced. Surprisingly, this first dated figurine has had very little collectible significance to the avid collector to date. I have found dated ornaments more popular among collectors than the dated figurines. Reported with Dove mark. Very slow seller on the secondary market.
Personal Data: _____
____Want Mark ____ Mark _____ Purch. 19__ Pd $ _____

E-5384 Miniature Drummer Boy
"I'll Play My Drum For Him"

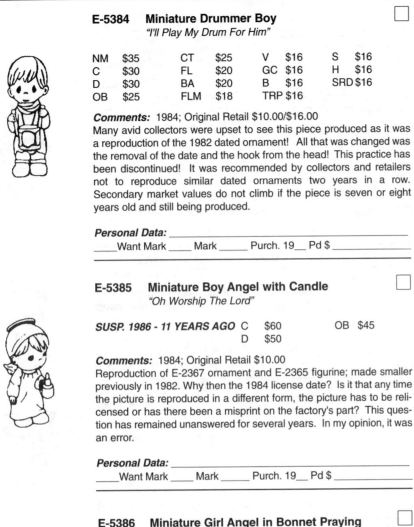

NM	$35	CT	$25	V	$16	S	$16
C	$30	FL	$20	GC	$16	H	$16
D	$30	BA	$20	B	$16	SRD	$16
OB	$25	FLM	$18	TRP	$16		

Comments: 1984; Original Retail $10.00/$16.00
Many avid collectors were upset to see this piece produced as it was a reproduction of the 1982 dated ornament! All that was changed was the removal of the date and the hook from the head! This practice has been discontinued! It was recommended by collectors and retailers not to reproduce similar dated ornaments two years in a row. Secondary market values do not climb if the piece is seven or eight years old and still being produced.

Personal Data: _____
____Want Mark ____ Mark _____ Purch. 19__ Pd $ _____

E-5385 Miniature Boy Angel with Candle
"Oh Worship The Lord"

SUSP. 1986 - 11 YEARS AGO C $60   OB $45
                               D $50

Comments: 1984; Original Retail $10.00
Reproduction of E-2367 ornament and E-2365 figurine; made smaller previously in 1982. Why then the 1984 license date? Is it that any time the picture is reproduced in a different form, the picture has to be relicensed or has there been a misprint on the factory's part? This question has remained unanswered for several years. In my opinion, it was an error.

Personal Data: _____
____Want Mark ____ Mark _____ Purch. 19__ Pd $ _____

E-5386 Miniature Girl Angel in Bonnet Praying
"Oh Worship The Lord"

SUSP. 1986 - 11 YEARS AGO C $70   OB $60
                               D $60

Comments: 1984; Original Retail $10.00
A reproduction of E-2366 and retired ornament E-2368. Changes: no hook (as ornament had) and smaller than the figurine.

Personal Data: _____
____Want Mark ____ Mark _____ Purch. 19__ Pd $ _____

E-5387 ORNAMENT – Choir Girl
"Wishing You A Merry Christmas"

DATED 1984   C $35

Comments: 1984; Original Retail $10.00
The fourth dated ornament.

Personal Data: _____
____Want Mark ____ Mark _____ Purch. 19__ Pd $ _____

E-5388 ORNAMENT – Shepherd Playing Harp
"Joy To The World"

RETIRED 1987 - 10 YEARS AGO
          C $45   OB $45
          D $45   CT $40

Comments: 1984; Original Retail $10.00/$11.00
First appeared on a tin container in 1981 but the license date on the ornament is 1984. Very small amount of trading found in recent years.

Personal Data: _____
____Want Mark ____ Mark _____ Purch. 19__ Pd $ _____

E-5389 ORNAMENT – Choir Boy
"Peace On Earth"

SUSP. 1986 - 11 YEARS AGO C $45
                               D $40
                               OB $35

Comments: 1984; Original Retail $10.00

Personal Data: _____
____Want Mark ____ Mark _____ Purch. 19__ Pd $ _____

E-5390 ORNAMENT – Girl/Birdhouse
"May God Bless You With A Perfect Holiday Season"

SUSP. 1989 - 8 YEARS AGO
          C $38   CT $30
          D $35   FL $30
          OB $35   BA $30

Comments: 1984; Original Retail $10.00/$13.50
Same girl that was in figurine E-0503.

Personal Data: _____
____Want Mark ____ Mark _____ Purch. 19__ Pd $ _____

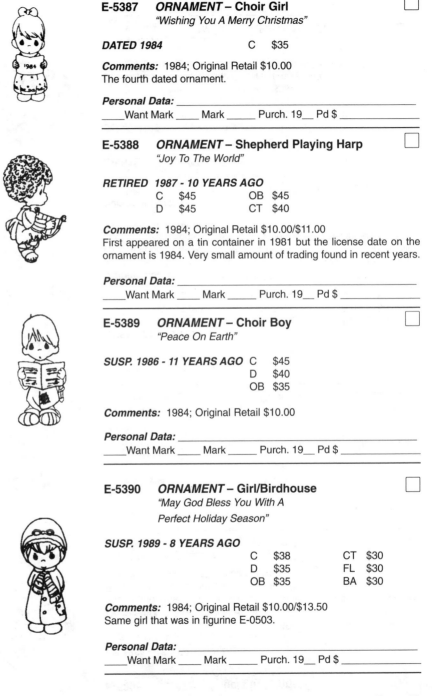
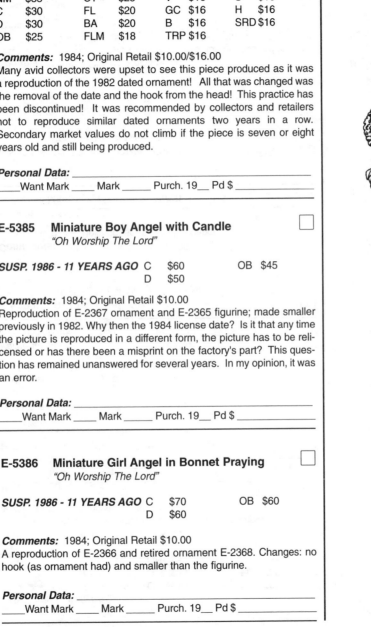

E-5391 **_ORNAMENT_** – Girl w/Cheese w/Bow
"Love Is Kind"

SUSP. 1989 - 8 YEARS AGO

C	$40	CT	$35
D	$38	FL	$35
OB	$35	BA	$35

Comments: 1984; Original Retail $10.00/$13.50
Several figurines and ornaments have the same inscription. E-1379A also has the same inscription as this one.

Personal Data: _____
____Want Mark ____ Mark _____ Purch. 19__ Pd $ _____

E-5392 **_ORNAMENT_** – Baby in Cradle
"Blessed Are The Pure In Heart"

DATED 1984 C $40

Comments: 1983; Original Retail $10.00
1984 Annual Edition. **_See #29, page XIV._**

Personal Data: _____
____Want Mark ____ Mark _____ Purch. 19__ Pd $ _____

E-5393 **_BELL_** – Choir Girl
"Wishing You A Merry Christmas"

DATED 1984 C $45

Comments: 1984; Original Retail $19.00
Fourth dated bell. Bells not selling in abundance!

Personal Data: _____
____Want Mark ____ Mark _____ Purch. 19__ Pd $ _____

E-5394 ♪ **_MUSICAL_** – Girls with Puppy
"Wishing You A Merry Christmas"

SUSP. 1986 - 11 YEARS AGO	C	$125
	D	$120
	OB	$105

Comments: 1984; Original Retail $55.00
Plays _We Wish You A Merry Christmas_. Also has been found to play Joy To The World. This piece has been found with NM. Not easily found.

Personal Data: _____
____Want Mark ____ Mark _____ Purch. 19__ Pd $ _____

E-5395 **_PLATE_** – Angels in Chariot
"Unto Us A Child Is Born"

LE 1984 - 13 YEARS OLD

MM	$50
C	$45

Comments: 1984; Original Retail $40.00
Fourth and Final Edition of _Christmas Collection Series_; 1984 Limited Edition 15,000. Several have been found without a mark. Marks are placed in the mold, not pressed in later.

Personal Data: _____
____Want Mark ____ Mark _____ Purch. 19__ Pd $ _____

E-5396 **_PLATE_** – Boy/Girl/Sled
"The Wonder Of Christmas"

DATED 1984 MM $48
        C $40

Comments: 1984; Original Retail $40.00
Third issue in _Joy of Christmas Series_. Plates are beautiful, but not in demand by collectors.

Personal Data: _____
____Want Mark ____ Mark _____ Purch. 19__ Pd $ _____

E-5397 **_DOLL_** – Jogger
"Timmy"

SUSP. 1991 - 6 YEARS

MM	$165	OB	$150	BA	$150
C	$160	CT	$150	FLM	$150
D	$155	FL	$150	V	$150

Comments: 1984; Original Retail $125/$150
Most dolls, if marked, are marked on the back of their necks. (Bride/Groom are hand-numbered on foot.) Notice the price differences in retail. Some collectors may be willing to sell for less because they paid the lower price.

Personal Data: _____
____Want Mark ____ Mark _____ Purch. 19__ Pd $ _____

E-5619 **_NATIVITY_** – Baby Sleeping in Manger
"Come Let Us Adore Him"

SUSP. 1985 - 12 YEARS AGO

NM	$55	F	$35
T	$45	C	$35
HG	$35	D	$35

Comments: 1980; Original Retail $10.00/$11.00
Abundant in 1982.

Personal Data: _____
____Want Mark ____ Mark _____ Purch. 19__ Pd $ _____

E-5620   **BELL** – Shepherd
"We Have Seen His Star"

SUSP. 1985 - 12 YEARS AGO

MM	$40	C	$35
HG	$35	D	$35

Comments: 1980; Original Retail $15.00/$19.00
Most bells not marked.

Personal Data: _____
____Want Mark ____ Mark _____ Purch. 19__ Pd $ _____

E-5621   **Donkey**

MM	$30	FL	$15	B	$15
C	$18	BA	$15	TRP	$15
D	$18	FLM	$15	S	$15
OB	$16	V	$15	H	$15
CT	$15	GC	$15	SRD	$15

Comments: 1980; Original Retail $6.00/$15.00
Very few sales reported - easily found at retail.

Personal Data: _____
____Want Mark ____ Mark _____ Purch. 19__ Pd $ _____

SAM LOVES LI'L CHILDREN.

1996

LICENSEE CONVENTION

Next Event: July 31-August 2, 1997

Sam presents a
plaque to Dave and Rosie for
their participation
as Licensees.

**Brenda Owensby
has her bag
full of
goodies to
show Rosie!**

How many does this make
for you, Marilyn?
Marilyn's button collection
is on display
at the chapel's art gallery.

E-5622 BELL – Angel
"Let The Heavens Rejoice"

DATED 1981 NM $190

Comments: 1980; Original Retail $15.00
This is the first dated bell. This li'l angel is in stone along the path to the Chapel. Would be ideal for our outside gardens! Most sought after bell in my opinion. 1981 ornament has same li'l angel. Considered a No Mark because it was produced before mid '81, before pieces were produced with the Triangle mark.

Personal Data: _____
____Want Mark ____ Mark _____ Purch. 19__ Pd $ _____

E-5623 BELL – Shepherd with Staff
"Jesus Is Born"

SUSP. 1984 – 13 YEARS AGO MM $55 C $45

Comments: 1980; Original Retail $15.00/$19.00

Personal Data: _____
____Want Mark ____ Mark _____ Purch. 19__ Pd $ _____

E-5624 NATIVITY – Camels with Wise Men (3 pc.)
"They Followed The Star"

NM	$340	D	$230	FLM	$230	S	$225
T	$280	OB	$230	V	$230	H	$225
HG	$255	CT	$230	GC	$225	SRD	$225
F	$245	FL	$230	B	$225		
C	$230	BA	$230	TRP	$225		

Comments: 1980; Original Retail $130.00/$225.00
It's been said some camels had no blankets. It's my opinion only sample pieces had no blankets. Large pieces usually do not rise on the secondary market as fast as smaller figurines. Very few secondary market sales reported on this set in past four years. Time for suspension. Really don't think retailers are ordering many sets.

Personal Data: _____
____Want Mark ____ Mark _____ Purch. 19__ Pd $ _____

E-5627 ORNAMENT – Boy Angel on Cloud
"But Love Goes On Forever"

SUSP. 1985 -12 YEARS AGO	NM $135	F	$100
	T $130	C	$90
	HG $115	D	$90

Comments: 1981; Original Retail $6.00/$10.00
Scarce since 1989. Due to scarcity, prices are still quite high.

Personal Data: _____
____Want Mark ____ Mark _____ Purch. 19__ Pd $ _____

E-5628 ORNAMENT – Girl Angel on Cloud
"But Love Goes On Forever"

SUSP. 1985 -12 YEARS AGO	NM $145	F	$100
	T $125	C	$90
	HG $115	D	$90

Comments: 1981; Original Retail $6.00/$10.00
Scarce. Tends to be more sought after than the Boy Angel, E-5627. Insure at these prices.

Personal Data: _____
____Want Mark ____ Mark _____ Purch. 19__ Pd $ _____

E-5629 ORNAMENT – Angel
"Let The Heavens Rejoice"

DATED 1981

Most sought after ornament...	NM	$235
	T	$215
No patch on gown.......... Rare!	NM	$275
	T	$270
Patch w/no paint..... Very Rare!	NM	$315
	T	$310

Comments: 1981; Original Retail $6.00
Patch missing on limited amount – sought after on secondary market. Significant piece for the avid collector. The patch with no paint is very rare. I have owned both errors. **See #29, page XIV.**

Personal Data: _____
____Want Mark ____ Mark _____ Purch. 19__ Pd $ _____

E-5630 ORNAMENT – Shepherd
"Unto Us A Child Is Born"

SUSP. 1985 -12 YEARS AGO	NM $70	F	$50
	T $60	C	$50
	HG $55	D	$50

Comments: 1981; Original Retail $6.00/$10.00
(A small figurine identical to this ornament was placed in approx. 5000 of small Nativity Set E-2395.) If the "correct one" as shown on the box from Enesco was requested, then the retailer replaced the incorrect one with the correct shepherd. This is why we are finding the "lone" Turban Boy on the secondary market. He was not necessarily being sold separately from the set. Some collectors were able to purchase the correct piece if ordered by their retailer and they kept the turban boy. Has been found with "Isn't He Wonderful" on the box.

Personal Data: _____
____Want Mark ____ Mark _____ Purch. 19__ Pd $ _____

E-5631 ORNAMENT – Boy with Teddy
"Baby's First Christmas"

SUSP. 1985 -12 YEARS AGO

NM	$78	F	$50
T	$65	C	$45
HG	$50	D	$45

Comments: 1980; Original Retail $6.00/$10.00

Personal Data: _____
____Want Mark ____ Mark ____ Purch. 19__ Pd $ _____

E-5632 ORNAMENT – Girl with Bunny
"Baby's First Christmas"

SUSP. 1985 -12 YEARS AGO

NM	$80	F	$50
T	$75	C	$50
HG	$55	D	$45

Comments: 1980; Original Retail $6.00/$10.00
Suspension has increased demand.

Personal Data: _____
____Want Mark ____ Mark ____ Purch. 19__ Pd $ _____

E-5633 NATIVITY – ORNAMENT - 4 pc. Set
"Come Let Us Adore Him"

SUSP. 1984 - 13 YEARS AGO

NM	$150	F	$120
T	$145	C	$120
HG	$135		

Comments: 1981; Original Retail $20.00/$31.50
Not easily found.

Personal Data: _____
____Want Mark ____ Mark ____ Purch. 19__ Pd $ _____

E-5634 ORNAMENT – Set of Three Kings
"Wee Three Kings"

SUSP. 1984 - 13 YEARS AGO

NM	$140	HG	$130	C	$115
T	$135	F	$120		

Comments: 1980; Original Retail $25.00/$27.50
Scarce.

Personal Data: _____
____Want Mark ____ Mark ____ Purch. 19__ Pd $ _____

E-5635 NATIVITY – Set of Three Kings
"Wee Three Kings"

NM	$145	D	$85	FLM	$75	S	$75
T	$120	OB	$80	V	$75	H	$75
HG	$110	CT	$80	GC	$75	SRD	$75
F	$85	FL	$80	B	$75		
C	$85	BA	$80	TRP	$75		

Comments: 1980; Original Retail $40.00/$75.00
Originals were very colorful. NMs were somewhat scarce. See the section on pewter for the Three Kings pewter prices. When a piece is still in production, as in this case, collectors feel no need to pay much more than retail on most pieces except for the first three marks (NM, T and HG). **See #13, page XII.**

Personal Data: _____
____Want Mark ____ Mark ____ Purch. 19__ Pd $ _____

E-5636 NATIVITY – Angel with Trumpet
"Rejoice O Earth"

NM	$80	D	$45	FLM	$30	S	$30
T	$75	OB	$35	V	$30	H	$30
HG	$60	CT	$35	GC	$30	SRD	$30
F	$55	FL	$35	B	$30		
C	$45	BA	$30	TRP	$30		

Comments: 1980; Original Retail $15.00/$30.00
Abundant - good candidate for suspension or retirement! Nativity pieces market well for sets.

Personal Data: _____
____Want Mark ____ Mark ____ Purch. 19__ Pd $ _____

E-5637 NATIVITY – Angel with Flashlight
"The Heavenly Light"

NM	$90	D	$40	FLM	$30	S	$30
T	$75	OB	$40	V	$30	H	$30
HG	$55	CT	$38	GC	$30	SRD	$30
F	$50	FL	$35	B	$30		
C	$40	BA	$35	TRP	$30		

Comments: 1980; Original Retail $15.00/$30.00
Perfect for retirement, but pieces that go with the Nativity set tend to remain on the market.

Personal Data: _____
____Want Mark ____ Mark ____ Purch. 19__ Pd $ _____

E5638 *NATIVITY* – Cow with Bell

NM	$55	CT	$40	V	$32.50	S	$32.50
C	$45	FL	$35	GC	$32.50	H	$32.50
D	$45	BA	$35	B	$32.50	SRD	$32.50
OB	$40	FLM	$35	TRP	$32.50		

Comments: 1980; Original Retail $16.00/$32.50
Most were never marked; abundant in 1983. Originals never had license date. The longer a piece is produced (6 to 8 years or more), the less we've found an increase in price. Suspension has been an answer in helping the secondary market values rise on many. Nativity pieces not being suspended or retired as they go well with the Nativity set.

Personal Data: _____
____Want Mark ____ Mark _____ Purch. 19__ Pd $ _____

E-5639 Angel with Harp
"Isn't He Wonderful"

SUSP. 1985 -12 YEARS AGO

NM	$80	HG	$65	C	$55
T	$70	F	$55	D	$55

Comments: 1980; Original Retail $12.00/$17.00

Personal Data: _____
____Want Mark ____ Mark _____ Purch. 19__ Pd $ _____

E-5640 Kneeling Girl Angel with Harp
"Isn't He Wonderful"

SUSP. 1985 -12 YEARS AGO

NM	$75	HG	$65	C	$65
T	$70	F	$65	D	$55

Comments: 1980; Original Retail $12.00/$17.00

Personal Data: _____
____Want Mark ____ Mark _____ Purch. 19__ Pd $ _____

E-5641 "Follow Me" Angel with Three Kings
"They Followed The Star"

SUSP. 1985 -12 YEARS AGO

NM	$250	F	$190	
T	$230	C	$185	
HG	$200	D	$185	

Comments: 1980; Original Retail $75/$100
Extra large and heavy piece; four figures on base. ***See #20, page XIII.***

Personal Data: _____
____Want Mark ____ Mark _____ Purch. 19__ Pd $ _____

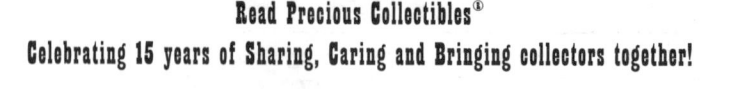

E-5642 ♪ *MUSICAL* – Sleeping Knight with Angel
"Silent Knight"

SUSP. 1985 -12 YEARS AGO

NM	$300	F	$250	
T	$275	C	$250	
HG	$255	D	$235	

Comments: 1980; Original Retail $45.00/$60.00
Plays *Silent Night*. Hard to find, especially NM and T. Escalated in price since '93. This is probably because there is no figurine similar to this piece. Look for this if you're wanting the unusual pieces. Seemed to be more trading on the pieces marked F through D last year than now. Do not over insure!
See #21, page XIII.

Personal Data: _____
____Want Mark ____ Mark _____ Purch. 19__ Pd $ _____

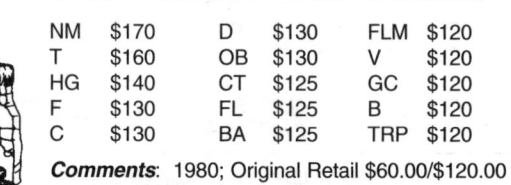

E-5644 *NATIVITY* – Walls - 2 Sections

NM	$170	D	$130	FLM	$120	S	$120
T	$160	OB	$130	V	$120	SRD	$120
HG	$140	CT	$125	GC	$120		
F	$130	FL	$125	B	$120		
C	$130	BA	$125	TRP	$120		

Comments: 1980; Original Retail $60.00/$120.00
It hasn't been a necessity, for some reason, to own the first marks of the buildings and walls. ***See #15, page XIII.***

Personal Data: _____
____Want Mark ____ Mark _____ Purch. 19__ Pd $ _____

E-5645 ♪ *MUSICAL* – Angel with Trumpet
"Rejoice O Earth"

RETIRED 1988 - 9 YEARS AGO

NM	$150	D	$85	
T	$145	OB	$85	
HG	$125	CT	$85	
F	$100	FL	$80	
C	$100			

Comments: 1980; Original Retail $35.00/$55.00
Plays *Joy To The World*. Musicals together are a nice presentation.

Personal Data: _____
____Want Mark ____ Mark _____ Purch. 19__ Pd $ _____

E-5646　PLATE – Nativity
"Come Let Us Adore Him"

LE 1981 - 16 YEARS OLD

NM $50

Comments: 1980; Original Retail $40.00
First in *Christmas Collection Series*. 1981 Limited Edition 15,000. This piece is a favorite of many.

Personal Data: _____
____Want Mark ____ Mark _____ Purch. 19__ Pd $ _____

E-6118　CANDLE CLIMBERS – Boy/Girl Angels
"But Love Goes On Forever"

SUSP. 1988 - 9 YEARS AGO

NM $110	C $90	FL $80
T $95	D $90	CT $80
F $90	OB $85	

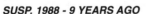

Comments: 1981; Original Retail $14.00/$25.00
Pair of Candle Climbers. Most were not marked. Only two different styles of candle climbers were produced. Adorable in a candle display. Not easily located anymore. Can be found in those collections of those who began collecting in the early 80's.

Personal Data: _____
____Want Mark ____ Mark _____ Purch. 19__ Pd $ _____

E-6120　ORNAMENT – Boy Carrying Lamb
"We Have Seen His Star"

RETIRED 1984 - 13 YEARS AGO

NM $75	F $60	HG $60
T $65	C $55	

Comments: 1980; Original Retail $9.00/$10.00

Personal Data: _____
____Want Mark ____ Mark _____ Purch. 19__ Pd $ _____

E-6214B　DOLL – "Mikey"

SUSP. 1985 -12 YEARS AGO

NM $245	C $205
HG $240	D $205
F $205	

Comments: 1980; Original Retail $175.00/$200.00
This doll is usually purchased along with the Debbie doll as a set. Mark is found on neck.

Personal Data: _____
____Want Mark ____ Mark _____ Purch. 19__ Pd $ _____

E-6214G　DOLL – "Debbie"

SUSP. 1985 -12 YEARS AGO

NM $250	F $205	C $205
HG $240	D $205	

Comments: 1980; Original Retail $175/$200
Marks began in 1983 on back of neck with HG mark. Produced in '82 but arrived for '83 sales. Very little trading on dolls in the past six years.

Personal Data: _____
____Want Mark ____ Mark _____ Purch. 19__ Pd $ _____

E-6613　Girl with Present and Kitten
"God Sends The Gift Of His Love"

SUSP. 1987 - 10 YEARS AGO

F $75	D $65	CT $60
C $70	OB $60	

Comments: 1984; Original Retail $22.50/$25.00

Personal Data: _____
____Want Mark ____ Mark _____ Purch. 19__ Pd $ _____

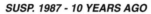

E-6901　PLAQUE – Oval Shaped with Boy Angel
"Precious Moments Last Forever"

SUSP. 1986 - 11 YEARS AGO

HG $125	C $50	OB $40
F $55	D $45	CT $40

Comments: 1981; Original Retail $19.00/$20.00
Was available in 1982 but very few appeared on merchants' shelves due to E-6901 being left off the retailers' order blanks. Large production in '84 and '85. A new plaque debuted in 1990, #230448. Many retailers learned of this piece by reading *Precious Collectibles*®! Another reason you should subscribe! ☺

Personal Data: _____
____Want Mark ____ Mark _____ Purch. 19__ Pd $ _____

E-7153　Boy Holding Heart
"God Is Love, Dear Valentine"

SUSP. 1986 - 11 YEARS AGO

NM $65	F $40	OB $30
T $55	C $35	
HG $45	D $35	

Comments: 1981; Original Retail $16.00/$17.00
Boy was a slower seller than the girl (E-7154) at retail. Not hard to locate on the secondary market.

Personal Data: _____
____Want Mark ____ Mark _____ Purch. 19__ Pd $ _____

E-7154 Girl Holding Heart
"God Is Love, Dear Valentine"

SUSP. 1986 - 11 YEARS AGO

NM	$70	C	$35
T	$60	D	$30
HG	$45	OB	$30
F	$35		

Comments: 1981; Original Retail $16.00/$17.00
Quite abundant.

Personal Data: _____
____Want Mark ____ Mark _____ Purch. 19__ Pd $ _____

E-7155 Praying Girl
"Thanking Him For You"

SUSP. 1984 - 13 YEARS AGO

HG	$65	C	$45
F	$55		

Comments: 1981; Original Retail $16.00/$17.00
Very plain figurine. Also appeared on bell. Was not a "best seller."

Personal Data: _____
____Want Mark ____ Mark _____ Purch. 19__ Pd $ _____

E-7156 Boy Holding Yellow Chick
"I Believe In Miracles"

SUSP. 1985 - 12 YEARS AGO
REISSUED IN 1987 AS E-7156R

HG	$120	D	$90
F	$110	FL	$85
C	$95	BA	$100

Comments: 1981; Original Retail $17.00/$19.00
Original piece, J&D licensee, no "Sam B." embossed on side. Boy with Yellow Chick was reissued in 1987. The only change was the color of the chick to blue. New mold later produced including large head, blue bird, etc. Order number was changed to E-7156R (see next entry). Has been found with MM. It has been stated that no suspended piece will be retired unless it has been brought back from suspension. (E-7156R), it is my opinion that this piece should also now be considered "retired" as it came back from suspension and the new piece was retired! This piece has been reported with a BA mark even though it was suspended earlier.

Personal Data: _____
____Want Mark ____ Mark _____ Purch. 19__ Pd $ _____

E-7156R Boy Holding Blue Bird
"I Believe In Miracles"

RETIRED 1992 - 5 YEARS AGO
RETURNED FROM SUSPENSION IN 1987

Large Head, Blue Chick, has "Sam B."

CT	$80	FLM	$60
FL	$70	V	$60
BA	$65		

Small Head, Blue Bird, no "Sam B."	RARE	CT	$205
Large Head, Yellow Chick, no "Sam B."	RARE	FL	$165

Comments: 1985; Original Retail $22.50/$27.50
R = Returned from Suspension.
Licensee Samuel J. Butcher Co. Made from Original Mold E-7156 with blue bird; then remolded with blue bird, large head on boy. Most avid collectors had this piece at the time of the Retirement announcement. This can be very confusing. If you want an avid collector's piece, it would be E-7156 (HG) and E-7156R with yellow chick. Very little trading in recent years for this piece. *See #5, 24, & 25, pages XI & XIV.*

Personal Data: _____
____Want Mark ____ Mark _____ Purch. 19__ Pd $ _____

E-7157 Waitress
"There Is Joy In Serving Jesus"

RETIRED 1986 - 11 YEARS AGO

HG	$65	D	$50
F	$55	OB	$45
C	$55		

Comments: 1981; Original Retail $17.00/$19.00
OB abundant! Display with *Eggs Over Easy* on a kitchen shelf!

Personal Data: _____
____Want Mark ____ Mark _____ Purch. 19__ Pd $ _____

E-7158 Nurse with Bear
"Love Beareth All Things"

HG	$70	CT	$45	GC	$45	SRD	$45
F	$55	FL	$45	B	$45		
C	$55	BA	$45	TRP	$45		
D	$50	FLM	$45	S	$45		
OB	$45	V	$45	H	$45		

Comments: 1981; Original Retail $25.00/$45.00
Still in production; this causes a slow secondary market. Very cute piece. Popular gift item. If it sells well then it won't get retired or suspended, but it is 16 years old!

Personal Data: _____
____Want Mark ____ Mark _____ Purch. 19__ Pd $ _____

E-7159   Bandaged Boy by Sign
"Lord Give Me Patience"

SUSP. 1985 - 12 YEARS AGO

HG	$60	D	$45
F	$55	OB	$45
C	$50		

Comments: 1981; Original Retail $25.00/$27.50
No decal on sign, add $100 to above prices. This happens to most figurines that require similar decals; only a few are considered an error. Add $100 for decals missing from figurines (not on base).
See #15, page XIII.

Personal Data: _____
____Want Mark ____ Mark ____ Purch. 19__ Pd $ _____

E-7160   Grandpa in Rocking Chair with Dog
"The Perfect Grandpa"

SUSP. 1986 - 11 YEARS AGO

HG	$80	D	$70
F	$75	OB	$60
C	$70		

Comments: 1981; Original Retail $25.00/$27.50
The Grandpa ornament was suspended in 1990.

Personal Data: _____
____Want Mark ____ Mark ____ Purch. 19__ Pd $ _____

E-7161   Boy Painting Lamb
"His Sheep Am I"

SUSP. 1984 - 13 YEARS AGO

MM	$100	F	$75	HG	$80	C	$70

Comments: 1981; Original Retail $25.00/$27.50
Some crosses on sheep were not painted. Rare! Add $75-$100 to the above values. Another collector reported her HG marked piece was missing the word "paint" on the bucket; add $50-$75 for this error. We have had "one" report of MM; this has occurred on many recent figurines (the mark has been left off from the mold).

Personal Data: _____
____Want Mark ____ Mark ____ Purch. 19__ Pd $ _____

E-7162   Girl at School Desk
"Love Is Sharing"

SUSP. 1984 - 13 YEARS AGO

HG	$170	C	$155	F	$160

Comments: 1981; Original Retail $25.00/$27.50
Was in production only three years.

Personal Data: _____
____Want Mark ____ Mark ____ Purch. 19__ Pd $ _____

E-7163   Boy with Ice Bag
"God Is Watching Over You"

SUSP. 1984 - 13 YEARS AGO

HG	$115	C	$90	F	$95

Comments: 1981; Original Retail $27.50/$30.00
This piece is scarce - only produced three years. I purchased one that had nothing on the base, no decal - nothing!

Personal Data: _____
____Want Mark ____ Mark ____ Purch. 19__ Pd $ _____

E-7164   Boy/Girl Painting Dog House
"Bless This House"

SUSP. 1984 - 13 YEARS AGO

HG	$225	C	$180	F	$205

Comments: 1981; Original Retail $45.00/$50.00
Not easily found on the secondary market. Only available three years. Between 1982-1984, large pieces were not ordered by retailers as often as smaller pieces. Becoming harder to find each year.

Personal Data: _____
____Want Mark ____ Mark ____ Purch. 19__ Pd $ _____

E-7165   Boy/Girl in Tub
"Let The Whole World Know"

SUSP. 1987 - 10 YEARS AGO

HG	$135	C	$130	OB	$100
F	$130	D	$110	CT	$95

Comments: 1981; Original Retail $45.00/$55.00
HG was hard to find when it debuted in '82. I drove many a mile to find it. Cute piece! *See #23, page XIII.*

Personal Data: _____
____Want Mark ____ Mark ____ Purch. 19__ Pd $ _____

E-7166   FRAME – Bride and Groom
"The Lord Bless You And Keep You"

SUSP. 1993 - 4 YEARS AGO

HG	$65	OB	$50	FLM	$45
F	$60	CT	$50	V	$45
C	$55	FL	$45	GC	$40
D	$55	BA	$45	B	$40

Comments: 1982; Original Retail $22.50/$32.50
See #8, page XII

Personal Data: _____
____Want Mark ____ Mark ____ Purch. 19__ Pd $ _____

E-7167 CONTAINER – Bride and Groom
"The Lord Bless You And Keep You"

SUSP. 1985 -12 YEARS

HG	$60	C	$50
F	$55	D	$45

Comments: 1981; Original Retail $22.50/$25.00
Container with lid. Not a popular seller when it debuted.

Personal Data: _____
____Want Mark ____ Mark ____ Purch. 19__ Pd $ _____

E-7168 FRAME – Boy Angel
"My Guardian Angel"

SUSP. 1984 - 13 YEARS AGO

HG	$75	C	$70
F	$70		

Comments: 1981; Original Retail $18.00/$19.00
Here's a challenge... find all of the frames!! Very scarce.
See #8, page XII

Personal Data: _____
____Want Mark ____ Mark ____ Purch. 19__ Pd $ _____

E-7169 FRAME – Girl Angel
"My Guardian Angel"

SUSP. 1984 - 13 YEARS AGO

HG	$75
F	$70
C	$70

Comments: 1981; Original Retail $18.00/$19.00
Very scarce. ***See #8, page XII***

Personal Data: _____
____Want Mark ____ Mark ____ Purch. 19__ Pd $ _____

E-7170 FRAME – Boy with Teddy
"Jesus Loves Me"

SUSP. 1985 - 12 YEARS AGO

HG	$60	C	$55
F	$55	D	$55

Comments: 1981; Original Retail $17.00/$19.00
See #8, page XII.

Personal Data: _____
____Want Mark ____ Mark ____ Purch. 19__ Pd $ _____

E-7171 FRAME – Girl with Bunny
"Jesus Loves Me"

SUSP. 1985 - 12 YEARS AGO

HG	$75	C	$55
F	$65	D	$55

Comments: 1981; Original Retail $17.00/$19.00
E-7170 and this piece are equally scarce! ***See #8, page XII.***

Personal Data: _____
____Want Mark ____ Mark ____ Purch. 19__ Pd $ _____

E-7172 PLATE – Christening
"Rejoicing With You"

SUSP. 1985 - 12 YEARS AGO

MM	$40	C	$35
D	$35		

Comments: 1981; Original Retail $30.00
7" Plate. ***See #1, page XI.***

Personal Data: _____
____Want Mark ____ Mark ____ Purch. 19__ Pd $ _____

E-7173 PLATE – Perfect Grandma
"The Purr-fect Grandma"

LE 1982 - 15 YEARS AGO

MM	$45
C	$40

Comments: 1981; Original Retail $40.00
8½" Plate. 1982 Limited Edition 15,000. Second issue of *Mother's Love Series.* ***See #1, page XI .***

Personal Data: _____
____Want Mark ____ Mark ____ Purch. 19__ Pd $ _____

E-7174 PLATE – Goose Girl
"Make A Joyful Noise"

LE 15,000

NM	$45
C	$40

Comments: 1981; Original Retail $40.00
8½" Plate. Limited Edition 15,000. Second issue of *Inspired Thoughts Series.* Debuted in '82. ***See #1, page XI.***

Personal Data: _____
____Want Mark ____ Mark ____ Purch. 19__ Pd $ _____

E-7175 *BELL* – Boy Graduate
"The Lord Bless You And Keep You"

SUSP. 1985 -12 YEARS AGO

MM	$50	D	$40
C	$45		

Comments: 1980; Original Retail $17.00/$19.00
Most bells unmarked. Debuted in '82. Seem to be more graduate bells than others. Girl is harder to locate as more bells are given to girl graduates than to boy graduates.
Personal Data: _____
____Want Mark ____ Mark _____ Purch. 19__ Pd $ _____

E-7176 *BELL* – Girl Graduate
"The Lord Bless You And Keep You"

SUSP. 1985 -12 YEARS AGO

MM	$65	D	$55
C	$60		

Comments: 1980; Original Retail $17.00/$19.00
Most bells unmarked.
Personal Data: _____
____Want Mark ____ Mark _____ Purch. 19__ Pd $ _____

E-7177 *FRAME* – Boy Graduate
"The Lord Bless You And Keep You"

SUSP. 1987 - 10 YEARS AGO

NM	$70	F	$45	OB	$40
T	$60	C	$40	CT	$40
HG	$58	D	$45		

Comments: 1980; Original Retail $18.00/$20.00
Frames are not easily found. Have been told by several collectors that frames are now their ultimate goal to collect. *See #8, page XII.*
Personal Data: _____
____Want Mark ____ Mark _____ Purch. 19__ Pd $ _____

E-7178 *FRAME* – Girl Graduate
"The Lord Bless You And Keep You"

SUSP. 1987 - 10 YEARS AGO

NM	$80	F	$65	OB	$60
T	$75	C	$65	CT	$55
HG	$65	D	$65		

Comments: 1980; Original Retail $18.00/$20.00
D through CT are more easily found than previous marks. Frames and Containers are becoming harder to find as they were not collected by the avid collector in the 70s and early 80s. Girls harder to find than boys. *See #8, page XII*
Personal Data: _____
____Want Mark ____ Mark _____ Purch. 19__ Pd $ _____

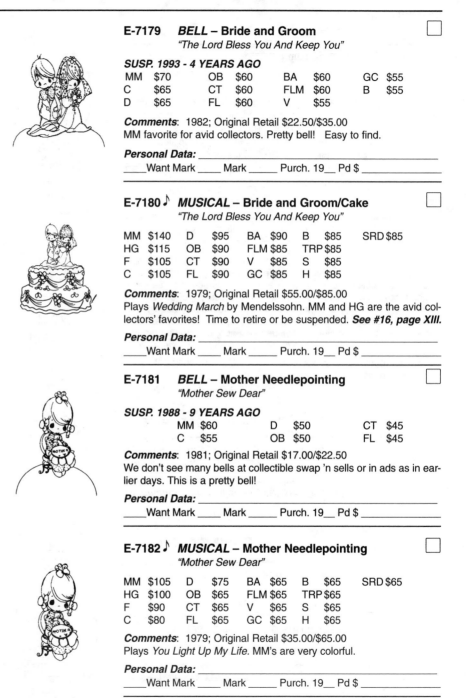

E-7179 *BELL* – Bride and Groom
"The Lord Bless You And Keep You"

SUSP. 1993 - 4 YEARS AGO

MM	$70	OB	$60	BA	$60	GC	$55
C	$65	CT	$60	FLM	$60	B	$55
D	$65	FL	$60	V	$55		

Comments: 1982; Original Retail $22.50/$35.00
MM favorite for avid collectors. Pretty bell!   Easy to find.
Personal Data: _____
____Want Mark ____ Mark _____ Purch. 19__ Pd $ _____

E-7180 ♪ *MUSICAL* – Bride and Groom/Cake
"The Lord Bless You And Keep You"

MM	$140	D	$95	BA	$90	B	$85	SRD	$85
HG	$115	OB	$90	FLM	$85	TRP	$85		
F	$105	CT	$90	V	$85	S	$85		
C	$105	FL	$90	GC	$85	H	$85		

Comments: 1979; Original Retail $55.00/$85.00
Plays *Wedding March* by Mendelssohn. MM and HG are the avid collectors' favorites! Time to retire or be suspended. *See #16, page XIII.*
Personal Data: _____
____Want Mark ____ Mark _____ Purch. 19__ Pd $ _____

E-7181 *BELL* – Mother Needlepointing
"Mother Sew Dear"

SUSP. 1988 - 9 YEARS AGO

MM	$60	D	$50	CT	$45
C	$55	OB	$50	FL	$45

Comments: 1981; Original Retail $17.00/$22.50
We don't see many bells at collectible swap 'n sells or in ads as in earlier days. This is a pretty bell!
Personal Data: _____
____Want Mark ____ Mark _____ Purch. 19__ Pd $ _____

E-7182 ♪ *MUSICAL* – Mother Needlepointing
"Mother Sew Dear"

MM	$105	D	$75	BA	$65	B	$65	SRD	$65
HG	$100	OB	$65	FLM	$65	TRP	$65		
F	$90	CT	$65	V	$65	S	$65		
C	$80	FL	$65	GC	$65	H	$65		

Comments: 1979; Original Retail $35.00/$65.00
Plays *You Light Up My Life*. MM's are very colorful.
Personal Data: _____
____Want Mark ____ Mark _____ Purch. 19__ Pd $ _____

E-7183 *BELL* – Grandma in Rocker
"The Purr-fect Grandma"

SUSP. 1988 - 9 YEARS AGO   Inked C $90

MM	$55	OB	$50
C	$50	CT	$45
D	$50	FL	$45

Comments: 1981; Original Retail $17.00/22.50
Found with an inked C mark above. RARE!

Personal Data: _____
____Want Mark ____ Mark ____ Purch. 19__ Pd $ _____

E-7184 ♪ *MUSICAL* – Grandma in Rocker
"The Purr-fect Grandma"

SUSP. 1993 - 4 YEARS AGO

MM	$105	D	$80	BA	$65	B	$60
HG	$95	OB	$75	FLM	$60		
F	$80	CT	$70	V	$60		
C	$80	FL	$70	GC	$60		

Comments: 1979; Original Retail $35.00/$60.00
Plays *Always In My Heart*. Great gift for Grandma on Mother's Day! Easy to find; do not over insure.

Personal Data: _____
____Want Mark ____ Mark ____ Purch. 19__ Pd $ _____

E-7185 ♪ *MUSICAL* – Girl at School Desk
"Love Is Sharing"

RETIRED 1985 - 12 YEARS AGO

HG	$185	C	$160
F	$170	D	$155

Comments: 1981; Original Retail $40.00/$45.00
Plays *School Days*. This piece is hard to find, mainly because it was produced only four years before retirement.

Personal Data: _____
____Want Mark ____ Mark ____ Purch. 19__ Pd $ _____

E-7186 ♪ *MUSICAL* – Boy/Girl in Tub
"Let the Whole World Know"

SUSP. 1986 - 11 YEARS AGO

MM	$165	F	$135	D	$130
HG	$155	C	$130	OB	$120

Comments: 1981; Original Retail $60.00/$65.00
Plays *What A Friend We Have In Jesus*. Not plentiful. MM and HG most coveted by avid collectors.

Personal Data: _____
____Want Mark ____ Mark ____ Purch. 19__ Pd $ _____

E-7241 *FRAME* – Mother Needlepointing
"Mother Sew Dear"

SUSP. 1986 - 11 YEARS AGO

HG	$60	C	$55	OB	$45
F	$55	D	$50		

Comments: 1981; Original Retail $18.00/$19.00

Personal Data: _____
____Want Mark ____ Mark ____ Purch. 19__ Pd $ _____

E-7242 *FRAME* – Grandma in Rocker
"The Purr-fect Grandma"

SUSP. 1988 - 9 YEARS AGO

HG	$55	C	$50	OB	$50	FL	$45
F	$50	D	$50	CT	$50		

Comments: 1981; Original Retail $18.00/$22.50
Suspended eight years ago... not easily found!

Personal Data: _____
____Want Mark ____ Mark ____ Purch. 19__ Pd $ _____

E-7267B *DOLL* – Groom
"Cubby"

LE 1981 - 15 YEARS OLD

Usually sold as set only	NM Set	$850
Individual DOLL	NM	$450

Comments: 1981; Original Retail $200.00
Hand-numbered on foot. Has certificate. Limited Edition 5,000. A few sets are signed on the foot by Sam's daughter and son-in-law, "Tammy and Cubby Bearinger." They attended our *Precious Collectibles®* Convention in '84 and signed several sets as well as cards, posters, figurines, ornaments, etc. Very few sets have been signed by them. Add $85 per set to these signed dolls. Appears prices are higher when sold individually rather than as a set.

Personal Data: _____
____Want Mark ____ Mark ____ Purch. 19__ Pd $ _____

E-7267G *DOLL* – Bride
"Tammy"

LE 1981 - 16 YEARS OLD

Usually sold as set only	NM Set	$850
Individual DOLL	NM	$525

Comments: 1981; Original Retail $300.00
Hand-numbered on foot. Has certificate. Limited Edition 5,000. Most popular PM "Collectible DOLL" set to date. See comments for E-7267B above.

Personal Data: _____
____Want Mark ____ Mark ____ Purch. 19__ Pd $ _____

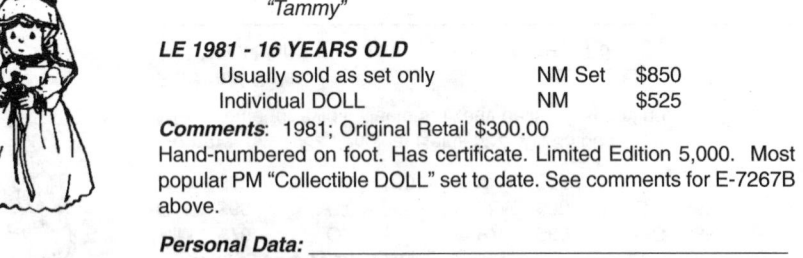

E-7350 Dome with Kids on Cloud Figurine

MM $825-850   C $750-800

Comments: Gift to Centers by Enesco.
Appears to be same as E-5207 night light. Has gold plaque on dome's base. Ask your local retailer. He or she may have one and just might sell! A collector commented that this was the same size as the night light with no cord cutout. The second dome for retailers debuted in '93 with the 15-year piece.

Personal Data: _____

____Want Mark ____ Mark _____ Purch. 19__ Pd $ _____

E-9251 Boy with Teacher
"Love Is Patient"

SUSP. 1985 - 12 YEARS AGO

*Decaled	C	$105		
	HG	$100	C	$85
	F	$95	D	$75

Comments: 1982; Original Retail $35.00
*Inked decal C has been found. The F marked piece has been the most available piece traded. We need a $30 teacher figurine, an affordable piece for some to give to teachers. ***See #24, page XIV.***

Personal Data: _____

____Want Mark ____ Mark _____ Purch. 19__ Pd $ _____

E-9252 Boy/Girl Making Up
"Forgiving Is Forgetting"

SUSP. 1989 - 8 YEARS AGO

Decaled	F	$110	D	$75
	MM	$125	OB	$75
	HG	$95	CT	$75
	F	$90	FL	$70
	C	$80	BA	$65

Comments: 1981; Original Retail $37.50/$47.50
Reported with no black eyes on little boy, insure for $75-100.
See #24, page XIV.

Personal Data: _____

____Want Mark ____ Mark _____ Purch. 19__ Pd $ _____

E-9253 Boy with Dog Ripping Britches
"The End Is In Sight"

SUSP. 1985 - 12 YEARS AGO

Decaled	F	$115	F	$75
	MM	$110	C	$70
	HG	$85	D	$60

Comments: 1982; Original Retail $25.00
Many reported sales. ***See #40, page XV.***

Personal Data: _____

____Want Mark ____ Mark _____ Purch. 19__ Pd $ _____

E-9254 Secretary
"Praise The Lord Anyhow"

RETIRED 1994 - 3 YEARS AGO

"Erasable" Decaled Mark (Inked)	Very Rare		F	$195
		Decaled	F	$150
MM $110				
HG $140	CT	$90	GC	$80
F $110	FL	$90	B	$75
C $105	BA	$85	TRP	$70
D $100	FLM	$85		
OB $90	V	$85		

Comments: 1982; Original Retail $35.00/$55.00
Out in early '83 with HG, later in '83 with F mark. Approx. 200 pieces appeared stamped with "inked" F mark in late '83. *Precious Collectibles®* magazine was the first to report decal marks and erasable marks to collectors. Our subscribers alert us to many rarities so that we can share them with you. We have been informed of this piece having two marks — a CT and FL — one on top of the other and of having an unpainted dress. Errors such as this have a value of $200 up. This piece has been found with a MM. Finding MM more often on new pieces than in the past since 1993.

Personal Data: _____

____Want Mark ____ Mark _____ Purch. 19__ Pd $ _____

E-9255 Groom Carrying Bride
"Bless You Two"

F	$55	CT	$50	V	$50	S	$45
C	$50	FL	$50	GC	$50	H	$45
D	$50	BA	$50	B	$45	SRD	$45
OB	$50	FLM	$50	TRP	$45		

Comments: 1982; Original Retail $21.00/$45.00
Not a lot of trading on this piece. This piece is not as popular as the original Bride 'n Groom couple. This is a good candidate for suspension or retirement because of the new piece that debuted in 1995.
See #16, page XIII.

Personal Data: _____

____Want Mark ____ Mark _____ Purch. 19__ Pd $ _____

E-9256 *PLATE* – Mother at Cradle
"The Hand That Rocks The Future"

LE 15,000

MM $38   C $35

Comments: 1983; Original Retail $40.00
Third issue of *Mother's Love Series*. Limited Edition 15,000.

Personal Data: _____

____Want Mark ____ Mark _____ Purch. 19__ Pd $ _____

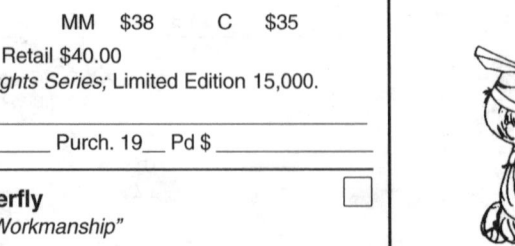

E-9257 PLATE – Boy Holding Chick
"I Believe In Miracles"

LE 15,000   MM $38   C $35

Comments: 1982; Original Retail $40.00
Third issue of *Inspired Thoughts Series;* Limited Edition 15,000.

Personal Data: _____
____Want Mark ____ Mark _____ Purch. 19__ Pd $ _____

E-9258 Girl with Butterfly
"We Are God's Workmanship"

HG	$65	OB	$40	FLM	$35	TRP	$35
F	$45	CT	$40	V	$35	S	$35
C	$40	FL	$40	GC	$35	H	$35
D	$40	BA	$35	B	$35	SRD	$35

Comments: 1982; Original Retail $19.00/$35.00
This was the same design used for the 1991 9" Easter Seals piece. Good candidate for suspension. This figurine was bought by a collector friend in Hawaii in '84 with the girl holding a bluebird not a butterfly. It was recommended that she insure for $500 over secondary market value. **See #25, page XIV.**

Personal Data: _____
____Want Mark ____ Mark _____ Purch. 19__ Pd $ _____

E-9259 Boy and Pig in Mud
"We're In It Together"

SUSP. 1990 - 7 YEARS AGO

HG	$95	D	$60	FL	$60
F	$75	OB	$60	BA	$55
C	$70	CT	$60	FLM	$55

Comments: 1982; Original Retail $24.00/$35.00
1983 piece came out early with HG mark which is the most difficult to find.

Personal Data: _____
____Want Mark ____ Mark _____ Purch. 19__ Pd $ _____

E-9260 Angel/Rainbow
"God's Promises Are Sure"

SUSP. 1987 - 10 YEARS AGO

Decaled	F	$100	HG	$100	D	$65
			F	$85	OB	$65
			C	$80	CT	$65

Comments: 1983; Original Retail $30.00/$33.50
Part of *Angels on a Cloud Series.* I always thought the inscription for E-9288 would have been great on this piece. Angel pieces are a favorite for many to collect.

Personal Data: _____
____Want Mark ____ Mark _____ Purch. 19__ Pd $ _____

E-9261 Boy Graduate with Scroll
"Seek Ye The Lord"

SUSP. 1986 - 11 YEARS AGO

"No Capital letters" error	F	$60		
	C	$55	D	$55
Corrected to capital letters	F	$50	D	$45
	C	$50	OB	$45

Comments: 1982; Original Retail $21.00
"Him" not capitalized in verse on scroll. (Actually, it isn't capitalized in the Holy Bible.) **See #9, page XII.**

Personal Data: _____
____Want Mark ____ Mark _____ Purch. 19__ Pd $ _____

E-9262 Girl Graduate with Scroll
"Seek Ye The Lord"

SUSP. 1986 - 11 YEARS AGO

"No Capital letters" error	F	$75		
	C	$65		
Corrected to capital letters	F	$50	D	$45
	C	$50	OB	$40

Comments: 1982; Original Retail $21.00
Same as E-9261. "He" not capitalized in verse on scroll. (Actually, it isn't capitalized in the Holy Bible.) **See #9, page XII.**

Personal Data: _____
____Want Mark ____ Mark _____ Purch. 19__ Pd $ _____

E-9263 Boy/Girl in Horse Costume
"How Can Two Walk Together Except They Agree"

SUSP. 1985 - 12 YEARS AGO

HG	$185	C	$140
F	$150	D	$140

Comments: 1982; Original Retail $35.00
Debuted in early 1983 with HG - scarce! The F mark began to appear about four weeks later. No question mark after the verse. *Precious Collectibles®* was first to picture the 1983 pieces with the 1982 mark. This was the first "notice" by *Precious Collectibles®* to collectors that last year's mark could be on new year's pieces! Very hard to find! **See #26, page XIV.**

Personal Data: _____
____Want Mark ____ Mark _____ Purch. 19__ Pd $ _____

E-9265 Girl Ironing
"Press On"

HG	$115	OB	$70	FLM	$65	TRP	$65
F	$85	CT	$70	V	$65	S	$65
C	$75	FL	$70	GC	$65	H	$65
D	$75	BA	$65	B	$65	SRD	$65

Comments: 1982; Original Retail $40.00/$65.00
Debuted early 1983 with HG - later with F.

Personal Data: _____
____Want Mark ____ Mark _____ Purch. 19__ Pd $ _____

E-9266 *CONTAINER* with Lid - 2 styles
(1) Lamb/Skunk and (2) Lamb/Bunny

(1) Our Love Is Heaven-Scent

(2) I'm Falling for Some Bunny and It Happens To Be You

SUSP. 1988 - 9 YEARS AGO

Decaled	F	$85	
MM	$55	D	$45
HG	$55	OB	$45
F	$45	CT	$35
C	$45	FL	$35

Comments: 1983 Original Retail $18.50/$25.00
Heart-shaped Container. Several reports of the base saying "Some Bunny Cares." Add $50 to the secondary market value for this error. Price is for each.

Personal Data: _____
____Want Mark ____ Mark _____ Purch. 19__ Pd $ _____

E-9267 Animal Figurines – Set of Six

E-9267A	Teddy Bear	E-9267D	Cat
E-9267B	Dog with Slipper	E-9267E	Lamb
E-9267C	Bunny with Carrot	E-9267F	Pig

SUSP. 1991 - 6 YEARS AGO

MM set	$160-170				
MM	$35 ea.	OB	$25 ea.	FLM	$25 ea.
F	$30 ea.	CT	$25 ea.	V	$25 ea.
C	$30 ea.	FL	$25 ea.		
D	$30 ea.	BA	$25 ea.		

Comments: 1982; Original Retail $6.50/$11.00
Originally a set of six - renumbered A-F in 1987. Different errors with the "DAD" decals on E-9267B have been reported (decals upside down or backwards). Teddy Bear is smiling, not frowning as shown in line art.
See #15, page XIII.

Personal Data: _____
____Want Mark ____ Mark _____ Purch. 19__ Pd $ _____

E-9268 Dunce Boy
"Nobody's Perfect"

RETIRED 1990 - 7 YEARS AGO

Error — "Smilie the Dunce" with smiling mouth				HG	$550	
Corrected	HG	$90	D	$75	FL	$65
	F	$80	OB	$75	BA	$65
	C	$75	CT	$70	FLM	$55

Comments: 1982; Original Retail $21.00/$30.00
Out in late 1982 with HG, then F later in 1983. Error on approx. first 5,000 pieces; had smile instead of circle mouth. Secondary market as high as $675 by mid 1983; down to $350 in mid 1987. Just because the Dunce Boy was retired, this should not have affected "Smilie" very much as he was rare (changed in 1982 after 5,000 were produced) and was considered to have had "retired" status from day one. Prices increased on "Smilie"!

Personal Data: _____
____Want Mark ____ Mark _____ Purch. 19__ Pd $ _____

E-9273 Girl with Umbrella
"Let Love Reign"

RETIRED 1987 - 10 YEARS AGO

HG	$95	D	$75
F	$80	OB	$70
C	$80	CT	$65

Comments: 1982; Original Retail $22.50/$30.00
Chicks have been found with unpainted eyes... Add $50 to the secondary market value.

Personal Data: _____
____Want Mark ____ Mark _____ Purch. 19__ Pd $ _____

E-9274 Girl Making Angel Food
"Taste And See That The Lord Is Good"

RETIRED 1986 - 11 YEARS AGO

F	$75	D	$65
C	$70	OB	$60

Comments: 1982; Original Retail $22.50
Part of *Angels on a Cloud Series.*

Personal Data: _____
____Want Mark ____ Mark _____ Purch. 19__ Pd $ _____

E-9275 *PLATE* – Boy with Teddy
"Jesus Loves Me"

SUSP. 1985 - 12 YEARS AGO

MM	$45	F	$35
C	$35		

Comments: 1982; Original Retail $30.00
Trading slow on this plate.

Personal Data: _____
____Want Mark ____ Mark _____ Purch. 19__ Pd $ _____

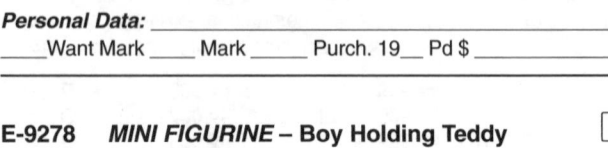

E-9276   *PLATE* – Girl with Bunny
"Jesus Loves Me"

SUSP. 1985 - 12 YEARS AGO

MM	$42.50	F	$35
C	$35		

Comments: 1982; Original Retail $30.00
Trading slow on this plate.

Personal Data: _____
____Want Mark ____ Mark _____ Purch. 19__ Pd $ _____

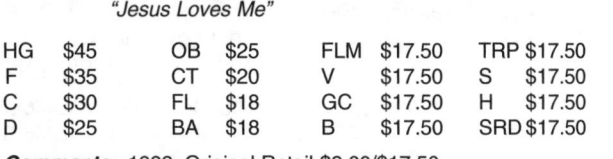

E-9278   *MINI FIGURINE* – Boy Holding Teddy
"Jesus Loves Me"

HG	$45	OB	$25	FLM	$17.50	TRP	$17.50
F	$35	CT	$20	V	$17.50	S	$17.50
C	$30	FL	$18	GC	$17.50	H	$17.50
D	$25	BA	$18	B	$17.50	SRD	$17.50

Comments: 1982; Original Retail $9.00/$17.50
HG limited in production. He's 15 years old this year! MM has been reported on this piece. Retail price increased in 1995 and 1996.

Personal Data: _____
____Want Mark ____ Mark _____ Purch. 19__ Pd $ _____

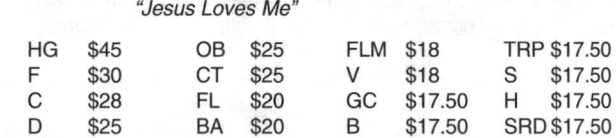

E-9279   *MINI FIGURINE* – Girl Holding Bunny
"Jesus Loves Me"

HG	$45	OB	$25	FLM	$18	TRP	$17.50
F	$30	CT	$25	V	$18	S	$17.50
C	$28	FL	$20	GC	$17.50	H	$17.50
D	$25	BA	$20	B	$17.50	SRD	$17.50

Comments: 1982; Original Retail $9.00/$17.50
HG limited in first shipment – more F. Has been found with J&D 1977 licensee and T mark; insure for $300 up.

Personal Data: _____
____Want Mark ____ Mark _____ Purch. 19__ Pd $ _____

E-9280   *CONTAINER* – Boy with Teddy
"Jesus Loves Me"

SUSP. 1985 - 12 YEARS AGO

HG	$55	C	$45
F	$50	D	$45

Comments: 1982; Original Retail $17.50/$19.00
Price down from last year.

Personal Data: _____
____Want Mark ____ Mark _____ Purch. 19__ Pd $ _____

E-9281   *CONTAINER* – Girl with Bunny
"Jesus Loves Me"

SUSP. 1985 - 12 YEARS AGO

HG	$70	C	$60
F	$60	D	$55

Comments: 1982; Original Retail $17.50/$19.00
Not easily found. Was not popular in the early '80s when it debuted. Containers are beginning to become more popular now.

Personal Data: _____
____Want Mark ____ Mark _____ Purch. 19__ Pd $ _____

E-9282A   Bunny with Carrot/Heart-Shaped Base
"To Some Bunny Special"

SUSP. 1990 - 7 YEARS AGO   Decaled   F $65

MM	$45	D	$35	FL	$30
HG	$45	OB	$35	BA	$30
F	$40	CT	$30	FLM	$30
C	$40				

Comments: 1982; Original Retail $8.00/$13.50
Comes in a set of three, *Especially For Ewe, You're Worth Your Weight In Gold,* and *To Some Bunny Special*. Has been found with decaled F. More trading on earlier marks than later... Heart-shaped base not shown on line drawing at left. This piece has not been found with a no mark but with a missing mark 1985.

Personal Data: _____
____Want Mark ____ Mark _____ Purch. 19__ Pd $ _____

E-9282B   Pig on Heart–Shaped Base
"You're Worth Your Weight In Gold"

SUSP. 1990 - 7 YEARS AGO

Decaled		F	$65		
MM	$45	D	$35	FL	$30
HG	$40	OB	$30	BA	$30
F	$38	CT	$30	FLM	$30
C	$35				

Comments: 1982; Original Retail $8.00/$13.50
Set of Three. Very popular piece. Has slot in top (piggy bank). Some have been found with two or three coins. Coins tend to be losing their shine on many pieces. Has been found with decaled F mark. Heart-shaped base not shown on original line drawing at left.

Personal Data: _____
____Want Mark ____ Mark _____ Purch. 19__ Pd $ _____

E-9282C Lamb on Heart-Shaped Base
"Loving Ewe" changed to
"Especially For Ewe"

SUSP. 1990 - 7 YEARS AGO

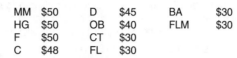

MM	$50	D	$45	BA	$30
HG	$50	OB	$40	FLM	$30
F	$50	CT	$30		
C	$48	FL	$30		

Comments: 1982; Original Retail $8.00/$13.50
Set of Three. Loving Ewe pieces, add $25 more on value. A decaled F has been reported. Heart-shaped base not shown on original line drawing at left. The bird is actually sitting on the back of the ewe. Popular.

Personal Data: _____
____Want Mark ____ Mark _____ Purch. 19__ Pd $ _____

E-9283 CONTAINERS – "Forever Friends"
1) *Dog on Heart-Shaped Container*
2) *Cat on Heart-Shaped Container*

SUSP. 1984 - 13 YEARS AGO

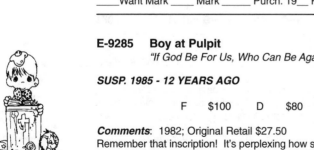

"Cat" Container - Decaled F	$85		
	MM	$75 ea.	F	$65 ea.
	T	$75 ea.	C	$60 ea.
	HG	$75 ea.	D	$60 ea.

Comments: 1981; Original Retail $15 ea./$17 ea.
Two styles; cat on one box and dog on other. Somewhat more popular than other "Covered Containers." Containers are becoming more sought after. They were slow sellers in early collector days. Not many out there for sale. Scarce! Very few T marks! Very little trading in past few years.

Personal Data: _____
____Want Mark ____ Mark _____ Purch. 19__ Pd $ _____

E-9285 Boy at Pulpit
"If God Be For Us, Who Can Be Against Us"

SUSP. 1985 - 12 YEARS AGO

F	$100	D	$80	C	$85

Comments: 1982; Original Retail $27.50
Remember that inscription! It's perplexing how some pieces are pulled from production so quickly. It's been said some inscriptions affect sales.
Personal Data: _____
____Want Mark ____ Mark _____ Purch. 19__ Pd $ _____

E-9287 Girl with Lion and Lamb
"Peace On Earth"

SUSP. 1986 - 11 YEARS AGO

F	$170	D	$150
C	$165	OB	$150

Comments: 1982; Original Retail $37.50
Most figurines produced for only 3-4 years and then suspended tend to rise faster on the secondary market than pieces that have been produced for more years before suspension. This is not an easy piece to find! In my opinion, as scarce as this piece is, buy any mark if you want it!

Personal Data: _____
____Want Mark ____ Mark _____ Purch. 19__ Pd $ _____

E-9287R Girl with Lion and Lamb
"And A Child Shall Lead Them"

RETURNED FROM SUSPENSION IN 1997

H	$50	SRD	$50

Comments: 1996; Original Retail $50.00

Personal Data: _____
____Want Mark ____ Mark _____ Purch. 19__ Pd $ _____

E-9288 Girl Angel with Sprinkling Can
"Sending You A Rainbow"

SUSP. 1986 - 11 YEARS AGO

F	$100-110	D	$90	C	$95	OB	$85

Comments: 1982; Original Retail $22.50
Becoming scarce on the secondary market.

Personal Data: _____
____Want Mark ____ Mark _____ Purch. 19__ Pd $ _____

E-9289 Boy Pilot Angel
"Trust In The Lord"

SUSP. 1987 - 10 YEARS AGO

F	$85	D	$75	CT	$60
C	$80	OB	$70		

Comments: 1982; Original Retail $20.00/$23.00
Title written on back of book; not an error. The original art was produced this way so the book could be under that arm.
Personal Data: _____
____Want Mark ____ Mark _____ Purch. 19__ Pd $ _____

12009   Girl with Quilt - Valentine Piece
"Love Covers All"

SUSP. 1991 - 6 YEARS AGO

C	$80	CT	$65	FLM	$60
D	$75	FL	$65	V	$60
OB	$70	BA	$60		

Comments: 1984; Original Retail $27.50/$37.50
Valentine pieces tend to be more available than others. A similar Club Membership piece debuted in 1990 (PM-902), a girl sewing a patch on a teddy bear. Nice piece!

Personal Data: _____
____Want Mark ____ Mark _____ Purch. 19__ Pd $ _____

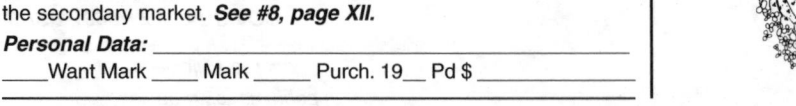

12017   *FRAME* – Boy Holding Heart
"Loving You"

SUSP. 1987 - 10 YEARS AGO

C	$60	OB	$55
D	$55	CT	$50

Comments: 1984; Original Retail $19.00/$20.00
Frames not easily attainable as in earlier years. ***See #8, page XII.***

Personal Data: _____
____Want Mark ____ Mark _____ Purch. 19__ Pd $ _____

12025   *FRAME* – Girl Holding Heart
"Loving You"

SUSP. 1987 - 10 YEARS AGO

C	$60	OB	$55
D	$55	CT	$50

Comments: 1984; Original Retail $19.00/$20.00
See #8, page XII.

Personal Data: _____
____Want Mark ____ Mark _____ Purch. 19__ Pd $ _____

12033   *FRAME* – Baby Boy
"God's Precious Gift"

SUSP. 1987 - 10 YEARS AGO

C	$110	OB	$75
D	$105	CT	$65

Comments: 1984; Original Retail $19.00/$20.00
Frames, as well as plates, dolls and bells, were not as popular as the figurines when they debuted. This frame has been very hard to find on the secondary market. ***See #8, page XII.***

Personal Data: _____
____Want Mark ____ Mark _____ Purch. 19__ Pd $ _____

12041   *FRAME* – Baby Girl
"God's Precious Gift"

SUSP. 1992 - 5 YEARS AGO

C	$55	CT	$45	FLM	$40
D	$50	FL	$45	V	$40
OB	$45	BA	$45	GC	$40

Comments: 1984; Original Retail $19.00/$27.50
Produced *longer than* 12033 Baby Boy frame. ***See #8, page XII.***

Personal Data: _____
____Want Mark ____ Mark _____ Purch. 19__ Pd $ _____

12068   Girl Holding Bible
"The Voice Of Spring"

LE 1985 - 12 YEARS OLD   C $250-295   D $275

Comments: 1984; Original Retail $30.00
First issue of *Four Seasons Series.* Limited Edition (one year only); coordinating plate, 12106. (All Four Seasons figurines are larger in height than regular pieces.) *Spring* and *Summer* figurines were produced in 1985 and were not difficult to locate as this new size was hard for collectors to accept. The size is now more accepted. It now appears that hindsight is better than foresight (should have bought many for future trading). The original artwork shown at left is the design for the plate; the figurine has a partial fence, shorter than the one shown, and the thimble has no fence. She's a favorite!

Personal Data: _____
____Want Mark ____ Mark _____ Purch. 19__ Pd $ _____

12076   Girl Holding Rose
"Summer's Joy"

LE 1985 - 12 YEARS OLD   C $105   D $90

Comments: 1984; Original Retail $30.00
Second issue of *Four Seasons Series.* Limited Edition figurine. The coordinating plate is 12114.

Personal Data: _____
____Want Mark ____ Mark _____ Purch. 19__ Pd $ _____

12084   Girl with Hair Blowing
"Autumn's Praise"

LE 1986 - 11 YEARS OLD   D $80   OB $65

Comments: 1984; Original Retail $30.00
Third Issue of *Four Seasons Series.* No total production figures were ever released. The coordinating plate for this figurine is 12122.

Personal Data: _____
____Want Mark ____ Mark _____ Purch. 19__ Pd $ _____

12092   **Girl with Birds**
"Winter's Song"

LE 1986 - 11 YEARS OLD

D	$130	FL $175
OB	$120	

Comments: 1984; Original Retail $30.00
Fourth Issue of *Four Seasons Series*. Refer to 12084 comments; same comments apply here. This piece has been found with the FL mark, which is very unusual as it is a 1986 Limited Edition piece. Insure the FL piece for $175 up.

Personal Data: _____
____Want Mark ____ Mark _____ Purch. 19__ Pd $ _____

12106   *PLATE* – **Girl Holding Bible**
"The Voice Of Spring"

LE 1985 - 12 YEARS OLD

C	$100	OB $65
D	$80	

Comments: 1984; Original Retail $40.00
1985 Limited Edition - First Edition in *Four Seasons Series*. Limited Edition Figurine 12068 also produced in 1985.

Personal Data: _____
____Want Mark ____ Mark _____ Purch. 19__ Pd $ _____

12114   *PLATE* – **Girl Holding Rose**
"Summer's Joy"

LE 1985 - 12 YEARS OLD   C $80   D $70

Comments: 1984; Original Retail $40.00
1985 Limited Edition - Second Edition in *Four Seasons Series*. Limited Edition figurine also produced in 1985.

Personal Data: _____
____Want Mark ____ Mark _____ Purch. 19__ Pd $ _____

12122   *PLATE* – **Girl with Hair Blowing**
"Autumn's Praise"

LE 1986 - 11 YEARS OLD   OB $30

Comments: 1984; Original Retail $40.00
1986 Limited Edition - Third Edition in *Four Seasons Series*. Many sales even at $25 were found! Price fell from '96.

Personal Data: _____
____Want Mark ____ Mark _____ Purch. 19__ Pd $ _____

12130   *PLATE* – **Girl with Birds**
"Winter's Song"

LE 1986 - 11 YEARS OLD   D $60   OB $45

Comments: 1984; Original Retail $40.00
1986 Limited Edition - Fourth Edition in *Four Seasons Series*.
Price fell on OB mark in "96!
Personal Data: _____
____Want Mark ____ Mark _____ Purch. 19__ Pd $ _____

12149   **Angel in Devil's Suit – Valentine Piece**
"Part Of Me Wants To Be Good"

SUSP. 1989 - 8 YEARS AGO	C	$100	CT	$75
	D	$85	FL	$70
	OB	$75	BA	$65

Comments: 1984; Original Retail $19.00/$25.00
Sam spoke to a group of collectors in 1984 concerning this piece. He painted the original drawing, remembering a special employee of his who always seemed to try to do what was right but still seemed not to get the job done! Debuted with C, then D later in 1985. Very little trading found on this piece.

Personal Data: _____
____Want Mark ____ Mark _____ Purch. 19__ Pd $ _____

12157   **Birthday Boy**
"This Is The Day The Lord Has Made"

SUSP. 1990 - 7 YEARS AGO
Error: "...Which The Lord Has Made"

	OB	$90	BA	$50
	CT	$75	FLM	$50
	FL	$65		

Corrected:	OB	$40	BA	$35
	CT	$40	FLM	$35
	FL	$35		

Comments: 1986; Original Retail $20.00/$30.00
First pieces were produced with error "...Which The Lord Has Made" then changed to omit the word "Which." Unlike other error pieces which were corrected, this piece continued to be produced both with the error and with the correction for several years. Slow seller on the secondary market.

Personal Data: _____
____Want Mark ____ Mark _____ Purch. 19__ Pd $ _____

12165 ♪ MUSICAL – Boy/Piano (2 pc. set)
"Lord, Keep My Life In Tune"

SUSP. 1989 - 8 YEARS AGO

D	$150	CT	$125	BA	$120
OB	$125	FL	$120		

Comments: 1984; Original Retail $37.50/$50.00
Rejoice In The Lord Band Series. Plays *Amazing Grace*.

Personal Data: _____
____Want Mark ____ Mark _____ Purch. 19__ Pd $ _____

12173 Girl Playing Triangle
"There's A Song In My Heart"

SUSP. 1990 - 7 YEARS AGO

D	$55	CT	$50	BA	$40
OB	$50	FL	$50	FLM	$40

Comments: 1984; Original Retail $11.00/$16.50
Rejoice In The Lord Band Series.

Personal Data: _____
____Want Mark ____ Mark _____ Purch. 19__ Pd $ _____

12203 Nun Figurine
"Get Into The Habit Of Prayer"

SUSP. 1986 - 11 YEARS AGO C $55   OB $40
D $45

Comments: 1984; Original Retail $19.00
This piece did not sell well. Scarce now due to low production, but not being sought after. It's my opinion this piece will be considered scarce in a few years due to only a 3 year production, then value could probably increase.

Personal Data: _____
____Want Mark ____ Mark _____ Purch. 19__ Pd $ _____

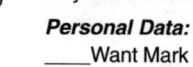

12211 Baby Getting Haircut
"Baby's First Haircut"

SUSP. 1987 - 10 YEARS AGO D $170   CT $160
OB $160

Comments: 1984; Original Retail $32.50/$37.00
Third issue in *Baby's First Series*. This series in the last two years has increased in value due to collector demand. It sometimes takes 6 to 8 years for a piece to become scarce. More trading found on D than any other mark. Has been found with wrong inspiration on bottom, reportedly "God Bless Our Home."

Personal Data: _____
____Want Mark ____ Mark _____ Purch. 19__ Pd $ _____

12238 Four Assorted Clowns (Mini pieces)
12238A Boy Balancing Ball
12238C Boy Handing Ball
12238B Girl w/Balloon
12238D Girl w/Flower Pot

ALL SUSP. 1996 - 1 YEAR AGO

Error "Crowns" instead of "Clowns" on Base   D $70 ea.

Corrected	D	$40 ea.	BA	$25 ea.	B	$25 ea.
	OB	$35 ea.	FLM	$25 ea.	TRP	$25 ea.
	CT	$30 ea.	V	$25 ea.	S	$25 ea.
	FL	$30 ea.	GC	$25 ea.		

Comments: 1984; Original Retail $13.50/$20.00
Set of Four. Smaller than regular figurines. Two girls and two boys. Some retailers sell sets only; others sell individually. Renumbered A-D in late 1987. **See #9, page XII.**

Personal Data: _____
____Want Mark ____ Mark _____ Purch. 19__ Pd $ _____

12246 MEDALLION – 1984
"Precious Moments Last Forever"
C $100

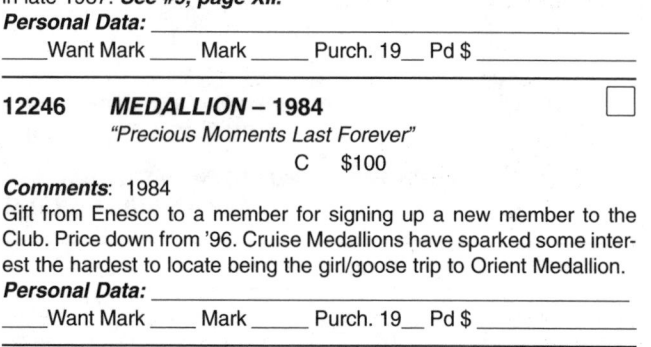

Comments: 1984
Gift from Enesco to a member for signing up a new member to the Club. Price down from '96. Cruise Medallions have sparked some interest the hardest to locate being the girl/goose trip to Orient Medallion.

Personal Data: _____
____Want Mark ____ Mark _____ Purch. 19__ Pd $ _____

12254 THIMBLE – Girl Stitching Quilt
"Love Covers All"

SUSP. 1990 - 7 YEARS AGO

C	$35	OB	$18	FL	$12	FLM	$12
D	$20	CT	$15	BA	$12	V	$12

Comments: 1984; Original Retail $5.50/$8.00
C mark recently found. Insure at $35.

Personal Data: _____
____Want Mark ____ Mark _____ Purch. 19__ Pd $ _____

12262 Clown Holding Balloons
"I Get A Bang Out Of You"

RETIRED 1997

D	$95	BA	$80	B	$70
OB	$90	FLM	$80	TRP	$70
CT	$80	V	$75	S	$70
FL	$80	GC	$75	H	$70

Comments: 1985; Original Retail $35.00/$45.00
First issue in *Clown Series*. Several clown figurines have been retired. Colorful! This is a very popular piece. Many report underline on "Bang."

Personal Data: _____
____Want Mark ____ Mark _____ Purch. 19__ Pd $ _____

12270   Clown on Ball
"Lord Keep Me On The Ball"

OB $70	FLM $50	TRP $45
CT $55	V $50	S $45
FL $50	GC $50	H $45
BA $50	B $50	SRD $45

Comments: 1985; Original Retail $35.00/$45.00
Fourth issue in *Clown Series*. Good suspension or retirement candidate.

Personal Data: _____
____Want Mark ____ Mark _____ Purch. 19__ Pd $ _____

12297   Policeman
"It Is Better To Give Than To Receive"

SUSP. 1987 - 10 YEARS AGO

D $155	CT $140	
OB $145		

Comments: 1984; Original Retail $19.00/$21.00
Price fell from '96. Perhaps the hype will be over once the new policeman debuts.

Personal Data: _____
____Want Mark ____ Mark _____ Purch. 19__ Pd $ _____

12300   Teacher with Report Card
"Love Never Fails"

D $65	BA $45	B $40	SRD $40
OB $55	FLM $40	TRP $40	
CT $55	V $40	S $40	
FL $50	GC $40	H $40	

Comments: 1984; Original Retail $25.00/$40.00
Teacher misspelled "Faithfulness." Probably a misspelling on "original" drawing. It's spelled "Faithfullness" with two "l's" instead of one "l." Not corrected to date. Very little trading reported on this piece for the past several years. It's time for suspension or retirement.

Personal Data: _____
____Want Mark ____ Mark _____ Purch. 19__ Pd $ _____

12319   Boy and Girl/Sandcastle
"God Bless Our Home"

D $85	BA $70	B $65	SRD $65
OB $80	FLM $65	TRP $65	
CT $75	V $65	S $65	
FL $75	GC $65	H $65	

Comments: 1984; Original Retail $40.00/$65.00
One report received of decal "HOWSE" in the D mark. It's time to see this one retired or suspended.

Personal Data: _____
____Want Mark ____ Mark _____ Purch. 19__ Pd $ _____

12335   Boy Angel on Cloud
"You Can Fly"

SUSP. 1988 - 9 YEARS AGO

OB $75	FL $65
CT $65	

Comments: 1985; Original Retail $25.00/$30.00
Display the angels on "clouds" together. This makes a great theme display in "cotton" or angel hair.

Personal Data: _____
____Want Mark ____ Mark _____ Purch. 19__ Pd $ _____

"Send In The Clowns." How many clowns have been retired or suspended?

109584 Retired '92	104396 Susp. '90	101850 Retired '92	520632 Retired '95	101842 Retired '91
15504 Retired '89	113964 Susp.'93	106216 Susp. '90	12467 Retired '88	12459 Retired '89
15822 Susp. '89	100668 Susp. '88	15830 Susp. '89	113972 Susp. '91	

12343 **Mary Knitting Booties**
"Jesus Is Coming Soon"

SUSP. 1986 - 11 YEARS AGO D $55   OB $50

Comments: 1985; Original Retail $19.00/$22.50
Reaction to this piece "varied" among collectors. It was probably the reason for suspension. This piece is hard to find! It was only in production two years! I feel it's a very pretty piece and I'd suggest you add it to your collection!

Personal Data: _____
____Want Mark ____ Mark _____ Purch. 19__ Pd $ _____

12351 **Two Angels Making Snowman**
"Halo, And Merry Christmas"

SUSP. 1988 - 9 YEARS AGO

D	$200	CT	$185
OB	$185	FL	$175

Comments: 1985; Original Retail $40.00/$47.50
This is a gorgeous piece! Another snowman piece (524913) debuted in 1990.

Personal Data: _____
____Want Mark ____ Mark _____ Purch. 19__ Pd $ _____

12378 **Boy Banjo Player**
"Happiness Is The Lord"

SUSP. 1990 - 7 YEARS AGO

C	$55	OB	$45	FL	$40	BA	$35
D	$40	CT	$40	BA	$35		

Comments: 1984; Original Retail $15.00/$22.50
Rejoice In The Lord Band Series. The Band Series was a "slow seller." Many D sales reported. Few C marks produced.

Personal Data: _____
____Want Mark ____ Mark _____ Purch. 19__ Pd $ _____

12386 **Girl/Harmonica**
"Lord Give Me A Song"

SUSP. 1990 - 7 YEARS AGO

F	$55	D	$50	CT	$40	BA	$35
C	$50	OB	$45	FL	$40	FLM	$35

Comments: 1984; Original Retail $15.00/$22.50
Rejoice In The Lord Band Series. First marks on this series are becoming harder to find. Sorry, our error. F and C marks were left off in '96.

Personal Data: _____
____Want Mark ____ Mark _____ Purch. 19__ Pd $ _____

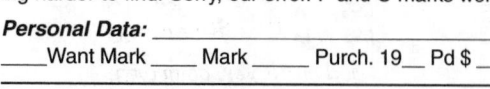

12394 **Boy/Trumpet/Dog (2 pc.)**
"He Is My Song"

SUSP. 1990 - 7 YEARS AGO

F	$60	D	$50	CT	$40	BA	$35
C	$55	OB	$45	FL	$40	FLM	$35

Comments: 1984; Original Retail $17.50/$27.50
Rejoice In The Lord Band Series. Very little trading found; may be awhile before value increases.

Personal Data: _____
____Want Mark ____ Mark _____ Purch. 19__ Pd $ _____

12408 ♪ *MUSICAL* – Angels Making Star (3-pc. set)
"We Saw A Star"

SUSP. 1987 - 10 YEARS AGO

F	$140	D	$130	CT	$115
C	$135	OB	$120		

Comments: 1984; Original Retail $50.00/$55.00
Plays *Joy To The World.* Collectors voiced their opinion that the star was "too plain" for display. Was very slow seller at retail. Price up from '96.

Personal Data: _____
____Want Mark ____ Mark _____ Purch. 19__ Pd $ _____

12416 ***ORNAMENT* - Boy in Airplane**
"Have A Heavenly Christmas"

Upside down error....$125-135

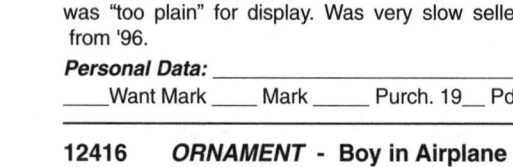

MM	$45	FL	$20	GC	$18.50	H	$18.50
D	$38	BA	$20	B	$18.50	SRD	$18.50
OB	$30	FLM	$20	TRP	$18.50		
CT	$25	V	$20	S	$18.50		

Comments: 1984; Original Retail $12.00/$18.50
Some of these appeared with decaled words "Heaven Bound" upside down on the plane. Also found with MM. Would be a great retirement piece. Found with patch not painted.

Personal Data: _____
____Want Mark ____ Mark _____ Purch. 19__ Pd $ _____

12424 ***DOLL* - Boy Angel**
"Aaron"

SUSP. 1986 - 11 YEARS AGO D $145   OB $140

Comments: 1984; Original Retail $135.00
12" Boy Angel. The embossed mark is on the neck. Dolls have been in less demand than the figurines.

Personal Data: _____
____Want Mark ____ Mark _____ Purch. 19__ Pd $ _____

12432 DOLL – Girl Angel
"Bethany"

SUSP. 1986 - 11 YEARS AGO   D $145   B $140

Comments: 1985; Original Retail $135.00
12" Girl Angel. The embossed D is on the neck. Dolls have been in less demand than the figurines.

Personal Data: _____
____Want Mark ____ Mark _____ Purch. 19__ Pd $ _____

12440 Commemorative Ed. 5th Anniversary
"God Bless Our Years Together"

D $265

Comments: 1984; Original Retail $175.00
Approx. 10-12 were shipped to retailers' shelves unpainted. Value $800 up.

Personal Data: _____
____Want Mark ____ Mark _____ Purch. 19__ Pd $ _____

12459 Girl Clown with Goose
"Waddle I Do Without You"

RETIRED 1989 - 8 YEARS AGO

C	$115	OB	$95	FL	$90
D	$105	CT	$90	BA	$90

Comments: 1985; Original Retail $30.00/$40.00
Second issue in *Clown Series*. (The first was 12262. It did not say "First of Series" on it.) A very colorful piece.

Personal Data: _____
____Want Mark ____ Mark _____ Purch. 19__ Pd $ _____

12467 Clown with Dog and Hoop
"The Lord Will Carry You Through"

RETIRED 1988 - 9 YEARS AGO

D	$90	CT	$80
OB	$85	FL	$75

Comments: 1985; Original Retail $30.00/$35.00
Third issue in *Clown Series*. Tends to be more OB marks for sale than any other mark in recent years.

Personal Data: _____
____Want Mark ____ Mark _____ Purch. 19__ Pd $ _____

12475 DOLL – Baby Boy
"P. D."

SUSP. 1986 - 11 YEARS AGO   MM $80   OB $70
                                 D $75

Comments: 1985; Original Retail $50.00
P.D. is for Philip Dale Jr., Philip Butcher's son and Sam's grandson. (Philip Sr. was killed Sept. 1990 in a car accident in Joplin, Missouri.) MM has been reported.

Personal Data: _____
____Want Mark ____ Mark _____ Purch. 19__ Pd $ _____

12483 DOLL – Baby Girl
"Trish"

SUSP. 1986 - 11 YEARS AGO

           MM $80   OB $70
           D $75

Comments: 1985; Original Retail $50.00
Trish is Philip and Connie Butcher's daughter (Sam's granddaughter). MM has been reported to us by several collectors.

Personal Data: _____
____Want Mark ____ Mark _____ Purch. 19__ Pd $ _____

12491 DOLL – Nurse
"Angie, The Angel Of Mercy"

LE 1986 - 11 YEARS OLD   CT $225   ·

Comments: 1986; Original Retail $160.00
Limited Edition 12,500. Several sales found at this price – Dolls have slowed on the secondary market rising in value.

Personal Data: _____
____Want Mark ____ Mark _____ Purch. 19__ Pd $ _____

12580 ♪ MUSICAL – Girl with Piano (2 pc. set)
"Lord, Keep My Life In Tune"

SUSP. 1990 - 7 YEARS AGO

OB	$250	FL	$200	BA	$150
CT	$240	BA	$200	FLM	$150

Comments: 1986; Original Retail $37.50/$55.00
Plays *I'd Like To Teach The World To Sing*. It seems she has been more sought after the last two years than the Boy (12165) but he's popular too! Value up from '96.

Personal Data: _____
____Want Mark ____ Mark _____ Purch. 19__ Pd $ _____

13293 THIMBLE – Mother with Needlepoint
"Mother Sew Dear"

C	$30	FL	$12	GC	$12	H	$8
D	$20	BA	$12	B	$10	SRD	$8
OB	$15	FLM	$12	TRP	$10		
CT	$12	V	$12	S	$8		

Comments: 1984; Original Retail $5.50/$8.00
See #27, page XIV. Very few C marks reported.

Personal Data: _____
____Want Mark ____ Mark _____ Purch. 19__ Pd $ _____

13307 THIMBLE – Grandma in Rocking Chair
"The Purr-fect Grandma"

C	$30	FL	$15	GC	$10	H	$8
D	$20	BA	$15	B	$10	SRD	$8
OB	$15	FLM	$12	TRP	$8		
CT	$15	V	$12	S	$8		

Comments: 1984; Original Retail $5.50/$8.00

Personal Data: _____
____Want Mark ____ Mark _____ Purch. 19__ Pd $ _____

15237 PLATE – Girl Story Teller
"Tell Me The Story Of Jesus"

DATED 1985   D $65

Comments: 1984; Original Retail $40.00
Fourth issue in *Joy of Christmas Series*. More scarce than other dated plates. Price down from '96.
See #1, page XI.

Personal Data: _____
____Want Mark ____ Mark _____ Purch. 19__ Pd $ _____

15482 Boy Tangled in Lights
"May Your Christmas Be Delightful"

SUSP. 1994 - 3 YEARS AGO

D	$70	FL	$55	V	$55	TRP	$45
OB	$65	BA	$55	GC	$55		
CT	$60	FLM	$55	B	$50		

Comments: 1985; Original Retail $25.00/$35.00
Also an ornament (#15849).

Personal Data: _____
____Want Mark ____ Mark _____ Purch. 19__ Pd $ _____

15490 Goose in Bonnet with Babies (2 pc. set)
"Honk If You Love Jesus"

D	$35	BA	$25	B	$20	SRD	$20
OB	$30	FLM	$25	TRP	$20		
CT	$30	V	$25	S	$20		
FL	$25	GC	$20	H	$20		

Comments: 1985; Original Retail $13.00/$20.00
Delicate! Be careful when dusting! Many goose necks have been broken, including my goose! Ha!

Personal Data: _____
____Want Mark ____ Mark _____ Purch. 19__ Pd $ _____

15504 ♪ MUSICAL – Jack in the Box
"God Sent You Just In Time"

RETIRED 1989 - 8 YEARS AGO

D	$118	FL	$95	OB	$100
BA	$90	CT	$95		

Comments: 1985; Original Retail $45.00/$60.00
Plays *We Wish You A Merry Christmas*.

Personal Data: _____
____Want Mark ____ Mark _____ Purch. 19__ Pd $ _____

15539 Baby Boy Holding Bottle
"Baby's First Christmas"

DATED 1985 -12 YEARS AGO   D $40

Comments: 1985; Original Retail $13.00
The first marked *Baby's First Christmas* dated pieces (cradle) debuted in 1983. Secondary market dealers report dated *Baby's First* is not traded as often as in years past. **See #29, page XIV.**

Personal Data: _____
____Want Mark ____ Mark _____ Purch. 19__ Pd $ _____

15547 Baby Girl Holding Bottle
"Baby's First Christmas"

DATED 1985   D $35

Comments: 1985; Original Retail $13.00
See #29, page XIV.

Personal Data: _____
____Want Mark ____ Mark _____ Purch. 19__ Pd $ _____

15768 *ORNAMENT* – **Angel with Holly Wreath**
"God Sent His Love"

DATED 1985   D $28

Comments: 1985; Original Retail $10.00
This ornament is the fifth in the dated ornament series (not including *Baby's First Christmas* dated ornaments). **See #29, page XIV.**

Personal Data: _____
___Want Mark ___ Mark ____ Purch. 19__ Pd $ _____

15776   **Mother with Cookies**
"May You Have The Sweetest Christmas"

SUSP. 1992 - 5 YEARS AGO

D $50	FL $45	V $40
OB $50	BA $42	GC $35
CT $45	FLM $42	

Comments: 1985; Original Retail $17.00/$25.00
First issue in the *Family Christmas Scene Series*. This series was also produced in "painted pewter" in 1990. Painted pewter is not as collectible as some thought it would become. The eyes were not painted well and paint chipped on first years' production. It will be interesting to watch the collectibility of the Goebel miniatures.

Personal Data: _____
___Want Mark ___ Mark ____ Purch. 19__ Pd $ _____

15784   **Father in Chair Reading Bible**
"The Story Of God's Love"

SUSP. 1992 - 5 YEARS AGO

D $65	FL $55	V $50	OB $55
BA $55	GC $47	CT $55	FLM $50

Comments: 1985; Original Retail $22.50/$35.00
Second issue in the *Family Christmas Scene Series* D mark only one being sought on secondary market. **See 15776, pewter.**

Personal Data: _____
___Want Mark ___ Mark ____ Purch. 19__ Pd $ _____

A gardener is someone who believes that what goes down must come up.

15792   **Little Boy Sitting**
"Tell Me A Story"

SUSP. 1992 - 5 YEARS AGO

D $40	FL $30	V $25
OB $30	BA $25	GC $22
CT $30	FLM $25	

Comments: 1985; Original Retail $10.00/$15.00
Third issue in the *Family Christmas Scene Series*. Only piece in demand to date is D mark. **See 15776, pewter.**

Personal Data: _____
___Want Mark ___ Mark ____ Purch. 19__ Pd $ _____

15806   **Girl Hanging an** *Ornament*
"God Gave His Best"

SUSP. 1992 - 5 YEARS AGO

D $50	FL $35	V $35
OB $45	BA $35	GC $30
CT $40	FLM $35	

Comments: 1985; Original Retail $13.00/$19.00
Fourth issue in the *Family Christmas Scene Series*. Do not over inflate prices as seen in other guides! **See 15776, pewter.**

Personal Data: _____
___Want Mark ___ Mark ____ Purch. 19__ Pd $ _____

15814 ♪   *MUSICAL* – **Tree**
"Silent Night"

SUSP. 1992 - 5 YEARS AGO

D $105	FL $90	V $75
OB $100	BA $80	GC $75
CT $95	FLM $75	

Comments: 1985; Original Retail $37.50/$55.00
Plays *Silent Night*. Fifth issue in *Family Christmas Scene Series*. Not being sought after heavily to date. **See 15776, pewter.**

Personal Data: _____
___Want Mark ___ Mark ____ Purch. 19__ Pd $ _____

Happy 15th Anniversary
PRECIOUS COLLECTIBLES®
Thank you Subscribers!

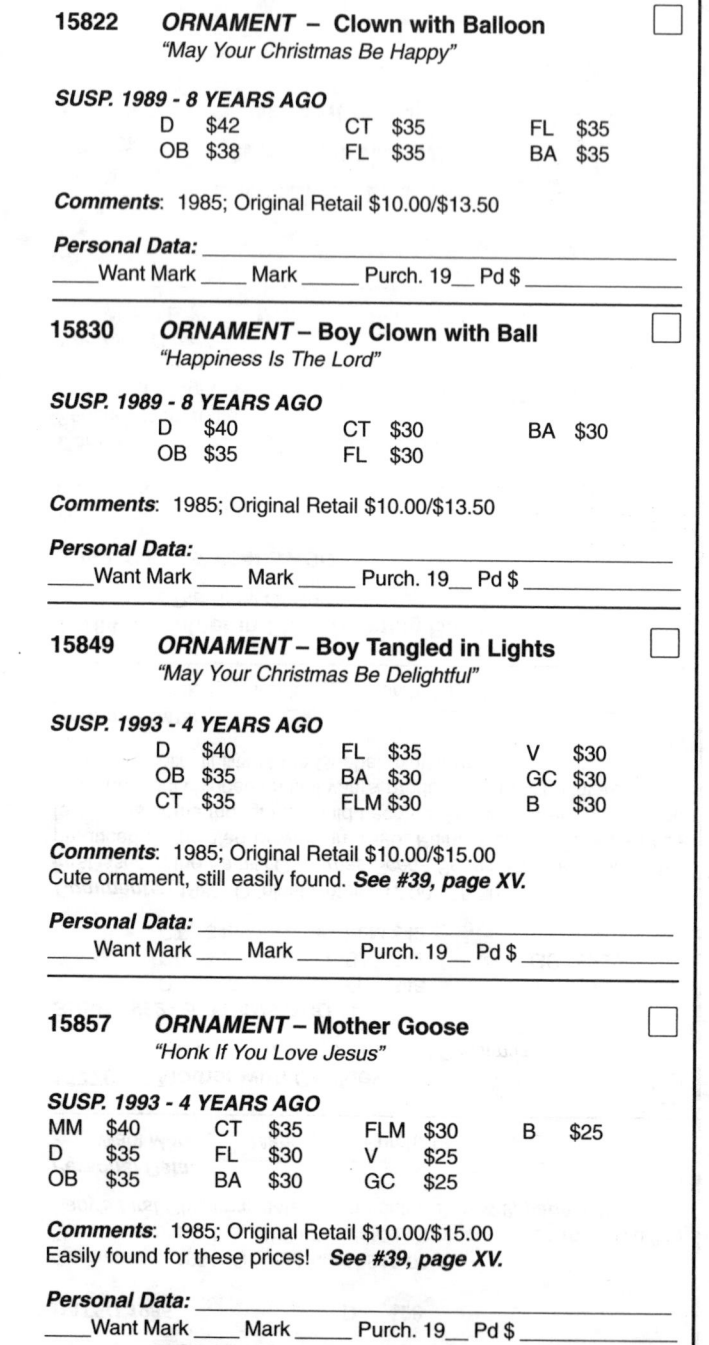

15822 ORNAMENT – Clown with Balloon
"May Your Christmas Be Happy"

SUSP. 1989 - 8 YEARS AGO

D	$42	CT	$35	FL	$35
OB	$38	FL	$35	BA	$35

Comments: 1985; Original Retail $10.00/$13.50

Personal Data: _____
____Want Mark ____ Mark _____ Purch. 19__ Pd $ _____

15830 ORNAMENT – Boy Clown with Ball
"Happiness Is The Lord"

SUSP. 1989 - 8 YEARS AGO

D	$40	CT	$30	BA	$30
OB	$35	FL	$30		

Comments: 1985; Original Retail $10.00/$13.50

Personal Data: _____
____Want Mark ____ Mark _____ Purch. 19__ Pd $ _____

15849 ORNAMENT – Boy Tangled in Lights
"May Your Christmas Be Delightful"

SUSP. 1993 - 4 YEARS AGO

D	$40	FL	$35	V	$30
OB	$35	BA	$30	GC	$30
CT	$35	FLM	$30	B	$30

Comments: 1985; Original Retail $10.00/$15.00
Cute ornament, still easily found. ***See #39, page XV.***

Personal Data: _____
____Want Mark ____ Mark _____ Purch. 19__ Pd $ _____

15857 ORNAMENT – Mother Goose
"Honk If You Love Jesus"

SUSP. 1993 - 4 YEARS AGO

MM	$40	CT	$35	FLM	$30	B	$25
D	$35	FL	$30	V	$25		
OB	$35	BA	$30	GC	$25		

Comments: 1985; Original Retail $10.00/$15.00
Easily found for these prices! ***See #39, page XV.***

Personal Data: _____
____Want Mark ____ Mark _____ Purch. 19__ Pd $ _____

15865 THIMBLE – Angel/Wreath
"God Sent His Love"

DATED 1985

D $50

Comments: 1985; Original Retail $5.50
Only scarce thimble to date, but trading slow in past year with lower prices. Embossed D mark, not decaled as on first three thimbles which debuted in 1985 (12254, 13293, and 13307).

Personal Data: _____
____Want Mark ____ Mark _____ Purch. 19__ Pd $ _____

15873 BELL – Angel with Holly Wreath
"God Sent His Love"

DATED 1985

D $25

Comments: 1985; Original Retail $19.00
1993 was the last year for dated bells of this design. Secondary market prices fell in '96.

Personal Data: _____
____Want Mark ____ Mark _____ Purch. 19__ Pd $ _____

15881 Angel with Holly Wreath
"God Sent His Love"

DATED 1985   D $45

Comments: 1985; Original Retail $17.00

Personal Data: _____
____Want Mark ____ Mark _____ Purch. 19__ Pd $ _____

15903 ORNAMENT – Boy Holding Bottle
"Baby's First Christmas"

DATED 1985   D $40

Comments: 1985; Original Retail $10.00

Personal Data: _____
____Want Mark ____ Mark _____ Purch. 19__ Pd $ _____

15911 ORNAMENT – Girl Holding Bottle
"Baby's First Christmas"

DATED 1985 D $40

Comments: 1985; Original Retail $10.00
There were more girls "for sale" in '93 and '94 than boys.

Personal Data: _____
____Want Mark ____ Mark _____ Purch. 19__ Pd $ _____

15938 Baby – Teddy/Caboose
"May Your Birthday Be Warm"

D	$40	BA	$20	B	$15	SRD $15
OB	$25	FLM	$18	TRP	$15	
CT	$20	V	$15	S	$15	
FL	$20	GC	$15	H	$15	

Comments: 1985; Original Retail $10.00/$15.00
Part of *Birthday Train Series*. **See #30, page XIV.**

Personal Data: _____
____Want Mark ____ Mark _____ Purch. 19__ Pd $ _____

15946 Age 1 – Lamb
"Happy Birthday Little Lamb"

D	$45	BA	$20	B	$15	SRD $15
OB	$25	FLM	$20	TRP	$15	
CT	$20	V	$18	S	$15	
FL	$20	GC	$15	H	$15	

Comments: 1985; Original Retail $10.00/$15.00
Part of *Birthday Train Series*. Many of the Birthday Train animals have been found with the numeral decals missing. Very limited. Add $75 on such an error. **See #30, page XIV.**

Personal Data: _____
____Want Mark ____ Mark _____ Purch. 19__ Pd $ _____

15954 Age 3 – Pig
"Heaven Bless Your Special Day"

D	$40	BA	$20	B	$17.50	SRD $17.50
OB	$25	FLM	$20	TRP	$17.50	
CT	$22	V	$17.50	S	$17.50	
FL	$20	GC	$17.50	H	$17.50	

Comments: 1985; Original Retail $11.00/$17.50
Part of *Birthday Train Series*.
See #30, page XIV.

Personal Data: _____
____Want Mark ____ Mark _____ Purch. 19__ Pd $ _____

15962 Age 2 – Seal
"God Bless You On Your Birthday"

D	$45	BA	$25	B	$20	SRD $17.50
OB	$30	FLM	$25	TRP	$17.50	
CT	$25	V	$25	S	$17.50	
FL	$25	GC	$20	H	$17.50	

Comments: 1985; Original Retail $11.00/$17.50
Part of *Birthday Train Series*. Children's "age" pieces usually are traded most on ages Baby through #2.
See #30, page XIV.

Personal Data: _____
____Want Mark ____ Mark _____ Purch. 19__ Pd $ _____

15970 Age 4 – Elephant
"May Your Birthday Be Gigantic"

D	$45	BA	$25	B	$20	SRD $20
OB	$30	FLM	$25	TRP	$20	
CT	$25	V	$25	S	$20	
FL	$25	GC	$20	H	$20	

Comments: 1985; Original Retail $12.50/$20.00
Part of *Birthday Train Series*. Retail rising faster than secondary market. **See #30, page XIV.**

Personal Data: _____
____Want Mark ____ Mark _____ Purch. 19__ Pd $ _____

Collectors waited patiently in line to meet Rosie at the Secaucus Expo.
Be sure to meet Rosie and Dave this April in Long Beach, CA and
Tulsa, OK and in June at the Expo in Rosemont, IL!

15989 Age 5 – Lion
"This Day Is Something To Roar About"

D	$40	BA	$30	B	$25	SRD $22.50
OB	$30	FLM	$30	TRP	$22.50	
CT	$30	V	$25	S	$22.50	
FL	$30	GC	$25	H	$22.50	

Comments: 1985; Original Retail $13.50/$22.50
Part of *Birthday Train Series*. Most collectors are not seeking these pieces after their child reaches age five or more. **See #30, page XIV.**

Personal Data: _____
____Want Mark ____ Mark _____ Purch. 19__ Pd $ _____

15997 Age 6 – Giraffe
"Keep Looking Up"

D	$40	BA	$28	B	$25	SRD $22.50
OB	$30	FLM	$28	TRP	$22.50	
CT	$28	V	$25	S	$22.50	
FL	$28	GC	$25	H	$22.50	

Comments: 1985; Original Retail $13.50/$22.50
Part of *Birthday Train Series*. Giraffe collectors enjoy this piece! **See #30, page XIV**.

Personal Data: _____
____Want Mark ____ Mark _____ Purch. 19__ Pd $ _____

16004 Clown Pulling Train
"Bless The Days Of Our Youth"

D	$38	BA	$25	B	$22.50	SRD $22.50
OB	$25	FLM	$25	TRP	$22.50	
CT	$25	V	$22.50	S	$22.50	
FL	$25	GC	$22.50	H	$22.50	

Comments: 1985; Original Retail $15.00/$22.50
Part of *Birthday Train Series*. **See #30, page XIV.**

Personal Data: _____
____Want Mark ____ Mark _____ Purch. 19__ Pd $ _____

How beautiful a day can be when kindness touches it.

16012 Angel Pushing Buggy
"Baby's First Trip"

SUSP. 1989 - 8 YEARS AGO

D	$300	CT	$285	BA	$265
OB	$295	FL	$265		

Comments: 1985; Original Retail $32.50/$45.00
Fourth in *Baby's First Series*. This series is very popular and this is a great piece! Not easy to find.

Personal Data: _____
____Want Mark ____ Mark _____ Purch. 19__ Pd $ _____

16020 *NIGHT LIGHT* – Angel Behind Rainbow
"God Bless You With Rainbows"

SUSP. 1989 - 8 YEARS AGO

D	$125	FL	$100
OB	$115	BA	$90
CT	$105		

Comments: 1985; Original Retail $45.00/$57.50
This piece has not been easy to find since 1989. Very pretty. Three rainbow pieces have been produced.

Personal Data: _____
____Want Mark ____ Mark _____ Purch. 19__ Pd $ _____

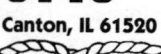

Michael Belofsky holds the attention of his audience while demonstrating the benefits of the computer inventory program he designed especially for Precious Moments collectors by using this guide's price values. *See MSdataBase Solutions, Inc.'s full page advertisement in this guide for more information.*

100021   Boy Sitting with Teddy
"To My Favorite Paw"

SUSP. 1988 - 9 YEARS AGO

D	$65	CT	$60
OB	$60	FL	$52

Comments: 1985; Original Retail $22.50/$27.00
Figurines for "Dad" are not top retail sellers as those for "Mom."

Personal Data: _____
____Want Mark ____ Mark _____ Purch. 19__ Pd $ _____

100048   Girl with Fawn
"To My Deer Friend"

OB	$95	FLM	$50	TRP	$50
CT	$70	V	$50	S	$50
FL	$60	GC	$50	H	$50
BA	$60	B	$50	SRD	$50

Comments: 1986; Original Retail $33.00/$50.00
Suspension coming soon, in my opinion, as demand is decreasing after twelve years; prices have been found below retail on several ads recently.

Personal Data: _____
____Want Mark ____ Mark _____ Purch. 19__ Pd $ _____

100056   Boy on Cloud with Bow and Arrow
"Sending My Love"

SUSP. 1991 - 6 YEARS AGO

D	$65	BA	$45
OB	$55	FLM	$45
CT	$50	V	$45
FL	$45		

Comments: 1985; Original Retail $22.50/$32.50
First appeared on a Halo Card, H039-B. May be considered a part of the *Halo Series* produced previously (Cloud as the base). First appeared on dealers' shelves in late Nov. 1985 for early 1986 Valentine's sales; had 1985 mark. This is the "norm" for Valentine pieces. (100250 also reached shelves at the same time.)
See #31, page XIV.

Personal Data: _____
____Want Mark ____ Mark _____ Purch. 19__ Pd $ _____

100064   Girl Kneeling at Church Window
"O Worship The Lord"

D	$60	BA	$40	B	$40	SRD	$40
OB	$50	FLM	$40	TRP	$40		
CT	$45	V	$40	S	$40		
FL	$40	GC	$40	H	$40		

Comments: 1985; Original Retail $24.00/$40.00
Appeared on J&D Card, A197-B. I feel this would be a good one to suspend or retire as it is a large piece that does not display as well with others due to its size. (Same for the Boy at Church Window, 102229.) Has been found with and without the "O" in title. No significant difference in secondary market. Perfect candidate for suspension or possible retirement.

Personal Data: _____
____Want Mark ____ Mark _____ Purch. 19__ Pd $ _____

100072   Two Girls Holding Flowers
"To My Forever Friend"

D	$100	BA	$55	B	$55	SRD	$55
OB	$65	FLM	$55	TRP	$55		
CT	$65	V	$55	S	$55		
FL	$55	GC	$55	H	$55		

Comments: 1985; Original Retail $33.00/$55.00
There have not been many double-figured pieces with two girls. This is an attractive piece! More colorful than most. (So colorful and time consuming to produce; it may be a good candidate for retirement.) The 1995 Easter Seals piece resembles this piece with flowers, etc.

Personal Data: _____
____Want Mark ____ Mark _____ Purch. 19__ Pd $ _____

100080 Girl/Boy Mending Broken Heart
"He's The Healer Of Broken Hearts"

OB	$65	FLM	$50	TRP	$50
CT	$62	V	$50	S	$50
FL	$60	GC	$50	H	$50
BA	$60	B	$50	SRD	$50

Comments: 1986; Original Retail $33.00/$50.00
Candidate for suspension?

Personal Data: _____
____Want Mark ____ Mark _____ Purch. 19__ Pd $ _____

100102 Girl with Sick Bear
"Make Me A Blessing"

RETIRED 1990 – 7 YEARS AGO

OB	$135	FL	$70	FLM	$60
CT	$90	BA	$65		

Comments: 1986; Original Retail $35.00/$50.00
Most available of the 1990 retirement pieces after retirement announcement... but not for long.

Personal Data: _____
____Want Mark ____ Mark _____ Purch. 19__ Pd $ _____

100110 Baseball Player with Bat
"Lord, I'm Coming Home"

D	$65	BA	$42	B	$35	SRD	$35
OB	$55	FLM	$42	TRP	$35		
CT	$45	V	$40	S	$35		
FL	$45	GC	$40	H	$35		

Comments: 1985; Original Retail $22.50/$35.00
Sports themes began in 1986. Slow secondary market seller. Good potential for retirement or suspension because of that.

Personal Data: _____
____Want Mark ____ Mark _____ Purch. 19__ Pd $ _____

100129 Ballerina
"Lord, Keep Me On My Toes"

RETIRED 1988 - 9 YEARS AGO

D	$110	CT	$85
OB	$85	FL	$80

Comments: 1985; Original Retail $22.50/$27.00

Personal Data: _____
____Want Mark ____ Mark _____ Purch. 19__ Pd $ _____

100137 Mom with Babies
"The Joy Of The Lord Is My Strength"

D	$110	BA	$55	B	$55	SRD	$55
OB	$80	FLM	$55	TRP	$55		
CT	$60	V	$55	S	$55		
FL	$55	GC	$55	H	$55		

Comments: 1985; Original Retail $35.00/$55.00
Cute piece, much detail. Easy to find. This piece was reported found with a C Mark. Very Rare!

Personal Data: _____
____Want Mark ____ Mark _____ Purch. 19__ Pd $ _____

100145 Mom/Dad/Girl Adoption
"God Bless The Day We Found You"

SUSP. 1990 - 7 YEARS AGO
RETURNED FROM SUSPENSION 1995

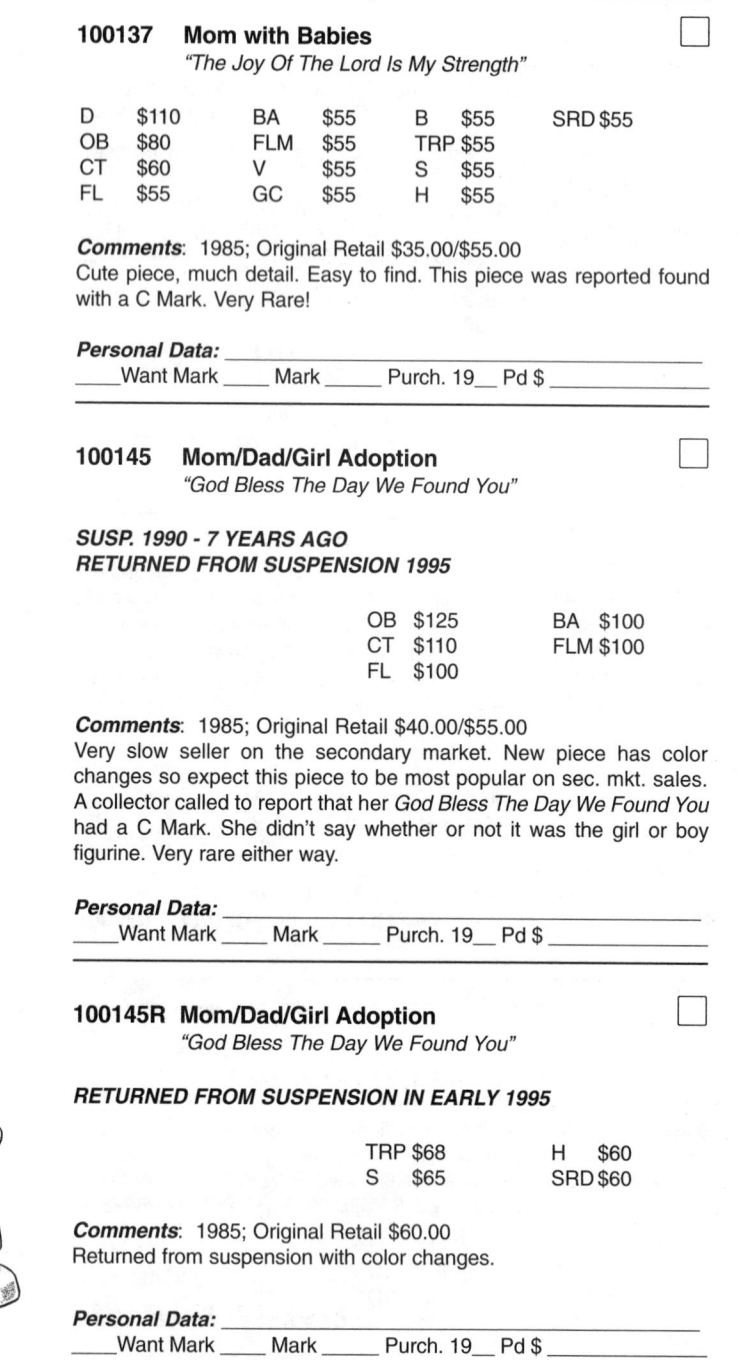

OB	$125	BA	$100
CT	$110	FLM	$100
FL	$100		

Comments: 1985; Original Retail $40.00/$55.00
Very slow seller on the secondary market. New piece has color changes so expect this piece to be most popular on sec. mkt. sales. A collector called to report that her *God Bless The Day We Found You* had a C Mark. She didn't say whether or not it was the girl or boy figurine. Very rare either way.

Personal Data: _____
____Want Mark ____ Mark _____ Purch. 19__ Pd $ _____

100145R Mom/Dad/Girl Adoption
"God Bless The Day We Found You"

RETURNED FROM SUSPENSION IN EARLY 1995

TRP	$68	H	$60
S	$65	SRD	$60

Comments: 1985; Original Retail $60.00
Returned from suspension with color changes.

Personal Data: _____
____Want Mark ____ Mark _____ Purch. 19__ Pd $ _____

100153 Mom/Dad/Boy Adoption
"God Bless The Day We Found You"

SUSP. 1990 - 7 YEARS AGO
RETURNED FROM SUSPENSION 1995

OB	$110	BA	$90
CT	$105	FLM	$90
FL	$100		

Comments: 1985; Original Retail $40.00/$55.00

Personal Data: _____
____Want Mark ____ Mark _____ Purch. 19__ Pd $ _____

100153R Mom/Dad/Boy Adoption
"God Bless The Day We Found You"

RETURNED FROM SUSPENSION IN 1995

TRP	$62.50	SRD	$60
S	$60.00		
H	$60.00		

Comments: 1985; Original Retail $60.00
Returned from suspension.

Personal Data: _____
____Want Mark ____ Mark _____ Purch. 19__ Pd $ _____

100161 Girl Tennis Player
"Serving The Lord"

SUSP. 1990 - 7 YEARS AGO

D	$75	FL	$45
OB	$65	BA	$40
CT	$55	FLM	$40

Comments: 1985; Original Retail $19.00/$27.50
See #32, page XIV.

Personal Data: _____
____Want Mark ____ Mark _____ Purch. 19__ Pd $ _____

100188 Boy with Football
"I'm A Possibility"

RETIRED 1993 - 4 YEARS AGO

OB	$85	BA	$65	GC	$60
CT	$75	FLM	$65	B	$60
FL	$70	V	$65		

Comments: 1985; Original Retail $22.00/$35.00

Personal Data: _____
____Want Mark ____ Mark _____ Purch. 19__ Pd $ _____

100196 Girl on Scales
"The Spirit Is Willing But The Flesh Is Weak"

RETIRED 1991 - 6 YEARS AGO

D	$105	CT	$80	BA	$65	V	$55
OB	$100	FL	$75	FLM	$60		

Comments: 1986; Original Retail $19.00/$30.00
From letters I've received, this piece slowed the demand to purchase the only other Curler Girl piece. Collectors wanted the Curler Girl, thus this piece made a good substitute. Figurine actually shows one hand holding candy box and one hand taking piece of candy, unlike line cut... often line cuts are different than the figurines.

Personal Data: _____
____Want Mark ____ Mark _____ Purch. 19__ Pd $ _____

100226 Girl/Cat and Bird Cage
"The Lord Giveth And The Lord Taketh Away"

RETIRED 1995 - 2 YEARS AGO

CT	$90	FLM	$70	B	$60
FL	$85	V	$65	TRP	$60
BA	$75	GC	$65	S	$55

Comments: 1986; Original Retail $33.50/$40.00
Sam relates this piece to when Katy lost her bird to a feline! I know how she felt!!! Mine never had a feather left!

Personal Data: _____
____Want Mark ____ Mark _____ Purch. 19__ Pd $ _____

100250 Boy and Girl in Boat
"Friends Never Drift Apart"

D	$85	BA	$60	B	$60	SRD	$60
OB	$70	FLM	$60	TRP	$60		
CT	$70	V	$60	S	$60		
FL	$60	GC	$60	H	$60		

Comments: 1985; Original Retail $35.00/$60.00
1986 Valentine piece. Produced in late months of 1985, thus first pieces had D mark. Some heads touch due to mold shrinkage. Have had one report of missing oars. This would be a good retirement piece. Lots of work in production but suspension more likely. Similar style ornament (522937) retired in 1995.

Personal Data: _____
____Want Mark ____ Mark _____ Purch. 19__ Pd $ _____

100269 Boy/Ink Spot
"Help, Lord I'm In A Spot"

RETIRED 1989 - 8 YEARS AGO

OB	$75	FL	$65
CT	$70	BA	$60

Comments: 1985; Original Retail $18.50/$25.00
Definitely did not sell well, not even on the secondary market after being retired. The ink spot was "too light" in color to be effective! One collector reported the ink bottle sitting straight up instead of on its side. Add $100 to the secondary market value for this error.

Personal Data: _____
____Want Mark ____ Mark ____ Purch. 19__ Pd $ _____

100277 Girl in Bathtub
"He Cleansed My Soul"

D	$60	BA	$40	B	$40	SRD	$40
OB	$50	FLM	$40	TRP	$40		
CT	$45	V	$40	S	$40		
FL	$45	GC	$40	H	$40		

Comments: 1985; Original Retail $24.00/$40.00
Has been found without "Holy Bible" decal on Bible. This increases the value by $75 on the secondary market. Place iridescent beads around this piece. It makes a delightful display in the bathroom!

Personal Data: _____
____Want Mark ____ Mark ____ Purch. 19__ Pd $ _____

100285 ♪ MUSICAL – Baby with Toys
"Heaven Bless You"

SUSP. 1993 - 4 YEARS AGO

D	$95	FL	$65	V	$65
OB	$85	BA	$65	GC	$65
CT	$70	FLM	$65	B	$65

Comments: 1984; Original Retail $45.00/$60.00
Plays *Brahm's Lullaby*.

Personal Data: _____
____Want Mark ____ Mark ____ Purch. 19__ Pd $ _____

$\mathcal{L}$ord, help me to be the person my dog thinks I am.

100293 Boy Tennis Player
"Serving The Lord"

SUSP. 1990 - 7 YEARS AGO

D	$60	FL	$35
OB	$50	BA	$35
CT	$40	FLM	$35

Comments: 1985; Original Retail $19.00/$27.50
See #32, page XIV.

Personal Data: _____
____Want Mark ____ Mark ____ Purch. 19__ Pd $ _____

100455 DOLL – Boy Clown
"Bong Bong"

LE 1985 - 12 YEARS OLD   OB $200-265

Comments: 1985; Original Retail $150.00
Limited Ed. 12,000. Very colorful – nice. Secondary market prices affecting slow sales. Insure at $265, but to sell quickly price may have to be reduced.

Personal Data: _____
____Want Mark ____ Mark ____ Purch. 19__ Pd $ _____

100463 DOLL – Girl Clown
"Candy"

LE 1985 - 12 YEARS OLD   OB $200-265

Comments: 1985; Original Retail $150.00
Limited Ed. 12,000. Pretty! Scarce. Not easily found - very colorful! See 100455 for same comments.

Personal Data: _____
____Want Mark ____ Mark ____ Purch. 19__ Pd $ _____

100498 Parents of the Groom
"God Bless Our Family"

CT	$65	FLM	$55	B	$50	H	$50
FL	$60	V	$50	TRP	$50	SRD	$50
BA	$55	GC	$50	S	$50		

Comments: 1986; Original Retail $35.00/$50.00
Not easily found. Slow seller; retailers don't order in volume. Cute piece. Potential for suspension, in my opinion, as $50 for a wedding gift usually isn't affordable for most.

Personal Data: _____
____Want Mark ____ Mark ____ Purch. 19__ Pd $ _____

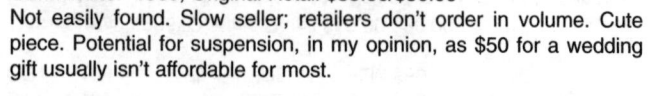

100501   Parents of the Bride
"God Bless Our Family"

CT	$62	FLM	$50	B	$50	H	$50
FL	$55	V	$50	TRP	$50	SRD	$50
BA	$55	GC	$50	S	$50		

Comments: 1986; Original Retail $35.00/$50.00
Not easily found. Slow seller; retailers don't order in volume. (I feel these would sell faster if the price could have been held lower. See 100498; same opinion.) This is probably a suspension candidate.

Personal Data: _____
____Want Mark ____ Mark _____ Purch. 19__ Pd $ _____

100528   Girl with Skunk
"Scent From Above"

RETIRED 1991 - 6 YEARS AGO

OB	$80	BA	$55
CT	$65	FLM	$40
FL	$65	V	$40

Comments: 1986; Original Retail $19.00/$27.50
Is this Diane and Beau K?

Personal Data: _____
____Want Mark ____ Mark _____ Purch. 19__ Pd $ _____

100536   Boy with Flower and Mom
"I Picked A Very Special Mom"

LE 1987 - 10 YEARS OLD   OB $80
                               CT $75

Error   *"I Picked A Special Mom"* OB $85
                                    CT $70

Comments: 1986; Original Retail $37.50/$40.00
1987 Limited Edition piece. Mainly CT pieces being sold...
OB not as abundant.

Personal Data: _____
____Want Mark ____ Mark _____ Purch. 19__ Pd $ _____

100544   Pilgrim/Indian/Turkey
"Brotherly Love"

SUSP. 1989 - 8 YEARS AGO   OB $110   FL $75
                               CT $90   BA $75

Comments: 1985; Original Retail $37.00/$47.50
Ideal for "Thanksgiving Theme." I was quite surprised when this was suspended! This is an unusual piece, different than the "norm."

Personal Data: _____
____Want Mark ____ Mark _____ Purch. 19__ Pd $ _____

100625   THIMBLE – Girl Holding Heart
"God Is Love, Dear Valentine"

SUSP. 1989 - 8 YEARS AGO   D $22   FL $12
                               OB $18   BA $12
                               CT $15

Comments: 1985; Original Retail $5.50/$8.00

Personal Data: _____
____Want Mark ____ Mark _____ Purch. 19__ Pd $ _____

100633   THIMBLE – Bride
"The Lord Bless You And Keep You"

SUSP. 1991 - 6 YEARS AGO   D $22   BA $12
                                OB $18   FLM $12
                                CT $14   V $12
                                FL $14

Comments: 1979; Original Retail $5.50/$8.00
As the original artwork of the Bride/Groom was sold to Enesco in 1979, I'm assuming the thimble would carry the same license date. Research found very little trading in thimbles.

Personal Data: _____
____Want Mark ____ Mark _____ Purch. 19__ Pd $ _____

100641   THIMBLES – "Four Seasons" (Set of 4)
"Worship The Lord"

LE 1985 - 12 YEARS OLD   OB $95 set
                                    $25 ea.

Comments: 1985; Original Retail $20.00
1985 Limited Edition.

Personal Data: _____
____Want Mark ____ Mark _____ Purch. 19__ Pd $ _____

100668   THIMBLES – (Set of 2)
"Clowns"

SUSP. 1988 - 9 YEARS AGO
                    OB $35 set   FL $35 set
                    CT $35 set   BA $35 set
Comments: 1985; Original Retail $11.00/$14.00

Personal Data: _____
____Want Mark ____ Mark _____ Purch. 19__ Pd $ _____

101702 ♪ *MUSICAL* – Boy and Girl in Box
"Our First Christmas Together"

RETIRED 1992 - 5 YEARS AGO

OB	$110	FLM	$100
CT	$105	V	$90
FL	$100	GC	$90
BA	$100		

Comments: 1985; Original Retail $50.00/$70.00
Plays *We Wish You A Merry Christmas*. In the 1990 guide I predicted suspension or retirement of this Musical due to its size. Did not see many FLM marks in 1990. Judge each piece carefully and you'll soon recognize candidates for suspension or retirement, especially after 7 or 8 years of production. Prices reflect a decrease in secondary market value.

Personal Data: _____
____Want Mark ____ Mark _____ Purch. 19__ Pd $ _____

101826 Angel and Girl at Heaven's Gate
"No Tears Past The Gate"

OB	$115	FLM	$70	TRP	$70
CT	$100	V	$70	S	$70
FL	$75	GC	$70	H	$70
BA	$75	B	$70	SRD	$70

Comments: 1986; Original Retail $40.00/$70.00
The front mural in the Precious Moments Chapel depicts a similar scene. Has been found without decal on bucket. Older marks demanding more on this figurine.

Personal Data: _____
____Want Mark ____ Mark _____ Purch. 19__ Pd $ _____

101834 *PLATE* – Girl at Mailbox
"I'm Sending You A White Christmas"

DATED 1986   OB $45

Comments: 1986; Original Retail $45.00
First issue in *Christmas Love Series*. A "flaw" similar to an HG mark appeared on most plates. Price down from '96.

Personal Data: _____
____Want Mark ____ Mark _____ Purch. 19__ Pd $ _____

101842 Clown Upside Down on Drum
"Smile Along The Way"

RETIRED 1991 - 6 YEARS AGO

MM	$195	BA	$135
OB	$180	FLM	$130
CT	$170	V	$125
FL	$145		

Comments: 1986; Original Retail $30.00/$45.00
Extra pieces were not produced after the retirement announcement. This piece is colorful and popular. Most of the trading was found on CT mark in '93, '94 and '95.

Personal Data: _____
____Want Mark ____ Mark _____ Purch. 19__ Pd $ _____

101850 Clown on Unicycle
"Lord, Help Us Keep Our Act Together"

RETIRED 1992 - 5 YEARS AGO	D	$150	BA	$115
	OB	$130	FLM	$115
	CT	$120	V	$100
	FL	$115		

Comments: 1986; Original Retail $35.00/$50.00
Much trading found for OB and V marks in '96! D Scarce!

Personal Data: _____
____Want Mark ____ Mark _____ Purch. 19__ Pd $ _____

102229 Boy Kneeling at Church Window
"O Worship The Lord"

D	$50	BA	$40	B	$40	SRD	$40
OB	$45	FLM	$40	TRP	$40		
CT	$40	V	$40	S	$40		
FL	$40	GC	$40	H	$40		

Comments: 1985; Original Retail $24.00/$40.00
Notice the great difference between this piece's order number and the Kneeling Girl's number (100064). Most generally "similar" pieces as these have similar order numbers. Not a best seller. Look for possible suspension. Found with and without "O" in title.

Personal Data: _____
____Want Mark ____ Mark _____ Purch. 19__ Pd $ _____

102253 *DOLL*
"Connie"

OB $200-225

Comments: 1985; Original Retail $160.00
Limited Edition 7,500. Named after Sam's daughter-in-law (Philip Butcher's wife). A very pretty doll. Price dropped considerably from '96.

Personal Data: _____
____Want Mark ____ Mark _____ Purch. 19__ Pd $ _____

102261 *MINI NATIVITY* – Angel with Lamb
"Shepherd Of Love"

OB	$32	BA	$17	GC	$16	S	$16
CT	$20	FLM	$16	B	$16	H	$16
FL	$17	V	$16	TRP	$16	SRD	$16

Comments: 1985; Original Retail $10.00/$16.00
Addition to Miniature Nativity.

Personal Data: _____
____Want Mark ____ Mark _____ Purch. 19__ Pd $ _____

102288 *ORNAMENT* – Angel with Lamb
"Shepherd Of Love"

SUSP. 1993 - 4 YEARS AGO

OB	$40	BA	$25	GC	$22
CT	$30	FLM	$25	B	$22
FL	$30	V	$22		

Comments: 1985; Original Retail $10.00/$15.00
Very popular ornament. Easily found.

Personal Data: _____
____Want Mark ____ Mark _____ Purch. 19__ Pd $ _____

Celebrating 15 years of
"Bringing Collectors
Together!"

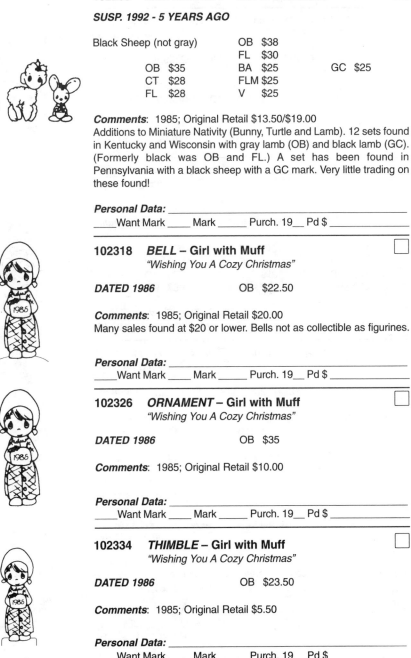

102296 *MINI NATIVITY* – Set of 3 Animals

SUSP. 1992 - 5 YEARS AGO

Black Sheep (not gray)		OB	$38		
		FL	$30		
OB	$35	BA	$25	GC	$25
CT	$28	FLM	$25		
FL	$28	V	$25		

Comments: 1985; Original Retail $13.50/$19.00
Additions to Miniature Nativity (Bunny, Turtle and Lamb). 12 sets found in Kentucky and Wisconsin with gray lamb (OB) and black lamb (GC). (Formerly black was OB and FL.) A set has been found in Pennsylvania with a black sheep with a GC mark. Very little trading on these found!

Personal Data: _____
____Want Mark ____ Mark _____ Purch. 19__ Pd $ _____

102318 *BELL* – Girl with Muff
"Wishing You A Cozy Christmas"

DATED 1986   OB $22.50

Comments: 1985; Original Retail $20.00
Many sales found at $20 or lower. Bells not as collectible as figurines.

Personal Data: _____
____Want Mark ____ Mark _____ Purch. 19__ Pd $ _____

102326 *ORNAMENT* – Girl with Muff
"Wishing You A Cozy Christmas"

DATED 1986   OB $35

Comments: 1985; Original Retail $10.00

Personal Data: _____
____Want Mark ____ Mark _____ Purch. 19__ Pd $ _____

102334 *THIMBLE* – Girl with Muff
"Wishing You A Cozy Christmas"

DATED 1986   OB $23.50

Comments: 1985; Original Retail $5.50

Personal Data: _____
____Want Mark ____ Mark _____ Purch. 19__ Pd $ _____

102342 FIGURINE – Girl with Muff
"Wishing You A Cozy Christmas"

DATED 1986 OB $40

Comments: 1985; Original Retail $18.00
Dated figurines have not made "news" recently on the secondary market.

Personal Data: _____
____Want Mark ____ Mark _____ Purch. 19__ Pd $ _____

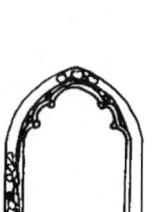

102350 ORNAMENT – Boy/Girl in Gift Box
"Our First Christmas Together"

DATED 1986 OB $30

Comments: 1985; Original Retail $10.00
This ornament was also produced in 1987 (112399) and 1988 (520233). The only differences were the marks, style numbers and the dates. *See #29, page XIV.*

Personal Data: _____
____Want Mark ____ Mark _____ Purch. 19__ Pd $ _____

102369 ARCH – Bridal Series
"Wedding Arch"

SUSP. 1992 - 5 YEARS AGO

OB $45	BA $30	GC $30
CT $40	FLM $30	
FL $30	V $30	

Comments: 1986; Original Retail $22.50/$30.00
Not sought after on the secondary market; not a collectible piece.

Personal Data: _____
____Want Mark ____ Mark _____ Purch. 19__ Pd $ _____

102377 ORNAMENT – Policeman
"Trust And Obey"

OB $25	BA $18	GC $17	S $17
CT $25	FLM $17	B $17	H $17
FL $20	V $17	TRP $17	SRD $17

Comments: 1985; Original Retail $10.00/$17.00

Personal Data: _____
____Want Mark ____ Mark _____ Purch. 19__ Pd $ _____

102385 ORNAMENT – Fireman
"Love Rescued Me"

OB $28	BA $18	GC $17	S $17
CT $22	FLM $17	B $17	H $17
FL $20	V $17	TRP $17	SRD $17

Comments: 1985; Original Retail $10.00/$17.00
The ornament does not have the water hose on his foot as shown; the similar figurine does.

Personal Data: _____
____Want Mark ____ Mark _____ Purch. 19__ Pd $ _____

102393 Fireman
"Love Rescued Me"

OB $50	FLM $37.50	TRP $37.50
CT $45	V $37.50	S $37.50
FL $40	GC $37.50	H $37.50
BA $38	B $37.50	SRD $37.50

Comments: 1985; Original Retail $22.50/$37.50

Personal Data: _____
____Want Mark ____ Mark _____ Purch. 19__ Pd $ _____

102407 ORNAMENT – Nurse
"Angel Of Mercy"

OB $30	FLM $20	TRP $17
CT $25	V $18	S $17
FL $20	GC $17	H $17
BA $20	B $17	SRD $17

Comments: 1985; Original Retail $10.00/$17.00
This is a popular gift item.

Personal Data: _____
____Want Mark ____ Mark _____ Purch. 19__ Pd $ _____

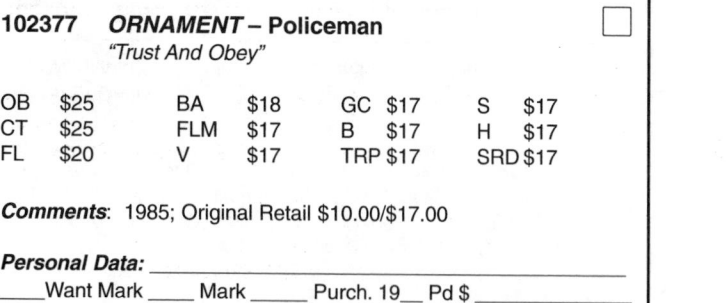

102415 ORNAMENT – Doctor
"It's A Perfect Boy"

SUSP. 1989 - 8 YEARS AGO

OB $30	FL $23
CT $25	BA $23

Comments: 1985; Original Retail $10.00/$13.50

Personal Data: _____
____Want Mark ____ Mark _____ Purch. 19__ Pd $ _____

102423 ORNAMENT – Ballerina
"Lord, Keep Me On My Toes"

RETIRED 1990 - 7 YEARS AGO

OB	$50	BA	$35
CT	$50	FLM	$35
FL	$40		

Comments: 1985; Original Retail $10.00/$15.00
Was a popular ornament but had to be hung in order to be displayed. Not abundant before or after retirement.

Personal Data: _____
____Want Mark ____ Mark _____ Purch. 19__ Pd $ _____

102431 ORNAMENT – Tennis Boy
"Serve With A Smile"

SUSP. 1988 - 9 YEARS AGO

OB	$25
CT	$20
FL	$20

Comments: 1985; Original Retail $10.00/$12.50

Personal Data: _____
____Want Mark ____ Mark _____ Purch. 19__ Pd $ _____

102458 ORNAMENT – Tennis Girl
"Serve With A Smile"

SUSP. 1988 - 9 YEARS AGO

OB	$32
CT	$28
FL	$25

Comments: 1985; Original Retail $10.00/$12.50

Personal Data: _____
____Want Mark ____ Mark _____ Purch. 19__ Pd $ _____

102466 ORNAMENT – Reindeer

DATED 1986

MM	$195
D	$185
OB	$165

Comments: 1986; Original Retail $11.00
Scarce! First ornament for *Birthday Club Series*. D mark found on leg. Rose to $125 on the secondary market by Dec. 1987, went down to $95, and up to $150-160 in 1991; down to $145-150 in 1992 and up to $190 in 1993. This piece appeared only on a few retailers' shelves as it was not placed on order forms. *Precious Collectibles®* was the first to alert collectors to search for this piece and several were found from our advertisers. Fun time in collecting!

Personal Data: _____
____Want Mark ____ Mark _____ Purch. 19__ Pd $ _____

102474 ORNAMENT – Rocking Horse

SUSP. 1991 - 6 YEARS AGO

OB	$30	BA	$20
CT	$25	FLM	$18
FL	$22	V	$18

Comments: 1985; Original Retail $10.00/$15.00

Personal Data: _____
____Want Mark ____ Mark _____ Purch. 19__ Pd $ _____

102482 Nurse with Flower
"Angel Of Mercy"

OB	$48	FLM	$32.50	TRP	$32.50
CT	$38	V	$32.50	S	$32.50
FL	$35	GC	$32.50	H	$32.50
BA	$35	B	$32.50	SRD	$32.50

Comments: 1985; Original Retail $20.00/$32.50

Personal Data: _____
____Want Mark ____ Mark _____ Purch. 19__ Pd $ _____

102490 Dad/Mom/Cookies/Dog
"Sharing Our Christmas Together"

SUSP. 1988 - 9 YEARS AGO

OB	$85
CT	$80
FL	$65

Comments: 1986; Original Retail $37.00/$45.00

Personal Data: _____
____Want Mark ____ Mark _____ Purch. 19__ Pd $ _____

102504 ORNAMENT – Girl with Candy Cane
"Baby's First Christmas"

DATED 1986   OB $25

Comments: 1985; Original Retail $10.00
Secondary Market prices decreased in '96.

Personal Data: _____
____Want Mark ____ Mark _____ Purch. 19__ Pd $ _____

102512 **_ORNAMENT_ – Boy with Candy Cane**
"Baby's First Christmas"

DATED 1986   OB $25

Comments: 1985; Original Retail $10.00
Seek and you might find below $20. Price down from '96.

Personal Data: _____
____Want Mark _____ Mark _____ Purch. 19__ Pd $ _____

102520 ♪ **_MUSICAL_ – Clown on Elephant**
"Let's Keep In Touch"

OB	$120	FLM	$95	TRP	$90
CT	$105	V	$95	S	$90
FL	$100	GC	$95	H	$90
BA	$100	B	$90	SRD	$90

Comments: 1985; Original Retail $65.00/$90.00
Plays _Be A Clown_. "Babe" was the name of Sam's secretary when he was a part of the J&D Co. "Babe" is written on the elephant's blanket. Retirement or suspension candidate? It's my opinion a $90 figurine is more likely to be suspended than retired because of collector reaction to the price at retirement announcement time.

Personal Data: _____
____Want Mark _____ Mark _____ Purch. 19__ Pd $ _____

102903 **Girl with Pearl**
"We Are All Precious In His Sight"

LE 1987 - 10 YEARS OLD   MM $80   CT $70

Comments: 1986; Original Retail $30.00
1987 Limited Edition. The inspiration was omitted from all pieces and the figurine was not marked "Limited." Several have been found without a mark which is an error. This piece was abundant during the issue year.

Personal Data: _____
____Want Mark _____ Mark _____ Purch. 19__ Pd $ _____

102938 **Uncle Sam**
"God Bless America"

LE 1986 - 11 YEARS OLD   OB $65

Comments: 1985; Original Retail $30.00
1986 Limited Edition. Very colorful and cute! Somewhat scarce starting mid-'92. This piece was abundant in '86. Display him with the service people and a small flag, a red carnation, etc.

Personal Data: _____
____Want Mark _____ Mark _____ Purch. 19__ Pd $ _____

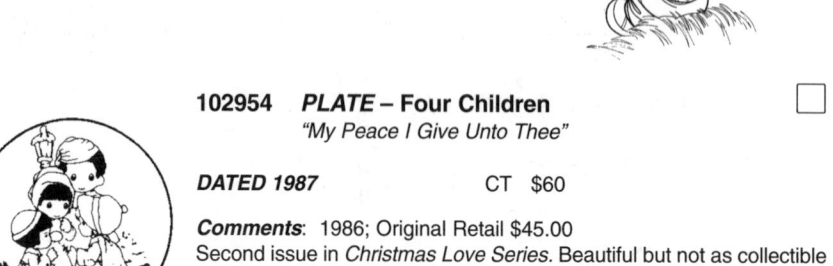

> _The way to tell a child is growing up is when he stops asking where he came from and starts refusing to tell you where he's going._

102954 **_PLATE_ – Four Children**
"My Peace I Give Unto Thee"

DATED 1987   CT $60

Comments: 1986; Original Retail $45.00
Second issue in _Christmas Love Series_. Beautiful but not as collectible as the figurines. Do not over insure!

Personal Data: _____
____Want Mark _____ Mark _____ Purch. 19__ Pd $ _____

102962 **Boy Angel/Birthday Cake**
"It's The Birthday Of A King"

SUSP. 1989 - 8 YEARS AGO

OB	$45	FL	$35
CT	$38	BA	$35

Comments: 1985; Original Retail $19.00/$25.00
Was a "slow" seller at retail.

Personal Data: _____
____Want Mark _____ Mark _____ Purch. 19__ Pd $ _____

102970 **Baby with Tub**
"I Would Be Sunk Without You"

CT	$29	V	$20	S	$20
FL	$25	GC	$20	H	$20
BA	$23	B	$20	SRD	$20
FLM	$20	TRP	$20		

Comments: 1986; Original Retail $15.00/$20.00

Personal Data: _____
____Want Mark _____ Mark _____ Purch. 19__ Pd $ _____

103004   Damien-Dutton Figurine and Bible
"We Belong To The Lord"

| SPECIAL EDITION | DIAMOND MARK | Fig. | $200 |
| | | Bible | $35 |

Comments: 1986; Original Retail $50.00
Special Edition produced for and sold by Damien-Dutton Society. A leather Bible accompanied this piece. The Damien-Dutton Society for Leprosy Aid was founded in 1944 by Howard Crouch for lepers in the USA and other parts of the world. The Damien-Dutton Society celebrated their 50th anniversary in September '94. This Society operates two gift shops in Bellmore and Port Jefferson, Long Island, NY. All profits from their sales go to this charity. I was privileged to speak at a meeting for the Damien-Dutton Society and Precious Moments® collectors in November 1988. This was the first trip to New York for Dave and me – a limo and all the fancies! It was a great time! We walked 26 blocks to the Statue of Liberty! Passed the Enesco Showroom on the way.

Personal Data: _____
____Want Mark ____ Mark _____ Purch. 19__ Pd $ _____

103497   Boy with Fish
"My Love Will Never Let You Go"

OB	$60	BA	$40	GC	$40	S	$37.50
CT	$55	FLM	$40	B	$40	H	$37.50
FL	$45	V	$40	TRP	$37.50	SRD	$37.50

Comments: 1986; Original Retail $25.00/$37.50
A great piece! Great gift for men/sportsmen. May be suspended as a new fisherman debuted in '95.

Personal Data: _____
____Want Mark ____ Mark _____ Purch. 19__ Pd $ _____

103632   Girl with Cross
"I Believe In The Old Rugged Cross"

D	$55	BA	$40	B	$35	SRD	$35
OB	$50	FLM	$40	TRP	$35		
CT	$40	V	$40	S	$35		
FL	$40	GC	$35	H	$35		

Comments: 1985; Original Retail $25.00/$35.00
Very popular figurine. Ideal to display with the '92-'93 Limited Edition pieces (526185 and 523593). Perfect "retirement" piece, wouldn't you say?

Personal Data: _____
____Want Mark ____ Mark _____ Purch. 19__ Pd $ _____

104000   *NATIVITY* – 9 pc. with Cassette
"Come Let Us Adore Him"

D	$145	BA	$130	B	$130	SRD	$130
OB	$140	FLM	$130	TRP	$130		
CT	$135	V	$130	S	$130		
FL	$135	GC	$130	H	$130		

Comments: 1986; Original Retail $95/$130
Changed from original set, E-2800. Heads now are larger. Sets produced in 1991 included a 16-page booklet featuring the Christmas story and family traditions. No demand on secondary market (E-2800 more popular). Maybe it's time for a new Nativity set?

Personal Data: _____
____Want Mark ____ Mark _____ Purch. 19__ Pd $ _____

104019   Boy Giving Girl Ring
"With This Ring I..."

CT	$70	FLM	$70	B	$65	H	$65
FL	$65	V	$65	TRP	$65	SRD	$65
BA	$65	GC	$65	S	$65		

Comments: 1986; Original Retail $40.00/$65.00
Due to price increase, retailers are reporting that this piece has "slowed" on retail sales as $40 was more affordable for a gift item. The collection could use a less expensive "engagement" figurine for a gift item.

Personal Data: _____
____Want Mark ____ Mark _____ Purch. 19__ Pd $ _____

104027   Boy/Hobby Horse
"Love Is The Glue That Mends"

SUSP. 1990 - 7 YEARS AGO			
CT	$70	BA	$55
FL	$60	FLM	$55

Comments: 1986; Original Retail $33.50/$40.00
This is a nice piece! Not many out there with only four years of production.

Personal Data: _____
____Want Mark ____ Mark _____ Purch. 19__ Pd $ _____

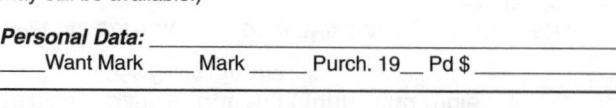

104035 Girl Cheerleader
"Cheers To The Leader"

RETIRED 1997

CT	$70	V	$50	S	$45
FL	$65	GC	$50	H	$45
BA	$60	B	$50		
FLM	$55	TRP	$45		

Comments: 1986; Original Retail $22.50/$32.50
A collector found this piece with a double V mark, which is an error; add $100 to secondary market value.

Personal Data: _____
____Want Mark ____ Mark ____ Purch. 19__ Pd $ _____

104396 Clown with Books
"Happy Days Are Here Again"

SUSP. 1990 - 7 YEARS AGO

CT	$70	BA	$55	FL	$65	FLM	$50

Comments: 1986; Original Retail $25.00/$32.50
Several other clowns have been suspended or retired. May become harder to find as it was produced for only four years!

Personal Data: _____
____Want Mark ____ Mark ____ Purch. 19__ Pd $ _____

104418 Rhino with Bird
"Friends To The End"

SUSP. 1993 - 4 YEARS AGO

MM	$55	FLM	$25	B	$21
FL	$45	V	$22		
BA	$25	GC	$21		

Comments: 1988; Original Retail $15.00/$18.50
(A shiny glass Rhino night light was available on retailers' shelves; it may still be available.)

Personal Data: _____
____Want Mark ____ Mark ____ Purch. 19__ Pd $ _____

104515 ORNAMENT – Bear in Tub/Skis
"Bear The Good News Of Christmas"

DATED 1987   CT $20

Comments: 1986; Original Retail $12.50
Second *Birthday Club Series* ornament. Quite abundant! Scarce at first. Secondary market dealers bought all they could find... then very large shipments arrived by mid-December.

Personal Data: _____
____Want Mark ____ Mark ____ Purch. 19__ Pd $ _____

104523 NATIVITY - 9" Dealer
"Come Let Us Adore Him"

OB $430

Comments: 1986; Original Retail $400.00
Produced for dealers, but collectors purchased them at $400 plus tax. These would have been a very much sought-after collectible, and collectors thought so too, buying several sets. But the following year Enesco produced almost the same set for retail, diminishing demand for the Dealer Nativity Sets. If you're brave, sell these pieces individually. You'll get more! If you price them at $50 for sheep, $50 for Baby and $100 for other pieces, it would total $650! Sell this way for other sets, too; you'll get more. It may take longer, though. Many reports of sales at above price!

Personal Data: _____
____Want Mark ____ Mark ____ Purch. 19__ Pd $ _____

104531 9" - 1988 EASTER SEALS – Girl w/Bunny
"Jesus Loves Me"

LE 1988 - 9 YEARS AGO   CT $1600-1750
                                      FL $1450-1500

Comments: 1988; Original Retail $500.00
1988 - 9" Figurine. Same as E-1372G. Limited Edition 1000 pcs. Most limited of the 9" Easter Seals pieces. Most sought after. Production on current 9" pieces is now at 2000; they are not scarce. 9" Boy with Teddy to match should be produced. ***See #25, page XIV.***

Personal Data: _____
____Want Mark ____ Mark ____ Purch. 19__ Pd $ _____

104817 Baby Boy/Tub
"A Tub Full Of Love"

CT	$45	FLM	$32.50	B	$32.50	H	$32.50
FL	$38	V	$32.50	TRP	$32.50	SRD	$32.50
BA	$35	GC	$32.50	S	$32.50		

Comments: 1986; Original Retail $22.50/$32.50

Personal Data: _____
____Want Mark ____ Mark ____ Purch. 19__ Pd $ _____

104825   Angel On Stool
"Sitting Pretty"

SUSP. 1990 - 7 YEARS AGO

CT	$60	FLM	$40
FL	$55	V	$38
BA	$40		

Comments: 1986; Original Retail $22.50/$30.00
Slow seller. Although suspended in 1990, collectors have reported that they have found this piece with the V (1991) mark; in my opinion, a slip-up at the factory. Not a sought – after piece.

Personal Data: _____
___Want Mark ___ Mark _____ Purch. 19__ Pd $ _____

105635   Boy with Scroll
"Have I Got News For You"

SUSP. 1991 - 6 YEARS AGO

CT	$60	FLM	$40
FL	$50	V	$35
BA	$40		

Comments: 1986; Original Retail $22.50/$30.00
Slow seller on the secondary market.

Personal Data: _____
___Want Mark ___ Mark _____ Purch. 19__ Pd $ _____

105643   Girl Holding Doll with Dog
"Something's Missing When You're Not Around"

SUSP. 1991 - 6 YEARS AGO

FL	$85	FLM	$60
BA	$75	V	$60

Comments: 1988; Original Retail $32.50/$37.50
Figurine has base. Prices increased more than most pieces since last year.

Personal Data: _____
___Want Mark ___ Mark _____ Purch. 19__ Pd $ _____

105813   Dentist with Boy's Tooth
"To Tell The Tooth You're Special"

SUSP. 1990 - 7 YEARS AGO

CT	$185	BA	$150
FL	$165	FLM	$150

Comments: 1986; Original Retail $38.50/$50.00
Becoming scarce! Many looking for this piece. Price increased 20% from mid '96! Seems to me more FL sales than others.

Personal Data: _____
___Want Mark ___ Mark _____ Purch. 19__ Pd $ _____

105821   Cowboy on Fence
"Hallelujah Country"

CT	$250	FLM	$50	B	$45	H	$45
FL	$65	V	$50	TRP	$45	SRD	$45
BA	$60	GC	$45	S	$45		

Comments: 1986; Original Retail $35.00/$45.00
CT marks are very scarce. I only know of a few collectors who have the CT mark. Do you? This li'l guy is on our cover this year. Hope you like our country-western theme in this year's guide!

Personal Data: _____
___Want Mark ___ Mark _____ Purch. 19__ Pd $ _____

105945   Elephant Showering Mouse
"Showers·Of Blessing"

RETIRED 1993 - 4 YEARS AGO

CT	$60	BA	$40	V	$35	B	$35
FL	$45	FLM	$35	GC	$35		

Comments: 1986; Original Retail $16.00/$20.00
Birthday Series. Smaller than the average piece.

Personal Data: _____
___Want Mark ___ Mark _____ Purch. 19__ Pd $ _____

105953   Skunk and Mouse
"Brighten Someone's Day"

SUSP. 1993 - 4 YEARS AGO

CT	$40	BA	$30	V	$24	B	$22
FL	$35	FLM	$27	GC	$24		

Comments: 1986; Original Retail $12.50/15.00
Several pieces found with decal missing from paint can. Add $50 to price.

Personal Data: _____
___Want Mark ___ Mark _____ Purch. 19__ Pd $ _____

106151   Boy with Donkey
"We're Pulling For You"

SUSP. 1991 - 6 YEARS AGO

CT	$80	BA	$65	V	$65
FL	$70	FLM	$65		

Comments: 1986; Original Retail $40.00/$55.00
Different colored strings have been found but have not made a significant secondary market difference to date.

Personal Data: _____
___Want Mark ___ Mark _____ Purch. 19__ Pd $ _____

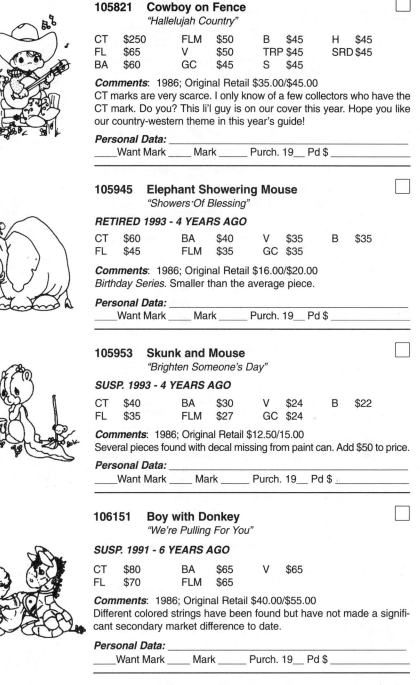

106194 Boy Graduate
"God Bless You Graduate"

OB	$50	FLM	$35	TRP	$35
CT	$38	V	$35	S	$35
FL	$35	GC	$35	H	$35
BA	$35	B	$35	SRD	$35

Comments: 1986; Original Retail $20.00/$35.00

Personal Data: _____
____Want Mark ____ Mark _____ Purch. 19__ Pd $ _____

106208 Girl Graduate
"Congratulations, Princess"

OB	$45	FLM	$35	TRP	$35
CT	$40	V	$35	S	$35
FL	$35	GC	$35	H	$35
BA	$35	B	$35	SRD	$35

Comments: 1986; Original Retail $20.00/$35.00
Not sought after to date on secondary market.

Personal Data: _____
____Want Mark ____ Mark _____ Purch. 19__ Pd $ _____

106216 Clown Going to School
"Lord, Help Me Make The Grade"

SUSP. 1990 - 7 YEARS AGO

CT	$60	BA	$50
FL	$55	FLM	$45

Comments: 1987; Original Retail $25.00/$32.50
Time for retirement.

Personal Data: _____
____Want Mark ____ Mark _____ Purch. 19__ Pd $ _____

106755 Groom Popping Out of Trunk
"Heaven Bless Your Togetherness"

CT	$105	V	$90	S	$90
FL	$90	GC	$90	H	$90
BA	$90	B	$90	SRD	$90
FLM	$90	TRP	$90		

Comments: 1986; Original Retail $65.00/$90.00
I look for this piece to be suspended or retired as, in my opinion, it was intended as a special gift item and a $90 retail limits many gift buyers! Not being traded often on today's secondary market; this seems to be the norm for pieces priced over $55. Insure at these prices.

Personal Data: _____
____Want Mark ____ Mark _____ Purch. 19__ Pd $ _____

106763 Couple on Couch Reading
"Precious Memories"

CT	$75	FLM	$50	B	$50	H	$50
FL	$60	V	$50	TRP	$50	SRD	$50
BA	$58	GC	$50	S	$50		

Comments: 1986; Original Retail $37.50/$50.00

Personal Data: _____
____Want Mark ____ Mark _____ Purch. 19__ Pd $ _____

106798 Anniversary Couple with Puppy
"Puppy Love Is From Above"

RETIRED 1995 - 2 YEARS AGO

CT	$95	FLM	$75	B	$75
FL	$90	V	$75	TRP	$75
BA	$75	GC	$75	S	$70

Comments: 1987; Original Retail $45.00/$55.00
Anniversary pieces not traded a lot on secondary market. This one is cuter than several of the others.

Personal Data: _____
____Want Mark ____ Mark _____ Purch. 19__ Pd $ _____

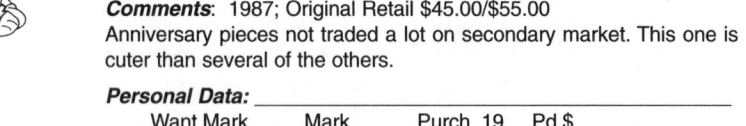

106836 Girl/Poppy Plant
"Happy Birthday Poppy"

SUSP. 1993 - 4 YEARS AGO

CT	$55	FLM	$50	B	$40
FL	$50	V	$50		
BA	$50	GC	$45		

Comments: 1987; Original Retail $27.50/$35.00
Inspiration eliminates many sales for birthdays as not many buy figurines for "Pop" on birthdays. Another "Poppy" figurine (604208) debuted in 1994.

Personal Data: _____
____Want Mark ____ Mark _____ Purch. 19__ Pd $ _____

106844 Girl Sewing Boy's Pants
"Sew In Love"

RETIRED 1997

CT	$100	FLM	$85	B	$80	H	$80
FL	$90	V	$85	TRP	$80		
BA	$85	GC	$80	S	$80		

Comments: 1987; Original Retail $45.00/$55.00
She reminds us of the li'l girl sewing the quilt.

Personal Data: _____
____Want Mark ____ Mark _____ Purch. 19__ Pd $ _____

107999   *EASTER SEALS* **– Girl On Crutches**
"He Walks With Me"

LE 1987/88   OB $45   CT $40

Comments: 1986; Original Retail $25.00
Commemorative Easter Seals Figurine 1987 Limited Edition w/decaled Lily Mark. Easter Seals Logo on base. Produced in great abundance that year. Easily found at these prices! Collector reported this with a C mark. Very Rare indeed!

Personal Data: _____
____Want Mark ____ Mark _____ Purch. 19__ Pd $ _____

108243   *MINI NATIVITY* **– Three Kings on Camels**
"They Followed The Star"

CT	$135	FLM	$120	B	$120	H	$120
FL	$120	V	$120	TRP	$120	SRD	$120
BA	$120	GC	$120	S	$120		

Comments: 1986; Original Retail $75.00/$120.00
Addition to Miniature Nativity. Only CT sales reported. Not much trading on these pieces has been reported the past five years!

Personal Data: _____
____Want Mark ____ Mark _____ Purch. 19__ Pd $ _____

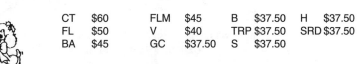

109231   **Baby Boy with Dog/Stocking**
"The Greatest Gift Is A Friend"

CT	$60	FLM	$45	B	$37.50	H	$37.50
FL	$50	V	$40	TRP	$37.50	SRD	$37.50
BA	$45	GC	$37.50	S	$37.50		

Comments: 1986; Original Retail $30.00/$37.50
This is a great title. It needs to have been on an everyday figurine as retailers say "Friends" figurines are great sellers for gift items. Retirement candidate.

Personal Data: _____
____Want Mark ____ Mark _____ Purch. 19__ Pd $ _____

109401   *ORNAMENT* **– Girl/Rocking Horse**
"Baby's First Christmas"

DATED 1987   CT $40

Comments: 1986; Original Retail $12.00
We received a report of OB marks. Rare!

Personal Data: _____
____Want Mark ____ Mark _____ Purch. 19__ Pd $ _____

109428   *ORNAMENT* **– Boy/Rocking Horse**
"Baby's First Christmas"

DATED 1987   CT $40

Comments: 1986; Original Retail $12.00
We have received one report of OB mark.

Personal Data: _____
____Want Mark ____ Mark _____ Purch. 19__ Pd $ _____

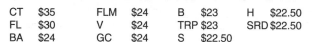

109460   **Age 8 - Ostrich**
"Isn't Eight Just Great"

CT	$35	FLM	$24	B	$23	H	$22.50
FL	$30	V	$24	TRP	$23	SRD	$22.50
BA	$24	GC	$24	S	$22.50		

Comments: 1985; Original Retail $18.50/$22.50
Part of the *Birthday Train Series*. Ages 7 and 8 debuted in 1988.
See #30, page XIV.

Personal Data: _____
____Want Mark ____ Mark _____ Purch. 19__ Pd $ _____

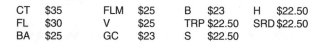

109479   **Age 7 - Leopard**
"Wishing You Grr-eatness"

CT	$35	FLM	$25	B	$23	H	$22.50
FL	$30	V	$25	TRP	$22.50	SRD	$22.50
BA	$25	GC	$23	S	$22.50		

Comments: 1985; Original Retail $18.50/$22.50
Part of the *Birthday Train Series*. Ages 7 and 8 debuted in 1988.
See #30, page XIV.

Personal Data: _____
____Want Mark ____ Mark _____ Purch. 19__ Pd $ _____

109487   **Boy with Barbells**
"Believe The Impossible"

SUSP. 1991 - 6 YEARS AGO

CT	$105	FLM	$60
FL	$65	V	$60
BA	$60		

Comments: 1987; Original Retail $35.00/$45.00
CT is scarce! Retailers reported "broken" bars when received. No doubt biggest reason for suspension.

Personal Data: _____
____Want Mark ____ Mark _____ Purch. 19__ Pd $ _____

109584 Clown Angel/Bouquet
"Happiness Divine"

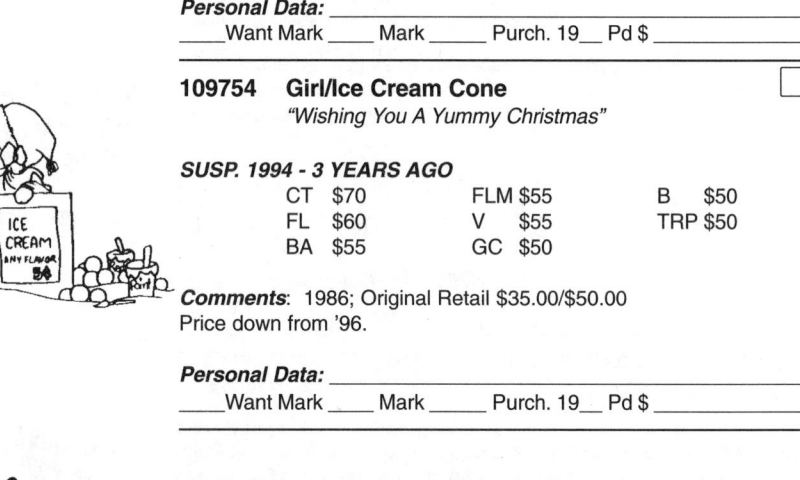

RETIRED 1992 - 5 YEARS AGO

FL	$85	V	$65
BA	$70	GC	$55
FLM	$65		

Comments: 1987; Original Retail $25.00/$30.00
The only figurine in the 1988 First Allotment not found with CT mark. On figurine clown is holding bouquet instead of halo (as shown at left). GC easiest to find.

Personal Data: _____
____Want Mark ____ Mark _____ Purch. 19__ Pd $ _____

109746 ♪ *MUSICAL* – Kids Caroling
"Peace On Earth"

SUSP. 1993 - 4 YEARS AGO

CT	$175	FLM	$150	B	$150
FL	$160	V	$150		
BA	$160	GC	$150		

Comments: 1988; Original Retail $100.00/$130.00
Plays *Hark The Herald Angels Sing.* Nice!

Personal Data: _____
____Want Mark ____ Mark _____ Purch. 19__ Pd $ _____

109754 Girl/Ice Cream Cone
"Wishing You A Yummy Christmas"

SUSP. 1994 - 3 YEARS AGO

CT	$70	FLM	$55	B	$50
FL	$60	V	$55	TRP	$50
BA	$55	GC	$50		

Comments: 1986; Original Retail $35.00/$50.00
Price down from '96.

Personal Data: _____
____Want Mark ____ Mark _____ Purch. 19__ Pd $ _____

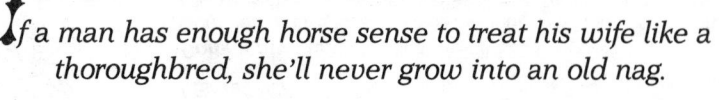

𝓘f a man has enough horse sense to treat his wife like a thoroughbred, she'll never grow into an old nag.

109762 Family/Thanksgiving
"We Gather Together To Ask The Lord's Blessing"

RETIRED 1995 - 2 YEARS AGO

CT	$270	FLM	$200	B	$200
FL	$200	V	$200	TRP	$200
BA	$200	GC	$200	S	$200

Comments: 1986; Original Retail $130.00/$150.00
Contains several separate pieces. We've seen many figurines debut using song titles or verses from songs and hymns as the inspiration. Collectors have reported sets containing two fathers or two mothers, rather than one of each. Adorable addition to your collection! Most sales found were on CT marks.

Personal Data: _____
____Want Mark ____ Mark _____ Purch. 19__ Pd $ _____

109770 *ORNAMENT* – Girl with Presents
"Love Is The Best Gift Of All"

DATED 1987   CT $42

Comments: 1986; Original Retail $11.00
This piece has been found without the date decal. Add $50-60 to the secondary market value.

Personal Data: _____
____Want Mark ____ Mark _____ Purch. 19__ Pd $ _____

109800 Girl with Kitten
"Meowie Christmas"

FL	$55	V	$35	TRP	$35	SRD	$35
BA	$42	GC	$35	S	$35		
FLM	$40	B	$35	H	$35		

Comments: 1988; Original Retail $30.00/$35.00
Retirement Candidate.

Personal Data: _____
____Want Mark ____ Mark _____ Purch. 19__ Pd $ _____

109819 Grandma in Rocking Chair "Sled"
"Oh What Fun It Is To Ride"

CT	$135	FLM	$115	B	$110	H	$110
FL	$125	V	$110	TRP	$110	SRD	$110
BA	$120	GC	$110	S	$110		

Comments: 1986; Original Retail $85.00/$110.00
Retailers do not order this piece in large quantities due to the high price. It's a cute piece. Great for a winter display.

Personal Data: _____
____Want Mark ____ Mark _____ Purch. 19__ Pd $ _____

109835 **BELL** – Girl with Present
"Love Is The Best Gift Of All"

DATED 1987   CT $30

Comments: 1986; Original Retail $22.50
Slow seller on the secondary market.

Personal Data: _____
____Want Mark ____ Mark _____ Purch. 19__ Pd $ _____

109843 **THIMBLE** – Girl with Present
"Love Is The Best Gift Of All"

DATED 1987   CT $32

Comments: 1987; Original Retail $6.00

Personal Data: _____
____Want Mark ____ Mark _____ Purch. 19__ Pd $ _____

109886 **Girl/Bunny in Hands**
"Wishing You A Happy Easter"

CT $45	FLM $35	B $35	H $35
FL $42	V $35	TRP $35	SRD $35
BA $35	GC $35	S $35	

Comments: 1987; Original Retail $23.00/$35.00
Suspension candidate – very similar to other pieces. Easter pieces do not sell well all year for retailers. Retirement or suspension candidate.

Comments: 1988; Original Retail $30.00/$35.00

Personal Data: _____
____Want Mark ____ Mark _____ Purch. 19__ Pd $ _____

109924 **Boy/Basket with Chick**
"Wishing You A Basket Full Of Blessings"

CT $50	FLM $38	B $35	H $35
FL $45	V $35	TRP $35	SRD $35
BA $40	GC $35	S $35	

Comments: 1987; Original Retail $23.00/35.00
Pretty! Pretty!

Personal Data: _____
____Want Mark ____ Mark _____ Purch. 19__ Pd $ _____

109967 **Girl on Cloud Dropping Hearts**
"Sending You My Love"

CT $70	FLM $50	B $45	H $45
FL $55	V $50	TRP $45	SRD $45
BA $55	GC $45	S $45	

Comments: 1987; Original Retail $35.00/$45.00

Personal Data: _____
____Want Mark ____ Mark _____ Purch. 19__ Pd $ _____

109975 **Boy with Flower**
"Mommy, I Love You"

CT $40	FLM $35	B $30	H $30
FL $38	V $30	TRP $30	SRD $30
BA $38	GC $30	S $30	

Comments: 1987: Original Retail $22.50/$30.00
Slow seller on the secondary market. Suspension or retirement candidate.

Personal Data: _____
____Want Mark ____ Mark _____ Purch. 19__ Pd $ _____

109983 **Girl Pushing Doll/Sleigh**
"January"

CT $55	FLM $50	B $45	H $45
FL $50	V $45	TRP $45	SRD $45
BA $50	GC $45	S $45	

Comments: 1987; Original Retail $37.50/$45.00
January Calendar Girl. Look for calendar pieces to phase out in a few years as retail price is increasing and may soon be out of the reach of "Birthday" gift buyers.

Personal Data: _____
____Want Mark ____ Mark _____ Purch. 19__ Pd $ _____

109991 **Girl Looking at Plant in Snow**
"February"

CT $55	FLM $38	B $37.50	H $37.50
FL $42	V $37.50	TRP $37.50	SRD $37.50
BA $40	GC $37.50	S $37.50	

Comments: 1987; Original Retail $27.50/$37.50
February Calendar Girl. Wouldn't a birthstone be nice in a Precious Moments® figurine for birthdays?! Hint, hint, to Enesco and Sam. (This was written '95, and in '96 the birthstone name appeared.) ☺

Personal Data: _____
____Want Mark ____ Mark _____ Purch. 19__ Pd $ _____

110019 Girl with Kite
"March"

CT	$60	FLM	$40	B	$37.50	H	$37.50
FL	$45	V	$37.50	TRP	$37.50	SRD	$37.50
BA	$45	GC	$37.50	S	$37.50		

Comments: 1987; Original Retail $27.50/$37.50
March Calendar Girl. A very popular piece. Seems to be an abundant due to gift buyer demand.

Personal Data: _____
____Want Mark ____ Mark _____ Purch. 19__ Pd $ _____

110027 Girl with Umbrella
"April"

CT	$110	V	$40	S	$40
FL	$50	GC	$40	H	$40
BA	$45	B	$40	SRD	$40
FLM	$45	TRP	$40		

Comments: 1987; Original Retail $27.50/$40.00
April Calendar Girl. CT mark harder to find. Sells at retail more quickly than other calendar pieces. Attractive piece. CT price down from '96!

Personal Data: _____
____Want Mark ____ Mark _____ Purch. 19__ Pd $ _____

110035 Girl with Potted Plant
"May"

CT	$115	FLM	$42	B	$35	H	$35
FL	$45	V	$35	TRP	$35	SRD	$35
BA	$42	GC	$35	S	$35		

Comments: 1987; Original Retail $27.50/$35.00
May Calendar Girl. Very few sales found.

Personal Data: _____
____Want Mark ____ Mark _____ Purch. 19__ Pd $ _____

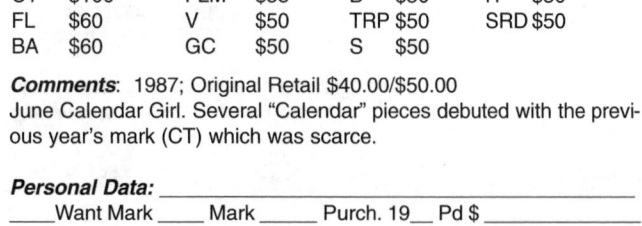

110043 Girl Dressing Up As Bride
"June"

CT	$100	FLM	$58	B	$50	H	$50
FL	$60	V	$50	TRP	$50	SRD	$50
BA	$60	GC	$50	S	$50		

Comments: 1987; Original Retail $40.00/$50.00
June Calendar Girl. Several "Calendar" pieces debuted with the previous year's mark (CT) which was scarce.

Personal Data: _____
____Want Mark ____ Mark _____ Purch. 19__ Pd $ _____

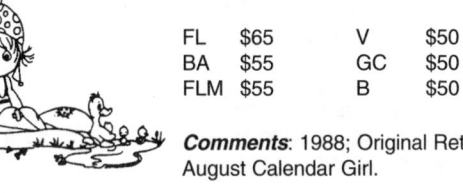

110051 Girl with Puppy in Basket
"July"

FL	$55	V	$45	TRP	$45	SRD $45
BA	$50	GC	$45	S	$45	
FLM	$50	B	$45	H	$45	

Comments: 1988; Original Retail $35.00/$45.00
July Calendar Girl.

Personal Data: _____
____Want Mark ____ Mark _____ Purch. 19__ Pd $ _____

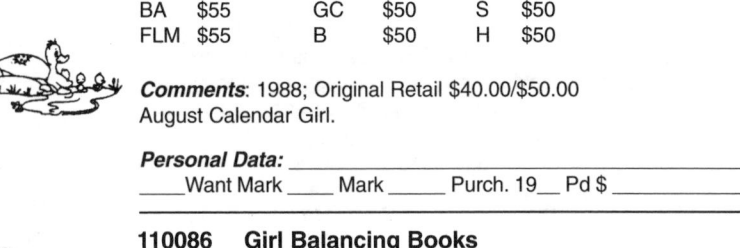

110078 Girl in Pool
"August"

FL	$65	V	$50	TRP	$50	SRD $50
BA	$55	GC	$50	S	$50	
FLM	$55	B	$50	H	$50	

Comments: 1988; Original Retail $40.00/$50.00
August Calendar Girl.

Personal Data: _____
____Want Mark ____ Mark _____ Purch. 19__ Pd $ _____

110086 Girl Balancing Books
"September"

FL	$50	V	$37.50	TRP	$37.50	SRD $37.50
BA	$42	GC	$37.50	S	$37.50	
FLM	$40	B	$37.50	H	$37.50	

Comments: 1988; Original Retail $27.50/$37.50
September Calendar Girl.

Personal Data: _____
____Want Mark ____ Mark _____ Purch. 19__ Pd $ _____

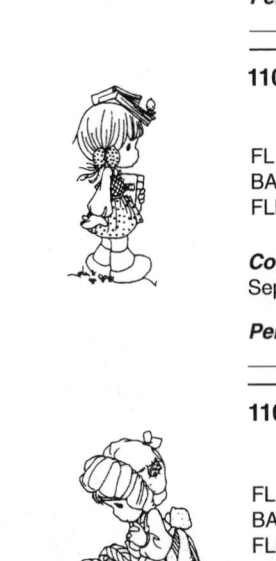

110094 Girl with Pumpkins
"October"

FL	$55	V	$45	TRP	$45	SRD $45
BA	$50	GC	$45	S	$45	
FLM	$45	B	$45	H	$45	

Comments: 1988; Original Retail $35.00/$45.00
October Calendar Girl. Pretty piece!

Personal Data: _____
____Want Mark ____ Mark _____ Purch. 19__ Pd $ _____

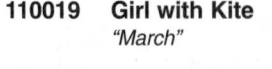

110108 Girl in Pilgrim Dress
"November"

FL	$55	V	$40	TRP	$37.50	SRD	$37.50
BA	$45	GC	$37.50	S	$37.50		
FLM	$40	B	$37.50	H	$37.50		

Comments: 1988; Original Retail $32.50/$37.50
November Calendar Girl.

Personal Data: _____
____Want Mark ____ Mark _____ Purch. 19__ Pd $ _____

110116 Girl with Christmas Candle
"December"

CT	$100	FLM	$35	B	$35	H	$35
FL	$52	V	$35	TRP	$35	SRD	$35
BA	$40	GC	$35	S	$35		

Comments: 1988; Original Retail $27.50/$35.00
December Calendar Girl. Reported with CT mark, Scarce!

Personal Data: _____
____Want Mark ____ Mark _____ Purch. 19__ Pd $ _____

110930 Girl with Present
"Love Is The Best Gift Of All"

DATED 1987   CT $40

Comments: 1986; Original Retail $22.50
Dated figurines have not been as popular with the avid collector as the dated ornaments (but the 1993 dated figurine was maybe more popular than ever!!)

Personal Data: _____
____Want Mark ____ Mark _____ Purch. 19__ Pd $ _____

111120 ORNAMENT – Football Player
"I'm A Possibility"

SUSP. 1990 - 7 YEARS AGO

CT	$35	BA	$25
FL	$30	FLM	$25

Comments: 1986; Original Retail $11.00/15.00
Similar figurine was retired in '93.

Personal Data: _____
 ____Want Mark ____ Mark _____ Purch. 19__ Pd $ _____

111155 Girl with Plunger
"Faith Takes The Plunge"

PUCKERED MOUTH (frown w/pucker in lip)

CT	$55	FLM	$40	B	$35	H	$35
FL	$45	V	$35	TRP	$35	SRD	$35
BA	$40	GC	$35	S	$35		

SMILE - Error

CT	$60
FL	$50
BA	$50

CIRCLE MOUTH VERY RARE (Estimated value)

FL	$200
BA	$200

Comments: 1987; Original Retail $27.50/$35.00
This piece debuted with the Smile and was immediately changed to a Puckered Mouth. We have heard of a Circle Mouth from a "good source" but we have never actually seen one. Excellent candidate for suspension or retirement. Very few sales found higher than '96 prices and lower for errored piece.

Personal Data: _____
____Want Mark ____ Mark _____ Purch. 19__ Pd $ _____

111163 Girl Adding Seasoning to Batter
"Tis The Season"

SUSP. 1996 - 1 YEAR AGO

FL	$50	V	$40	TRP	$35
BA	$40	GC	$35	S	$35
FLM	$40	B	$35	H	$35

Comments: 1988; Original Retail $27.50/$35.00
Slower seller for some reason.

Personal Data: _____
____Want Mark ____ Mark _____ Purch. 19__ Pd $ _____

111333 NATIVITY (4 pc.)
"O Come Let Us Adore Him"

SUSP. 1991 - 6 YEARS AGO

CT	$250	V	$220
FLM	$230	BA	$220
FL	$225		

Comments: 1987; Original Retail $200.00/$220.00
This is the set that detracted from the Dealer Set's rise on the secondary market (104523).
Personal Data: _____
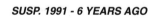 ____Want Mark ____ Mark _____ Purch. 19__ Pd $ _____

112143 Girl with Flowers
"Mommy, I Love You"

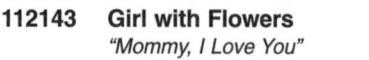

CT	$45	FLM	$30	B	$30	H	$30
FL	$40	V	$30	TRP	$30	SRD	$30
BA	$35	GC	$30	S	$30		

Comments: 1987; Original Retail $22.50/$30.00
Suspension or retirement candidate. Slow seller on secondary market.

Personal Data: _____
____Want Mark ____ Mark _____ Purch. 19__ Pd $ _____

112313 Baby Girl in Tub
"A Tub Full Of Love"

CT	$45	FLM	$32	B	$32	H	$32
FL	$35	V	$32	TRP	$32	SRD	$32
BA	$35	GC	$32	S	$32		

Comments: 1987; Original Retail $22.50/$32.00
I look for her and the boy in tub to be suspended in the future due to retail price increase to $30 for a smaller than normal piece. Price increased to $32 in 1996.

Personal Data: _____
____Want Mark ____ Mark _____ Purch. 19__ Pd $ _____

112356 ORNAMENT – Girl with String of Hearts
"You Have Touched So Many Hearts"

RETIRED 1997

CT	$43	FLM	$33	B	$33	H	$32
FL	$37	V	$33	TRP	$32		
BA	$33	GC	$33	S	$32		

Comments: 1986; Original Retail $11.00/$17.00
Appeared as the 1990 9" Easter Seals figurine. Perfect retirement candidate. Very few sales found to determine any change for this guide.

Personal Data: _____
____Want Mark ____ Mark _____ Purch. 19__ Pd $ _____

112364 ORNAMENT – Girl Clown with Goose
"Waddle I Do Without You"

CT	$39	FLM	$20	B	$18	H	$17
FL	$22	V	$18	TRP	$17	SRD	$17
BA	$20	GC	$18	S	$17		

Comments: 1986; Original Retail $11.00/$17.00
Maybe a retirement candidate... Why? Because of the many colors and time consuming design; also, she's a clown.

Personal Data: _____
____Want Mark ____ Mark _____ Purch. 19__ Pd $ _____

112372 ORNAMENT – Girl Mailing Snowball
"I'm Sending You A White Christmas"

SUSP. 1992 - 5 YEARS AGO

MM	$45	BA	$25	GC	$20
CT	$35	FLM	$24		
FL	$30	V	$22		

Comments: 1986; Original Retail $11.00/15.00
Musical of similar design retired in 1993. Reportedly found with no mark.

Personal Data: _____
____Want Mark ____ Mark _____ Purch. 19__ Pd $ _____

112380 ORNAMENT - Girl in Tub
"He Cleansed My Soul"

CT	$30	FLM	$18	B	$17	H	$17
FL	$25	V	$18	TRP	$17	SRD	$17
BA	$20	GC	$17	S	$17		

Comments: 1986; Original Retail $12.00/$17.00
Cute ornament, very popular!

Personal Data: _____
____Want Mark ____ Mark _____ Purch. 19__ Pd $ _____

112399 ORNAMENT – Boy/Girl in Package
"Our First Christmas Together"

DATED 1987 CT $30

Comments: 1986; Original Retail $11.00
This ornament was also produced in 1986 (102350) and 1988 (520233). The only differences were the marks, style numbers and the dates.

Personal Data: _____
____Want Mark ____ Mark _____ Purch. 19__ Pd $ _____

112402 ♪ MUSICAL – Girl Mailing Snowball
"I'm Sending You A White Christmas"

RETIRED 1993 - 4 YEARS AGO

OB	$150	BA	$125	GC	$110
CT	$150	FLM	$125	B	$110
FL	$130	V	$125		

Comments: 1987; Original Retail $55.00/$75.00
Plays *White Christmas*.

Personal Data: _____
____Want Mark ____ Mark _____ Purch. 19__ Pd $ _____

112577 ♪ **MUSICAL - Girl with String of Hearts**
"You Have Touched So Many Hearts"

SUSP. 1996 - 1 YEAR AGO

CT	$75	FLM	$65	B	$65	H	$65
FL	$65	V	$65	TRP	$65		
BA	$65	GC	$65	S	$65		

Comments: 1988; Original Retail $50.00/$65.00
Plays *Everybody Loves Somebody*. Musicals are becoming more popular on the secondary market. Notice retail price increase again for '96. Double FLM mark found – insure for $100 over secondary market value. Up $15 since 1994, secondary market up but so was retail!

Personal Data: _____
____Want Mark ____ Mark _____ Purch. 19__ Pd $ _____

113956 **ORNAMENT – Two Girls Holding Basket/Wreath**
"To My Forever Friend"

FL	$40	V	$20	TRP	$18.50	SRD	$18.50
BA	$30	GC	$18.50	S	$18.50		
FLM	$25	B	$18.50	H	$18.50		

Comments: 1988; Original Retail $16.00/$18.50
Pretty! Pretty! The actual ornament is different from the original artwork shown at left. The ornament is of one girl with holly in her hair, holding a basket, and another girl holding a wreath.

Personal Data: _____
____Want Mark ____ Mark _____ Purch. 19__ Pd $ _____

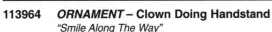

113964 **ORNAMENT – Clown Doing Handstand**
"Smile Along The Way"

SUSP. 1993 - 4 YEARS AGO

FL	$35	FLM	$28	GC	$20
BA	$30	V	$25	B	$20

Comments: 1988; Original Retail $15.00/$17.50

Personal Data: _____
____Want Mark ____ Mark _____ Purch. 19__ Pd $ _____

113972 **ORNAMENT – Clown with Jack-in-Box**
"God Sent You Just In Time"

SUSP. 1991 - 6 YEARS AGO

FL	$35	FLM	$32
BA	$32	V	$30

Comments: 1988; Original Retail $13.50/$15.00
We predicted this piece would be either retired or suspended in 1991... It was suspended! Poor li'l clowns! Display with Sammy's Circus.

Personal Data: _____
____Want Mark ____ Mark _____ Purch. 19__ Pd $ _____

113980 **ORNAMENT – Angel with Trumpet**
"Rejoice O Earth"

RETIRED 1991 - 6 YEARS AGO

		FL	$45	FLM	$30
		BA	$40	V	$25

Comments: 1988; Original Retail $13.50/$15.00
Four years of production.

Personal Data: _____
____Want Mark ____ Mark _____ Purch. 19__ Pd $ _____

113999 **ORNAMENT – Cheerleader**
"Cheers To The Leader"

SUSP. 1991 - 6 YEARS AGO | FL | $32 | FLM | $25 |
|---|---|----|-----|-----|-----|
| | | BA | $25 | V | $22 |

Comments: 1988; Original Retail $13.50/$15.00
Four years in production. Price down from '96.

Personal Data: _____
____Want Mark ____ Mark _____ Purch. 19__ Pd $ _____

114006 **ORNAMENT – Fisherman**
"My Love Will Never Let You Go"

SUSP. 1991 - 6 YEARS AGO | FL | $32 | FLM | $25 |
|---|---|----|-----|-----|-----|
| | | BA | $28 | V | $22 |

Comments: 1988; Original Retail $13.50/$15.00
Four years of production.

Personal Data: _____
____Want Mark ____ Mark _____ Purch. 19__ Pd $ _____

114014 **Boy with Broken Heart**
"This Too Shall Pass"

CT	$40	FLM	$30	B	$30	H	$30
FL	$35	V	$30	TRP	$30	SRD	$30
BA	$32	GC	$30	S	$30		

Comments: 1987; Original Retail $23.00/$30.00
This piece was designed when Sam was feeling sad... Retailers report that he's too sad for a sale. Suspension or retirement candidate?

Personal Data: _____
____Want Mark ____ Mark _____ Purch. 19__ Pd $ _____

114022　Couple with Dog and Puppies
"The Good Lord Has Blessed Us Tenfold"

 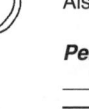

LE 1988 - 9 YEARS OLD	CT	$215
	FL	$160

Comments: 1987; Original Retail $90.00
10-Year Club Anniversary Piece. 1988 Limited Edition. Twelve unpainted pieces were released accidentally from the factory!
See #19, page XIII.

Personal Data: _____
____Want Mark _____ Mark _____ Purch. 19__ Pd $ _____

115231　Girl Carrying Bag/Balloons
"You Are My Main Event"

Pink Strings	CT	$80
White Strings	CT	$45
	FL	$50

Comments: 1987; Original Retail $30.00
1988 Special Events Piece, for Special Events only. *Precious Collectibles®* was first to announce the "pink strings" difference to collectors. These debuted early in the year. For some reason CT less than FL sales. Seemed to be an overabundance of both sales. Many, many "For Sale" quotes on this piece, few sales found.

Personal Data: _____
____Want Mark _____ Mark _____ Purch. 19__ Pd $ _____

115274　Bunnies
"Some Bunny's Sleeping"

SUSP. 1996 - 1 YEAR AGO

FL	$35	V	$25	TRP	$20
BA	$25	GC	$25	S	$20
FLM	$25	B	$22	H	$20

Comments: 1988; Original Retail $15.00/$18.50

Personal Data: _____
____Want Mark _____ Mark _____ Purch. 19__ Pd $ _____

115282　*ORNAMENT* – Boy with Bear in Sleigh
"Baby's First Christmas"

DATED 1988	FL	$25

Comments: 1988; Original Retail $15.00
Also produced in 1989 (523194). ***See #29, page XIV.***

Personal Data: _____
____Want Mark _____ Mark _____ Purch. 19__ Pd $ _____

115290　Couple with Gifts
"Our First Christmas Together"

SUSP. 1991 - 6 YEARS AGO			
FL	$85	FLM	$75
BA	$75	V	$75

Comments: 1988; Original Retail $50.00/$60.00
Popular piece, very cute! Give this piece a few more years to be in demand. Easily found at these prices.

Personal Data: _____
____Want Mark _____ Mark _____ Purch. 19__ Pd $ _____

115304　*BELL* – Girl with Calendar/Clock
"Time To Wish You A Merry Christmas"

DATED 1988	FL	$28

Comments: 1988; Original Retail $25.00

Personal Data: _____
____Want Mark _____ Mark _____ Purch. 19__ Pd $ _____

115312　*THIMBLE* – Girl with Calendar/Clock
"Time To Wish You A Merry Christmas"

DATED 1988	FL	$45

Comments: 1988; Original Retail $7.00
Most thimbles have gone up since '96.

Personal Data: _____
____Want Mark _____ Mark _____ Purch. 19__ Pd $ _____

115320　*ORNAMENT* – Girl with Calendar/Clock
"Time To Wish You A Merry Christmas"

DATED 1988	FL	$45

Comments: 1988; Original Retail $13.00
Has been found without the 1988 date. Add $50 to the secondary market price.

Personal Data: _____
____Want Mark _____ Mark _____ Purch. 19__ Pd $ _____

115339　*FIGURINE* – Girl with Calendar/Clock
"Time To Wish You A Merry Christmas"

DATED 1988	FL	$35

Comments: 1988; Original Retail $24.00
Personal Data: _____
____Want Mark _____ Mark _____ Purch. 19__ Pd $ _____

115479 **_EASTER SEALS_** – Boy/Arm Braces/Dog
"Blessed Are They That Overcome"

LE 1988 - 9 YEARS AGO   CT $35
                                 FL $28

Comments: 1987; Original Retail $27.50
Commemorative Easter Seals Figurine. 1988 Limited Edition. Large quantity produced. None of the pieces had the normally printed "Easter Seals Lily" mark on base. An error, no doubt, but by the time it was realized, it was too late to remedy. Easter Seals pieces are produced in large quantities for this special charity. Pieces have also been done for the Damien-Dutton Society (103004), St. Jude Children's Research Hospital (E-1381R), Disaster Relief (603864), Child Evangelism Fellowship, American Legion Auxiliary (604208) and Boys and Girls Clubs of America (521701) (See descriptive index).

Personal Data: _____
____Want Mark ____ Mark _____ Purch. 19__ Pd $ _____

127019 **Girl Kneeling at Flowered Cross**
"Love Blooms Eternal"

DATED 1995   TRP $40
                      S $35

Comments: 1994; Original Retail $35.00
A collector reported her decal was slanted on the front. First issue of *Dated Cross Series*.

Personal Data: _____
____Want Mark ____ Mark _____ Purch. 19__ Pd $ _____

127809 **Two Zebras**
"Congratulations, You Earned Your Stripes"

       S $20   H $15   SRD $15

Comments: 1994; Original Retail $15.00
Addition to *Two By Two, Noah's Ark*.

Personal Data: _____
____Want Mark ____ Mark _____ Purch. 19__ Pd $ _____

128295A **_ORNAMENT_** – Girl with Umbrella
"An Event Showered With Love"

DATED 1994   TRP $75-80

Comments: 1994; Original Retail $30.00
Regional event piece in Wisconsin.

Personal Data: _____
____Want Mark ____ Mark _____ Purch. 19__ Pd $ _____

128295C **_ORNAMENT_** – Girl with Umbrella
"An Event Showered With Love"

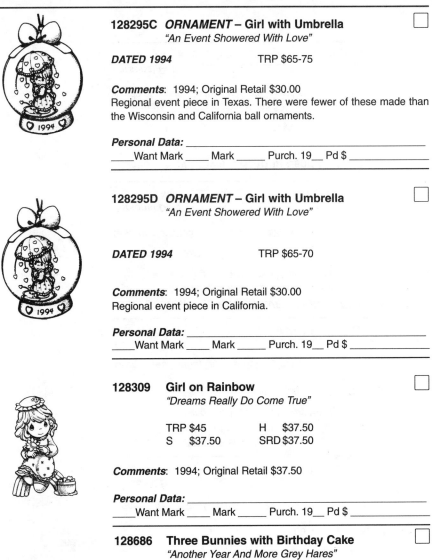

DATED 1994   TRP $65-75

Comments: 1994; Original Retail $30.00
Regional event piece in Texas. There were fewer of these made than the Wisconsin and California ball ornaments.

Personal Data: _____
____Want Mark ____ Mark _____ Purch. 19__ Pd $ _____

128295D **_ORNAMENT_** – Girl with Umbrella
"An Event Showered With Love"

DATED 1994   TRP $65-70

Comments: 1994; Original Retail $30.00
Regional event piece in California.

Personal Data: _____
____Want Mark ____ Mark _____ Purch. 19__ Pd $ _____

128309 **Girl on Rainbow**
"Dreams Really Do Come True"

       TRP $45   H $37.50
       S $37.50   SRD $37.50

Comments: 1994; Original Retail $37.50

Personal Data: _____
____Want Mark ____ Mark _____ Purch. 19__ Pd $ _____

128686 **Three Bunnies with Birthday Cake**
"Another Year And More Grey Hares"

       TRP $25   H $18.50
       S $20   SRD $18.50

Comments: 1994; Original Retail $17.50/$18.50
Birthday Series addition.

Personal Data: _____
____Want Mark ____ Mark _____ Purch. 19__ Pd $ _____

128694 Girl in Hula Dress
"Happy Hula Days"

| S | $35 | H | $32 | SRD $30 |

Comments: 1994; Original Retail $30.00
Because of her black hair, I look for suspension in a year or two. Cute piece.

Personal Data: _____
____Want Mark ____ Mark _____ Purch. 19__ Pd $ _____

128708 ORNAMENT – Owl on Branch
"Owl Be Home For Christmas"

DATED 1996   H $20

Comments: 1995; Original Retail $18.50
Birthday Series addition.

Personal Data: _____
____Want Mark ____ Mark _____ Purch. 19__ Pd $ _____

128899 EASTER SEALS – ORNAMENT
Girl w/ Roses
"Take Time To Smell The Roses"

DATED 1995   NM $10

Comments: 1994; Original Retail $7.50
1995 Commemorative Easter Seals two-dimensional Ornament.

Personal Data: _____
____Want Mark ____ Mark _____ Purch. 19__ Pd $ _____

129097 Anniversary Couple
"Love Vows To Always Bloom"

| S | $75 | H | $70 | SRD $70 |

Comments: 1995; Original Retail $70.00
Features the more "grown-up" look.

Personal Data: _____
____Want Mark ____ Mark _____ Purch. 19__ Pd $ _____

129100 Bride and Groom
"I Give You My Love Forever True"

| TRP $80 | H | $70 |
| S | $72 | SRD $70 |

Comments: 1994; Original Retail $70.00
This new Bride and Groom features a more "grown-up" appearance and is also more colorful.

Personal Data: _____
____Want Mark ____ Mark _____ Purch. 19__ Pd $ _____

129151 PLATE – Girl Bending Over Flowers
"He Hath Made Everything Beautiful In His Time"

DATED 1995   S $50

Comments: 1994; Original Retail $50.00
2nd Issue in *Mother's Day Plate Series*.

Personal Data: _____
____Want Mark ____ Mark _____ Purch. 19__ Pd $ _____

129259 CHAPEL EXCLUSIVE – Girl with Castle
"Grandpa's Island"

| S | $110 | H | $100 | SRD $100 |

Comments: 1995; Original Retail $100.00

Personal Data: _____
____Want Mark ____ Mark _____ Purch. 19__ Pd $ _____

129267 CHAPEL EXCLUSIVE
Boy Angel w/Candle and Teddy Bear
"Lighting The Way To A Happy Holiday"

| S | $35 | H | $30 | SRD $30 |

Comments: 1995; Original Retail $30.00

Personal Data: _____
____Want Mark ____ Mark _____ Purch. 19__ Pd $ _____

129275 CHAPEL EXCLUSIVE – ORNAMENT
Boy Angel w/Candle and Teddy Bear
"Lighting The Way To A Happy Holiday"

| S | $25 | H | $20 | SRD $20 |

Comments: 1995; Original Retail $20.00

Personal Data: _____
____Want Mark ____ Mark _____ Purch. 19__ Pd $ _____

129488 Boy Drawing Heart in Sand
"Love Letters In The Sand"

| H | $35 | SRD $35 |

Comments: 1996; Original Retail $35.00
Words drawn inside the heart are "God Loves You."

Personal Data: _____
____Want Mark ____ Mark _____ Purch. 19__ Pd $ _____

135992 ***CHAPEL EXCLUSIVE***
"Heaven Must Have Sent You"

SRD $45

Comments: 1996; Original Retail $45.00

Personal Data: _____
____Want Mark ____ Mark _____ Purch. 19__ Pd $ _____

136190 **Baby Girl with Cake**
"Age 1"

S $32   SRD $25
H $25

Comments: 1994; Original Retail $25.00
From the *Growing In Grace Series*. Baby with cake at age 1. Has been found with a 7 on the heart.

Personal Data: _____
____Want Mark ____ Mark _____ Purch. 19__ Pd $ _____

136204 **Angel with Announcement**
"Infant Angel With Newspaper"

S $28   SRD $22.50
H $22.50

Comments: 1994; Original Retail $22.50
From the *Growing In Grace Series*. Angel with newspaper announcing "It's A Girl."

Personal Data: _____
____Want Mark ____ Mark _____ Purch. 19__ Pd $ _____

136212 **Girl with Baby Blocks**
"Age 2"

S $30   SRD $25
H $25

Comments: 1994; Original Retail $25.00
From the *Growing In Grace Series*. Baby girl at age 2. No doubt, missing numerals have been found on one of these pieces. Add $50 to the secondary market value for that error.

Personal Data: _____
____Want Mark ____ Mark _____ Purch. 19__ Pd $ _____

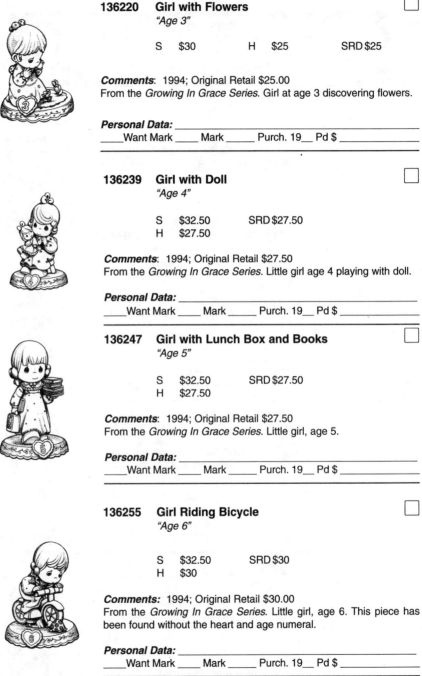

136220 **Girl with Flowers**
"Age 3"

S $30   H $25   SRD $25

Comments: 1994; Original Retail $25.00
From the *Growing In Grace Series*. Girl at age 3 discovering flowers.

Personal Data: _____
____Want Mark ____ Mark _____ Purch. 19__ Pd $ _____

136239 **Girl with Doll**
"Age 4"

S $32.50   SRD $27.50
H $27.50

Comments: 1994; Original Retail $27.50
From the *Growing In Grace Series*. Little girl age 4 playing with doll.

Personal Data: _____
____Want Mark ____ Mark _____ Purch. 19__ Pd $ _____

136247 **Girl with Lunch Box and Books**
"Age 5"

S $32.50   SRD $27.50
H $27.50

Comments: 1994; Original Retail $27.50
From the *Growing In Grace Series*. Little girl, age 5.

Personal Data: _____
____Want Mark ____ Mark _____ Purch. 19__ Pd $ _____

136255 **Girl Riding Bicycle**
"Age 6"

S $32.50   SRD $30
H $30

Comments: 1994; Original Retail $30.00
From the *Growing In Grace Series*. Little girl, age 6. This piece has been found without the heart and age numeral.

Personal Data: _____
____Want Mark ____ Mark _____ Purch. 19__ Pd $ _____

136263 **Girl Holding Sixteen Roses**
"Sweet Sixteen"

S $52.50   H $47   SRD $45

Comments: 1994; Original Retail $45.00
From the *Growing In Grace Series*. Sweet Sixteen with a bouquet of roses. Very similar to 1992 LE #526185.

Personal Data: _____
____Want Mark _____ Mark _____ Purch. 19__ Pd $ _____

136271 **Soldier Driving Car**
"You Will Always Be Our Hero"

LE 1995 - 2 YEARS OLD   S $45

Comments: 1994; Original Retail $40.00
Limited Edition figurine commemorating the 50th Anniversary of the return to peace and the end of WW II. The first shipments of this figurine were refused by Enesco due to some production problems.

Personal Data: _____
____Want Mark _____ Mark _____ Purch. 19__ Pd $ _____

139475   ***CENTURY CIRCLE***
Boy and Girl Riding Carousel
"Love Makes The World Go 'Round"

LE 15,000   S $450-500 up

Comments: 1995; Original Retail $200.00
The first Century Circle Exclusive piece. These figurines were offered at only 35 retailers nationwide. Features gold accents.

Personal Data: _____
____Want Mark _____ Mark _____ Purch. 19__ Pd $ _____

139491   **Girl Daydreaming**
"Where Would I Be Without You"

SRD $20

Comments: 1996; Original Retail $20.00
Part of the Little Moments Collection

Personal Data: _____
____Want Mark _____ Mark _____ Purch. 19__ Pd $ _____

139505   **Girl with Baby**
"All Things Grow With Love"

SRD $20

Comments: 1996; Original Retail $20.00
Part of the Little Moments Collection

Personal Data: _____
____Want Mark _____ Mark _____ Purch. 19__ Pd $ _____

139513   **Girl with Basket of Berries**
"You're The Berry Best"

SRD $20

Comments: 1996; Original Retail $20.00
Part of the Little Moments Collection

Personal Data: _____
____Want Mark _____ Mark _____ Purch. 19__ Pd $ _____

139521   **Girl with Candy**
"You Make The World A Sweeter Place"

SRD $20

Comments: 1996; Original Retail $20.00
Part of the Little Moments Collection

Personal Data: _____
____Want Mark _____ Mark _____ Purch. 19__ Pd $ _____

139548   **Boy and Girl Holding Hands**
"You're Forever In My Heart"

SRD $20

Comments: 1996; Original Retail $20.00
Part of the Little Moments Collection

Personal Data: _____
____Want Mark _____ Mark _____ Purch. 19__ Pd $ _____

A friend is one who helps you bridge the gaps between loneliness and fellowship, frustration and confidence, despair and hope, setbacks and success.

139556   Girl with Birthday Cake/Crown
"Birthday Wishes With Hugs And Kisses"

SRD $20

Comments: 1996; Original Retail $20.00
Part of the Little Moments Collection

Personal Data: _____
____Want Mark _____ Mark _____ Purch. 19__ Pd $ _____

139564   Boy Angel with Paper Airplane
"You Make My Spirit Soar"

SRD $20

Comments: 1996; Original Retail $20.00
Part of the Little Moments Collection

Personal Data: _____
____Want Mark _____ Mark _____ Purch. 19__ Pd $ _____

142654   Girl Holding Scissors/Snowflake
"He Covers The Earth With His Beauty"

DATED 1995   S $35

Comments: 1995; Original Retail $30.00

Personal Data: _____
____Want Mark _____ Mark _____ Purch. 19__ Pd $ _____

142662   ORNAMENT – Girl Holding Scissors/Snowflake
"He Covers The Earth With His Beauty"

DATED 1995   S $25

Comments: 1995; Original Retail $17.00

Personal Data: _____
____Want Mark _____ Mark _____ Purch. 19__ Pd $ _____

*F*aith is not like gasoline, which runs out as
you use it, but like a muscle, which grows
stronger as you exercise it.

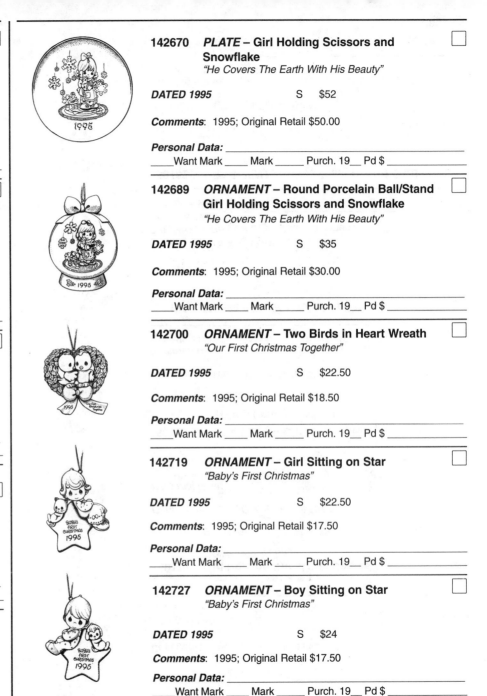

142670   PLATE – Girl Holding Scissors and Snowflake
"He Covers The Earth With His Beauty"

DATED 1995   S $52

Comments: 1995; Original Retail $50.00

Personal Data: _____
____Want Mark _____ Mark _____ Purch. 19__ Pd $ _____

142689   ORNAMENT – Round Porcelain Ball/Stand Girl Holding Scissors and Snowflake
"He Covers The Earth With His Beauty"

DATED 1995   S $35

Comments: 1995; Original Retail $30.00

Personal Data: _____
____Want Mark _____ Mark _____ Purch. 19__ Pd $ _____

142700   ORNAMENT – Two Birds in Heart Wreath
"Our First Christmas Together"

DATED 1995   S $22.50

Comments: 1995; Original Retail $18.50

Personal Data: _____
____Want Mark _____ Mark _____ Purch. 19__ Pd $ _____

142719   ORNAMENT – Girl Sitting on Star
"Baby's First Christmas"

DATED 1995   S $22.50

Comments: 1995; Original Retail $17.50

Personal Data: _____
____Want Mark _____ Mark _____ Purch. 19__ Pd $ _____

142727   ORNAMENT – Boy Sitting on Star
"Baby's First Christmas"

DATED 1995   S $24

Comments: 1995; Original Retail $17.50

Personal Data: _____
____Want Mark _____ Mark _____ Purch. 19__ Pd $ _____

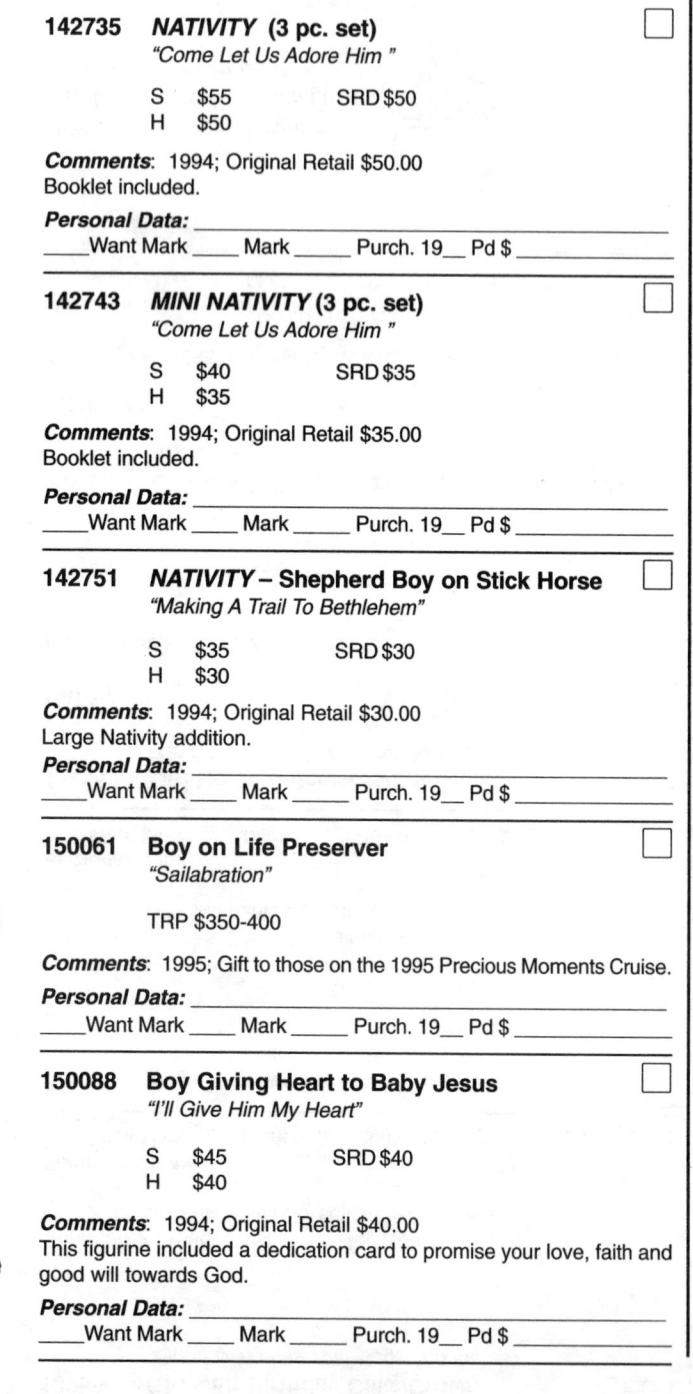

142735 **_NATIVITY_ (3 pc. set)**
"Come Let Us Adore Him"

| S | $55 | SRD $50 |
| H | $50 | |

Comments: 1994; Original Retail $50.00
Booklet included.

Personal Data: _____
____Want Mark ____ Mark _____ Purch. 19__ Pd $ _____

142743 **_MINI NATIVITY_ (3 pc. set)**
"Come Let Us Adore Him "

| S | $40 | SRD $35 |
| H | $35 | |

Comments: 1994; Original Retail $35.00
Booklet included.

Personal Data: _____
____Want Mark ____ Mark _____ Purch. 19__ Pd $ _____

142751 **_NATIVITY_ – Shepherd Boy on Stick Horse**
"Making A Trail To Bethlehem"

| S | $35 | SRD $30 |
| H | $30 | |

Comments: 1994; Original Retail $30.00
Large Nativity addition.

Personal Data: _____
____Want Mark ____ Mark _____ Purch. 19__ Pd $ _____

150061 **Boy on Life Preserver**
"Sailabration"

TRP $350-400

Comments: 1995; Gift to those on the 1995 Precious Moments Cruise.

Personal Data: _____
____Want Mark ____ Mark _____ Purch. 19__ Pd $ _____

150088 **Boy Giving Heart to Baby Jesus**
"I'll Give Him My Heart"

| S | $45 | SRD $40 |
| H | $40 | |

Comments: 1994; Original Retail $40.00
This figurine included a dedication card to promise your love, faith and good will towards God.

Personal Data: _____
____Want Mark ____ Mark _____ Purch. 19__ Pd $ _____

150096 **Boy Chimney Sweep**
"Soot Yourself To A Merry Christmas"

| S | $40 | SRD $35 |
| H | $35 | |

Comments: 1994; Original Retail $35.00

Personal Data: _____
____Want Mark ____ Mark _____ Purch. 19__ Pd $ _____

150118 **Girl Holding Christmas Candle**
"Making Spirits Bright"

| S | $40 | H | $37.50 | SRD $37.50 |

Comments: 1994; Original Retail $37.50

Personal Data: _____
____Want Mark ____ Mark _____ Purch. 19__ Pd $ _____

150126 **_ORNAMENT_ – Girl Holding Holly**
"Joy From Head To Mistletoe"

| S | $22 | H | $17 | SRD $17 |

Comments: 1994; Original Retail $17.00

Personal Data: _____
____Want Mark ____ Mark _____ Purch. 19__ Pd $ _____

150134 **Moose with Decorated Antlers**
"Merry Chrismoose"

DATED 1995   S $28

Comments: 1995; Original Retail $17.00
DSR Holiday Preview Event Dated ornament.

Personal Data: _____
____Want Mark ____ Mark _____ Purch. 19__ Pd $ _____

150142 **_ORNAMENT_ – Girl Holding Report Card**
"You're "A" Number One In My Book, Teacher"

| S | $22 | SRD $17 |
| H | $17 | |

Comments: 1994; Original Retail $17.00

Personal Data: _____
____Want Mark ____ Mark _____ Purch. 19__ Pd $ _____

150320 ORNAMENT – Angel Blowing Trumpet
"Joy To The World"

S $23   SRD $20
H $20

Comments: 1994; Original Retail $20.00

Personal Data: _____
____Want Mark ____ Mark _____ Purch. 19__ Pd $ _____

151114 PLATE – Girl with String of Hearts
"You Have Touched So Many Hearts"

Insure at retail.

Comments: 1995; Original Retail $35.00
This resin plate has a 3D effect. From the Sharing The Moments Plate collection. Plates are numbered.

Personal Data: _____
____Want Mark ____ Mark _____ Purch. 19__ Pd $ _____

152277 9" EASTER SEALS – Girl with Daisy
"HE Loves Me"

LE 1996   H $550

Comments: 1995; Original Retail $500.00
1996 Commemorative Limited Edition 9" Easter Seals figurine. Matching figurine 524263.

Personal Data: _____
____Want Mark ____ Mark _____ Purch. 19__ Pd $ _____

152579 EASTER SEALS – ORNAMENT
Girl with Piggy Bank
"You Can Always Count On Me"

LE 1996   H $6.50

Comments: 1995; Original Retail $6.50
1996 Commemorative Easter Seals ornament.

Personal Data: _____
____Want Mark ____ Mark _____ Purch. 19__ Pd $ _____

153338 ORNAMENT – Angel with Flute
"Joy To The World"

H $22   SRD $20

Comments: 1995; Original Retail $20.00

Personal Data: _____
____Want Mark ____ Mark _____ Purch. 19__ Pd $ _____

160334D ORNAMENT – Girl with String of Sunflowers
"An Event Filled With Sunshine And Flowers"

DATED 1995
S $70

Comments: 1995; Original Retail $35.00
Porcelain Ball Ornament for Regional Event in Missouri.

Personal Data: _____
____Want Mark ____ Mark _____ Purch. 19__ Pd $ _____

160334E ORNAMENT – Girl with String of Sunflowers
"An Event Filled With Sunshine And Flowers"

DATED 1995
S $70

Comments: 1995; Original Retail $35.00
Porcelain Ball Ornament for Regional Event in Maryland.

Personal Data: _____
____Want Mark ____ Mark _____ Purch. 19__ Pd $ _____

160334F ORNAMENT – Girl with String of Sunflowers
"An Event Filled With Sunshine And Flowers"

DATED 1995
S $68

Comments: 1995; Original Retail $35.00
Ball Ornament for Regional Event in Florida.

Personal Data: _____
____Want Mark ____ Mark _____ Purch. 19__ Pd $ _____

160334G ORNAMENT – Girl with String of Sunflowers
"An Event Filled With Sunshine And Flowers"

DATED 1995
S $70

Comments: 1995; Original Retail $35.00
Porcelain Ball Ornament for Regional Event in Ohio.

Personal Data:_____
____Want Mark ____ Mark _____ Purch. 19__ Pd $ _____

163597 Father Bandaging Doll's Foot
"You Are Always There For Me"

H $50   SRD $50

Comments: 1996; Original Retail $50.00

Personal Data: _____
____Want Mark ____ Mark _____ Purch. 19__ Pd $ _____

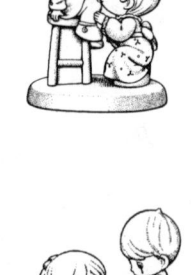

163600   **Mother & Daughter**
"You Are Always There For Me"

    S $55   H $50   SRD $50

Comments: 1995; Original Retail $50.00
Part of the *Family Series*.

Personal Data: _____
____Want Mark ____ Mark _____ Purch. 19__ Pd $ _____

163619   **Mother Bandaging Boy's Knee**
"You Are Always There For Me"

    H $50   SRD $50

Comments: 1996; Original Retail $50.00

Personal Data: _____
____Want Mark ____ Mark _____ Purch. 19__ Pd $ _____

163627   **Father & Son**
"You Are Always There For Me"

    S $55   H $50   SRD $50

Comments: 1995; Original Retail $50.00
Part of the *Family Series*.
Personal Data: _____
____Want Mark ____ Mark _____ Purch. 19__ Pd $ _____

163635   **Mother Comforting Daughter**
"You Are Always There For Me"

    H $55   SRD $50

Comments: 1995; Original Retail $50.00
Part of *Family Series*.

Personal Data: _____
____Want Mark ____ Mark _____ Purch. 19__ Pd $ _____

163694   **Goats**
"I'd Goat Anywhere With You"

    S $12   H $10   SRD $10

Comments: 1995; Original Retail $10.00
Addition to *Two By Two, Noah's Ark Series*.
Personal Data: _____
____Want Mark ____ Mark _____ Purch. 19__ Pd $ _____

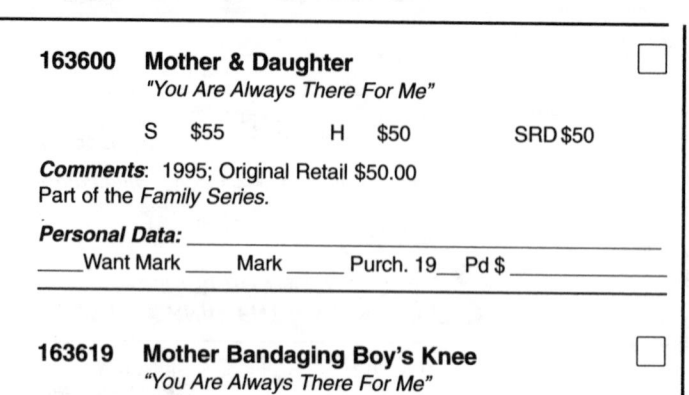

*D*on't laugh at those who
have fallen because there
may be some slippery
places in your own path.

163716   ***PLATE* – Girl with Spring Flowers**
*"Of All The Mother's I Have Known, There's None As
Precious As My Own"*

DATED 1996

    S $50   H $50

Comments: 1995; Original Retail $50.00
Third issue in the *Mother's Day Plate Series*.

Personal Data: _____
____Want Mark ____ Mark _____ Purch. 19__ Pd $ _____

163732   **Girl standing at Flowered Cross**
"Standing In The Presence Of The Lord"

DATED 1996

    S $40   H $37.50

Comments: 1995; Original Retail $37.50
Second issue of *Dated Cross Series*.

Personal Data: _____
____Want Mark ____ Mark _____ Purch. 19__ Pd $ _____

163740   **Girl Nursing Sick Kitten**
"Age 7"

    S $35   H $32.50   SRD $32.50

Comments: 1995; Original Retail $32.50
Heart missing reported by collector, add $100.

Personal Data: _____
____Want Mark ____ Mark _____ Purch. 19__ Pd $ _____

163759   **Girl with Puppy/and Marbles**
"Age 8"

    S $35   H $32.50   SRD $32.50

Comments: 1995; Original Retail $32.50

Personal Data: _____
____Want Mark ____ Mark _____ Purch. 19__ Pd $ _____

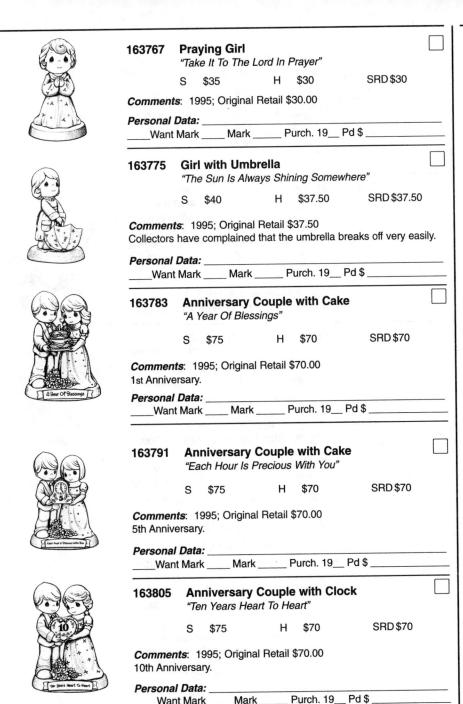

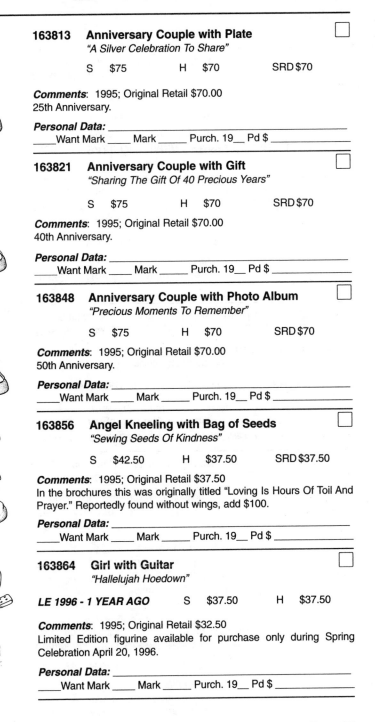

163767   Praying Girl
"Take It To The Lord In Prayer"

S $35   H $30   SRD $30

Comments: 1995; Original Retail $30.00

Personal Data: _____
____Want Mark ____ Mark _____ Purch. 19__ Pd $ _____

163775   Girl with Umbrella
"The Sun Is Always Shining Somewhere"

S $40   H $37.50   SRD $37.50

Comments: 1995; Original Retail $37.50
Collectors have complained that the umbrella breaks off very easily.

Personal Data: _____
____Want Mark ____ Mark _____ Purch. 19__ Pd $ _____

163783   Anniversary Couple with Cake
"A Year Of Blessings"

S $75   H $70   SRD $70

Comments: 1995; Original Retail $70.00
1st Anniversary.

Personal Data: _____
____Want Mark ____ Mark _____ Purch. 19__ Pd $ _____

163791   Anniversary Couple with Cake
"Each Hour Is Precious With You"

S $75   H $70   SRD $70

Comments: 1995; Original Retail $70.00
5th Anniversary.

Personal Data: _____
____Want Mark ____ Mark _____ Purch. 19__ Pd $ _____

163805   Anniversary Couple with Clock
"Ten Years Heart To Heart"

S $75   H $70   SRD $70

Comments: 1995; Original Retail $70.00
10th Anniversary.

Personal Data: _____
____Want Mark ____ Mark _____ Purch. 19__ Pd $ _____

163813   Anniversary Couple with Plate
"A Silver Celebration To Share"

S $75   H $70   SRD $70

Comments: 1995; Original Retail $70.00
25th Anniversary.

Personal Data: _____
____Want Mark ____ Mark _____ Purch. 19__ Pd $ _____

163821   Anniversary Couple with Gift
"Sharing The Gift Of 40 Precious Years"

S $75   H $70   SRD $70

Comments: 1995; Original Retail $70.00
40th Anniversary.

Personal Data: _____
____Want Mark ____ Mark _____ Purch. 19__ Pd $ _____

163848   Anniversary Couple with Photo Album
"Precious Moments To Remember"

S $75   H $70   SRD $70

Comments: 1995; Original Retail $70.00
50th Anniversary.

Personal Data: _____
____Want Mark ____ Mark _____ Purch. 19__ Pd $ _____

163856   Angel Kneeling with Bag of Seeds
"Sewing Seeds Of Kindness"

S $42.50   H $37.50   SRD $37.50

Comments: 1995; Original Retail $37.50
In the brochures this was originally titled "Loving Is Hours Of Toil And Prayer." Reportedly found without wings, add $100.

Personal Data: _____
____Want Mark ____ Mark _____ Purch. 19__ Pd $ _____

163864   Girl with Guitar
"Hallelujah Hoedown"

LE 1996 - 1 YEAR AGO   S $37.50   H $37.50

Comments: 1995; Original Retail $32.50
Limited Edition figurine available for purchase only during Spring Celebration April 20, 1996.

Personal Data: _____
____Want Mark ____ Mark _____ Purch. 19__ Pd $ _____

163880   CHAPEL EXCLUSIVE – ORNAMENT
Chapel as Manger for Baby Jesus
"His Presence is Felt In The Chapel"

SRD $25

Comments: 1996; Original Retail $25.00
Available exclusively at the Precious Moments® Chapel. Ornament is not marked.

Personal Data: _____
____Want Mark ____ Mark _____ Purch. 19__ Pd $ _____

163899   Boy with Lawnmower/Fence
"It May Be Greener, But It's Just As Hard To Cut"

S $42.50   H $37.50   SRD $37.50

Comments: 1995; Original Retail $37.50

Personal Data: _____
____Want Mark ____ Mark _____ Purch. 19__ Pd $ _____

170003   PLATE – Girls Sharing Tea
"Friendship Hits The Spot"

H $35   SRD $35

Comments: 1996; Original Retail $35.00
6 ¾" dia. resin plate.

Personal Data: _____
____Want Mark ____ Mark _____ Purch. 19__ Pd $ _____

175277   CENTURY CIRCLE – Girl at Vanity
"God's Love Is Reflected In You"

LE 15,000   H $200 up

Comments: 1995; Original Retail $150
Special details include real mirror, gold and pearlized accents and drop earrings on the girl. Attractive piece, may go higher in '97.
See #33 page XIV

Personal Data: _____
____Want Mark ____ Mark _____ Purch. 19__ Pd $ _____

If some people would be a little more careful where they step, those who follow wouldn't stumble.

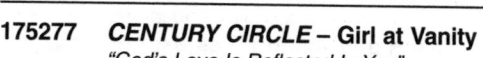
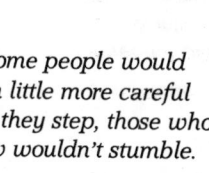
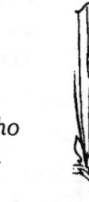

176958   Angel with Water Can
"Some Plant, Some Water, But God Giveth The Increase"

H $40   SRD $37.50

Comments: 1995; Original Retail $37.50
Listed on original sheets as *All Things Grow With Love.*
Part of *Garden Angels Series.*

Personal Data: _____
____Want Mark ____ Mark _____ Purch. 19__ Pd $ _____

Photo not available.

177083   MEDALLION – Girl Holds Figurine
"A Perfect Display Of 15 Happy Years"

S $275

Comments: 1995; Original Retail – Gift
Given as gift for attending convention.

Personal Data: _____
____Want Mark ____ Mark _____ Purch. 19__ Pd $ _____

177091   CENTURY CIRCLE ORNAMENT
Angel in Filigree Heart
"Peace On Earth"

LE 15,000 DATED 1995   S $42   SRD $25

Comments: 1995; Original Retail $25.00
This ornament is the second Century Circle Retailers' piece.

Personal Data: _____
____Want Mark ____ Mark _____ Purch. 19__ Pd $ _____

183342   Boy Angel with Slate
"Peace On Earth... Anyway"

H $35   SRD $32.50

Comments: 1995; Original Retail $32.50

Personal Data: _____
____Want Mark ____ Mark _____ Purch. 19__ Pd $ _____

183350   BALL ORNAMENT – Boy Angel with Slate
"Peace On Earth... Anyway"

H $35   SRD $30

Comments: 1995; Original Retail $30.00

Personal Data: _____
____Want Mark ____ Mark _____ Purch. 19__ Pd $ _____

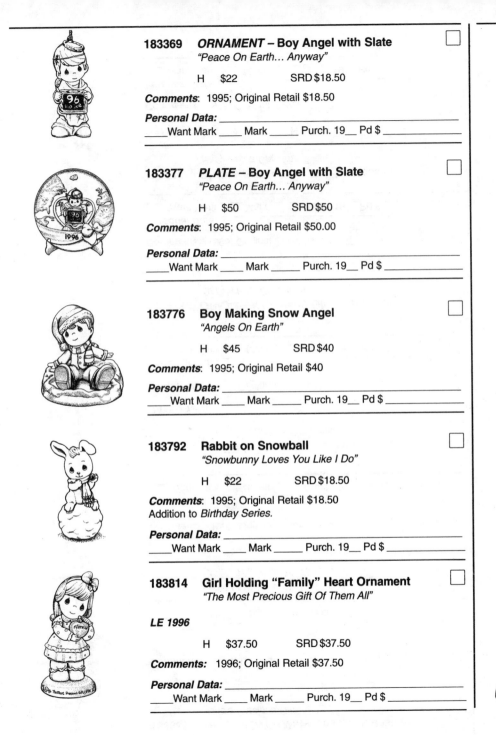

183369 ***ORNAMENT – Boy Angel with Slate***
"Peace On Earth... Anyway"

    H $22   SRD $18.50

Comments: 1995; Original Retail $18.50

Personal Data: _____
____Want Mark ____ Mark _____ Purch. 19__ Pd $ _____

183377 ***PLATE – Boy Angel with Slate***
"Peace On Earth... Anyway"

    H $50   SRD $50

Comments: 1995; Original Retail $50.00

Personal Data: _____
____Want Mark ____ Mark _____ Purch. 19__ Pd $ _____

183776 **Boy Making Snow Angel**
"Angels On Earth"

    H $45   SRD $40

Comments: 1995; Original Retail $40

Personal Data: _____
____Want Mark ____ Mark _____ Purch. 19__ Pd $ _____

183792 **Rabbit on Snowball**
"Snowbunny Loves You Like I Do"

    H $22   SRD $18.50

Comments: 1995; Original Retail $18.50
Addition to *Birthday Series.*

Personal Data: _____
____Want Mark ____ Mark _____ Purch. 19__ Pd $ _____

183814 **Girl Holding "Family" Heart Ornament**
"The Most Precious Gift Of Them All"

LE 1996

    H $37.50   SRD $37.50

Comments: 1996; Original Retail $37.50

Personal Data: _____
____Want Mark ____ Mark _____ Purch. 19__ Pd $ _____

183830 **9" Angel with Trumpet**
"Sing In Excelsis Deo"

    H $135   SRD $125

Comments: 1995; Original Retail $125.00
May sell quite well, as all other 9" pieces are the Easter Seals $500 pieces.

Personal Data: _____
____Want Mark ____ Mark _____ Purch. 19__ Pd $ _____

183849 **Boy Dressed as Scarecrow**
"You're Just Too Sweet To Be Scary"

    SRD $55

Comments: 1996; Original Retail $55.00

Personal Data: _____
____Want Mark ____ Mark _____ Purch. 19__ Pd $ _____

183857 **Boy as Jack Frost**
"Color Your World With Thanksgiving"

    H $60   SRD $60

Comments: 1995; Original Retail $60
First art work done for 25th Annual Carthage Maple Festival in 1991. I predict this will be the favorite figurine of the regular line.

Personal Data: _____
____Want Mark ____ Mark _____ Purch. 19__ Pd $ _____

183865 **Girl with Bird**
"Age 9"

    H $32   SRD $30

Comments: 1995; Original Retail $30
From the *Growing In Grace Series.*

Personal Data: _____
____Want Mark ____ Mark _____ Purch. 19__ Pd $ _____

183873 **Girl with Bowling Ball**
"Age 10"

    H $32.50   SRD $30.50

Comments: 1995; Original Retail $30.50
From the *Growing In Grace Series.* Found with 7 bowling pins on it.

Personal Data: _____
____Want Mark ____ Mark _____ Purch. 19__ Pd $ _____

183881 ORNAMENT – Mary, Joseph & Jesus
"God's Precious Gift"

H $22   SRD $20

Comments: 1995; Original Retail $20.00

Personal Data: _____
____Want Mark ____ Mark _____ Purch. 19__ Pd $ _____

183903 ORNAMENT – Dog in Skate
"When The Skating's Ruff, Try Prayer"

H $20   SRD $18.50

Comments: 1995; Original Retail $18.50

Personal Data: _____
____Want Mark ____ Mark _____ Purch. 19__ Pd $ _____

183911 ORNAMENT – Boy and Girl on Skis
"Our First Christmas Together"

DATED 1996   H $25

Comments: 1995; Original Retail $22.50

Personal Data: _____
____Want Mark ____ Mark _____ Purch. 19__ Pd $ _____

183938 ORNAMENT – Baby Girl in Stocking
"Baby's First Christmas"

DATED 1996   H $20

Comments: 1995; Original Retail $17.50

Personal Data: _____
____Want Mark ____ Mark _____ Purch. 19__ Pd $ _____

183946 ORNAMENT – Baby Boy in Stocking
"Baby's First Christmas"

DATED 1996   H $21

Comments: 1995; Original Retail $17.50

Personal Data: _____
____Want Mark ____ Mark _____ Purch. 19__ Pd $ _____

183954 NATIVITY – Shepherd with Lambs (3 pc)
"Shepherd With Lambs"

H $40   SRD $40

Comments: 1995; Original Retail $40
Set of three, addition to large Nativity.
Personal Data: _____
____Want Mark ____ Mark _____ Purch. 19__ Pd $ _____

183962 NATIVITY – Shepherd with Lambs (3 pc)
"Shepherd With Lambs"

SRD $40

Comments: 1996; Original Retail $40
Set of three, addition to large Nativity. Similar to 183954. Pictured in the 1997 Fall and Winter flyer as being identical to 183954, only photo proved to be that of a prototype.
Personal Data: _____
____Want Mark ____ Mark _____ Purch. 19__ Pd $ _____

184004 MINI NATIVITY – Boy on Stick Horse
"Making A Trail To Bethlehem"

H $25   SRD $25

Comments: 1995; Original Retail $25.00
Mini Nativity addition.
Personal Data: _____
____Want Mark ____ Mark _____ Purch. 19__ Pd $ _____

184012 NATIVITY – Girl with Bird Cage and Birds
"All Sing His Praises"

H $35   SRD $32.50

Comments: 1995; Original Retail $32.50
Large Nativity addition. Figurine produced was very different from prototype pictured in 1996 Fall and Winter flyer.
Personal Data: _____
____Want Mark ____ Mark _____ Purch. 19__ Pd $ _____

184209 CENTURY CIRLCE – ORNAMENT
Girl on Carousel Horse
"Love Makes The World Go 'Round"

LE 1996

H $30 and up
Comments: 1995; Original Retail $22.50
Personal Data: _____
____Want Mark ____ Mark _____ Purch. 19__ Pd $ _____

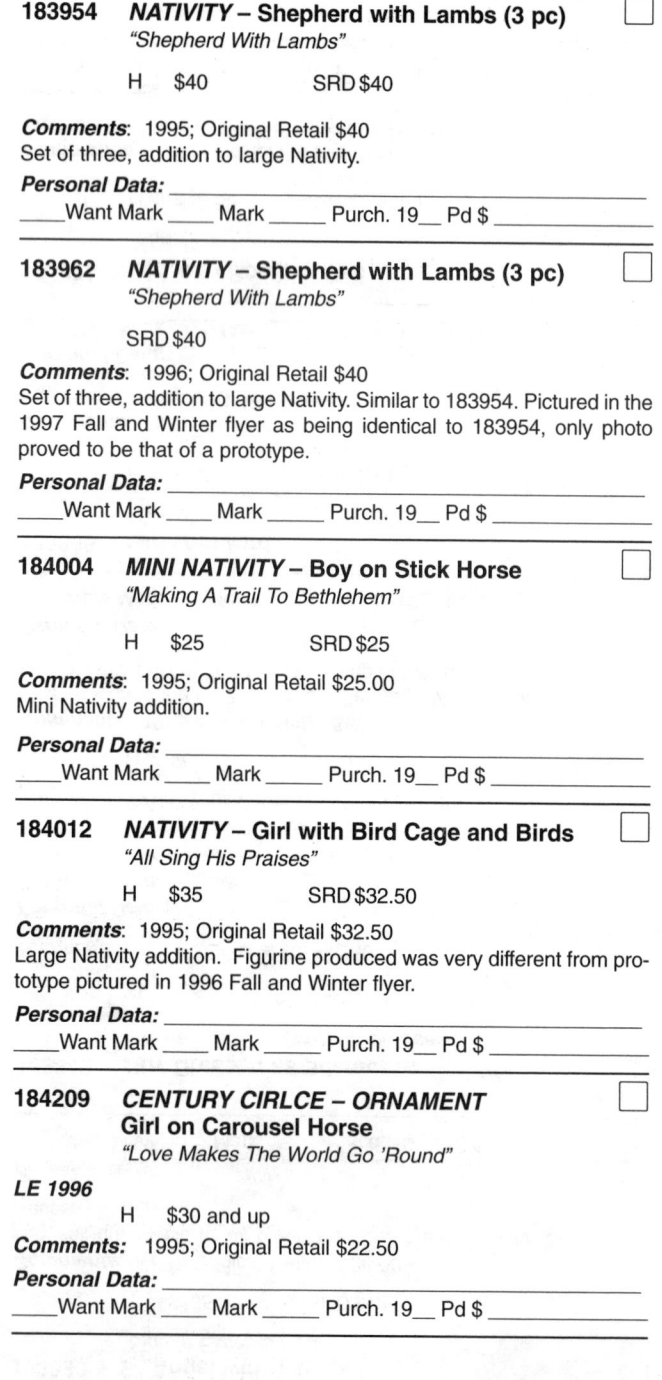

184217 *CENTURY CIRCLE*
Girl Holding String of Sunshine Faces
"May The Sun Always Shine On You"

H $50 and up
Comments: 1995; Original Retail $37.50

Personal Data: _____
____Want Mark ____ Mark _____ Purch. 19__ Pd $ _____

184268   Girl Angel with Bouquet of Flowers
"A Bouquet From God's Garden Of Love"

H $37.50   SRD $37.50

Comments: 1995; Original Retail $37.50
Third edition of *Growing In God's Garden Of Love Series*.

Personal Data: _____
____Want Mark ____ Mark _____ Purch. 19__ Pd $ _____

186384   *PLATE* – Girl with Bunny/Nursery Background
"Jesus Loves Me"

H $35   SRD $35

Comments: 1995; Original Retail $35.00
Very colorful resin plate; 6 ³/₄" dia.

Personal Data: _____
____Want Mark ____ Mark _____ Purch. 19__ Pd $ _____

186406   *PLATE* – Boy and Girl Sitting on Stump
"Love One Another"

SRD $35

Comments: 1996; Original Retail $35.00
Very colorful resin plate; 6 ¹/₂" dia.

Personal Data: _____
____Want Mark ____ Mark _____ Purch. 19__ Pd $ _____

186457   *PLATE* – Two Girls with Flowers
"Good Friends Are Forever"

SRD $35

Comments: 1996; Original Retail $35.00
Very colorful resin plate; 6 ¹/₄" dia.

Personal Data: _____
____Want Mark ____ Mark _____ Purch. 19__ Pd $ _____

192368   *EASTER SEALS*
Boy with Basketball in Wheelchair
"Give Ability A Chance"

LE 1997   H $30

Comments: 1995; Original Retail $30.00
1997 Easter Seals Commemorative figurine. Does not have Easter Seal symbol on them.

Personal Data: _____
____Want Mark ____ Mark _____ Purch. 19__ Pd $ _____

192376   9" *EASTER SEALS*
Girl Signing "I Love You"
"Love Is Universal"

LE 1997   SRD $500

Comments: 1995; Original Retail $500.00
1997 Easter Seals. For each figurine sold a $500 donation will be made. This figurine may be found with the H mark.

Personal Data: _____
____Want Mark ____ Mark _____ Purch. 19__ Pd $ _____

192384   *EASTER SEALS* – ORNAMENT
Boy with Basketball in Wheelchair
"Give Ability A Chance"

LE 1997   H $6

Comments: 1995; Original Retail $6.00
1997 Easter Seals Commemerative ornament. Two dimensional round ornament.

Personal Data: _____
____Want Mark ____ Mark _____ Purch. 19__ Pd $ _____

204854   Girl with Life Preserver
"You're A Life Saver To Me"

H $35   SRD $35

Comments: 1996; Original Retail $35.00
Personal Data: _____
____Want Mark ____ Mark _____ Purch. 19__ Pd $ _____

204862   *CHAPEL EXCLUSIVE*
Indian Chief with Headdress
"The Lord Is Our Chief Inspiration"

NM $45

Comments: 1996; Original Retail $45.00
A beautiful figurine depicting a Native American boy.

Personal Data: _____
____Want Mark ____ Mark _____ Purch. 19__ Pd $ _____

204870 *9" CHAPEL EXCLUSIVE*
Indian Chief with Headdress
"The Lord Is Our Chief Inspiration"

LE 1996-1997
  NM $250

Comments: 1996; Original Retail $250.00
Limited to year of production. This piece was first available at the Chapel September of 1996.

Personal Data: _____
____Want Mark ____ Mark _____ Purch. 19__ Pd $ _____

204889 *CHAPEL EXCLUSIVE*
Girl with Clown Doll
"Coleenia"

  NM $32.50

Comments: 1996; Original Retail $32.50
Personal Data: _____
____Want Mark ____ Mark _____ Purch. 19__ Pd $ _____

212563 **Girl Flying Heart Shaped Kite**
"Your Precious Spirit Comes Shining Through"

  H $35   SRD $35

Comments: 1995; Original Retail $35.00
1996 Knoxville Regional Conference Event figurine.

Personal Data: _____
____Want Mark ____ Mark _____ Purch. 19__ Pd $ _____

212563A **Girl Flying Heart Shaped Kite**
"Your Precious Spirit Comes Shining Through"

  H $35   SRD $35

Comments: 1995; Original Retail $32.50
1996 Indianapolis Regional Conference Event figurine.
Personal Data: _____
____Want Mark ____ Mark _____ Purch. 19__ Pd $ _____

212563B **Girl Flying Heart Shaped Kite**
"Your Precious Spirit Comes Shining Through"

  H $35   SRD $32.50

Comments: 1995; Original Retail $32.50
1996 Minneapolis Regional Conference Event figurine.
Personal Data: _____
____Want Mark ____ Mark _____ Purch. 19__ Pd $ _____

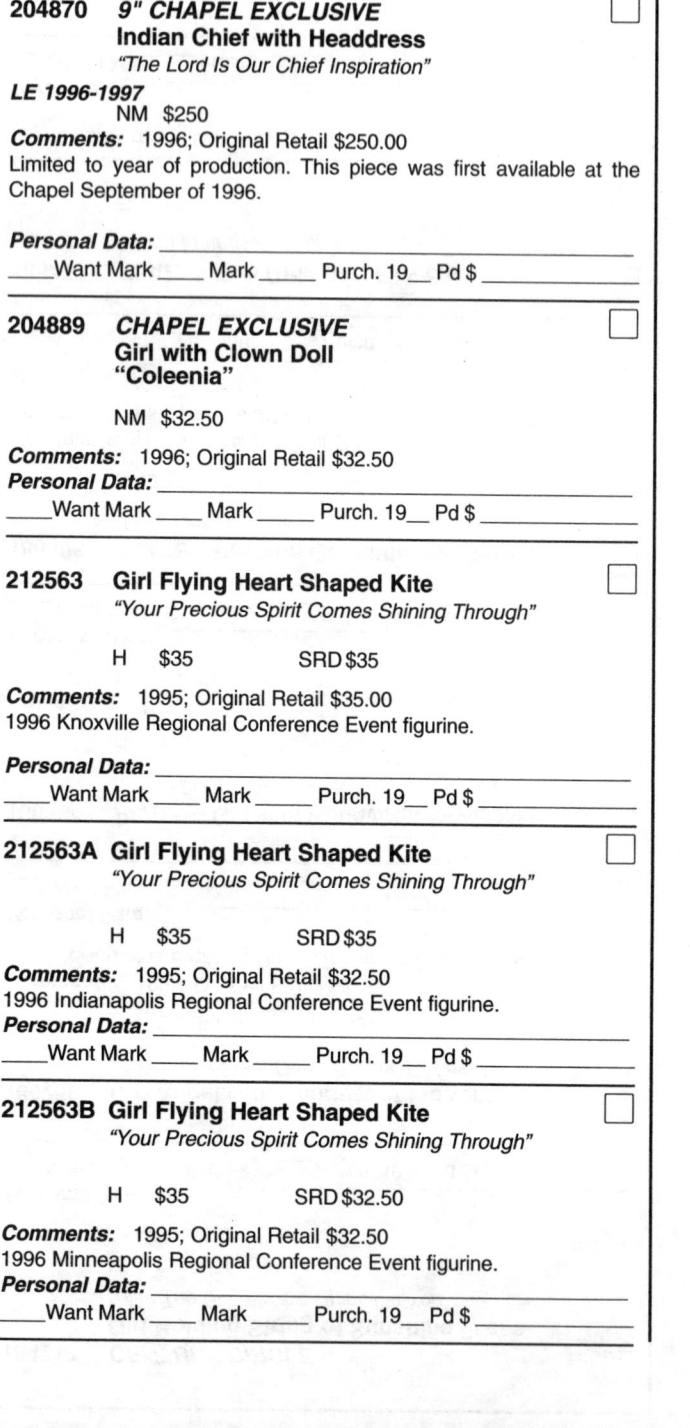

212520 *ORNAMENT–*
Girl on Heart Shaped Ornament
"The Most Precious Gift Of Them All"

LE 1996

  H $20

Comments: 1996; Original Retail $20.00
Catalog exclusive with special understamp.
Personal Data: _____
____Want Mark ____ Mark _____ Purch. 19__ Pd $ _____

213616 *MINI NATIVITY –* **Shepherd and Sheep**

  SRD $22.50

Comments: 1996; Original Retail $22.50
Two piece addition to mini nativity.
Personal Data: _____
____Want Mark ____ Mark _____ Purch. 19__ Pd $ _____

213624 *MINI NATIVITY –* **Three Kings with Gifts**
"Wee Three Kings"

  H $55   SRD $55

Comments: 1995; Original Retail $55.00
Three piece addition to mini Nativity set.

Personal Data: _____
____Want Mark ____ Mark _____ Purch. 19__ Pd $ _____

225290 *EASTER SEALS – ORNAMENT*
Girl with Chick in Egg
"Always In His Care"

DATED 1990   NM $10

Comments: 1989; Original Retail $8.00
1990 Commemorative Easter Seals two-dimensional ornament. Same shape as Easter Seals logo.
Personal Data: _____
____Want Mark ____ Mark _____ Purch. 19__ Pd $ _____

227986 *ORNAMENT –* Collectors' Club
"Celebrating A Decade Of Loving, Caring And Sharing"

DATED 1990   NM $10

Comments: 1989; Original Retail $7.00
Special Ten-Year ornament available to Club Members Only.
Personal Data: _____
____Want Mark ____ Mark _____ Purch. 19__ Pd $ _____

230448 PLAQUE
"The Enesco Precious Moments Collection"

MM	$22	V	$15	TRP	$15	SRD	$15
BA	$18	GC	$15	S	$15		
FLM	$18	B	$15	H	$15		

Comments: 1989; Original Retail $15.00

Personal Data: _____
____Want Mark ____ Mark _____ Purch. 19__ Pd $ _____

233196 ORNAMENT – Girl with Dove
"Sharing A Gift Of Love"

DATED 1991   NM $8.50

Comments: 1990; Original Retail $8.00
1991 Commemorative Easter Seals. Two-dimensional, heart-shaped ornament.

Personal Data: _____
____Want Mark ____ Mark _____ Purch. 19__ Pd $ _____

238899 EASTER SEALS – ORNAMENT
Envelope w/Girl Signing
"A Universal Love"

DATED 1992   NM $10

Comments: 1990; Original Retail $8.00
1992 Easter Seals Commemorative Ornament. No demand.

Personal Data: _____
____Want Mark ____ Mark _____ Purch. 19__ Pd $ _____

244570 EASTER SEALS – ORNAMENT
Girl with Pail of Shells
"It Is No Secret What God Can Do"

DATED 1994   NM $8

Comments: 1993; Original Retail $6.50
1994 Easter Seals Commemorative Ornament.

Personal Data: _____
____Want Mark ____ Mark _____ Purch. 19__ Pd $ _____

250112 ORNAMENT – Girl with Trophy Cup
"You're My Number One Friend"

DATED 1993   NM $10

Comments: 1992; Original Retail $8.00
1993 Easter Seals Commemorative Ornament.

Personal Data: _____
____Want Mark ____ Mark _____ Purch. 19__ Pd $ _____

260916 Girl with Lamb Standing by Cross
"Lead Me To Calvary"

DATED 1997

          H $37.50   SRD $37.50

Comments: 1996; Original Retail $37.50

Personal Data: _____
____Want Mark ____ Mark _____ Purch. 19__ Pd $ _____

260924 Girl with Dog and Sign
"Age 11"

          H $37.50   SRD $37.50

Comments: 1996; Original Retail $37.50
Growing In Grace Series. The girl's sign shows "11 flavors of ice cream."

Personal Data: _____
____Want Mark ____ Mark _____ Purch. 19__ Pd $ _____

260932 Girl with Dog Holding Alarm Clock
"Age 12"

          H $37.50   SRD $37.50

Comments: 1996; Original Retail $37.50
Growing In Grace Series

Personal Data: _____
____Want Mark ____ Mark _____ Purch. 19__ Pd $ _____

260940 Monkeys Painting Spots on Leopard
"From The First Time I Spotted You I Knew We'd Be Friends"

          H $18.50   SRD $18.50

Comments: 1996; Original Retail $18.50
Birthday Series. The prototype only shows one monkey, but we have heard the final production has two monkeys.

Personal Data: _____
____Want Mark ____ Mark _____ Purch. 19__ Pd $ _____

261068 Cave-Girl with Dinosaur
"Friends From The Very Beginning"

          H $50   SRD $50

Comments: 1996; Original Retail $50.00
Colorful! Prototype pictured in Enesco Spring and Summer 1997 flyer was different from actual figurine produced. Actual figurine has the dinosaur green and the girl's hair and position changed, along with the dinosaur's standing position.

Personal Data: _____
____Want Mark ____ Mark _____ Purch. 19__ Pd $ _____

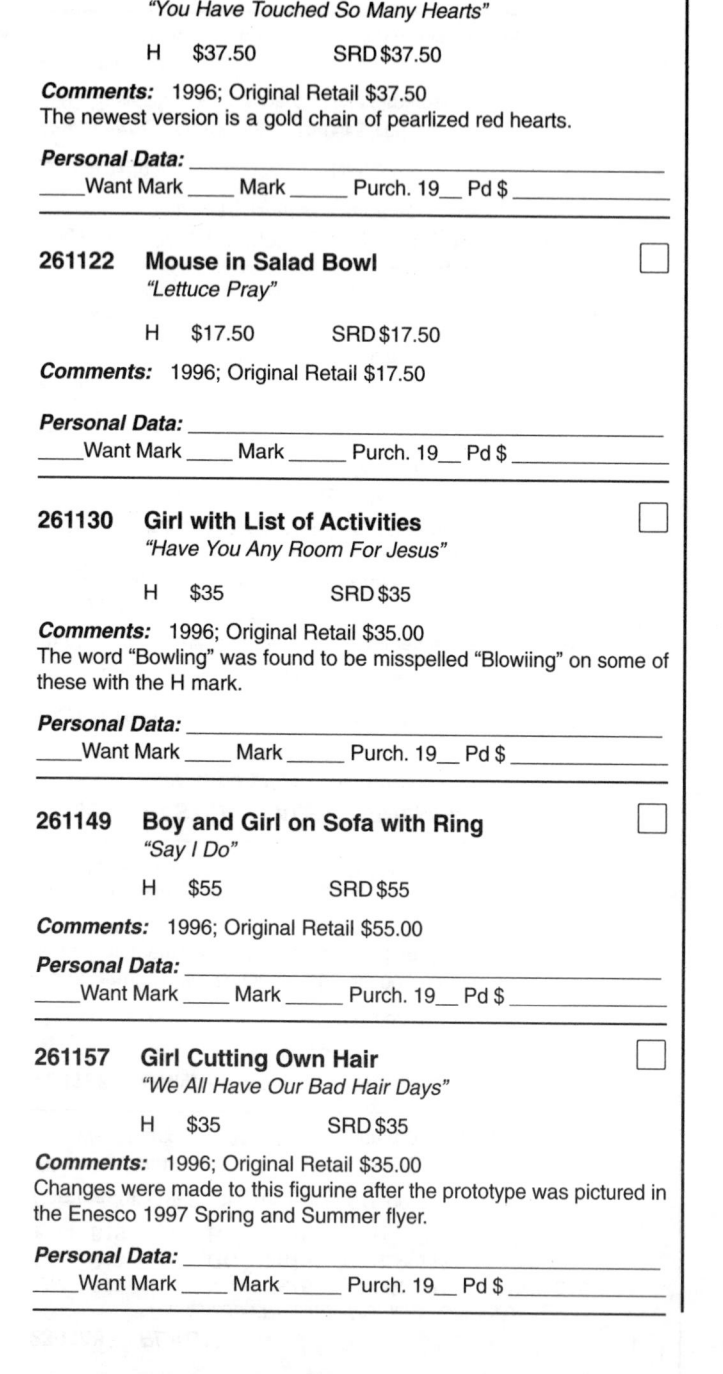

261084 **Girl with String of Hearts**
"You Have Touched So Many Hearts"

H $37.50   SRD $37.50

Comments: 1996; Original Retail $37.50
The newest version is a gold chain of pearlized red hearts.

Personal Data: _____
____Want Mark ____ Mark ____ Purch. 19__ Pd $ _____

261122 **Mouse in Salad Bowl**
"Lettuce Pray"

H $17.50   SRD $17.50

Comments: 1996; Original Retail $17.50

Personal Data: _____
____Want Mark ____ Mark ____ Purch. 19__ Pd $ _____

261130 **Girl with List of Activities**
"Have You Any Room For Jesus"

H $35   SRD $35

Comments: 1996; Original Retail $35.00
The word "Bowling" was found to be misspelled "Blowiing" on some of these with the H mark.

Personal Data: _____
____Want Mark ____ Mark ____ Purch. 19__ Pd $ _____

261149 **Boy and Girl on Sofa with Ring**
"Say I Do"

H $55   SRD $55

Comments: 1996; Original Retail $55.00

Personal Data: _____
____Want Mark ____ Mark ____ Purch. 19__ Pd $ _____

261157 **Girl Cutting Own Hair**
"We All Have Our Bad Hair Days"

H $35   SRD $35

Comments: 1996; Original Retail $35.00
Changes were made to this figurine after the prototype was pictured in the Enesco 1997 Spring and Summer flyer.

Personal Data: _____
____Want Mark ____ Mark ____ Purch. 19__ Pd $ _____

261203 **Girl Angel with Gem on Shoe**
"January"

SRD $20

Comments: 1996; Original Retail $20
Part of the Little Moments Birthstone Collection.

Personal Data: _____
____Want Mark ____ Mark ____ Purch. 19__ Pd $ _____

261211 **Girl Angel with Gem on Shoe**
"May"

SRD $20

Comments: 1996; Original Retail $20
Part of the Little Moments Birthstone Collection.

Personal Data: _____
____Want Mark ____ Mark ____ Purch. 19__ Pd $ _____

261238 **Girl Angel with Gem on Shoe**
"September"

SRD $20

Comments: 1996; Original Retail $20
Part of the Little Moments Birthstone Collection.

Personal Data: _____
____Want Mark ____ Mark ____ Purch. 19__ Pd $ _____

261246 **Girl Angel with Gem on Necklace**
"February"

SRD $20

Comments: 1996; Original Retail $20
Part of the Little Moments Birthstone Collection.

Personal Data: _____
____Want Mark ____ Mark ____ Purch. 19__ Pd $ _____

261254 **Girl Angel with Gem on Necklace**
"June"

SRD $20

Comments: 1996; Original Retail $20
Part of the Little Moments Birthstone Collection.

Personal Data: _____
____Want Mark ____ Mark ____ Purch. 19__ Pd $ _____

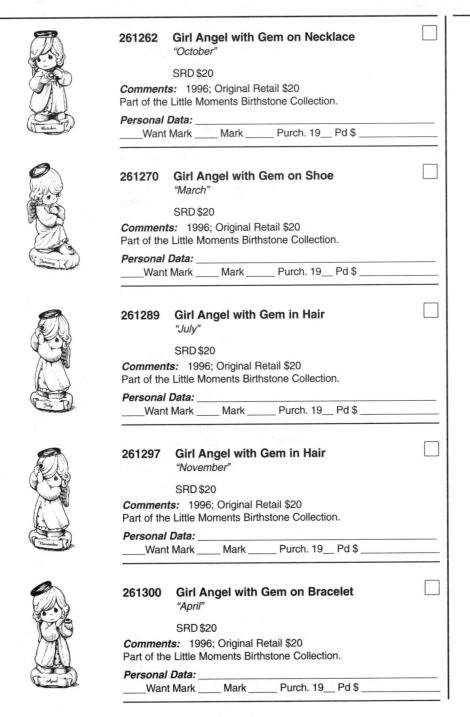

261262 Girl Angel with Gem on Necklace
"October"

SRD $20

Comments: 1996; Original Retail $20
Part of the Little Moments Birthstone Collection.

Personal Data: _____
____Want Mark _____ Mark _____ Purch. 19__ Pd $ _____

261270 Girl Angel with Gem on Shoe
"March"

SRD $20

Comments: 1996; Original Retail $20
Part of the Little Moments Birthstone Collection.

Personal Data: _____
____Want Mark _____ Mark _____ Purch. 19__ Pd $ _____

261289 Girl Angel with Gem in Hair
"July"

SRD $20

Comments: 1996; Original Retail $20
Part of the Little Moments Birthstone Collection.

Personal Data: _____
____Want Mark _____ Mark _____ Purch. 19__ Pd $ _____

261297 Girl Angel with Gem in Hair
"November"

SRD $20

Comments: 1996; Original Retail $20
Part of the Little Moments Birthstone Collection.

Personal Data: _____
____Want Mark _____ Mark _____ Purch. 19__ Pd $ _____

261300 Girl Angel with Gem on Bracelet
"April"

SRD $20

Comments: 1996; Original Retail $20
Part of the Little Moments Birthstone Collection.

Personal Data: _____
____Want Mark _____ Mark _____ Purch. 19__ Pd $ _____

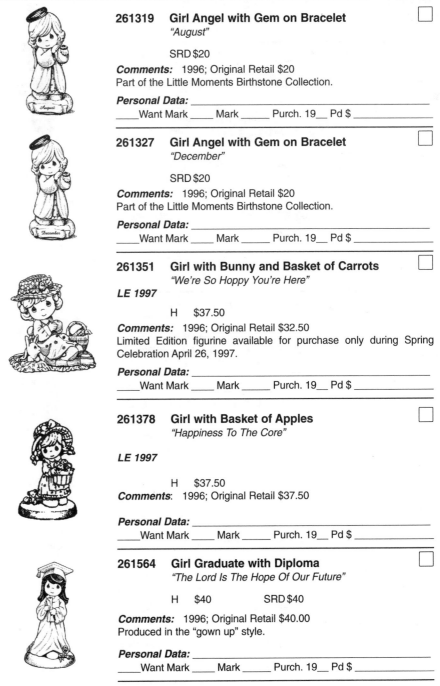

261319 Girl Angel with Gem on Bracelet
"August"

SRD $20

Comments: 1996; Original Retail $20
Part of the Little Moments Birthstone Collection.

Personal Data: _____
____Want Mark _____ Mark _____ Purch. 19__ Pd $ _____

261327 Girl Angel with Gem on Bracelet
"December"

SRD $20

Comments: 1996; Original Retail $20
Part of the Little Moments Birthstone Collection.

Personal Data: _____
____Want Mark _____ Mark _____ Purch. 19__ Pd $ _____

261351 Girl with Bunny and Basket of Carrots
"We're So Hoppy You're Here"

LE 1997

H $37.50

Comments: 1996; Original Retail $32.50
Limited Edition figurine available for purchase only during Spring Celebration April 26, 1997.

Personal Data: _____
____Want Mark _____ Mark _____ Purch. 19__ Pd $ _____

261378 Girl with Basket of Apples
"Happiness To The Core"

LE 1997

H $37.50

Comments: 1996; Original Retail $37.50

Personal Data: _____
____Want Mark _____ Mark _____ Purch. 19__ Pd $ _____

261564 Girl Graduate with Diploma
"The Lord Is The Hope Of Our Future"

H $40   SRD $40

Comments: 1996; Original Retail $40.00
Produced in the "gown up" style.

Personal Data: _____
____Want Mark _____ Mark _____ Purch. 19__ Pd $ _____

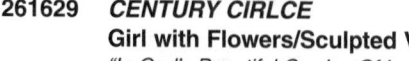

261629 *CENTURY CIRLCE*
Girl with Flowers/Sculpted Vine
"In God's Beautiful Garden Of Love"

LE 15,000 1997

    H $150   SRD $150
Look for this piece to go up on the secondary market.

Comments: 1996; Original Retail $150.00

Personal Data: _____
____Want Mark ____ Mark _____ Purch. 19__ Pd $ _____

272422   **Baby Girls with Flowers**
"Good Friends Are Forever"

    H $30   SRD $30

Comments: 1996; Original Retail $30.00
Baby Classics Series.

Personal Data: _____
____Want Mark ____ Mark _____ Purch. 19__ Pd $ _____

272434   **Baby Girl with Butterfly**
"We Are God's Workmanship"

    H $25   SRD $25

Comments: 1996; Original Retail $25
Baby Classics Series.

Personal Data: _____
____Want Mark ____ Mark _____ Purch. 19__ Pd $ _____

272450   **Baby Girl with Goose**
"Make A Joyful Noise"

    H $30   SRD $30

Comments: 1996; Original Retail $30.00
Baby Classics Series. Prototype pictured in Enesco flyer was different from actual figurine produced. Actual figurine produced shows open arms.

Personal Data: _____
____Want Mark ____ Mark _____ Purch. 19__ Pd $ _____

272469   **Baby Boy with Chick**
"I Believe In Miracles"

    H $25   SRD $25

Comments: 1996; Original Retail $25.00
Baby Classics Series.

Personal Data: _____
____Want Mark ____ Mark _____ Purch. 19__ Pd $ _____

272477   **Baby Girl with Puppies**
"God Loveth A Cheerful Giver"

    H $25   SRD $25

Comments: 1996; Original Retail $25.00
Baby Classics Series. Prototype pictured in Enesco flyer was different from actual figurine produced. Actual figurine produced shows girl holding a paper which says "Free Puppies".

Personal Data: _____
____Want Mark ____ Mark _____ Purch. 19__ Pd $ _____

272485   **Baby Girl with String of Hearts**
"You Have Touched So Many Hearts"

    H $25   SRD $25

Comments: 1996; Original Retail $25.00
Baby Classics Series.

Personal Data: _____
____Want Mark ____ Mark _____ Purch. 19__ Pd $ _____

272493   **Baby Boy Sharing Ice Cream w/Puppy**
"Love Is Sharing"

    H $25   SRD $25

Comments: 1996; Original Retail $25.00
Baby Classics Series.

Personal Data: _____
____Want Mark ____ Mark _____ Purch. 19__ Pd $ _____

272507   **Baby Couple with Seedling**
"Love One Another"

    H $30   SRD $30

Comments: 1996; Original Retail $30.00
Baby Classics Series.

Personal Data: _____
____Want Mark ____ Mark _____ Purch. 19__ Pd $ _____

272523   **Girl Holding Birthday Cake**
"Happy Birthday Jesus"
SRD $35

Comments: 1996; Original Retail $35.00
Personal Data: _____
____Want Mark ____ Mark _____ Purch. 19__ Pd $ _____

272531 **Girl Holding Candle**
"Sharing The Light Of Love"

SRD $35

Comments: 1996; Original Retail $35.00

Personal Data: _____
____Want Mark ____ Mark _____ Purch. 19__ Pd $ _____

272558 **Boy Angel Holding "Holy Cow" Sign**
"I Think You're Just Divine"

SRD $40

Comments: 1996; Original Retail $40.00

Personal Data: _____
____Want Mark ____ Mark _____ Purch. 19__ Pd $ _____

272566 ***ORNAMENT* – Girl Angel Flying w/Harp**
"Joy To The World"

SRD $20

Comments: 1996; Original Retail $20.00

Personal Data: _____
____Want Mark ____ Mark _____ Purch. 19__ Pd $ _____

272582 ***NATIVITY* – Palm Trees, Hay Bale and Baby Food**

SRD $60

Comments: 1996; Original Retail $60.00

Personal Data: _____
____Want Mark ____ Mark _____ Purch. 19__ Pd $ _____

272590 **Mouse Sleeping in Matchbox**
"Sharing The Light Of Love"

SRD $25

Comments: 1996; Original Retail $25.00

Personal Data: _____
____Want Mark ____ Mark _____ Purch. 19__ Pd $ _____

272647 **Girl Praying at Turtle Race**
"Age 13"

SRD $40

Comments: 1996; Original Retail $40.00

Personal Data: _____
____Want Mark ____ Mark _____ Purch. 19__ Pd $ _____

272655 **Girl Holding Diary**
"Age 14"

SRD $35

Comments: 1996; Original Retail $35.00

Personal Data: _____
____Want Mark ____ Mark _____ Purch. 19__ Pd $ _____

272663 **Girl withPuppy Holding List**
"Age 15"

SRD $40

Comments: 1996; Original Retail $40.00

Personal Data: _____
____Want Mark ____ Mark _____ Purch. 19__ Pd $ _____

272671 **Girl Holding Heart Shaped Candy Cane**
"Cane You Join Us For A Merry Christmas"

DATED 1997
SRD $30

Comments: 1996; Original Retail $30.00

Personal Data: _____
____Want Mark ____ Mark _____ Purch. 19__ Pd $ _____

272698 ***ORNAMENT* –**
Girl Holding Heart Shaped Candy Cane
"Cane You Join Us For A Merry Christmas"

DATED 1997
SRD $40

Comments: 1996; Original Retail $40.00

Personal Data: _____
____Want Mark ____ Mark _____ Purch. 19__ Pd $ _____

272701   **PLATE – Girl Holding Heart-Shaped Candy Cane**
"Cane You Join Us For A Merry Christmas"

DATED 1997

SRD $50

Comments: 1996; Original Retail $50.00

Personal Data: _____
____Want Mark ____ Mark _____ Purch. 19__ Pd $ _____

272728   **BALL ORNAMENT – Girl Holding Heart Shaped Candy Cane**
"Cane You Join Us For A Merry Christmas"

DATED 1997

SRD $30

Comments: 1996; Original Retail $30.00

Personal Data: _____
____Want Mark ____ Mark _____ Purch. 19__ Pd $ _____

272736   **ORNAMENT – Boy and Girl Sitting on Locomotive**
"Our First Christmas Together"

DATED 1997

SRD $20

Comments: 1996; Original Retail $20.00

Personal Data: _____
____Want Mark ____ Mark _____ Purch. 19__ Pd $ _____

272744   **ORNAMENT – Baby Girl Sitting in Flower Pot**
"Baby's First Christmas"

DATED 1997

SRD $18.50

Comments: 1996; Original Retail $18.50

Personal Data: _____
____Want Mark ____ Mark _____ Purch. 19__ Pd $ _____

272752   **ORNAMENT – Baby Boy Sitting in Flower Pot**
"Baby's First Christmas"

DATED 1997   SRD $18.50

Comments: 1996; Original Retail $18.50

Personal Data: _____
____Want Mark ____ Mark _____ Purch. 19__ Pd $ _____

272760   **ORNAMENT – Snail**
"Slow Down For The Holidays"

DATED 1997   SRD $18.50

Comments: 1996; Original Retail $18.50
Part of the *Birthday Series.*

Personal Data: _____
____Want Mark ____ Mark _____ Purch. 19__ Pd $ _____

272787   **NATIVITY – Boy with Halo Wearing Star**
"And You Shall See A Star"

SRD $32.50

Comments: 1996; Original Retail $32.50

Personal Data: _____
____Want Mark ____ Mark _____ Purch. 19__ Pd $ _____

272892   **ORNAMENT – Two Puppies with Sled**

SRD $18.50

Comments: 1996; Original Retail $18.50

Personal Data: _____
____Want Mark ____ Mark _____ Purch. 19__ Pd $ _____

272922   **EASTER SEALS – ORNAMENT**
Clown with Monkey
"Somebody Cares"

DATED 1998   SRD 6.50

Comments: 1996; Original Retail $6.50

Personal Data: _____
____Want Mark ____ Mark _____ Purch. 19__ Pd $ _____

279323   *MINI NATIVITY – CAMEL, COW AND DONKEY*

SRD 30.00

Comments: 1996; Original Retail $30.00
Three piece mini nativity addition.

Personal Data: _____
____Want Mark ____ Mark _____ Purch. 19__ Pd $ _____

283428   *NATIVITY – Lighted Inn*

SRD 100.00

Comments: 1996; Original Retail $100.00

Personal Data: _____
____Want Mark ____ Mark _____ Purch. 19__ Pd $ _____

283436   *MINI NATIVITY – Wall*

SRD 40.00

Comments: 1996; Original Retail $40.00

Personal Data: _____
____Want Mark ____ Mark _____ Purch. 19__ Pd $ _____

283444   *MINI NATIVITY – Girl Angel Sitting*
"For An Angel You're So Down To Earth"

SRD 17.50

Comments: 1996; Original Retail $17.50

Personal Data: _____
____Want Mark ____ Mark _____ Purch. 19__ Pd $ _____

291293   *MINI NATIVITY – Cats with Kittens*

SRD 18.50

Comments: 1996; Original Retail $18.50

Personal Data: _____
____Want Mark ____ Mark _____ Purch. 19__ Pd $ _____

292753   *NATIVITY – Wishing Well*

SRD 30.00

Comments: 1996; Original Retail $30.00

Personal Data: _____
____Want Mark ____ Mark _____ Purch. 19__ Pd $ _____

408735 ♪ *MUSICAL – JACK-IN-THE-BOX*
Four Seasons Spring
"The Voice Of Spring"

LE 1990/91- 6 YEARS OLD   FLM $140
                                                    V $120

Comments: 1984; Original Retail $200.00
Limited to two years' production. Plays *April Love.* In my opinion, this style of doll did not have great appeal for most collectors. Why were these dolls "unpopular?" Maybe they could not be held and loved?

Personal Data: _____
____Want Mark ____ Mark _____ Purch. 19__ Pd $ _____

408743 ♪ *MUSICAL – JACK-IN-THE-BOX*
Four Seasons Summer
"Summer's Joy"

LE 1990/91 - 6 YEARS OLD   FLM $135
                                                    V $115

Comments: 1984; Original Retail $200.00
Limited to two year's production. Plays *You Are My Sunshine.* Good source reported seeing these dolls being destroyed at the Enesco warehouse in Elk Grove. Not good sellers. ***See note on 408735.***

Personal Data: _____
____Want Mark ____ Mark _____ Purch. 19__ Pd $ _____

408751 ♪ *MUSICAL – JACK-IN-THE-BOX*
Four Seasons Autumn

"Autumn's Praise"

LE 1990/91 - 6 YEARS OLD   FLM $130
                                                    V $110

Comments: 1984; Original Retail $200.00
Limited to two years' production. Plays *Autumn Leaves.*
See note on 408735.

Personal Data: _____
____Want Mark ____ Mark _____ Purch. 19__ Pd $ _____

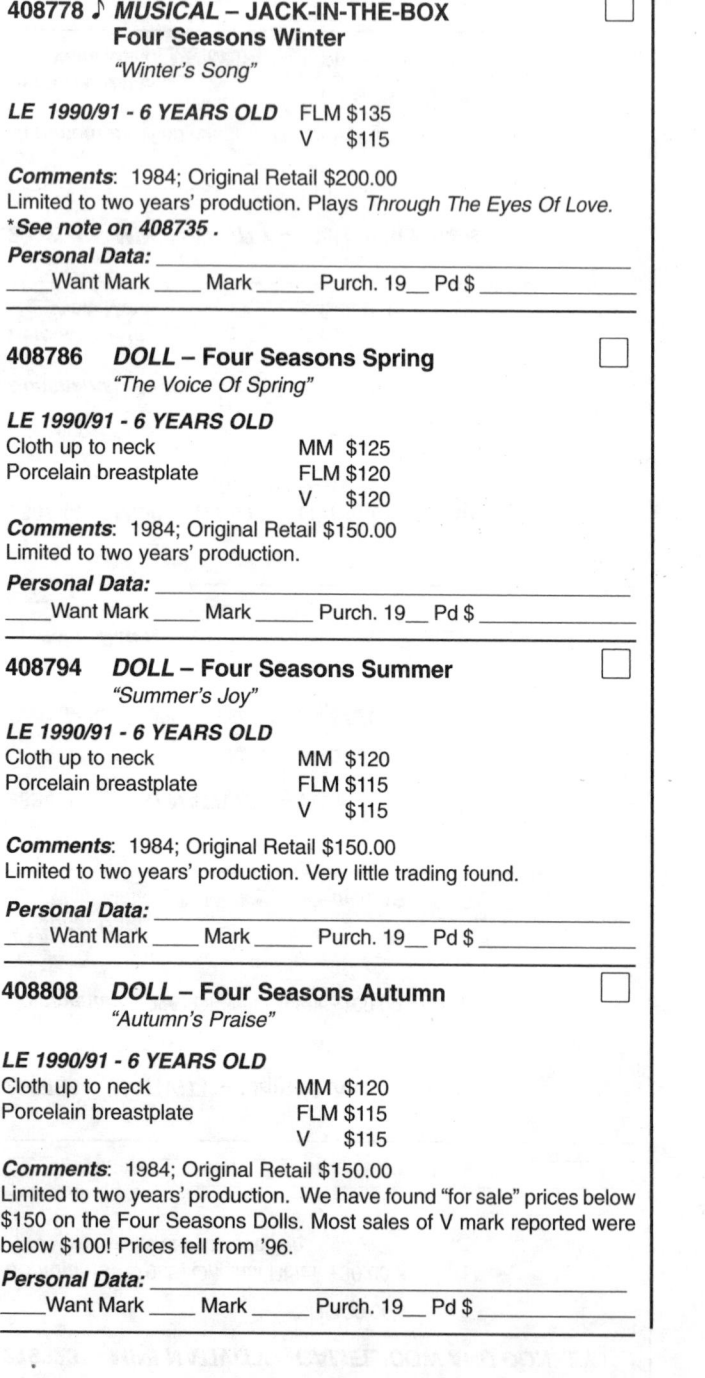

408778 ♪ *MUSICAL – JACK-IN-THE-BOX*
Four Seasons Winter

"Winter's Song"

LE 1990/91 - 6 YEARS OLD   FLM $135
                               V $115

Comments: 1984; Original Retail $200.00
Limited to two years' production. Plays *Through The Eyes Of Love.*
*See note on 408735 .
Personal Data: _____
___Want Mark ____ Mark _____ Purch. 19__ Pd $ _____

408786   **DOLL** – Four Seasons Spring
"The Voice Of Spring"

LE 1990/91 - 6 YEARS OLD
Cloth up to neck   MM $125
Porcelain breastplate   FLM $120
                            V $120

Comments: 1984; Original Retail $150.00
Limited to two years' production.
Personal Data: _____
___Want Mark ____ Mark _____ Purch. 19__ Pd $ _____

408794   **DOLL** – Four Seasons Summer
"Summer's Joy"

LE 1990/91 - 6 YEARS OLD
Cloth up to neck   MM $120
Porcelain breastplate   FLM $115
                            V $115

Comments: 1984; Original Retail $150.00
Limited to two years' production. Very little trading found.

Personal Data: _____
___Want Mark ____ Mark _____ Purch. 19__ Pd $ _____

408808   **DOLL** – Four Seasons Autumn
"Autumn's Praise"

LE 1990/91 - 6 YEARS OLD
Cloth up to neck   MM $120
Porcelain breastplate   FLM $115
                            V $115

Comments: 1984; Original Retail $150.00
Limited to two years' production. We have found "for sale" prices below $150 on the Four Seasons Dolls. Most sales of V mark reported were below $100! Prices fell from '96.

Personal Data: _____
___Want Mark ____ Mark _____ Purch. 19__ Pd $ _____

408816   **DOLL** – Four Seasons Winter
"Winter's Song"

LE 1990/91 - 6 YEARS OLD
Cloth up to neck   NM $125
Porcelain breastplate   FLM $115
                            V $115

Comments: 1984; Original Retail $150.00
Limited to two years' production.
Personal Data: _____
___Want Mark ____ Mark _____ Purch. 19__ Pd $ _____

417777 ♪ *MUSICAL – JACK-IN-THE-BOX*
Christmas Girl

"May You Have An Old Fashioned Christmas"

LE 1991/92 - 5 YEARS OLD   FLM $135   GC $115
                               V $135

Comments: 1990; Original Retail $200.00
Limited to two years' production. Plays *Have Yourself A Merry Little Christmas.* No sales reported. Did not sell well.
Personal Data: _____
___Want Mark ____ Mark _____ Purch. 19__ Pd $ _____

417785   **DOLL** – Christmas Girl
"May You Have An Old Fashioned Christmas"

LE 1991/92 - 5 YEARS OLD MM $145
                              V   NE   GC NE   FLM NE

Comments: 1990; Original Retail $150.00
Limited to two years' production. No sales found in research.
Personal Data: _____
___Want Mark ____ Mark _____ Purch. 19__ Pd $ _____

422282 ♪ *MUSICAL – JACK-IN-THE-BOX*
- Girl with Hearts
"You Have Touched So Many Hearts"

LE 1991/92 - 5 YEARS OLD   FLM $120
                               V $110
                               GC $100

Comments: 1990; Original Retail $175.00
Limited to two years' production. Plays *Everybody Loves Somebody.* No reports of this being sold on the secondary market for three years. Not a popular style; poor retail seller. Overproduced; many were destroyed at company. **See #35, page XIV.**
Personal Data: _____
___Want Mark ____ Mark _____ Purch. 19__ Pd $ _____

427527   *DOLL* – Girl with Hearts
"You Have Touched So Many Hearts"

LE 1991/92 - 5 YEARS OLD   FLM $90
                                  V $90
                                  GC $85

Comments: 1990; Original Retail $90.00
Limited to two years' production. No reported sales on the secondary market for three years. ***See #35, page XIV.***
Personal Data: _____
____Want Mark ____ Mark _____ Purch. 19__ Pd $ _____

429570 ♪ *MUSICAL ACTION DOLL* – Blue
Baby Boy Doll on Pillow, straight hair

"The Eyes Of The Lord Are Upon You"

SUSP. 1994 - 3 YEARS AGO

                    FLM $75   B $65
                    V $65   TRP $65
                    GC $65

Comments: 1990; Original Retail $65.00
Plays *Brahm's Lullaby*. Fewer FLM marks. Reported with Missing Mark.
Personal Data: _____
____Want Mark ____ Mark _____ Purch. 19__ Pd $ _____

429589 ♪ *MUSICAL ACTION DOLL* – Pink
Baby Girl Doll on Pillow, curly hair

"The Eyes Of The Lord Are Upon You"

SUSP. 1994 - 3 YEARS AGO   FLM $75   B $65
                                  V $65   TRP $65
                                  GC $65

Comments: 1990; Original Retail $65.00
Plays *Brahm's Lullaby*. Very cute doll. Fewer FLM marks.

Personal Data: _____
____Want Mark ____ Mark _____ Purch. 19__ Pd $ _____

A successful marriage is built on trust – and an occasional compliment.

*S*am first drew this in 1991 as the symbol for the 25th Annual Carthage Maple Leaf Festival. Doesn't it resemble the 1996 "Color Your World With Thanksgiving" figurine? See page 89.

520233 ORNAMENT – Boy and Girl/Box
"Our First Christmas Together"

DATED 1988   FL $18.50

Comments: 1988; Original Retail $13.00
This ornament was also produced in 1986 (102350) and 1987 (112399). The only differences were the marks, style numbers and the dates. Secondary market has been thus affected. **See #28, page XIV.**

Personal Data: _____
____Want Mark ____ Mark _____ Purch. 19__ Pd $ _____

520241 ORNAMENT – Girl in Sleigh
"Baby's First Christmas"

DATED 1988   FL $25

Comments: 1988; Original Retail $15.00
Also produced in 1989 (523208). The Baby Boy Ornament for 1988 was 115282. **See #28, page XIV.**

Personal Data: _____
____Want Mark ____ Mark _____ Purch. 19__ Pd $ _____

520268 Angel with Trumpet (Miniature)
"Rejoice O Earth"

FL	$35	V	$20	TRP	$17	SRD	$17
FLM	$22	GC	$17	S	$17		
BA	$20	B	$17	H	$17		

Comments: 1988; Original Retail $13.00/$17.00
Rarely will one pay extra for a figurine on the secondary market when it's still in production. If the first mark is scarce, then the secondary market is higher. Generally Christmas pieces' first marks are not scarce.

Personal Data: _____
____Want Mark ____ Mark _____ Purch. 19__ Pd $ _____

520276 ORNAMENT – Puppy in Stocking
"You Are My Gift Come True"

DATED 1988   FL $23

Comments: 1988; Original Retail $12.50
10th Anniversary Ornament. No inspiration on base.
Easily found under $20 even after nine years.

Personal Data: _____
____Want Mark ____ Mark _____ Purch. 19__ Pd $ _____

520284 PLATE – Girl with Reindeer
"Merry Christmas Deer"

DATED 1988   FL $50

Comments: 1988; Original Retail $50
Third issue of *Christmas Love Series*. Plates are not trading much over retail; many even for less. Easily found at above price for several years.

Personal Data: _____
____Want Mark ____ Mark _____ Purch. 19__ Pd $ _____

520292 ORNAMENT – Kitten Hanging on Wreath
"Hang On For The Holly Days"

DATED 1988   FL $28

Comments: 1988; Original Retail $13.00
Birthday Series Ornament. Easily found at the above prices! Read *Precious Collectibles*® ads for this ornament and others. A collector reported finding this one with the BA mark.

Personal Data: _____
____Want Mark ____ Mark _____ Purch. 19__ Pd $ _____

520322 9" EASTER SEALS – Girl with Goose w/Dome
"Make A Joyful Noise"

LE 1989 - 8 YEARS AGO   BA $900-950

Comments: 1988; Original Retail $500.00
Limited Edition 1,500 pieces. 1989 Easter Seals 9" figurine. Similar to E-1374G. Debuted with a dome and is a very pretty piece.

Personal Data: _____
____Want Mark ____ Mark _____ Purch. 19__ Pd $ _____

520349 SHARING ORNAMENT – Girl with Sunflower
"A Growing Love"

DATED 1988   FL $78

Comments: 1988; 1988 Growing Season Ornament
Given by Enesco for signing up new collectors to the Club.

Personal Data: _____
____Want Mark ____ Mark _____ Purch. 19__ Pd $ _____

You're As Pretty As A Picture

A little girl named Katie wrote to Sam asking that he make a Precious Moments figurine with bangs and a cowlick. Sam responded by drawing You're As Pretty As A Picture. The frame on the prototype Katie figurine covered too much of the little girl's head, so Sam redesigned the figurine, raising the frame so that her face showed through. Sam then presented Katie with her very own figurine. This figurine has been produced as the 1996 Enesco Precious Moments Collectors' Club membership piece.

520357   Angel with Newspaper and Dog
"Jesus The Savior Is Born"

SUSP. 1993 - 4 YEARS AGO	FL	$65	V	$45
	BA	$50	GC	$45
	FLM	$50	B	$40

Comments: 1988; Original Retail $25.00/$32.50
Not easily found. May be due to retailers not ordering. Suspended in late '93. We predicted this in the '92 guide! What are some of your predictions?

Personal Data: _____
____Want Mark ____ Mark _____ Purch. 19__ Pd $ _____

520403   ORNAMENT – Hippo
       "Hippo Holidays"

DATED 1995   S $22

Comments: 1995; Original Retail $17.00
Birthday Series Ornament.

Personal Data: _____
____Want Mark ____ Mark _____ Purch. 19__ Pd $ _____

520411   ORNAMENT – Squirrel on Log
       "I'm Nuts About You"

DATED 1992   GC $23

Comments: 1992; Original Retail $16.00
Birthday Series Ornament.
Personal Data: _____
____Want Mark ____ Mark _____ Purch. 19__ Pd $ _____

520438   ORNAMENT – Bunny on Ice Skates
       "Sno-Bunny Falls For You Like I Do"

DATED 1991   V $30

Comments: 1990; Original Retail $15.00
Birthday Series Ornament. Oops! The li'l silver skates made this ornament popular. Found without a date! Add $50 to secondary market value. Not marked as *Birthday Series*. Found many listed for sale in late '94 for $20!

Personal Data: _____
____Want Mark ____ Mark _____ Purch. 19__ Pd $ _____

520462   ORNAMENT – Dog/Gift Box
       "Christmas Is Ruff Without You"

DATED 1989   FL $40   BA $35

Comments: 1988; Original Retail $13.00
Birthday Series Ornament. Was somewhat plentiful but popular. More trading was found on BA than FL mark the last three years.
See #29, page XIV.

Personal Data: _____
____Want Mark ____ Mark _____ Purch. 19__ Pd $ _____

520470   ORNAMENT – Christmas Puppy
       "Take A Bow Cuz You're My Christmas Star"

DATED 1994   TRP $15

Comments: 1993; Original Retail $16.00
Price dropped from '96!

Personal Data: _____
____Want Mark ____ Mark _____ Purch. 19__ Pd $ _____

520489   ORNAMENT – Turtle with Gift/Antlers
       "Slow Down And Enjoy The Holidays"

PLEASE DON'T RUN OVER THE TURTLES

THANK YOU

DATED 1993   B $22

Comments: 1992; Original Retail $16.00
Birthday Series Ornament. Sam has a super cute outdoor sign along Chapel Road requesting that we not run over the turtles.

Personal Data: _____
____Want Mark ____ Mark _____ Purch. 19__ Pd $ _____

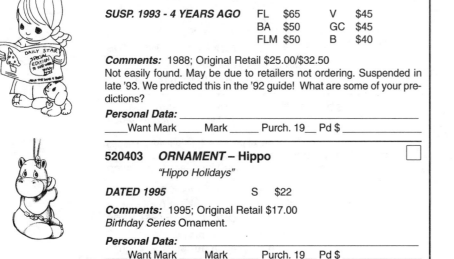

520497 ORNAMENT – Kitten with Ornament
"Wishing You A Purr-fect Holiday"

DATED 1990 FLM $38

Comments: 1989; Original Retail $15.00
Birthday Series Ornament. Found without date; add $50 to the secondary market value.

Personal Data: _____
____Want Mark ____ Mark _____ Purch. 19__ Pd $ _____

520535 Ballerina in Red Tutu
"The Lord Turned My Life Around"

SUSP. 1996 - 1 YEAR AGO

V	$45	B	$42	S	$42
GC	$45	TRP	$42	H	$40

Comments: 1992; Original Retail $35.00/$37.50
Because there are other Ballerinas, maybe this one, 520578 or 520551. Retail price increased in '96.

Personal Data: _____
____Want Mark ____ Mark _____ Purch. 19__ Pd $ _____

520543 Ballerina in Pink Tutu
"In The Spotlight Of His Grace"

SUSP. 1996 - 1 YEAR AGO

FLM	$50	B	$45	H	$40
V	$45	TRP	$45		
GC	$45	S	$45		

Comments: 1990; Original Retail $35.00/$37.50
Retail price increased in '96, just before suspension date.

Personal Data: _____
____Want Mark ____ Mark _____ Purch. 19__ Pd $ _____

520551 Ballerina in Blue Tutu
"Lord, Turn My Life Around"

SUSP. 1996 - 1 YEAR AGO

BA	$60	GC	$45	S	$45
FLM	$45	B	$45	H	$40
V	$45	TRP	$45		

Comments: 1988; Original Retail $35.00/$37.50
Retail price increased in '96. A little more popular than the other 3 on this page.

Personal Data: _____
____Want Mark ____ Mark _____ Purch. 19__ Pd $ _____

520578 Ballerina in Purple Tutu
"You Deserve An Ovation"

GC	$42	TRP	$40	H	$40
B	$40	S	$40	SRD	$37.50

Comments: 1990; Original Retail $35.00/$37.50
Very little trading found on this piece. Too many ballerinas at the present time – adorable but perfect for retirement or suspension. Retail price increased in '96.

Personal Data: _____
____Want Mark ____ Mark _____ Purch. 19__ Pd $ _____

520624 Boy with X-Ray Machine
"My Heart Is Exposed With Love"

FL	$70	V	$60	TRP	$60	SRD	$60
BA	$65	GC	$60	S	$60		
FLM	$65	B	$60	H	$60		

Comments: 1988; Original Retail $45.00/$60.00
I predict suspension or retirement for this piece as retailers say it is accepted mainly by the medical field/gift buyers and the nurse figurine outsells this piece. Cute piece! A must for X-ray technicians. Retail price increased to $60 in '96. Secondary market did increase but so did retail.

Personal Data: _____
____Want Mark ____ Mark _____ Purch. 19__ Pd $ _____

520632 Clown with Mouse Wiping Tears
"A Friend Is Someone Who Cares"

RETIRED 1995 - 2 YEARS AGO

FL	$90	V	$60	TRP	$55
BA	$78	GC	$60	S	$55
FLM	$60	B	$60		

Comments: 1988; Original Retail $30.00/$35.00
Fourteen clowns have been retired or suspended since 1988.

Personal Data: _____
____Want Mark ____ Mark _____ Purch. 19__ Pd $ _____

520640 Angel with Butterfly
"I'm So Glad You Fluttered Into My Life"

RETIRED 1991 - 6 YEARS AGO

FL	$335	FLM	$260
BA	$265	V	$250

Comments: 1988; Original Retail $40.00/$45.00
First mark very scarce. Very few V marks as well as FL marks. Prices skyrocketed after retirement. The main reason? No "after" production!! Called "Drop Dead." High prices now coming down after an all time high in 93/94. Was up to $400 on FL. Big drop in prices in '95 and '96.

Personal Data: _____

___ Want Mark ___ Mark ___ Purch. 19__ Pd $ _____

520659 Bear with Cake
"Wishing You A Happy Bear Hug"

SUSP. 1996 - 1 YEAR AGO

TRP $42		S	$38	H	$35

Comments: 1992; Original Retail $27.50
Birthday Series addition.

Personal Data: _____

___ Want Mark ___ Mark ___ Purch. 19__ Pd $ _____

520667 Girl with Bucket of Eggs/Chicken
"Eggspecially For You"

FL	$75	V	$55	TRP	$50	SRD	$50
BA	$70	GC	$55	S	$50		
FLM	$60	B	$50	H	$50		

Comments: 1988; Original Retail $45.00/$50.00
Many call her "Rosie." I autograph this one (okayed by Sam). I write about my chickens in "Down on the Farm" articles for the *Precious Collectibles®* magazine. Now we have ostriches, too! Maybe Sam will let me sign the Ostrich birthday piece, too. ☺

Personal Data: _____

___ Want Mark ___ Mark ___ Purch. 19__ Pd $ _____

520675 Boy Helping Girl at Fountain
"Your Love Is So Uplifting"

FL	$95	V	$75	TRP	$75	SRD	$75
BA	$90	GC	$75	S	$75		
FLM	$85	B	$75	H	$75		

Comments: 1988; Original Retail $60.00/$75.00
Somewhat limited, as are all the extra large pieces, but not sought after on the secondary market to date. Retail went up $15 in '95; thus when secondary market prices rose, it didn't appear there was any trading on this figurine. There has been no significant increase since.

Personal Data: _____

___ Want Mark ___ Mark ___ Purch. 19__ Pd $ _____

520683 Boy with Paper Over Head
"Sending You Showers Of Blessings"

RETIRED 1992 - 5 YEARS AGO

FL	$85	V	$65
BA	$75	GC	$65
FLM	$70		

Comments: 1988; Original Retail $32.50/$35.00
Very attractive piece! GC somewhat scarce when retired. Price leveled off for now.

Personal Data: _____

___ Want Mark ___ Mark ___ Purch. 19__ Pd $ _____

520691 ♪ MUSICAL – Ballerina on Base
"Lord, Keep My Life In Balance"

SUSP. 1993 - 4 YEARS AGO

V	$95	GC	$85	B	$75

Comments: 1990; Original Retail $60.00/$65.00
Plays *Music Box Dancer*.

Personal Data: _____

___ Want Mark ___ Mark ___ Purch. 19__ Pd $ _____

520705 Baby/Father, Puppy with Bottle
"Baby's First Pet"

SUSP. 1994 - 3 YEARS AGO

FL	$90	V	$65	TRP	$55
BA	$85	GC	$58		
FLM	$75	B	$58		

Comments: 1988; Original Retail $45.00/$50.00
Fifth issue in *Baby's First Series*. Most sought after series on secondary market in last three years. Found the most trading was on FL and BA mark.

Personal Data: _____

___ Want Mark ___ Mark ___ Purch. 19__ Pd $ _____

520721 Boy/Dog/Fishing Pole
"Just A Line To Wish You A Happy Day"

SUSP. 1996 - 1 YEAR AGO

FL	$110	V	$80	TRP	$80
BA	$95	GC	$80	S	$80
FLM	$90	B	$80	H	$80

Comments: 1988; Original Retail $65.00/$75.00
In my opinion, this is more scarce than collectors realize. This is true for most current large pieces. Another fisherman debuted in 1995, so this is probably why this was suspended. Usually large pieces get suspended over retirement.

Personal Data: _____

___ Want Mark ___ Mark ___ Purch. 19__ Pd $ _____

520748 Two Girls Having A Tea Party
"Friendship Hits The Spot"

FL	$90	V	$75	TRP $70	SRD $70
BA	$80	GC	$75	S $70	
FLM	$75	B	$70	H $70	
		ERROR - no table	$225-250		

Comments: 1988; Original Retail $55.00/$70.00
We have heard from several collectors that this piece has been found without the table. There is an "x" on one where the table was to be. Retail up to $70 in '96. Has been found with the word "Friendship" misspelled, "Friendship." (TRP and S) Add $25 for this error over the above. Spelling error found on S and TRP marks. Excellent candidate for retirement but perhaps a suspension will happen. $70 may be high for collectors if a retirement announcement was made.

Personal Data: _____
____Want Mark ____ Mark _____ Purch. 19__ Pd $ _____

520756 Boy by Sign Post with Bag
"Jesus Is The Only Way"

SUSP. 1993 - 4 YEARS AGO

CT	$90	FLM $70	B	$50
FL	$80	V $60		
BA	$75	GC $50		

Comments: 1988; Original Retail $40.00/$45.00
"Many" of the decals were placed on the sign incorrectly which caused collectors to believe the sign was spelled incorrectly. (ex. OVEP) C-0113, the 1993 Club Membership figurine, is very similar. Probably suspended due to all the decals. CT hard to find.

Personal Data: _____
____Want Mark ____ Mark _____ Purch. 19__ Pd $ _____

520764 Two Puppies
"Puppy Love"

FL	$35	V	$25	TRP $20	SRD $17.50
BA	$30	GC	$25	S $20	
FLM	$25	B	$20	H $17.50	

Comments: 1988; Original Retail $12.50/$17.50
Retail price increase in '95 and again in '96.

Personal Data: _____
____Want Mark ____ Mark _____ Purch. 19__ Pd $ _____

Unless we find beauty and happiness in our backyard, we will never find them in the mountains.

520772 Boy/Girl Indians in Canoe
"Many Moons In Same Canoe, Blessum You"

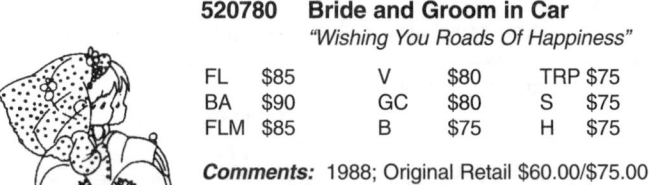

RETIRED 1990 - 7 YEARS AGO

FL	$295	FLM $270	BA	$285

Comments: 1988; Original Retail $50.00/$55.00
These Indians were changed from "gray" hair to darker hair on later pieces. Collectors wrote suggesting that clothes be painted. With all these problems, it's no wonder it was retired. This was the most scarce of the 1990 retired pieces. **Rosebud mark has been found insured for $425!**

Personal Data: _____
____Want Mark ____ Mark _____ Purch. 19__ Pd $ _____

520780 Bride and Groom in Car
"Wishing You Roads Of Happiness"

FL	$85	V	$80	TRP $75	SRD $75
BA	$90	GC	$80	S $75	
FLM	$85	B	$75	H $75	

Comments: 1988; Original Retail $60.00/$75.00
Also produced in crystal and as an ornament.

Personal Data: _____
____Want Mark ____ Mark _____ Purch. 19__ Pd $ _____

520799 Girl with Bridal Gown and Baseball/Bat
"Someday My Love"

RETIRED 1992 - 5 YEARS AGO

FL	$85	FLM $80	GC	$70
BA	$80	V $75		

Comments: 1988; Original Retail $40.00/$45.00

Personal Data: _____
____Want Mark ____ Mark _____ Purch. 19__ Pd $ _____

520802 Girl at Ladder/Blue Paint Spilled
"My Days Are Blue Without You"

SUSP. 1991 - 6 YEARS AGO

CIRCLE MOUTH		FL	$110	FLM $90
		BA	$100	V $95
SMILE (ERROR)		FL	$130	BA $115

Comments: 1988; Original Retail $65.00/$70.00
Find the smiling girl with FL mark as this piece has been changed to a circle mouth to represent being sad. This smile is more abundant than the Dunce's smile but as time goes by it will become scarce. Also found with frown.

Personal Data: _____
____Want Mark ____ Mark _____ Purch. 19__ Pd $ _____

520810   Grandpa with Dog
"We Need A Good Friend Through The Ruff Times"

SUSP. 1991 - 6 YEARS AGO

FL	$65	FLM	$55
BA	$60	V	$50

Comments: 1988; Original Retail $35.00/$37.50

Personal Data: _____
____Want Mark ____ Mark _____ Purch. 19__ Pd $ _____

520829   Girl with Trophy
"You Are My Number One"

FL	$50	V	$35	TRP	$35	SRD	$35
BA	$45	GC	$35	S	$35		
FLM	$40	B	$35	H	$35		

Comments: 1988; Original Retail $25.00/$35.00
I look for this to be suspended or retired in the future. Slow seller.

Personal Data: _____
____Want Mark ____ Mark _____ Purch. 19__ Pd $ _____

520837   Bride and Groom with Candle
"The Lord Is Your Light To Happiness"

FL	$75	V	$65	TRP	$65	SRD	$65
BA	$65	GC	$65	S	$65		
FLM	$65	B	$65	H	$65		

Comments: 1988; Original Retail $50.00/$65.00
Popular wedding gift. About fifty dollars was a price range more gift buyers were willing to pay. Found a few sales less than retail.

Personal Data: _____
____Want Mark ____ Mark _____ Purch. 19__ Pd $ _____

520845   Boy Kneeling with Engagement Ring
"Wishing You A Perfect Choice"

FL	$80	V	$65	TRP	$65	SRD	$65
BA	$75	GC	$65	S	$65		
FLM	$65	B	$65	H	$65		

Comments: 1988; Original Retail $55.00/$65.00
Price increase will slow retail sales for individuals, in my opinion. Not being sought after on secondary market at this time.

Personal Data: _____
____Want Mark ____ Mark _____ Purch. 19__ Pd $ _____

520853   Orphan Boy with Flowers
"I Belong To The Lord"

SUSP. 1991 - 6 YEARS AGO

FL	$50	FLM	$30	BA	$40	V	$30

Comments: 1988; Original Retail $25.00/$27.50
Definitely was a slow seller on gift market, no doubt the reason for suspension.

Personal Data: _____
____Want Mark ____ Mark _____ Purch. 19__ Pd $ _____

520861   Girl with Slate
"Sharing Begins In The Heart"

LE 1989 - 8 YEARS AGO   FL $80   BA $45

Comments: 1988; Original Retail $25.00
Second *Main Event* piece. No reference is written on the piece to signify "Main Event" piece. No doubt an error. Fewer events early in 1989, thus fewer first marks than BA marks.

Personal Data: _____
____Want Mark ____ Mark _____ Purch. 19__ Pd $ _____

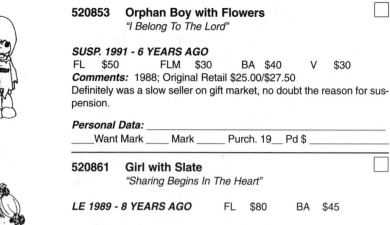

520934   Baby with Bunny, Turtle and Box
"Heaven Bless You"

BA	$60	GC	$35	S	$35
FLM	$50	B	$35	H	$35
V	$50	TRP	$35	SRD	$35

Comments: 1989; Original Retail $35.00
This figurine has been seen with an HG mark. It may have been a sample ($135-155).

Personal Data: _____
____Want Mark ____ Mark _____ Purch. 19__ Pd $ _____

521000   Boy Holding a Pearl
"There Is No Greater Treasure Than
To Have A Friend Like You"

GC	$40	TRP	$30	H	$30
B	$32	S	$30	SRD	$30

Comments: 1992; Original Retail $30.00
Display with 531111, *Girl with Pearl in Oyster*, for a perfect seaside theme. Use sand and sea shells, etc.

Personal Data: _____
____Want Mark ____ Mark _____ Purch. 19__ Pd $ _____

521043 Bird and Gorilla
"To My Favorite Fan"

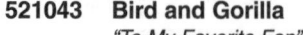

SUSP. 1993 - 4 YEARS AGO

BA	$55	GC	$24
FLM	$38	B	$24
V	$25		

Comments: 1989; Original Retail $16.00
First mark, BA, was somewhat scarce. Not marked *Birthday Series*.

Personal Data: _____
____Want Mark ____ Mark _____ Purch. 19__ Pd $ _____

521175 Kangaroo with Baby in Pouch
"Hello World!"

FL	$30	V	$17.50	TRP	$17.50	SRD	$17.50
BA	$25	GC	$17.50	S	$17.50		
FLM	$20	B	$17.50	H	$17.50		

Comments: 1988; Original Retail $13.50/$17.50
Not marked *Birthday Series*. Retail price increase in 1995 and in 1996.

Personal Data: _____
____Want Mark ____ Mark _____ Purch. 19__ Pd $ _____

521183 Two Girls Embracing
"That's What Friends Are For"

FLM	$55	B	$50	H	$50
V	$50	TRP	$50	SRD	$50
GC	$50	S	$50		

Comments: 1989; Original Retail $45.00/$50.00
Slow at retail. Retail price raised in 1996.

Personal Data: _____
____Want Mark ____ Mark _____ Purch. 19__ Pd $ _____

521191 Boy with Bowling Ball and Pins
"Lord, Spare Me"

H	$37.50	SRD	$37.50

Comments: 1996; Original Retail $37.50

Personal Data: _____
____Want Mark ____ Mark _____ Purch. 19__ Pd $ _____

521205 Girl with Stick Horse
"Hope You're Up And On The Trail Again"

SUSP. 1993 - 4 YEARS AGO

BA	$60	GC	$50
FLM	$55	B	$45
V	$50		

Comments: 1989; Original Retail $35.00
Cute piece.

Personal Data: _____
____Want Mark ____ Mark _____ Purch. 19__ Pd $ _____

521213 Girl with Bowl of Fruit
"The Fruit Of The Spirit Is Love"

B	$35	S	$32.50	SRD	$32.50
TRP	$32.50	H	$32.50		

Comments: 1992; Original Retail $30.00/$32.50
Seemed abundant in '93. Good suspension candidate.

Personal Data: _____
____Want Mark ____ Mark _____ Purch. 19__ Pd $ _____

521221 Boy with Basketball
"Enter His Courts With Thanksgiving"

S	$40	H	$35	SRD	$35

Comments: 1995; Original Retail $35.00

Personal Data: _____
____Want Mark ____ Mark _____ Purch. 19__ Pd $ _____

521272 Boy on Rocking Horse
"Take Heed When You Stand"

SUSP. 1994 - 3 YEARS AGO

V	$85	B	$65	S	$55
GC	$75	TRP	$60		

Comments: 1990; Original Retail $55.00
One report of an unpainted hat band. Most sales found at the V level.

Personal Data: _____
____Want Mark ____ Mark _____ Purch. 19__ Pd $ _____

521280 Girl on Skates
"Happy Trip"

SUSP. 1994 - 3 YEARS AGO

BA $95	V $50	B $50
FLM $55	GC $50	TRP $40

Comments: 1989; Original Retail $35.00
BA somewhat scarce. Slow on secondary market for past two years.

Personal Data: _____
____Want Mark ____ Mark _____ Purch. 19__ Pd $ _____

521299 Boy and Girl Hugging
"Hug One Another"

RETIRED 1995 - 2 YEARS AGO

FLM $65	B $75
V $75	TRP $65
GC $75	S $65

Comments: 1990; Original Retail $45.00/$50.00
This piece was portrayed as a "dancing" couple when we visited the Precious Moments® Studio in Japan. We all "danced" to music at the studio! First time visit to Japan! Enesco planned a lifetime of memories for us! Retirement brought secondary market from $50 to $100, but seeing a continuous fall since the rise.

Personal Data: _____
____Want Mark ____ Mark _____ Purch. 19__ Pd $ _____

521302 ORNAMENT – Little Girl with Snowball
"May All Your Christmases Be White"

SUSP. 1994 - 3 YEARS AGO	BA $32	GC $20
	FLM $28	B $20
	V $25	TRP $20

Comments: 1988; Original Retail $13.50/$16.00
This little girl was a tribute to Sam's mother. When she was a little girl she wanted to mail snowballs to her relatives in Florida. (See the display at the Chapel.)

Personal Data: _____
____Want Mark ____ Mark _____ Purch. 19__ Pd $ _____

521310 Girl with Apple
"Yield Not To Temptation"

SUSP. 1993 - 4 YEARS AGO

BA $55	V $45	B $37.50
FLM $45	GC $37.50	

Comments: 1989; Original Retail $27.50/$30.00
Very little trading on this piece for past three years.

Personal Data: _____
____Want Mark ____ Mark _____ Purch. 19__ Pd $ _____

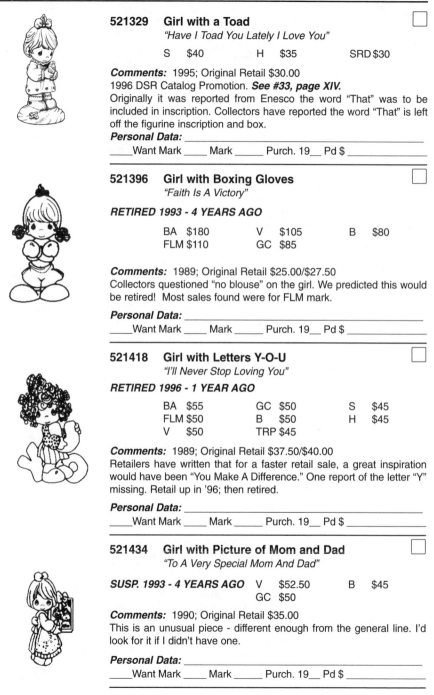

521329 Girl with a Toad
"Have I Toad You Lately I Love You"

S $40	H $35	SRD $30

Comments: 1995; Original Retail $30.00
1996 DSR Catalog Promotion. **See #33, page XIV.**
Originally it was reported from Enesco the word "That" was to be included in inscription. Collectors have reported the word "That" is left off the figurine inscription and box.

Personal Data: _____
____Want Mark ____ Mark _____ Purch. 19__ Pd $ _____

521396 Girl with Boxing Gloves
"Faith Is A Victory"

RETIRED 1993 - 4 YEARS AGO

BA $180	V $105	B $80
FLM $110	GC $85	

Comments: 1989; Original Retail $25.00/$27.50
Collectors questioned "no blouse" on the girl. We predicted this would be retired! Most sales found were for FLM mark.

Personal Data: _____
____Want Mark ____ Mark _____ Purch. 19__ Pd $ _____

521418 Girl with Letters Y-O-U
"I'll Never Stop Loving You"

RETIRED 1996 - 1 YEAR AGO

BA $55	GC $50	S $45
FLM $50	B $50	H $45
V $50	TRP $45	

Comments: 1989; Original Retail $37.50/$40.00
Retailers have written that for a faster retail sale, a great inspiration would have been "You Make A Difference." One report of the letter "Y" missing. Retail up in '96; then retired.

Personal Data: _____
____Want Mark ____ Mark _____ Purch. 19__ Pd $ _____

521434 Girl with Picture of Mom and Dad
"To A Very Special Mom And Dad"

SUSP. 1993 - 4 YEARS AGO	V $52.50	B $45
	GC $50	

Comments: 1990; Original Retail $35.00
This is an unusual piece - different enough from the general line. I'd look for it if I didn't have one.

Personal Data: _____
____Want Mark ____ Mark _____ Purch. 19__ Pd $ _____

521450 Girl with Glue on Foot
"Lord, Help Me Stick To My Job"

RETIRED 1997

BA $80	GC $65	S $60
FLM $75	B $65	H $60
V $65	TRP $60	

Comments: 1989; Original Retail $30.00/$35.00

Personal Data: _____

____Want Mark ____ Mark _____ Purch. 19__ Pd $ _____

521477 Girl with Telephone
"Tell It To Jesus"

BA $60	GC $40	S $40
FLM $45	B $40	H $40
V $45	TRP $40	SRD $40

Comments: 1988; Original Retail $35.00/$40.00
Popular piece. Display with PM811 *Hello, Lord It's Me Again.*

Personal Data: _____

____Want Mark ____ Mark _____ Purch. 19__ Pd $ _____

521485 Girl Looking Through Hollow Log
"There's A Light At The End Of The Tunnel"

SUSP. 1996 - 1 YEAR AGO

FLM $85	B $70	H $65
V $80	TRP $65	
GC $70	S $65	

Comments: 1990; Original Retail $55.00/$60.00
Retail price up in '96 then suspended.

Personal Data: _____

____Want Mark ____ Mark _____ Purch. 19__ Pd $ _____

521493 Girl with Baby
"A Special Delivery"

V $45	TRP $32.50	SRD $32.50
GC $40	S $32.50	
B $35	H $32.50	

Comments: 1990; Original Retail $30.00/$32.50

Personal Data: _____

____Want Mark ____ Mark _____ Purch. 19__ Pd $ _____

521507 ♪ *MUSICAL* – Girl by Lamppost
"The Light Of The World Is Jesus"

BA $90	GC $75	S $70
FLM $80	B $75	H $70
V $75	TRP $70	SRD $70

Comments: 1988; Original Retail $60.00/$70.00
Plays *White Christmas*. This was Philip Butcher's favorite piece as it resembled the *Connie* doll (Philip's wife). Philip, Sam's son, was killed in an auto accident in '90 in Joplin, MO. A Prayer Room featuring a special mural was added at the Chapel in his memory. A lithograph of *Phil's Mural* was also available. Perfect piece for retirement. A retirement piece is given a recognizable status of the collectible.

Personal Data: _____

____Want Mark ____ Mark _____ Purch. 19__ Pd $ _____

521558 *ORNAMENT* – Bride and Groom in Car
"Our First Christmas Together"

DATED 1989   BA $32

Comments: 1988; Original Retail $17.50
Also produced in 1990. This design was also produced as a "friction" car. Cute ornament! *See #28, page XIV.*

Personal Data: _____

____Want Mark ____ Mark _____ Purch. 19__ Pd $ _____

521566 *ORNAMENT* – Girl on Skates
"Glide Through The Holidays"

RETIRED 1992 - 5 YEARS AGO

FLM $40	GC $25	V $30

Comments: 1988; Original Retail $13.50
Several have been found with "Special Issue" on box. Prices found quite readily below $25 in early '96 on GC.

Personal Data: _____

____Want Mark ____ Mark _____ Purch. 19__ Pd $ _____

521574 *ORNAMENT* – Girl with Baby in Sleigh
"Dashing Through The Snow"

SUSP. 1994 - 3 YEARS AGO

FLM $32	GC $25	TRP $22
V $28	B $22	

Comments: 1987; Original Retail $15.00/$16.00
Same as *January* figurine, 109983. Price up since suspension.

Personal Data: _____

____Want Mark ____ Mark _____ Purch. 19__ Pd $ _____

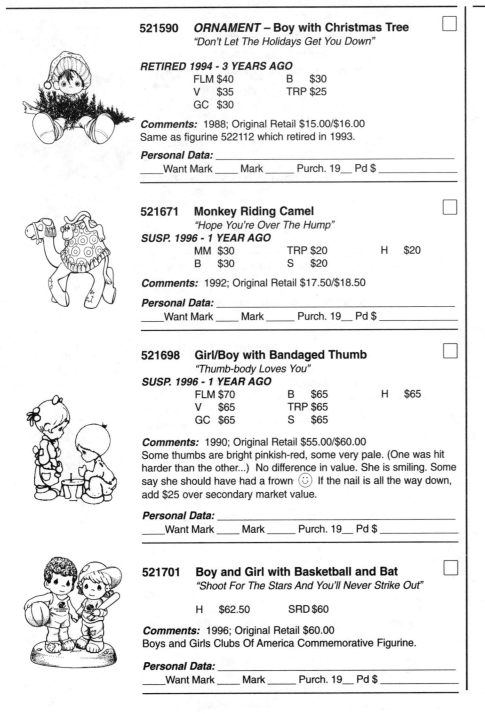

521590 ***ORNAMENT** – Boy with Christmas Tree*
"Don't Let The Holidays Get You Down"

RETIRED 1994 - 3 YEARS AGO

FLM	$40	B	$30
V	$35	TRP	$25
GC	$30		

Comments: 1988; Original Retail $15.00/$16.00
Same as figurine 522112 which retired in 1993.

Personal Data: _____
____Want Mark ____ Mark _____ Purch. 19__ Pd $ _____

521671 **Monkey Riding Camel**
"Hope You're Over The Hump"
SUSP. 1996 - 1 YEAR AGO

MM	$30	TRP	$20	H	$20
B	$30	S	$20		

Comments: 1992; Original Retail $17.50/$18.50

Personal Data: _____
____Want Mark ____ Mark _____ Purch. 19__ Pd $ _____

521698 **Girl/Boy with Bandaged Thumb**
"Thumb-body Loves You"
SUSP. 1996 - 1 YEAR AGO

FLM	$70	B	$65	H	$65
V	$65	TRP	$65		
GC	$65	S	$65		

Comments: 1990; Original Retail $55.00/$60.00
Some thumbs are bright pinkish-red, some very pale. (One was hit harder than the other...) No difference in value. She is smiling. Some say she should have had a frown ☺ If the nail is all the way down, add $25 over secondary market value.

Personal Data: _____
____Want Mark ____ Mark _____ Purch. 19__ Pd $ _____

521701 **Boy and Girl with Basketball and Bat**
"Shoot For The Stars And You'll Never Strike Out"

H	$62.50	SRD	$60

Comments: 1996; Original Retail $60.00
Boys and Girls Clubs Of America Commemorative Figurine.

Personal Data: _____
____Want Mark ____ Mark _____ Purch. 19__ Pd $ _____

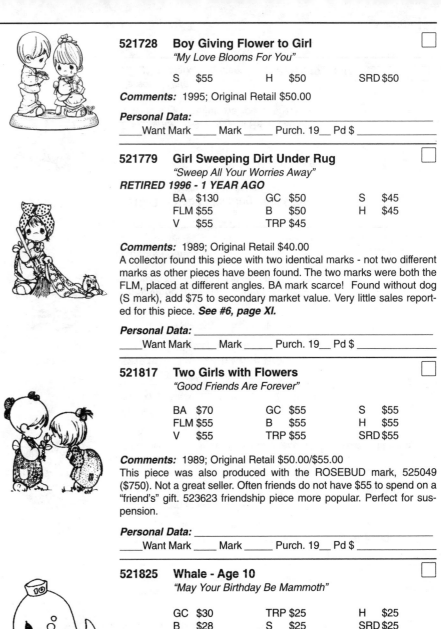

521728 **Boy Giving Flower to Girl**
"My Love Blooms For You"

S	$55	H	$50	SRD	$50

Comments: 1995; Original Retail $50.00

Personal Data: _____
____Want Mark ____ Mark _____ Purch. 19__ Pd $ _____

521779 **Girl Sweeping Dirt Under Rug**
"Sweep All Your Worries Away"
RETIRED 1996 - 1 YEAR AGO

BA	$130	GC	$50	S	$45
FLM	$55	B	$50	H	$45
V	$55	TRP	$45		

Comments: 1989; Original Retail $40.00
A collector found this piece with two identical marks - not two different marks as other pieces have been found. The two marks were both the FLM, placed at different angles. BA mark scarce! Found without dog (S mark), add $75 to secondary market value. Very little sales reported for this piece. ***See #6, page XI.***

Personal Data: _____
____Want Mark ____ Mark _____ Purch. 19__ Pd $ _____

521817 **Two Girls with Flowers**
"Good Friends Are Forever"

BA	$70	GC	$55	S	$55
FLM	$55	B	$55	H	$55
V	$55	TRP	$55	SRD	$55

Comments: 1989; Original Retail $50.00/$55.00
This piece was also produced with the ROSEBUD mark, 525049 ($750). Not a great seller. Often friends do not have $55 to spend on a "friend's" gift. 523623 friendship piece more popular. Perfect for suspension.

Personal Data: _____
____Want Mark ____ Mark _____ Purch. 19__ Pd $ _____

521825 **Whale - Age 10**
"May Your Birthday Be Mammoth"

GC	$30	TRP	$25	H	$25
B	$28	S	$25	SRD	$25

Comments: 1990; Original Retail $25.00
Part of the *Birthday Train Series*.

Personal Data: _____
____Want Mark ____ Mark _____ Purch. 19__ Pd $ _____

521833 Horse - Age 9
"Being Nine Is Just Divine"

GC $30	TRP $25	H $25
B $28	S $25	SRD $25

Comments: 1990; Original Retail $25.00
Part of the *Birthday Train Series*. Original drawing for age 9 was a Unicorn.

Personal Data: _____
____Want Mark ____ Mark _____ Purch. 19__ Pd $ _____

521841 Boy Whispering into Girl's Ear
"Love Is From Above"

SUSP. 1996 - 1 YEAR AGO

BA $60	GC $50	S $50
FLM $55	B $50	H $50
V $55	TRP $50	

Comments: 1989; Original Retail $45.00/$50.00
No action on secondary market.

Personal Data: _____
____Want Mark ____ Mark _____ Purch. 19__ Pd $ _____

521868 Angel Holding Commandments
"The Greatest Of These Is Love"

SUSP. 1991 - 6 YEARS AGO

BA $50	V $40
FLM $45	

Comments: 1988; Original Retail $27.50/$30.00

Personal Data: _____
____Want Mark ____ Mark _____ Purch. 19__ Pd $ _____

521884 Boy and Dog with Pizza
"Pizza On Earth"

SRD $55

Comments: 1996; Original Retail $55.00

Personal Data: _____
____Want Mark ____ Mark _____ Purch. 19__ Pd $ _____

When you think you have made your mark on the world, watch out for the guys with the erasers.

521892 Boy Pulling Girl with Lily in Wagon
"Easter's On Its Way"

BA $75	GC $65	S $65
FLM $72	B $65	H $65
V $70	TRP $65	SRD $65

Comments: 1989; Original Retail $60.00/$65.00
Suspension candidate in my opinion. Not enough secondary market sales to report from '96.

Personal Data: _____
____Want Mark ____ Mark _____ Purch. 19__ Pd $ _____

521906 Girl with Easter Basket Looking at Frogs
"Hoppy Easter, Friend"

FLM $50	B $40	H $40
V $45	TRP $40	SRD $40
GC $40	S $40	

Comments: 1990; Original Retail $40.00
Cute piece, affordable! Seasonal piece. No increase or much trading found for this piece.

Personal Data: _____
____Want Mark ____ Mark _____ Purch. 19__ Pd $ _____

521914 Boys with Song Book
"Perfect Harmony"

TRP $60	H $55
S $55	SRD $55

Comments: 1994; Original Retail $55.00
A suspension candidate in my opinion.

Personal Data: _____
____Want Mark ____ Mark _____ Purch. 19__ Pd $ _____

521922 Baby Sleeping on a Cloud
"Safe In The Arms Of Jesus"

GC $35	TRP $32.50	H $32.50
B $32.50	S $32.50	SRD $32.50

Comments: 1992; Original Retail $30.00/$32.50
Child Evangelism Fellowship Figurine.

Personal Data: _____
____Want Mark ____ Mark _____ Purch. 19__ Pd $ _____

521949   Boy Standing by Tree Stump/Squirrel
"Wishing You A Cozy Season"

SUSP. 1993 - 4 YEARS AGO

BA	$70	V	$60	B	$55
FLM	$65	GC	$55		

Comments: 1988; Original Retail $42.50/$45.00

Personal Data: _____
____Want Mark ____ Mark _____ Purch. 19___ Pd $ _____

521957   Boy with Kite
"High Hopes"

SUSP. 1993 - 4 YEARS AGO

BA	$50	V	$42	B	$30
FLM	$45	GC	$35		

Comments: 1989; Original Retail $30.00

Personal Data: _____
____Want Mark ____ Mark _____ Purch. 19___ Pd $ _____

521965   Boy with Potted Flower
"To A Special Mum"

FLM	$50	B	$40	H	$35
V	$45	TRP	$35	SRD	$35
GC	$40	S	$35		

Comments: 1990; Original Retail $30.00/$35.00

Personal Data: _____
____Want Mark ____ Mark _____ Purch. 19___ Pd $ _____

521981   Boy Marching with Drum
"Marching To The Beat Of Freedom's Drum"

S	$37.50	H	$35	SRD	$35

Comments: 1995; Original Retail $35.00

Personal Data: _____
____Want Mark ____ Mark _____ Purch. 19___ Pd $ _____

522015   Boy with Apple and School Book
"To The Apple Of God's Eye"

B	$38	S	$35	SRD	$35
TRP	$35	H	$35		

Comments: 1992; Original Retail $32.50
Slow seller. Cute piece.

Personal Data: _____
____Want Mark ____ Mark _____ Purch. 19___ Pd $ _____

522023   Football Player Among Leaves
"May Your Life Be Blessed With Touchdowns"

BA	$65	GC	$55	S	$50
FLM	$60	B	$50	H	$50
V	$55	TRP	$50	SRD	$50

Comments: 1988; Original Retail $45.00/$50.00

This was a very popular J&D poster. Figurines should have a leaf on the boy's leg; several have been found without the leaf. Add $45-50 over secondary market value for pieces without the leaf. Bases on these pieces and several others are a darker-toned tan compared to the general collection. A decision was evidently made at the factory during production, as we notified Enesco of this change and their response was that they would "look into it." Other pieces have also been found with dark-toned bases similar to another collectible (Memories of Yesterday) produced by the same factory. (In my opinion, the factory made this change and Enesco later okayed it as so many were already produced this way.) Very little trading found for this piece.

Personal Data: _____
____Want Mark ____ Mark _____ Purch. 19___ Pd $ _____

522031   Boy and Turkey at Thanksgiving Table
"Thank You Lord For Everything"

SUSP. 1993 - 4 YEARS AGO

BA	$90	V	$80	B	$80
FLM	$85	GC	$80		

Comments: 1988; Original Retail $55.00
This was different from the "norm." Really cute piece!

Personal Data: _____
____Want Mark ____ Mark _____ Purch. 19___ Pd $ _____

522058   Boy with Candle/Bedtime Stories
"Now I Lay Me Down To Sleep"

RETIRED 1997

TRP	$60	H	$57.50
S	$57.50		

Comments: 1994; Original Retail $30.00/$32.50
Color flyers from Enesco show the prototype for this figurine having a teddy bear by the boy's feet. Neither the actual figurine or the line art have the teddy bear.

Personal Data: _____
____Want Mark ____ Mark _____ Purch. 19___ Pd $ _____

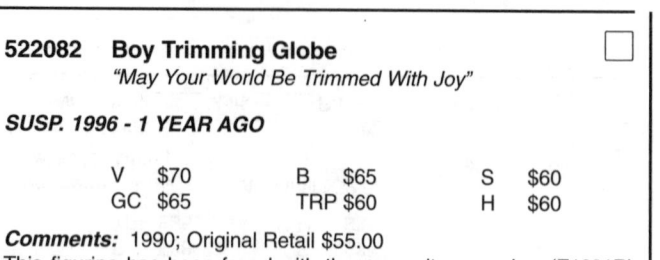

522082   Boy Trimming Globe
"May Your World Be Trimmed With Joy"

SUSP. 1996 - 1 YEAR AGO

V	$70	B	$65	S	$60
GC	$65	TRP	$60	H	$60

Comments: 1990; Original Retail $55.00
This figurine has been found with the wrong item number (E1381R) and wrong inspiration, "Jesus Is The Answer."

Personal Data: _____
____Want Mark ____ Mark _____ Purch. 19__ Pd $ _____

522090   Girl/Boy with Water Hose
"There Shall Be Showers Of Blessings"

BA	$80	GC	$75	S	$70
FLM	$75	B	$70	H	$70
V	$70	TRP	$70	SRD	$70

Comments: 1989; Original Retail $60.00/$70.00
Predict a suspension on this piece.

Personal Data: _____
____Want Mark ____ Mark _____ Purch. 19__ Pd $ _____

522104   Girl with Chickens/Dog/Eggs
"It's No Yoke When I Say I Love You"

SUSP. 1994 - 3 YEARS AGO	V	$95	B	$80
	GC	$95	TRP	$80

Comments: 1990; Original Retail $60.00/$65.00
The retail price made her a slow seller. She is a very attractive piece! Suspension usually increases the sales for earlier marks. Only produced four years. Price fell from '96!

Personal Data: _____
____Want Mark ____ Mark _____ Purch. 19__ Pd $ _____

522112   Boy with Christmas Tree Across Lap
"Don't Let The Holidays Get You Down"

RETIRED 1993 - 4 YEARS AGO

BA	$105	V	$85	B	$80
FLM	$85	GC	$80	MM	$95

Comments: 1988; Original Retail $42.50/$45.00
Not abundant at retirement time. Was found without the hatchet. Nice piece! Prices down from '96!

Personal Data: _____
____Want Mark ____ Mark _____ Purch. 19__ Pd $ _____

522120   Boy/Gift Box with Dog, Ball and Bat
"Wishing You A Very Successful Season"

BA	$80	GC	$70	S	$70
FLM	$75	B	$70	H	$70
V	$75	TRP	$70	SRD	$70

Comments: 1988; Original Retail $60.00/$70.00
Very limited amount of trading on this piece. In my opinion, higher priced figurines ($60-70), if not very scarce, do not become popular pieces in future trades on the secondary market. This baseball one is probably a "strike out." Insure at these prices.

Personal Data: _____
____Want Mark ____ Mark _____ Purch. 19__ Pd $ _____

522201   Boy and Girl on Motorcycle
"Bon Voyage"

SUSP. 1996 - 1 YEAR AGO

BA	$125	GC	$95	S	$95
FLM	$115	B	$95	H	$90
V	$100	TRP	$95	SRD	$90

Comments: 1988; Original Retail $75.00/$90.00
Super nice piece!

Personal Data: _____
____Want Mark ____ Mark _____ Purch. 19__ Pd $ _____

522244   ♪ MUSICAL – Boy Looking in Package
"Do Not Open Till Christmas"

SUSP. 1994 - 3 YEARS AGO

GC	$90	B	$85	TRP	$80

Comments: 1992; Original Retail $75.00
Plays *Toyland*. Very slow seller on secondary market since suspension.

Personal Data: _____
____Want Mark ____ Mark _____ Purch. 19__ Pd $ _____

522252   Angel on Cloud Decorating Manger
"He Is The Star Of The Morning"

SUSP. 1993 - 4 YEARS AGO

BA	$80	V	$72	B	$70
FLM	$75	GC	$70		

Comments: 1988; Original Retail $55.00/$60.00
(Also found with double GC mark - insure for $150 over secondary market value.)

Personal Data: _____
____Want Mark ____ Mark _____ Purch. 19__ Pd $ _____

522260   Giraffe with Baby in Mouth
"To Be With You Is Uplifting"

RETIRED 1994 - 3 YEARS AGO

BA $50	V $40	B $35
FLM $45	GC $35	TRP $30

Comments: 1988; Original Retail $20.00/$22.50
Part of the *Birthday Series*. Popular with giraffe collectors. Easily found at these prices. BA mark may be found for less if you look.

Personal Data: _____
____Want Mark ____ Mark _____ Purch. 19__ Pd $ _____

522279   Girl Looking in Bird Bath
"A Reflection Of His Love"

FLM $70	B $55	H $50
V $60	TRP $55	SRD $50
GC $55	S $50	

Comments: 1990; Original Retail $50.00
Reflection in birdbath – so clever! Prediction: retail price may go up on this piece. Buy now. She's different and nice to own. Has a white water reflection but has also been seen with a blue water reflection.

Personal Data: _____
____Want Mark ____ Mark _____ Purch. 19__ Pd $ _____

522287   Girl Kneeling
"Thinking Of You Is What I Really Like To Do"

SUSP. 1996 - 1 YEAR AGO

BA $50	GC $32.50	S $32.50
FLM $45	B $32.50	H $32.50
V $35	TRP $32.50	

Comments: 1989; Original Retail $30.00/$32.50

Personal Data: _____
____Want Mark ____ Mark _____ Purch. 19__ Pd $ _____

522317   Girl Putting Ornaments on Deer Antlers
"Merry Christmas Deer"

RETIRED 1997

BA $105	GC $85	S $85
FLM $95	B $85	H $85
V $90	TRP $85	

Comments: 1988; Original Retail $50.00/$60.00
"PM" logo omitted on all BA pieces. FLM and S marks are also being found without the "PM" logo.

Personal Data: _____
____Want Mark ____ Mark _____ Purch. 19__ Pd $ _____

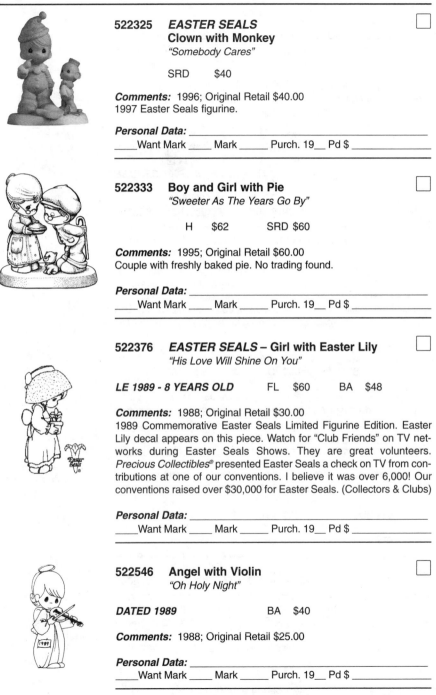

522325   *EASTER SEALS*
Clown with Monkey
"Somebody Cares"

SRD $40

Comments: 1996; Original Retail $40.00
1997 Easter Seals figurine.

Personal Data: _____
____Want Mark ____ Mark _____ Purch. 19__ Pd $ _____

522333   Boy and Girl with Pie
"Sweeter As The Years Go By"

H $62   SRD $60

Comments: 1995; Original Retail $60.00
Couple with freshly baked pie. No trading found.

Personal Data: _____
____Want Mark ____ Mark _____ Purch. 19__ Pd $ _____

522376   *EASTER SEALS* – Girl with Easter Lily
"His Love Will Shine On You"

LE 1989 - 8 YEARS OLD   FL $60   BA $48

Comments: 1988; Original Retail $30.00
1989 Commemorative Easter Seals Limited Figurine Edition. Easter Lily decal appears on this piece. Watch for "Club Friends" on TV networks during Easter Seals Shows. They are great volunteers. *Precious Collectibles®* presented Easter Seals a check on TV from contributions at one of our conventions. I believe it was over 6,000! Our conventions raised over $30,000 for Easter Seals. (Collectors & Clubs)

Personal Data: _____
____Want Mark ____ Mark _____ Purch. 19__ Pd $ _____

522546   Angel with Violin
"Oh Holy Night"

DATED 1989   BA $40

Comments: 1988; Original Retail $25.00

Personal Data: _____
____Want Mark ____ Mark _____ Purch. 19__ Pd $ _____

522554 THIMBLE – Angel with Violin
"Oh Holy Night"

DATED 1989 BA $25

Comments: 1988; Original Retail $7.50

Personal Data: _____
____Want Mark ____ Mark _____ Purch. 19__ Pd $ _____

522821 BELL – Angel with Violin
"Oh Holy Night"

DATED 1989 BA $35

Comments: 1988; Original Retail $25.00

Personal Data: _____
____Want Mark ____ Mark _____ Purch. 19__ Pd $ _____

522848 ORNAMENT – Angel with Violin
"Oh Holy Night"

DATED 1989 BA $30

Comments: 1988; Original Retail $13.50

Personal Data: _____
____Want Mark ____ Mark _____ Purch. 19__ Pd $ _____

522856 Bear in Rocking Chair
"Have A Beary Merry Christmas"

| SUSP. 1992 - 5 YEARS AGO | BA $38 | V $22 |
| | FLM $30 | GC $20 |

Comments: 1988; Original Retail $15.00/$16.50
Sixth addition to *Family Christmas Scene.*

Personal Data: _____
____Want Mark ____ Mark _____ Purch. 19__ Pd $ _____

522864 Grandpa Fishing with "Just Retired" on Chair
"Just A Line To Say You're Special"

| TRP $55 | H $48 |
| S $50 | SRD $45 |

Comments: 1994; Original Retail $45.00

Personal Data: _____
____Want Mark ____ Mark _____ Purch. 19__ Pd $ _____

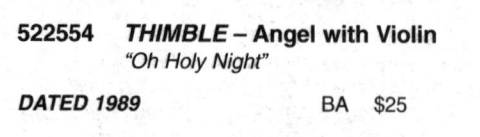

522872 Boy in Car with Dog and Suitcase
"On My Way To A Perfect Day"

| H $45 | SRD $45 |

Comments: 1996; Original Retail $45.00

Personal Data: _____
____Want Mark ____ Mark _____ Purch. 19__ Pd $ _____

522910 ORNAMENT – Girl with Goose
"Make A Joyful Noise"

SUSP. 1996 - 1 YEAR AGO

BA $30	GC $20	S $20
FLM $25	B $20	H $20
V $22	TRP $20	SRD $20

Comments: 1988; Original Retail $15.00/$17.00
Be sure to have this ornament. "Almost" the logo for this collection.

Personal Data: _____
____Want Mark ____ Mark _____ Purch. 19__ Pd $ _____

522929 ORNAMENT – Boy and Girl on Stump
"Love One Another"

BA $25	GC $20	S $18.50
FLM $22	B $20	H $18.50
V $22	TRP $20	SRD $18.50

Comments: 1976; Original Retail $17.50/$18.50
Very little trading found on this ornament. It's my opinion the avid collector should have this, as it is identical to E-1376 which is considered the first piece in the Precious Moments art collection. Still produced with Jonathan & David license name.

Personal Data: _____
____Want Mark ____ Mark _____ Purch. 19__ Pd $ _____

522937 ORNAMENT – Boy and Girl in Boat
"Friends Never Drift Apart"

RETIRED 1995 - 2 YEARS AGO

FLM $45	B $35
V $40	TRP $35
GC $40	S $30

Comments: 1989; Original Retail $17.50/$18.50
Somewhat heavier than others. Predicted this could be retired or suspended for that reason. Prediction came true Nov. 4, 1995!

Personal Data: _____
____Want Mark ____ Mark _____ Purch. 19__ Pd $ _____

522945   *ORNAMENT* – **Bride with Groom Popping Out of Trunk**
"Our First Christmas Together"

DATED 1991   V $30

Comments: 1989; Original Retail $17.50

Personal Data: _____
____Want Mark ____ Mark _____ Purch. 19__ Pd $ _____

522953   *ORNAMENT* – **Girl with Cross**
"I Believe In The Old Rugged Cross"

SUSP. 1994 - 3 YEARS AGO	BA	$40	GC	$25
	FLM	$35	B	$25
	V	$30	TRP	$20

Comments: 1988; Original Retail $15.00/$16.00
Popular ornament. Suspension has speeded up the trading!

Personal Data: _____
____Want Mark ____ Mark _____ Purch. 19__ Pd $ _____

522961   *SHARING SEASON ORNAMENT*
Girl with Box of Puppies
"Always Room For One More"

BA $95

Comments: 1988; 1989 Sharing Season Ornament given to collectors when they signed up two new Enesco Collector's Club Members. Yes, you may have more than one membership. Many signed up two new memberships for themselves. They received club pieces and free ornaments.

Personal Data: _____
____Want Mark ____ Mark _____ Purch. 19__ Pd $ _____

522988   *MINI NATIVITY* – **Girl Sweeping**
"Isn't He Precious"

SUSP. 1993 - 4 YEARS AGO				
BA	$35	V	$30	B	$25
FLM	$30	GC	$30		

Comments: 1988; Original Retail $15.00/$16.50
Addition to Miniature Nativity.

Personal Data: _____
____Want Mark ____ Mark _____ Purch. 19__ Pd $ _____

522996   *MINI NATIVITY* – Mama and Baby Bunnies
"Some Bunny's Sleeping"

SUSP. 1993 - 4 YEARS AGO	FLM	$30	GC	$20
	V	$25	B	$18

Comments: 1989; Original Retail $12.00
Addition to Miniature Nativity. Cute with Noah's Ark set, too.

Personal Data: _____
____Want Mark ____ Mark _____ Purch. 19__ Pd $ _____

523003   *PLATE* – *Family Series*
"May Your Christmas Be A Happy Home"

DATED 1989   BA $50

Comments: 1988; Original Retail $50.00
Fourth issue of *Christmas Love Series*. Attractive plate. Send us a photo of your plate displays. Not many plates being traded.

Personal Data: _____
____Want Mark ____ Mark _____ Purch. 19__ Pd $ _____

523011   **Chapel**
"There's A Christian Welcome Here"

SUSP. 1995 - 2 YEARS AGO			
NM WITHOUT BROW	$125		
NM WITH BROW	$110		
V	$60	GC	$55
TRP	$55	S	$55

Comments: 1988; Original Retail $45.00
The Chapel first debuted in 1989. The first allotment (several thousand) had no eyebrow. "NMs" were still being offered in 1991 at the Precious Moments Chapel in Carthage, Missouri. In late 1992 more "no eyebrow" NM figurines were found at the Chapel. This piece was sold only to visitors at the Chapel at $45 each. Many bought extra to bring back to collectors at home in the beginning. *Precious Collectibles®'* first convention at the Chapel drew over 1600 avid collectors. Many NMs were sold that weekend.

Personal Data: _____
____Want Mark ____ Mark _____ Purch. 19__ Pd $ _____

One of the greatest pleasures in life is doing what people say you can't.

523038 Boy Painting Picture with Animals
"He Is My Inspiration"

NM $60-70

Comments: 1990; Original Retail $60.00
Available only at the Chapel Gift Shoppe. Debuted in 1991. Some pieces found without palette, add $100 to secondary market price. As reported by Chapel Gift Shoppe, this piece has not been assigned a mark. "I would like to see the Chapel have an exclusive Chapel imprint with year mark on the bottom of such figurines." Hint! Hint!

Personal Data: _____
____Want Mark ____ Mark ____ Purch. 19__ Pd $ _____

523062 ORNAMENT – Round Porcelain Ball/Stand
"Peace On Earth"

DATED 1989   BA $68

Comments: 1988; Original Retail $25.00
First issue in *Masterpiece Series*; many damaged in production, thus over 30%-40% never reached retailers' shelves.

Personal Data: _____
____Want Mark ____ Mark ____ Purch. 19__ Pd $ _____

523097 Girl Angel with Book
"Jesus Is The Sweetest Name I Know"

SUSP. 1993 - 4 YEARS AGO

BA $45	V $40	B $30
FLM $40	GC $35	

Comments: 1988; Original Retail $22.50/$25.00

Personal Data: _____
____Want Mark ____ Mark ____ Purch. 19__ Pd $ _____

523178 Girl/Stork with Bundle
"Joy On Arrival"

FLM $75	B $55	H $55
V $65	TRP $55	SRD $55
GC $55	S $55	

Comments: 1990; Original Retail $50.00/$55.00
Very "sweet" piece. FLM not abundant in my opinion. Retail up in '96.

Personal Data: _____
____Want Mark ____ Mark ____ Purch. 19__ Pd $ _____

523194 ORNAMENT - Baby Boy in Sleigh with Bear
"Baby's First Christmas 1989"

DATED 1989   BA $22.50

Comments: 1988; Original Retail $15.00
Also produced in 1988 (115282). ***See #29, page XIV.***

Personal Data: _____
____Want Mark ____ Mark ____ Purch. 19__ Pd $ _____

523208 ORNAMENT - Baby Girl in Sleigh with Doll
"Baby's First Christmas 1989"

DATED 1989   BA $22

Comments: 1988; Original Retail $15.00
Identical to 1988 (520241). The identical design produced two years has kept the secondary market from increasing as compared to ornament designs produced for one year only. ***See #28, page XIV.***

Personal Data: _____
____Want Mark ____ Mark ____ Purch. 19__ Pd $ _____

523224 ORNAMENT – Girl with Stick Horse
"Happy Trails Is Trusting Jesus"

SUSP. 1994 - 3 YEARS AGO

	V $35	B $28	
	GC $30	TRP $25	

Comments: 1989; Original Retail $15.00/$16.00
Not easy to find. FLM reported. Do you have a FLM?

Personal Data: _____
____Want Mark ____ Mark ____ Purch. 19__ Pd $ _____

523283 **9" *EASTER SEALS* – Girl Holding String of Hearts with Dome**
"You Have Touched So Many Hearts"

LE 1990 - 7 YEARS OLD   BA $450-500 FLM $500

Comments: 1982; Original Retail $500.00
1990 Easter Seals 9" piece. Limited Edition 2000. Similar to figurine E-2821. Plentiful for demand. Prices below retail found! Thus lowering price found in '96. ***See #25, page XIV.***

Personal Data: _____
____Want Mark ____ Mark ____ Purch. 19__ Pd $ _____

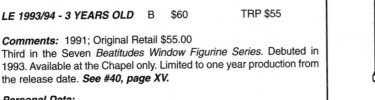

523291 **Girl Giving Alms to Poor Boy**
"Blessed Are The Merciful, For They Shall Obtain Mercy"

LE 1994 - 3 YEARS OLD   NM $70   TRP $60

Comments: 1991; Projected Original Retail $55.00
Fifth in the Seven *Beatitudes Window Figurine Series.* Debuted in 1994. Available at the Chapel only. Limited to one year production from the release date. Unpainted mouse has been reported. ***See #40, page XV.***

Personal Data: _____
____Want Mark ____ Mark ____ Purch. 19__ Pd $ _____

523313 **Indian with Deer**
"Blessed Are The Meek, For They Shall Inherit The Earth"

LE 1993/94 - 3 YEARS OLD   B $60   TRP $55

Comments: 1991; Original Retail $55.00
Third in the Seven *Beatitudes Window Figurine Series.* Debuted in 1993. Available at the Chapel only. Limited to one year production from the release date. ***See #40, page XV.***

Personal Data: _____
____Want Mark ____ Mark ____ Purch. 19__ Pd $ _____

523321 **Girl Praying**
"Blessed Are They Which Do Hunger And Thirst After Righteousness, For They Shall Be Filled"

LE 1993 - 4 YEARS OLD   B $60

Comments: 1991; Original Retail $55.00
Fourth in the Seven *Beatitudes Window Figurine Series.* Debuted in Sept. 1993. Available at the Chapel only. ***See #40, page XV.***

Personal Data: _____
____Want Mark ____ Mark ____ Purch. 19__ Pd $ _____

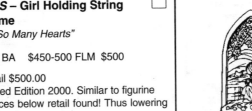

523348 **Girl with Butterfly**
"Blessed Are The Peacemakers, For They Shall Be Called The Children Of God"

LE 1995 - 2 YEARS OLD   TRP $55   S $55
                              H $55

Comments: 1991; Projected Original Retail $55.00
Seventh in the Seven *Beatitudes Window Figurine Series.* **This piece debuted in 1995.** Available at Chapel only. Limited to one year production from the release date. ***See #40, page XV.***

Personal Data: _____
____Want Mark ____ Mark ____ Purch. 19__ Pd $ _____

523380 **Girl Crying**
"Blessed Are They That Mourn, For They Shall Be Comforted"

LE 1991/92 - 5 YEARS OLD   GC $65   B $55

Comments: 1991; Original Retail $55.00
Second in the Seven *Beatitudes Window Figurine Series.* Available at Chapel only. Debuted in 1992. Limited to one year production from the release date. ***See #40, page XV.***

Personal Data: _____
____Want Mark ____ Mark ____ Purch. 19__ Pd $ _____

523399 **Girl Sitting with Birds**
"Blessed Are The Pure In Heart, For They Shall See God"

LE 1994/95 - 2 YEARS OLD   TRP $55   S $55

Comments: 1991; Projected Original Retail $55.00
Sixth in the Seven *Beatitudes Window Figurine Series.* This piece debuted in late '94. Available at Chapel only. Limited to one year production from the release date. ***See #40, page XV.***

Personal Data: _____
____Want Mark ____ Mark ____ Purch. 19__ Pd $ _____

523437 **Princess Washing Servant's Feet**
"Blessed Are The Poor In Spirit, For Theirs Is The Kingdom Of Heaven"

LE 1992 - 5 YEARS OLD   GC $70

Comments: 1991; Original Retail $55.00
First in the Seven *Beatitudes Window Figurine Series.* Debuted in 1992. Available through collectors' ads in *Precious Collectibles®.* Limited to one year production after release date. ***See #40, page XV.***

Personal Data: _____
____Want Mark ____ Mark ____ Purch. 19__ Pd $ _____

523453 Expectant Mother
"The Good Lord Always Delivers"

BA $40	GC $30	S $30
FLM $35	B $30	H $30
V $32	TRP $30	SRD $30

Comments: 1989; Original Retail $27.50/$30.00

Personal Data: _____
____Want Mark ____ Mark ____ Purch. 19__ Pd $ _____

523496 Girl with Bible and Cross
"This Day Has Been Made In Heaven"

BA $45	GC $35	S $35
FLM $40	B $35	H $35
V $35	TRP $35	SRD $35

Comments: 1989; Original Retail $30.00/$35.00
Could be a suspension candidate. Slow seller. A collector found this piece with double marks – B and TRP. Add $100 to the secondary market value. Retail price raised in 1996.

Personal Data: _____
____Want Mark ____ Mark ____ Purch. 19__ Pd $ _____

523518 Girl with Heart Behind Back
"God Is Love Dear Valentine"

BA $45	GC $30	S $30
FLM $38	B $30	H $30
V $35	TRP $30	SRD $30

Comments: 1989; Original Retail $27.50/$30.00

Personal Data: _____
____Want Mark ____ Mark ____ Purch. 19__ Pd $ _____

523526 Girl with Fan
"I'm A Precious Moments Fan"

LE 1990 - 7 YEARS OLD   BA $52
                              FLM $45

Comments: 1988; Original Retail $25.00
1990 Special Event figurine. Generally, Special Event figurines are easily found.

Personal Data: _____
____Want Mark ____ Mark ____ Purch. 19__ Pd $ _____

523534 *EGG WITH SEPARATE BASE –* Girl with Cross
"I Will Cherish The Old Rugged Cross"

DATED 1991   FLM $40
                        V $30

Comments: 1990; Original Retail $27.50
This egg is a "bas-relief" – the design is in the mold, rather than on a decal as the small, dated Easter eggs. This piece is also larger than the first dated porcelain eggs. Slow seller!

Personal Data: _____
____Want Mark ____ Mark ____ Purch. 19__ Pd $ _____

523542 Girl at Typewriter
"You Are The Type I Love"

V $55	TRP $45	SRD $45
GC $50	S $45	
B $45	H $45	

Comments: 1990; Original Retail $40.00/$45.00
Not being sought after on secondary market to date.

Personal Data: _____
____Want Mark ____ Mark ____ Purch. 19__ Pd $ _____

523593 Girl Holding a Bird
"The Lord Will Provide"

LE 1993 - 4 YEARS OLD   GC $60
                              B $55

Comments: 1993; Original Retail $40.00
1993 Limited Edition. Beautiful! Display her with the '92 Limited Edition piece, *You Are My Happiness*. A perfect display!

Personal Data: _____
____Want Mark ____ Mark ____ Purch. 19__ Pd $ _____

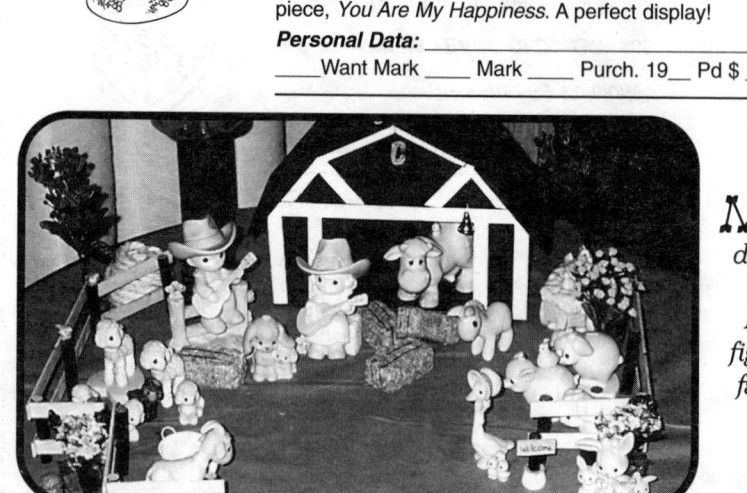

Millie Carey displays her Precious Moments® figurines in a farm scene.

523615 **Girl Climbing Ladder to "Air Mail" Box**
"Good News Is So Uplifting"

V	$80	TRP	$70	SRD	$70
GC	$75	S	$70		
B	$70	H	$70		

Comments: 1990; Original Retail $60.00/$70.00
A suspension candidate!

Personal Data: _____
____Want Mark ____ Mark ____ Purch. 19__ Pd $ _____

523623 **Two Girls Feeding a Kitten**
"I'm So Glad That God Blessed Me With A Friend Like You"

RETIRED 1995 - 2 YEARS AGO

| GC | $95 | TRP | $75 |
| B | $80 | S | $75 |

Comments: 1992; Original Retail $50.00/$55.00

Personal Data: _____
____Want Mark ____ Mark ____ Purch. 19__ Pd $ _____

523631 **Girl at Gate**
"I Will Always Be Thinking Of You"

RETIRED 1996 - 1 YEAR AGO

| B | $65 | S | $55 |
| TRP | $60 | H | $55 |

Comments: 1993; Original Retail $45.00
Has been found with the title decal placed backwards on the bottom.

Personal Data: _____
____Want Mark ____ Mark ____ Purch. 19__ Pd $ _____

523682 ♪ **MUSICAL – Girl with Bible and Cross**
"This Day Has Been Made In Heaven"

V	$75	TRP	$65	SRD	$65
GC	$70	S	$65		
B	$65	H	$65		

Comments: 1990; Original Retail $60.00/$65.00
Plays *Amazing Grace*.

Personal Data: _____
____Want Mark ____ Mark ____ Purch. 19__ Pd $ _____

523704 *ORNAMENT* – **Round Porcelain Ball/Stand**
"May Your Christmas Be A Happy Home"

DATED 1990

| FLM Blue Shirt | $40 |
| FLM Yellow Shirt | $65 |

Comments: 1989; Original Retail $27.50
Second issue of *Masterpiece Series*. The first shipments had yellow shirts on the little boy; the following shipments arrived with blue shirts. There are fewer yellow shirts. Easily found at above prices. Found in FLM with pink shirt.

Personal Data: _____
____Want Mark ____ Mark ____ Purch. 19__ Pd $ _____

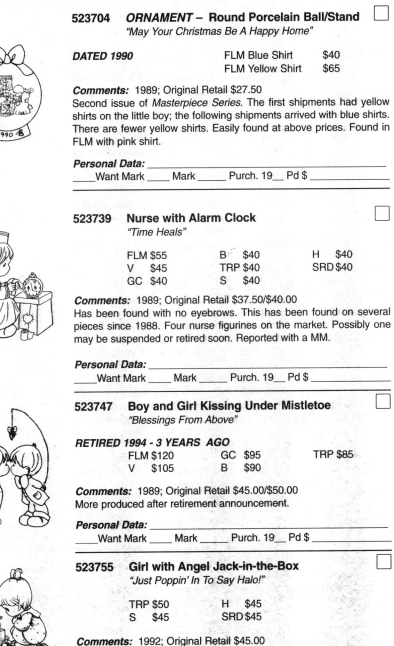

523739 **Nurse with Alarm Clock**
"Time Heals"

FLM	$55	B	$40	H	$40
V	$45	TRP	$40	SRD	$40
GC	$40	S	$40		

Comments: 1989; Original Retail $37.50/$40.00
Has been found with no eyebrows. This has been found on several pieces since 1988. Four nurse figurines on the market. Possibly one may be suspended or retired soon. Reported with a MM.

Personal Data: _____
____Want Mark ____ Mark ____ Purch. 19__ Pd $ _____

523747 **Boy and Girl Kissing Under Mistletoe**
"Blessings From Above"

RETIRED 1994 - 3 YEARS AGO

| FLM | $120 | GC | $95 | TRP | $85 |
| V | $105 | B | $90 | | |

Comments: 1989; Original Retail $45.00/$50.00
More produced after retirement announcement.

Personal Data: _____
____Want Mark ____ Mark ____ Purch. 19__ Pd $ _____

523755 **Girl with Angel Jack-in-the-Box**
"Just Poppin' In To Say Halo!"

| TRP | $50 | H | $45 |
| S | $45 | SRD | $45 |

Comments: 1992; Original Retail $45.00
Personal Data: _____
____Want Mark ____ Mark ____ Purch. 19__ Pd $ _____

523763 Boy with Alphabet Blocks
"I Can't Spell Success Without You"

SUSP. 1994 - 3 YEARS AGO	MM $85	GC $60
	FLM $80	B $60
	V $75	TRP $60

Comments: 1990; Original Retail $40.00/$45.00
Very little trading found on this piece. The mark most traded in the past two years seems to be the V mark. This piece has been found without the embossed *Sam B.* Add $25 to the secondary market value. This piece has also been reported with a MM. Look for a future piece with the same type of concept using letters…

Personal Data: _____
____Want Mark ____ Mark ____ Purch. 19__ Pd $ _____

523771 ORNAMENT – Girl with Pie
"Baby's First Christmas"

DATED 1990 FLM $25

Comments: 1989; Original Retail $15.00

Personal Data: _____
____Want Mark ____ Mark ____ Purch. 19__ Pd $ _____

523798 ORNAMENT – Boy with Pie
"Baby's First Christmas"

DATED 1990 FLM $25

Comments: 1989; Original Retail $15.00

Personal Data: _____
____Want Mark ____ Mark ____ Purch. 19__ Pd $ _____

523801 PLATE – Girl Selling Ice Cream
"Wishing You A Yummy Christmas"

DATED 1990 FLM $55

Comments: 1989; Original Retail $50.00
First issue of *Christmas Blessings Series.* Very few plates are being traded on the secondary market.

Personal Data: _____
____Want Mark ____ Mark ____ Purch. 19__ Pd $ _____

523828 BELL - Girl with Candle and Book
"Once Upon A Holy Night"

DATED 1990 FLM $35

Comments: 1989; Original Retail $25.00

Personal Data: _____
____Want Mark ____ Mark ____ Purch. 19__ Pd $ _____

523836 Girl with Candle and Book
"Once Upon A Holy Night"

DATED 1990 FLM $35

Comments: 1989; Original Retail $25.00
1990 is written for the viewer to read, not the little girl. Original pictures of the "sample piece" had "1990" turned toward the girl.
See #7, page VII.

Personal Data: _____
____Want Mark ____ Mark ____ Purch. 19__ Pd $ _____

523844 THIMBLE – Girl with Candle and Book
"Once Upon A Holy Night"

DATED 1990 FLM $20

Comments: 1989; Original Retail $8.00

Personal Data: _____
____Want Mark ____ Mark ____ Purch. 19__ Pd $ _____

523852 ORNAMENT – Girl with Candle and Book
"Once Upon A Holy Night"

DATED 1990 FLM $25

Comments: 1989; Original Retail $15.00

Personal Data: _____
____Want Mark ____ Mark ____ Purch. 19__ Pd $ _____

The average man has sixty-six pounds of muscle, forty pounds of bone, and three and a half pounds of brain – which seems to explain a lot of things.

523860 *PLATE* – Girl at Bird House
"Blessings From Me To Thee"

DATED 1991   V $50

Comments: 1990; Original Retail $50.00
Very little trading found.

Personal Data: _____
____Want Mark ____ Mark _____ Purch. 19__ Pd $ _____

523879 *9" EASTER SEALS* – Girl with Butterfly
with Dome
"We Are God's Workmanship"

LE 1990 - 7 YEARS OLD   FLM $650
                                         V $625

Comments: 1982; Original Retail $500.00
1990 Easter Seals 9" Figurine with Dome. Limited Edition 2,000 pieces.
Similar to E-9258. Prices seem to be decreasing somewhat on most of
the 9" Easter Seals pieces.

Personal Data: _____
____Want Mark ____ Mark _____ Purch. 19__ Pd $ _____

523941 **Mother Rocking Baby**
"Love Never Leaves A Mother's Arms"

     S $45   H $40   SRD $40

Comments: 1995; Original Retail $40.00

Personal Data: _____
____Want Mark ____ Mark _____ Purch. 19__ Pd $ _____

524069 **Boy Eating Cake with Fingers**
"Baby's First Birthday"

     GC $32   TRP $25   H $25
     B $25   S $25   SRD $25

Comments: 1992; Original Retail $25.00
Addition to *Baby's First Series*.

Personal Data: _____
____Want Mark ____ Mark _____ Purch. 19__ Pd $ _____

524077 **Baby in High Chair**
"Baby's First Meal'

FLM $60	B $40	H $40
V $50	TRP $40	SRD $40
GC $50	S $40	

Comments: 1990; Original Retail $35.00/$40.00
6th issue in *Baby's First Series*. Becoming a VERY popular series.
Baby's First Trip is the most sought after in the past year.

Personal Data: _____
____Want Mark ____ Mark _____ Purch. 19__ Pd $ _____

524085 **Girl in Tree Swing**
"My Warmest Thoughts Are You"

RETIRED 1996 - 1 YEAR AGO

V $75	TRP $60	S $60
GC $65	B $65	H $60

Comments: 1990; Original Retail $55.00/$60.00
This figurine differs from original artwork as shown at left; the figurine
has no hearts on the tree, the bluebird and leaves are in different positions and the girl has bows in her hair instead of wearing a bonnet.
Large pieces such as this, are not ordered in quantity due to retail
price. It is my opinion that the high retail price may be a reason for
retirement. Condsider this in the future with figurines priced similarly.

Personal Data: _____
____Want Mark ____ Mark _____ Purch. 19__ Pd $ _____

524123 **Girl in Coat with Bunny**
"Good Friends Are For Always"

V $40	B $32.50	S $32.50	SRD $32.50
GC $35	TRP $32.50	H $32.50	

Comments: 1990; Original Retail $27.50/$32.50
Retail price increased in 1995.

Personal Data: _____
____Want Mark ____ Mark _____ Purch. 19__ Pd $ _____

524131 *ORNAMENT* – Girl Holding Bunny
"Good Friends Are For Always"

RETIRED 1997

GC $35	TRP $32	H $32
B $32	S $32	

Comments: 1992; Original Retail $15.00/$17.00
Retail price last increased in 1995.

Personal Data: _____
____Want Mark ____ Mark _____ Purch. 19__ Pd $ _____

524158 Girl Kneeling at Altar with Bible
"Lord Teach Us To Pray"

TRP $45

Comments: 1993; Original Retail $35.00
Commemorative 1994 National Day of Prayer Figurine.

Personal Data: _____
___Want Mark ____ Mark _____ Purch. 19__ Pd $ _____

524166 Girl with Bird
"May Your Christmas Be Merry"

DATED 1991   V $35

Comments: 1990; Original Retail $27.50
It takes several years to see a large increase in the secondary market on dated pieces. This dated piece is not as scarce as previous years' dated figurines.

Personal Data: _____
___Want Mark ____ Mark _____ Purch. 19__ Pd $ _____

524174 ORNAMENT – Girl with Bird
"May Your Christmas Be Merry"

DATED 1991   V $28

Comments: 1990; Original Retail $15.00

Personal Data: _____
___Want Mark ____ Mark _____ Purch. 19__ Pd $ _____

524182 BELL – Girl with Bird
"May Your Christmas Be Merry"

DATED 1991   V $35

Comments: 1990; Original Retail $25.00

Personal Data: _____
___Want Mark ____ Mark _____ Purch. 19__ Pd $ _____

*T*he longest chapter in the Bible is
Numbers Chapter 7;
nearly two thousand words, all about giving.

524190 THIMBLE - Girl with Bird
"May Your Christmas Be Merry"

DATED 1991   V $22

Comments: 1990; Original Retail $8.00

Personal Data: _____
___Want Mark ____ Mark _____ Purch. 19__ Pd $ _____

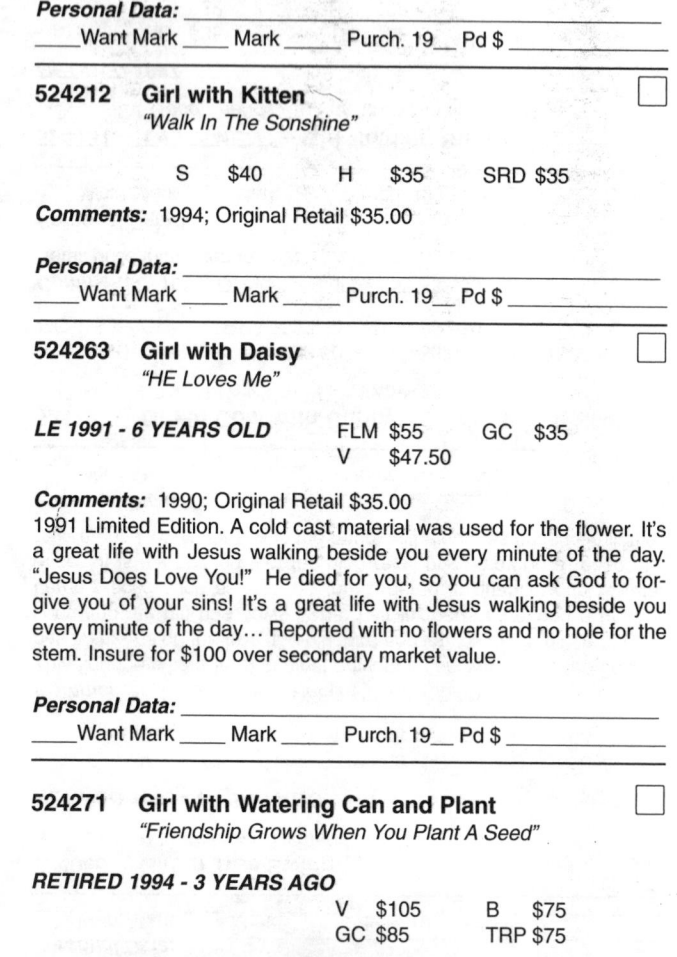

524212 Girl with Kitten
"Walk In The Sonshine"

S $40   H $35   SRD $35

Comments: 1994; Original Retail $35.00

Personal Data: _____
___Want Mark ____ Mark _____ Purch. 19__ Pd $ _____

524263 Girl with Daisy
"HE Loves Me"

LE 1991 - 6 YEARS OLD   FLM $55   GC $35
                          V $47.50

Comments: 1990; Original Retail $35.00
1991 Limited Edition. A cold cast material was used for the flower. It's a great life with Jesus walking beside you every minute of the day. "Jesus Does Love You!" He died for you, so you can ask God to forgive you of your sins! It's a great life with Jesus walking beside you every minute of the day… Reported with no flowers and no hole for the stem. Insure for $100 over secondary market value.

Personal Data: _____
___Want Mark ____ Mark _____ Purch. 19__ Pd $ _____

524271 Girl with Watering Can and Plant
"Friendship Grows When You Plant A Seed"

RETIRED 1994 - 3 YEARS AGO

                V $105   B $75
                GC $85   TRP $75

Comments: 1990; Original Retail $40.00
Hardest one of '94 retirement pieces to find. No production after announcement. Not a big increase seen in value on secondary market from last year's values. Many sales found.

Personal Data: _____
___Want Mark ____ Mark _____ Purch. 19__ Pd $ _____

524298　Girl Blowing Cake Off the Table
"May Your Every Wish Come True"

GC	$65	TRP	$55	H	$50
B	$60	S	$50	SRD	$50

Comments: 1992; Original Retail $50.00
The Enesco brochure shows four candles; the piece has five. (Just in case you get excited.)

Personal Data: _____
____Want Mark ____ Mark _____ Purch. 19__ Pd $ _____

524301　Girl with Birthday Cake
"May Your Birthday Be A Blessing"

FLM	$55	B	$35	H	$35
V	$45	TRP	$35	SRD	$35
GC	$40	S	$35		

Comments: 1990; Original Retail $30.00/$35.00
A cold cast material was used for the birthday cake and candles. Excellent gift which is affordable for birthdays. Retail price increase in '95 and '96. Hopefully this piece will remain at this price when received as a gift; just could "start a new collector." This figurine has been found with the cake missing. Insure for $100 over secondary market value for this error.

Personal Data: _____
____Want Mark ____ Mark _____ Purch. 19__ Pd $ _____

524336　Boy and Girl Sharing Soda
"Our Friendship Is Soda-Licious"

GC	$80	TRP	$75	H	$70
B	$78	S	$70	SRD	$70

Comments: 1992; Original Retail $65.00/$70.00
Higher priced retail pieces may be "hard to find" in the future. Retailers do not order as many of these pieces as the more "affordable" figurines under fifty dollars sell more quickly in the gift line. Not too abundant. Retail price up in 1996.

Personal Data: _____
____Want Mark ____ Mark _____ Purch. 19__ Pd $ _____

Money used to talk, then it whispered, now it just sneaks off.

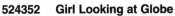

524352　Girl Looking at Globe
"What The World Needs Now"

RETIRED 1997

V	$85	B	$75	S	$75
GC	$80	TRP	$75	H	$75

Comments: 1990; Original Retail $50.00
Several have been found without the Bible.

Personal Data: _____
____Want Mark ____ Mark _____ Purch. 19__ Pd $ _____

524360　Girl Looking Into Baby Carriage
"Something Precious From Above"

H	$50	SRD	$50

Comments: 1996; Original Retail $50.00

Personal Data: _____
____Want Mark ____ Mark _____ Purch. 19__ Pd $ _____

524379　Girl/Flower Picked from Box Behind Her
"So Glad I Picked You As A Friend"

B	$55
TRP	$55

Comments: 1993; Original Retail $40.00
Only those DSR shops participating in the 1994 Spring catalog offer were able to order this figurine. **See #31, page XIV.**

Personal Data: _____
____Want Mark ____ Mark _____ Purch. 19__ Pd $ _____

524387　*EASTER SEALS* – Girl with Basket of Roses
"Take Time To Smell The Flowers"

LE 1995 - 2 YEARS OLD

TRP	$40	S	$35

Comments: 1994; Original Retail $30.00
1995 Easter Seals Commemorative Figurine. Pretty! Has been more popular than some of the other past Easter Seals pieces.

Personal Data: _____
____Want Mark ____ Mark _____ Purch. 19__ Pd $ _____

524395 Girl Holding Kitten
"You Are Such A Purr-fect Friend"

GC	$45	TRP	$35	H	$35
B	$40	S	$35	SRD	$35

Comments: 1992; Original Retail $35.00
Has been found with two B marks. Very similar to '95 piece #136263 and LE #526185. Pretty!

Personal Data: _____
___Want Mark ___ Mark ____ Purch. 19__ Pd $ _____

524425 Girl with Butterfly Net and Butterfly
"May Only Good Things Come Your Way"

FLM	$55	B	$37.50	H	$37.50
V	$48	TRP	$37.50	SRD	$37.50
GC	$40	S	$37.50		

Comments: 1990; Original Retail $30.00/$37.50
Many confuse this piece with the retired Butterfly Angel (520640). Retail price increased last in 1995. Do not over insure. Could get suspension or retirement soon.

Personal Data: _____
___Want Mark ___ Mark ____ Purch. 19__ Pd $ _____

524441 Boy and Girl Kissing
"Sealed With A Kiss"

RETIRED 1996 - 1 YEAR AGO

GC	$75	TRP	$60	H	$60
B	$60	S	$60		

Comments: 1992; Original Retail $50.00/$60.00
Retail price increase of 10% in 1995 and nearly that again in '96, then retired. Not sought after to date.

Personal Data: _____
___Want Mark ___ Mark ____ Purch. 19__ Pd $ _____

524468 Boy with Bell
"A Special Chime For Jesus"

RETIRED 1997

B	$63	S	$57.50	TRP	$60	H $57.50

Comments: 1992; Original Retail $32.50
Boy's pajamas found to be from very light to bright red and orange.

Personal Data: _____
___Want Mark ___ Mark ____ Purch. 19__ Pd $ _____

524476 Girl Decorating Christmas Tree
"God Cared Enough To Send His Best"

RETIRED 1996 - 1 YEAR AGO

TRP	$55	H	$55
S	$55		

Comments: 1994; Original Retail $50.00
Slow on the secondary market.

Personal Data: _____
___Want Mark ___ Mark ____ Purch. 19__ Pd $ _____

524484 Cat with Mouse on Cheese (2 pc. set)
"Not A Creature Was Stirring"

SUSP. 1994 - 3 YEARS AGO

FLM	$30	B	$22
V	$28	TRP	$22
GC	$25		

Comments: 1989; Original Retail $17.00
The cat has been found with only one eyebrow. Not unusual to hear about missing eyebrows.

Personal Data: _____
___Want Mark ___ Mark ____ Purch. 19__ Pd $ _____

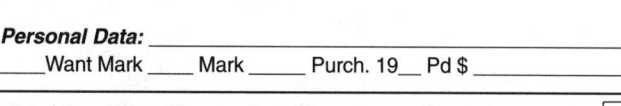

524492 Cat with Bird in Cage
"Can't Be Without You"

FLM	$25	B	$17.50	H	$17.50
V	$22	TRP	$17.50	SRD	$17.50
GC	$17.50	S	$17.50		

Comments: 1990; Original Retail $16.00/$17.50
Retail price increase in 1995 and 1996! Good retirement candidate.

Personal Data: _____
___Want Mark ___ Mark ____ Purch. 19__ Pd $ _____

524506 Pig with Gift
"Oinky Birthday"

B	$18	S	$14.50	SRD	$14.50
TRP	$14.50	H	$14.50		

Comments: 1993; Original Retail $13.50/$14.50
Birthday Series Addition. Retail up in 1996. Definitely a suspension or retirement candidate.

Personal Data: _____
___Want Mark ___ Mark ____ Purch. 19__ Pd $ _____

524522 EASTER SEALS – Girl with Chick in Egg
"Always In His Care"

LE 1990 - 7 YEARS OLD   BA $45
                                   FLM $40

Comments: 1989; Original Retail $30.00
1990 Easter Seals Limited Edition Figurine. Easter Seals Logo on base. Easter Seals pieces are usually abundant.

Personal Data: _____
____Want Mark _____ Mark _____ Purch. 19__ Pd $ _____

524875 Bear in Package
"Happy Birthday Dear Jesus"

SUSP. 1993 - 4 YEARS AGO   FLM $35   GC $20
                               V $22   B $20

Comments: 1989; Original Retail $13.50
Addition to regular Nativity Set.

Personal Data: _____
____Want Mark _____ Mark _____ Purch. 19__ Pd $ _____

524883 Christmas Fireplace

SUSP. 1992 - 5 YEARS AGO   FLM $55   GC $45
                               V $45

Comments: 1989; Original Retail $37.50
Seventh addition to *Family Christmas Scene*.

Personal Data: _____
____Want Mark _____ Mark _____ Purch. 19__ Pd $ _____

524905 Boy on Skis
"It's So Uplifting To Have A Friend Like You"

GC $50   TRP $45   H $45
B $45   S $45   SRD $45

Comments: 1992; Original Retail $40.00/$45.00
Retail price increased 10% in 1995.

Personal Data: _____
____Want Mark _____ Mark _____ Purch. 19__ Pd $ _____

524913 Girl with Melting Snowman
"We're Going To Miss You"

FLM $70   B $55   H $50
V $65   TRP $55   SRD $50
GC $60   S $50

Comments: 1989; Original Retail $50.00
This is an attractive piece. Three snowmen have been produced. 12351 was suspended in 1988, and there was a snowman added to the Sugar Town collection in 1993.

Personal Data: _____
____Want Mark _____ Mark _____ Purch. 19__ Pd $ _____

524921 Two Angels on Stool
"Angels We Have Heard On High"

RETIRED 1996 - 1 YEAR AGO
V $75   TRP $65
GC $70   S $65
B $70   H $65

Comments: 1990; Original Retail $60.00/$65.00
It's been reported the little black angel's hand is not painted on many.

Personal Data: _____
____Want Mark _____ Mark _____ Purch. 19__ Pd $ _____

525049 Two Girls with Flowers
"Good Friends Are Forever"

ROSEBUD MARK WITH EMBOSSED BA MARK $750

Comments: 1989. Also produced as 521817 in the regular line. Given away at store events – one per DSR. Many went to the "general public," not all to collectors. Under 500 produced. Would be hard to replace if broken. Very few sold or traded. Insure at $750 to replace.

Personal Data: _____
____Want Mark _____ Mark _____ Purch. 19__ Pd $ _____

PRECIOUS MOMENTS RETIRED FEBRUARY 3, 1997

12262 – I Get A Bang Out Of You
104035 – Cheers To The Leader
524468 – A Special Chime For Jesus
526150 – Friends To The Very End
522058 – Now I Lay Me Down To Sleep
522317 – Merry christmas Deer
521450 – Lord, Help Me Stick To My Job
529966 – Ring Out The Good News
527378 – You Are My Favorite Star
524352 – What The World Needs Now
106844 – Sew In Love
112356 – You Have Touched So Many Hearts
524131 – Good Friends Are For Always

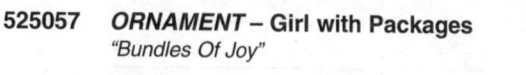

525057 **ORNAMENT** – Girl with Packages
"Bundles Of Joy"

LE 1990 - 7 YEARS OLD FLM $20

Comments: 1989; Original Retail $17.50
1990 Limited Edition. This ornament was available exclusively to
Precious Moments® Collectors Centers as a special sale item. Many
sales found below $20! Down from '96.

Personal Data: _____
____Want Mark ____ Mark _____ Purch. 19__ Pd $ _____

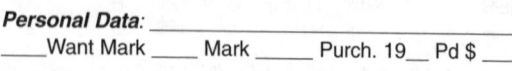

525278 **MINI NATIVITY** – Pig with Chicken on Back
"Tubby's First Christmas"

GC $18	TRP $10	H $10
B $10	S $10	SRD $10

Comments: 1992; Original Retail $10.00
Addition to the Miniature Nativity.

Personal Data: _____
____Want Mark ____ Mark _____ Purch. 19__ Pd $ _____

525286 **MINI NATIVITY** – Boy Angel with Doctor's Bag
"It's A Perfect Boy"

V $25	TRP $17	SRD $17
GC $20	S $17	
B $18.50	H $17	

Comments: 1990; Original Retail $16.50/$17.00
Addition to Miniature Nativity.

Personal Data: _____
____Want Mark ____ Mark _____ Purch. 19__ Pd $ _____

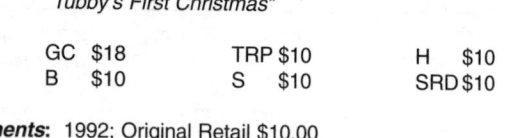

525316 **Girl Praying in Front of Window**
"May Your Future Be Blessed"

GC $45	TRP $40	H $40
B $40	S $40	SRD $40

Comments: 1992; Original Retail $35.00/$40.00
Suspension candidate.

Personal Data: _____
____Want Mark ____ Mark _____ Purch. 19__ Pd $ _____

525324 **ORNAMENT** – Bride and Groom in Car
"Our First Christmas Together"

DATED 1990 FLM $25

Comments: 1989; Original Retail $17.50
Same design as 521558. Debuted in crystal at $50. Crystal is not con-
sidered a "hot" Precious Moments® "collectible." Figurine Collectors collect mainly the figurines only. **See #28, page XIV.**

Personal Data: _____
____Want Mark ____ Mark _____ Purch. 19__ Pd $ _____

525332 **ORNAMENT** – Ballerina on One Toe
with Purple Tutu
"Lord Keep Me On My Toes"

GC $22	TRP $17	H $17
B $18	S $17	SRD $17

Comments: 1992; Original Retail $15.00/$17.00
Displays well hanging from a display ornament stand all year round.

Personal Data: _____
____Want Mark ____ Mark _____ Purch. 19__ Pd $ _____

525898 **Two Angels Ringing a Bell**
"Ring Those Christmas Bells"
RETIRED 1996 - 1 YEAR AGO

GC $135	TRP $100	H $105
B $120	S $105	

Comments: 1992; Original Retail $95.00/$100.00
This is a very large, attractive piece.

Personal Data: _____
____Want Mark ____ Mark _____ Purch. 19__ Pd $ _____

525960 **EGG WITH SEPARATE BASE** –
Girl with Butterfly
"We Are God's Workmanship"

DATED 1992 V $30 GC $27.50

Comments: 1990; Original Retail $27.50
Eggs are beautiful but not sought after.

Personal Data: _____
____Want Mark ____ Mark _____ Purch. 19__ Pd $ _____

THE CHAPEL

Errors & Variations

The Greatest of These Is Love, an angel holding the Ten Commandments, has been found with the crayons decal missing on the angel's pocket.

Compare these and you will see that paint variations can occur. This can happen because of more than one factory being used to produce Precious Moments pieces.

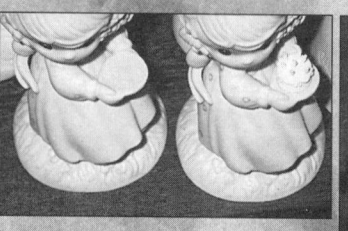

Rejoicing With You has been found with a missing Bible decal.

May Your Birthday Be A Blessing has been found with the cake missing. If you look closely at the photo, you can see a triangle shape where the cake should have been placed. An error such as this should be insured for $100 over the secondary market price.

Here we have a frowning *Faith Takes the Plunge* as well as a smiling one.

Jesus Loves Me shown with one bear's nose being painted dark brown, the other one light brown.

Figurines licensed by the Jonathan & David Co. were produced with smaller heads than later figurines licensed by the Samuel J. Butcher Co. Notice the difference in these two figurines.

Notice the differences between these two Birthday Train bears.

The decaled words "Heaven Bound" appeared upside down on some of these.

The artwork of *But Love Goes On Forever* was produced as a figurine and a night light as well as Membership Plaques and a Club Welcome Gift.

The 9" version of *Many Moons In Same Canoe, Bless-um You* appears in the Precious Moments Chapel display *Will You Be Ready When Jesus Comes?*

This picture of six fake Precious Moments figurines was sent to us by Helen Starling.

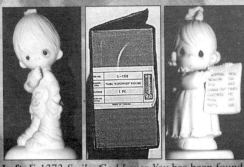

Left: E-1373 *Smile, God Loves You* has been found with a brown "black eye" as shown. There is no significance in this.
Center: The oldest Precious Moments boxes were plain brown cardboard with a simple paper label. This box is for the coveted Free Puppies.
Right: *Have You Any Room For Jesus,* a 1997 piece has been found with the word bowling misspelled "biowling".

This is another example of a decal which was put on incorrectly. Here we see E-9267B, one from a set of six animal figurines, with the "Dad" decal placed differently. (Which way should it be?)

Some of the puppies on *The Good Lord Has Blessed Us Tenfold* have unpainted eyes.

A good example of a missing decal can be seen on this photo of *Blessed Are The Peacemakers.*

I Believe In Miracles was suspended, then reissued. The reissued figurine is pictured on the left.

Tippy is missing his name decal on the *Puppy Love* figurine on the left.

Notice the two "fake" clowns to the right of the real thing.

Are they triplets? No, it's just three of *Nobody's Perfect,* known as Smiley the Dunce. Two versions were produced, one with a smile and one with a frown.

Notice the difference in the angle of the girl's head. The figurine on the left has a triangle mark, the one on the right is the NM E-3108.

Notice the two different inspirations on the bottom.

Dr. Sam Sugar (the doctor who delivered Sam Butcher) signed these two *Sugar Town* pieces for Millie Carey.

Exciting errors occasionally surface in the Precious Moments collection. *The Friendship Hits The Spot* figurine on the right is missing the table!

CLUBS

COLEENIA'S STORY

Taken from August, 1991 Precious Collectibles - Page 37

Collectors attending a Wednesday Night Chapel Dinner during Precious Collectibles' Christmas in June of 1991 were so inspired when Terri Heckmaster introduced Mike Sutton who spoke about his step-daughter, Coleenia.

Coleenia Louise - she would have been 23 in August, 1991. Her story isn't unusual, isn't different from many children. Unfortunately it has to do with a life of suffering, with a life of courage. Your theme this year is Christmas - a time to renew your faith, a time to show man's belief in God and faith in things being the way they are for a purpose. Coleenia served one such purpose, and that's what I'd like to share with you tonight.

Coleenia was born on August 28, 1968. She was well. It was six weeks into her life when she was struck with meningitis. She contracted encephalitis, she ran long bouts of high temperatures, continuing seizures and convulsions. Her mother had dreams in the beginning, as all mothers do, for their children. She had hopes and prayers of her own. These changed at that early age. But Coleenia was there and you had only to look into her eyes to know there was a reason.

The doctors told the mother at an early age to love her while she could. "You won't have her long. There's nothing we can do. This isn't to say that she will never grow to walk, for she will not even take a step. This isn't to say that she won't be able to talk very much, for she will never say a word. This isn't to say that she will have trouble standing, for she will never sit up. But you have her, so love her and keep her with you as long as possible." They told her, as good doctors do, that with much care and love perhaps she would see her teen years. They said, "Hope for no more; expect less. Do the best you can; leave her in God's hands."

Time went by. People would come up, some with all the sharing and care people could offer, some with stares, some that would flat shake their heads and turn away. People asked us at different times, "Why do you think this could be? There could be no reason for this. It's so unfair. It's such a waste." We questioned it ourselves at times. My wife, whose faith is as strong as any person's can be, was shaken many times

over. The doubts were there. The fears were there every day. You had to expect each day to be her last. You had to hope each day would stretch on into the next and if Coleenia could summon perhaps one smile, which she always seemed to do, that was the reward of the day itself. To the people that knew her and loved her and were around her, this was their message, this was all they needed.

Time went by, years passed. Coleenia not only indeed went into these teenage years, she went past them. Coleenia turned 21. Her mother had become an avid fan of Mr. Sam Butcher. She collected when she could. She loved his work very much. When the Chapel opened, she told me that we were going to visit one weekend. My sister lives in the area, and they were going to tour the Chapel. I told her that would be fine. Coleenia, by this time, was very ill and needed a suction machine at all times. She coughed continuously. She couldn't get out much and this was in the summer, the worst time of the year for her. But we thought my wife needed to get away herself for some sort of trip and I said, "we'll drive down in the car, we'll get a nice motel room, and Coleenia and I will stay there. We'll wait. You enjoy yourself. You go to the Chapel and we'll wait for you to get back."

My wife came out here -- she was moved. She came back that evening. She told me, "Coleenia needs to see the Chapel." I was against it. "I see no reason for that. I'm sure it's nice; I'm sure the man does good work." I've seen the figurines, I like them, but Coleenia has to be carried, Coleenia coughed continuously, she couldn't stand the heat. We still, on occasion, ran into people who didn't care, but were only curious. I could see no advantage to bringing her to this place. Her mother, knowing more than I (as always), continued her argument. Finally I gave in. Early the next morning we were here - the first tour - I might say right off that the only people we met were the kindest people I've ever met with regards to Coleenia. Both employees and visitors - the nicest people that Coleenia could hope to see. We brought her in, we carried in a lawn chair - we brought her suction machine. I carried her down to the Chapel; we were there almost an hour. I had her in my arms and she was totally at ease. She did not cough one time. She did not breathe heavy. The

machine was not turned on. She looked around the Chapel continuously. One smile would leave her face, only to be replaced by another. She was totally at peace. She was very much at home.

We finally left, both of us very happy for the experience, and returned home. Some time after that my wife wrote Mr. Butcher and thanked him for what this place did for her and most of all what it did for our daughter. Some time after that we received a very nice letter from Mr. Butcher. He said he would

This Chapel Exclusive Figurine is sculpted in memory of a young woman named Coleenia, whose favorite toy was a Precious Moments® clown doll.

like to meet Coleenia, that he was very proud to know that perhaps his work could inspire someone like her and that he would like to make her acquaintance. We brought her back. They met; they were together only a short time, but their souls touched. They were both at ease with one another. Again, she had no problem while here. Again, she was totally happy. She was very much at home.

We left after this meeting, and returned home. At that time we had hopes and plans of bringing her back, knowing that it probably would be occasionally, at least rarely we prayed. But time being as time is, she was not to stay. She was taken from us in October of last year.

I, in my anger and my lack of faith, lashed out at everything around me. I wrote Mr. Butcher a letter. I said it was brought to my attention that a friend of ours called you at your office, and they asked you if perhaps you could send a card or make a call because of the importance you held in the hearts of my wife, Carolyn, and Coleenia. I had heard this story and I knew there had been no card or no call and I was angry. I was angry at everyone. I was angry at God most of all, and everyone beneath Him. I sent this letter to Mr. Butcher, expecting to hear nothing in return and at the time, not caring.

Thinking that by lashing out at him, in some way it would help get even for what had been taken from me. A very short time after that a messenger came to our door. It was a letter from Mr. Butcher, asking to see my wife and I as soon as possible. I had not told my wife of my letter, for I was ashamed after I had sent it. She was very eager to go. She didn't know exactly why he wanted to see us, but she assumed it was because someone had made contact and let him know about Coleenia. I knew different. I didn't know why he wanted to see us, either. I was very apprehensive. We went anyway. All the way down there that day on that drive I said, "Lord God, I don't have the right to ask this, especially after all the things I've done, so let me walk down to the Chapel and look into Hallelujah Square and see a sign, see a child whose hair seems to be that color, or one who has a look that's slightly different from the others and I will know. I will know."

I didn't tell my wife of my prayer and we walked down that day and there was nothing. Everything was beautiful but everything was as it always was. There was no sign. I knew I wasn't entitled to one, so I stood there for the longest of times. Finally she came up to me. She said, "It's time for our appointment. What's wrong with you?" Nothing. Nothing I didn't expect, I told her. Let's go.

We went to Mr. Butcher's office. He came in and greeted us. He took us into a private room. He gave of himself to my wife, to console her; he told her of his grief and of how in the short time he knew Coleenia, she had come to mean so much to him for the very reason God makes these things happen. In the middle of the conversation the man paused, he looked me straight in the eye and said, "I was in Florida a short time ago and was awakened in the middle of the night. I don't know why but I had come to a decision. The message had been sent to me that Coleenia would be painted into Hallelujah Square. I would have had it done today when you

got here, but I wanted you to tell me of something she could hold, something so that in the future, when your friends and family and yourself come, you will always know she's there watching and safe." The tap on his shoulder I had asked for from the Lord turned into a sledge-hammer blow in the back of the head. I knew then Coleenia was where she should be. I knew then that she had done what she was supposed to do and that she was being rewarded.

We thanked Mr. Butcher and we left. I was overwhelmed. I told my wife of my prayers on my way down and how it all came together and what it meant to me. She was greatly touched. But as only a mother would, she continued to mourn her daughter's loss terribly.

Time passed. Mother's Day was upon us. My wife said, "I don't know what I'm going to do. I don't think I can stand it." We got a phone call - totally unexpected - from Terri. She said that Sam was in and would like to see us, and oh, by the way, she had his permission to let us know that not only had the painting been completed of Coleenia, but there would be a doll in her sake. I thanked her, turned when my wife came into the room, and told her. Once again, he had saved my wife without even knowing it. On what would have been the worst day of her life since our daughter's death, he saved her. We came down Mother's Day and talked with him.

Coleenia holding her Precious Moments® clown doll was painted into Hallelujah Square.

My wife was happy. A week before there was no way I would have thought there was a chance in the world she could smile on that day. If there's a story in there, I don't know. We are friends with Sam - we keep in touch. I, a man who at one time doubted the sincerity of his work, have been brought to realize this man does his art from the depths of his soul and heart. There are critics who say Sam Butcher's work is not a true art, but we say to those critics, we cannot judge what art is any more than we can judge the crippled people of this world. We don't know unless we have the feelings men like him possess. You people here tonight, I feel, are gifted in a sense that something brings you together, the fact that you want to be here. The fact that you sing together

and praise God and thank Mr. Butcher for his work in collecting. That shows me you have received the sign. You know I am not about to stand before you and say that we have Messiah or a great spiritual leader, but it goes far beyond a man that makes bigger names. I feel all of you are aware of this and for that I am happy for you. We came down off the mount, we walk down to the Chapel to see Coleenia. We thank Him every day for what He has done. We praise God for strength. We waited 22 years for our daughter to be taken from us. I knew that when she was, I would lose my wife. Sam Butcher, I feel, saved her by these short meetings and by the gestures he did on his own. No suggestions were made by me except for the first letter which asked simply for a phone call or a card. This man understands. When he talked to us he understood. He told my wife, "I know the sense of loss you have and I know that it must be even greater in your case because of the time you had to spend with this child. And it is true, it is true, that he has done so much for her. The reason I come before you tonight is, I am Coleenia's step-father. Her mother gave her 22 years; Mr. Butcher gave her immortal life. I offered her far less. I felt like tonight or sometime, somewhere I needed to speak out at least once in her behalf. We need to understand that when we see people that are handicapped, people that are in pain, there could be reasons that are far greater than those we are expected to know and will ever know. Everything in life is a balance and for all the evil that's out there, there must be that much good. People like her are God's warriors. They are suffering. They are going through this. But they make it, they continue to live, they do the best they can because they know things we don't know. They know where their next place will be, they are at peace. In spite of all that's around them, they are at peace. And it touches me very deeply to know that Mr. Butcher has this same sense of value about himself and all of the people he connects with. Most certainly, as the years go by, be proud of what you're involved in now because you're dealing with someone who is much more involved in life itself than in creating anything that anyone would simply set on a shelf. The people that say they don't even know for sure why, it's just that they love these things. Believe me, you've got the message. You just have to go with it from there.

Editor's Note: We thank Sharon Kamacho and Nancy Schowalter for supplying the tapes of this speech we were able to share with you. Sam asked that we not publish his speech from the video we heard on Saturday evening...

COUPLE FINDS NEW LIFE AFTER DEATH OF THEIR SON

Reprinted with permission from
December 17, 1996
Carthage Press article
by Amy Lamb Campbell

John and Sharon Shively left a note for their son Bradley just before they left their home in Monroe City Sept. 10, 1994.

"If you are here, stay here. We are out looking for you," the note read.

His two cousins had been in a serious car accident coming home from a football game and the Shivelys wanted to find and comfort their only son, who was 16 and had been close to his cousins.

Not until they reached the accident site, as a medical helicopter was taking off, did they realize their son had been in the car, too. He wasn't supposed to be with them.

All three teenagers died.

The loss of three high school students, who were all popular athletes, devastated the town of 2,700 in northeast Missouri. For the Shivelys, who lost their only child, there were no answers.

They barely left their house. They didn't want to go on with their lives.

"Nobody could help anybody," said John Shively. "We were starving for some kind of answers."

A friend of theirs who was a Precious Moments collector had visited the Chapel in Carthage, and told the Shivelys they should come to Carthage to see Sam Butcher, who had also lost a son.

"We didn't know anything about Precious Moments," Shively said. "It didn't mean a thing to us."

They traveled to Precious Moments and asked the information desk if there was a Sam Butcher there.

"We didn't know if he was the guy who mowed the lawn or who he was," Shively said.

The woman at the desk said he was the creator of everything they saw. She asked them to write their names down and Sam would be given the message when he got back into the country.

"We wrote that we were looking for some kind of direction because we'd lost our son," Mrs. Shively said.

The Shivelys didn't expect to hear from Sam, but he called them as soon as he got their note. He asked them to come to Carthage for lunch.

The Shivelys met Sam and a friendship soon developed. Sam, whose son Philip was killed in a car accident in 1990, tried to help them through this roughest time of their lives.

"I felt like Sharon lost it," Sam said. "She was full of emotion. It was John who I felt was concealing his emotion. I was really praying, 'How can I really bring the reality of his (Bradley's) being with the Lord to these people?'"

One day Sam's assistant asked Shively what his son's basketball number was. "Twenty," Shively replied. Suddenly, Sam had an idea.

"That was like an open door," Sam said. He began work on the Bradley figurine, a basketball player whose number is 20, immediately.

The process of making one of the Precious Moments figurines usually takes between 1½ to 2 years, Sam said. But the original Bradley prototypes were finished in just a few months.

"It was a first priority thing," Sam said.

Sam called the Shivelys and said he had something for them. It was around Christmas time.

"When he handed me mine, he said 'Be sad no more, you have your Bradley back,'" Mrs. Shively said.

"I still felt like with Sharon, it was hard to comfort her because she was too obsessed with the impossibility of all this," Sam said. "I felt I couldn't do anything to settle it. John, he didn't talk much. He was still behind the wall."

"But when I gave them their figurines, the wall was gone and the obsession vanished. It was like Bradley bounced into the room."

"I can remember it like it just happened." Shively said. "It was like Bradley said 'Dad, what else do you want me to do?'"

The next summer, Sam added another angel to Hallelujah Square, the mural of children in heaven at the front of the Precious Moments chapel. He added Bradley, the basketball player.

"It was not only done for John and Sharon's sake," Sam said, "I believe there

John and Sharon Shively are comforted by Sam Butcher over the loss of their son, Bradley.

are a million Bradleys out there. He brought a common ground to heaven."

Many people have been touched by not only Bradley's story, but by the other angels in Hallelujah Square, many of whom represent other real children.

"It's a relationship you can't even describe," Shively said. "It's like any bereaved parent who comes here, for them to know our children represents their children."

The Shivelys moved to Carthage eight months ago and both work at Precious Moments; Sharon works in special events and John at the RV Park.

They visit Bradley at the chapel every day.

"We don't feel like it's work," Shively said. "Plus, we get to work with Bradley. One of the benefits of working here is that we have a key and can get in any time day or night."

With the holidays coming, they are facing one of the toughest times of the year as a grieving family.

"We don't put up a tree or anything anymore," Mrs. Shively said. "We don't decorate at home. This (Precious Moments) is where our Christmas is now."

Mrs. Shively said her son loved Christmas, with one of the most important aspects for him being the Christmas is Caring program, where he helped less fortunate people have a good Christmas.

"He would come home and get stuff he had to give to the kids because he felt sorry for them," Mrs. Shively said.

Precious Moments started a program this year called Christmas is Sharing, where the company is working to make sure underprivileged children get toys on their wish list.

Sam attributes the company's involvement with the Salvation Army directly to the Shivelys and their ideas and contributions.

He said the company's charity involvement will increase in the future.

But the helping spirit is helping the Shivelys through the holiday season. Sam, too, has a difficult time during this time of year.

"The holidays are a pretty painful thing to me still," he said. "It's something I still haven't worked out. To me, Christmas is every day, when I feel something very special. For some reason, because of the death of Philip and other very painful experiences I've gone through, Christmas is something I don't try to stress."

About losing a child, Sam said it's something that's always with a grieving parent.

"I really believe you never really come out of it," he said. "As much as I feel I need

to minister to people, I don't feel like I have anybody to go to. The only way to get out of it is to be creative. It helps to talk to people, but there are times I have that people don't know about because I don't talk about it."

Sam's creativity has helped the Shivelys cope with their grief, and they have seen how he has helped other families, too.

"It seemed like when we were really down and needed something, he did something that would help us," Mrs. Shively said.

"He does that for everybody," added her husband. "He's doing it constantly."

Sam feels that helping others is a necessity that can't be shrugged away just because he has made a successful business.

Successful people who say they don't have time anymore for others "use that as an excuse to separate themselves from people because they think they've arrived at the point they're star-status or whatever," Sam said.

"When I meet someone who feels something, no one feels it more than I do," he said. "I feel like it would be betraying my character to say, 'I'm busy.'"

525979　Boy Hitching a Ride with Angel
"Going Home"

V	$75	B	$65	S	$60	SRD	$60
GC	$70	TRP	$60	H	$60		

Comments: 1991; Original Retail $60.00
Dedicated to the memory of Philip Butcher.

Personal Data: _____

____Want Mark ____ Mark _____ Purch. 19__ Pd $ _____

526010　*9" EASTER SEALS –*
Girl Holding Cat with Dome
"You Are Such A Purr-fect Friend"

LE 1992 - 5 YEARS OLD	V	$610-655
	GC	$550-600

Comments: 1990; Original Retail $500.00
1992 Easter Seals 9" Commemorative Figurine. At 2,000 production, this quantity supplied the demand. Not scarce as 1500. Very attractive piece!

Personal Data: _____

____Want Mark ____ Mark _____ Purch. 19__ Pd $ _____

526037　Boy with Gold Crown/Jeweled Ring
"A Prince Of A Guy"

S	$40	H	$35	SRD	$35

Comments: 1994; Original Retail $35.00
This figurine was available in the Fall of 1995 through special buying programs. Only the "catalog" exclusive figurines were to have the Ship mark and "1995 Catalog Exclusive" on the bases; however, the Princess did not come with the notation. The base of the Prince figurine did say "1995 Catalog Exclusive." In late '95, the Prince and Princess (from the Spring '96 line) arrived at retailers' with the Ship mark. In my opinion, it would be difficult to know whether the Princess was a part of the catalog exclusive or the '96 line. Will probably not be a best seller.

Personal Data: _____

____Want Mark ____ Mark _____ Purch. 19__ Pd $ _____

526053　Girl with Gold Crown/Jeweled Ring
"Pretty As A Princess"

S	$40	H	$35	SRD	$35

Comments: 1994; Original Retail $35.00
This figurine was available in the Spring of 1995 through special buying programs. See *Boy with Gold Crown/Jeweled Ring* for more information. Found with one of points on her crown left unpainted.

Personal Data: _____

____Want Mark ____ Mark _____ Purch. 19__ Pd $ _____

526061　Century Circle Exclusive
Little Mermaid Sitting on Oyster Shell
"The Pearl Of Great Price"

SRD $50

Comments: 1996; Original Retail $50.00
This figurine is the 1997 CCR event figurine.

Personal Data: _____

____Want Mark ____ Mark _____ Purch. 19__ Pd $ _____

526142　Girl Holding Map of Carthage
"I Would Be Lost Without You"

V	$38	B	$30	S	$30	SRD	$30
GC	$30	TRP	$30	H	$30		

Comments: 1990; Original Retail $27.50/$30.00
This was reported to be a First in Series, however no Second in Series followed. Most "gift buyers" will not understand why Carthage and Joplin are marked on the figurine. Probably a future suspension piece. Perhaps instead of "Carthage," chapel may have been more relevant for collectors.

Personal Data: _____

____Want Mark ____ Mark _____ Purch. 19__ Pd $ _____

526150　Boy with Duck
"Friends To The Very End"

RETIRED 1997

	B	$75	S	$70
	TRP	$70	H	$70

Comments: 1993; Original Retail $40.00/$45.00
Ouch! Cute piece! Retail up in 1996 – ouch!

Personal Data: _____

____Want Mark ____ Mark _____ Purch. 19__ Pd $ _____

526185　Girl Holding Bouquet of Roses
"You Are My Happiness"

LE 1992 - 5 YEARS OLD	V	$65
	GC	$60

Comments: 1990; Original Retail $37.50
Limited to One Year Production (1992). A beautiful piece! Expect a secondary market rise in another year or two. This was the easiest of pieces to sell as a gift item in 1992. Get this piece and display her with the '93 L.E. figurine 523593. She's so pretty and I feel she's a must for your collection. Price down from '96.

Personal Data: _____

____Want Mark ____ Mark _____ Purch. 19__ Pd $ _____

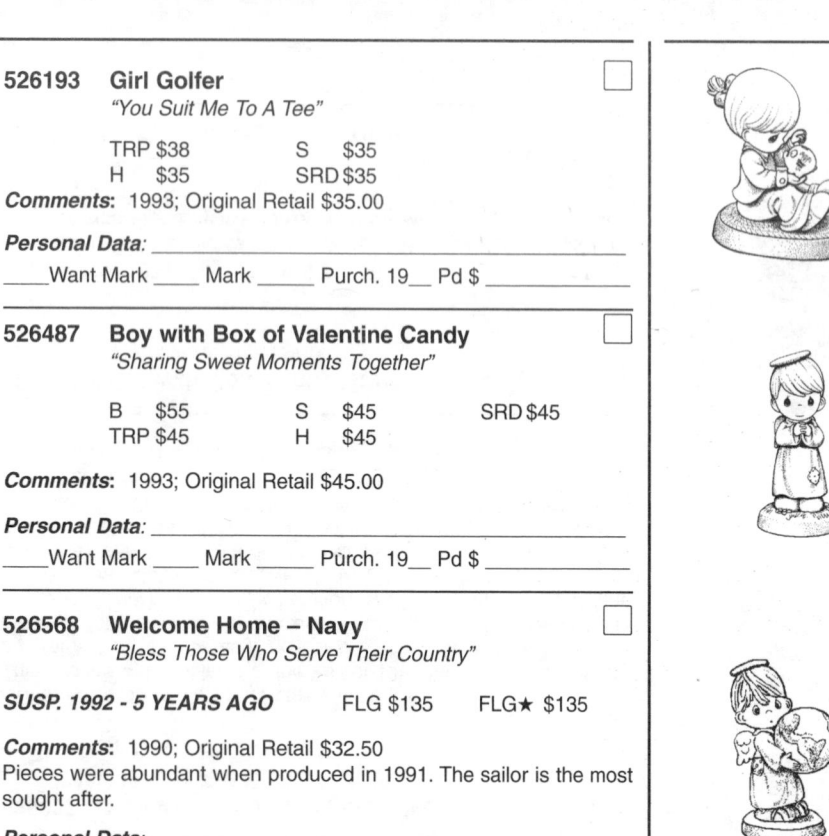

526193 Girl Golfer
"You Suit Me To A Tee"

TRP $38	S $35	
H $35	SRD $35	

Comments: 1993; Original Retail $35.00

Personal Data: _____

____Want Mark ____ Mark _____ Purch. 19__ Pd $ _____

526487 Boy with Box of Valentine Candy
"Sharing Sweet Moments Together"

B $55	S $45	SRD $45
TRP $45	H $45	

Comments: 1993; Original Retail $45.00

Personal Data: _____

____Want Mark ____ Mark _____ Purch. 19__ Pd $ _____

526568 Welcome Home – Navy
"Bless Those Who Serve Their Country"

SUSP. 1992 - 5 YEARS AGO FLG $135 FLG★ $135

Comments: 1990; Original Retail $32.50
Pieces were abundant when produced in 1991. The sailor is the most sought after.

Personal Data: _____

____Want Mark ____ Mark _____ Purch. 19__ Pd $ _____

526576 Welcome Home – Army
"Bless Those Who Serve Their Country"

SUSP. 1992 - 5 YEARS AGO FLG $50 FLG★ $45

Comments: 1990; Original Retail $32.50

Personal Data: _____

____Want Mark ____ Mark _____ Purch. 19__ Pd $ _____

526584 Welcome Home – Air Force
"Bless Those Who Serve Their Country"

SUSP. 1992 - 5 YEARS AGO FLG $50 FLG★ $45

Comments: 1990; Original Retail $32.50.

Personal Data: _____

____Want Mark ____ Mark _____ Purch. 19__ Pd $ _____

526827 *EASTER SEALS* – Girl with Piggy Bank/Coin
"You Can Always Count On Me"

S $35	H $30	SRD $30

Comments: 1995; Original Retail $30.00
Reported with an Easter Seal insignia backwards on pig. Add $50.

Personal Data: _____

____Want Mark ____ Mark _____ Purch. 19__ Pd $ _____

526835 Praying Angel
"The Lord Is With You"

S $30	H $27.50	SRD $27.50

Comments: 1995; Original Retail $27.50.

Personal Data: _____

____Want Mark ____ Mark _____ Purch. 19__ Pd $ _____

526886 *9" EASTER SEALS* –
Angel with World in Hands
"He's Got The Whole World In His Hands"

LE 1995 - 2 YEARS AGO
TRP $575-600 S $550-600 H $550

Comments: 1994; 9" Easter Seals Commemorative Figurine for '95 Limited to 2,000 Numbered Pieces. Nice! Nice! Does all this one million go to Easter Seals? *See #25, page XIV.*

Personal Data: _____

____Want Mark ____ Mark _____ Purch. 19__ Pd $ _____

526916 ♪ *MUSICAL* – Girl by Wishing Well
"Wishing You Were Here"

GC $125	TRP $110	H $100
B $110	S $100	SRD $100

Comments: 1992; Original Retail $100.00
Plays *When You Wish Upon A Star*. This is a large piece. Nice... not overproduced due to size. Since this has a higher retail price, retailers order less, thus not a big production is required for retailer demand. It is likely that this piece will be suspended. I feel she is different from the norm and a nice piece for you to include in your collection, if affordable for you. Place on bottom shelf in your cabinet with glass shelves.

Personal Data: _____

____Want Mark ____ Mark _____ Purch. 19__ Pd $ _____

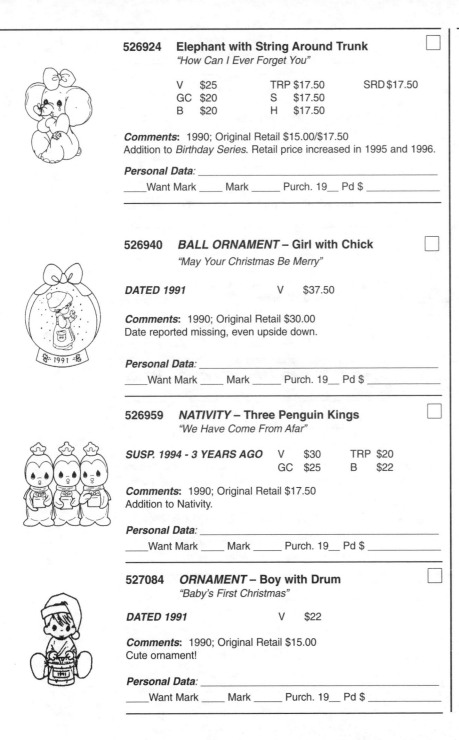

526924 **Elephant with String Around Trunk**
"How Can I Ever Forget You"

V	$25	TRP	$17.50	SRD	$17.50
GC	$20	S	$17.50		
B	$20	H	$17.50		

Comments: 1990; Original Retail $15.00/$17.50
Addition to *Birthday Series*. Retail price increased in 1995 and 1996.

Personal Data: _____
____Want Mark ____ Mark _____ Purch. 19__ Pd $ _____

526940 **BALL ORNAMENT – Girl with Chick**
"May Your Christmas Be Merry"

DATED 1991   V $37.50

Comments: 1990; Original Retail $30.00
Date reported missing, even upside down.

Personal Data: _____
____Want Mark ____ Mark _____ Purch. 19__ Pd $ _____

526959 **NATIVITY – Three Penguin Kings**
"We Have Come From Afar"

SUSP. 1994 - 3 YEARS AGO	V	$30	TRP	$20
	GC	$25	B	$22

Comments: 1990; Original Retail $17.50
Addition to Nativity.

Personal Data: _____
____Want Mark ____ Mark _____ Purch. 19__ Pd $ _____

527084 **ORNAMENT – Boy with Drum**
"Baby's First Christmas"

DATED 1991   V $22

Comments: 1990; Original Retail $15.00
Cute ornament!

Personal Data: _____
____Want Mark ____ Mark _____ Purch. 19__ Pd $ _____

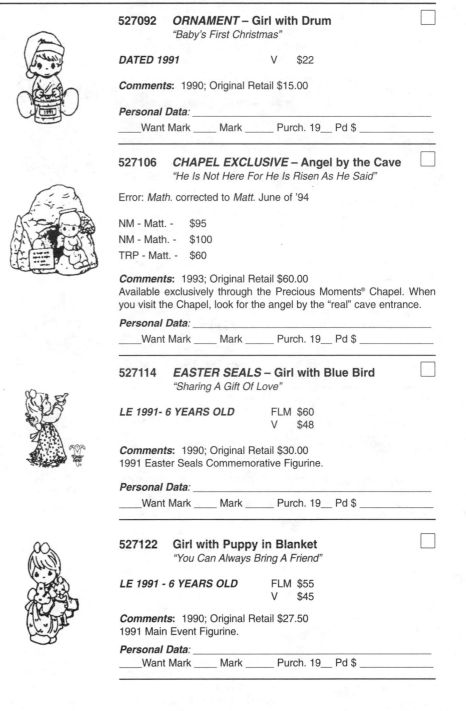

527092 **ORNAMENT – Girl with Drum**
"Baby's First Christmas"

DATED 1991   V $22

Comments: 1990; Original Retail $15.00

Personal Data: _____
____Want Mark ____ Mark _____ Purch. 19__ Pd $ _____

527106 **CHAPEL EXCLUSIVE – Angel by the Cave**
"He Is Not Here For He Is Risen As He Said"

Error: *Math.* corrected to *Matt.* June of '94

NM - Matt. -	$95
NM - Math. -	$100
TRP - Matt. -	$60

Comments: 1993; Original Retail $60.00
Available exclusively through the Precious Moments® Chapel. When you visit the Chapel, look for the angel by the "real" cave entrance.

Personal Data: _____
____Want Mark ____ Mark _____ Purch. 19__ Pd $ _____

527114 **EASTER SEALS – Girl with Blue Bird**
"Sharing A Gift Of Love"

LE 1991- 6 YEARS OLD	FLM	$60
	V	$48

Comments: 1990; Original Retail $30.00
1991 Easter Seals Commemorative Figurine.

Personal Data: _____
____Want Mark ____ Mark _____ Purch. 19__ Pd $ _____

527122 **Girl with Puppy in Blanket**
"You Can Always Bring A Friend"

LE 1991 - 6 YEARS OLD	FLM	$55
	V	$45

Comments: 1990; Original Retail $27.50
1991 Main Event Figurine.

Personal Data: _____
____Want Mark ____ Mark _____ Purch. 19__ Pd $ _____

527165 _ORNAMENT_ – Expectant Mother
"The Good Lord Always Delivers"

SUSP. 1993 - 4 YEARS AGO   V $30
             GC $22   B $20

Comments: 1990; Original Retail $15.00
Not sought after.

Personal Data: _____
___Want Mark ___ Mark ____ Purch. 19__ Pd $ _____

527173   Easter Seals – Girl Signing "I Love You"
"A Universal Love"

LE 1992 - 5 YEARS OLD   V $85   GC $75

Comments: 1990; Original Retail $32.50
1992 Limited Edition Commemorative Easter Seals Figurine. Easter Seals pieces quite abundant, but this piece is very, very sought after. Sought after but price fell from '96 somewhat.

Personal Data: _____
___Want Mark ___ Mark ____ Purch. 19__ Pd $ _____

527211   _ORNAMENT_ – Girl Carrying Candle
"Share In The Warmth Of Christmas"

    B $20   S $17   SRD $17
   TRP $18   H $17

Comments: 1992; Original Retail $15.00/$17.00
Retail price increased in 1995.

Personal Data: _____
___Want Mark ___ Mark ____ Purch. 19__ Pd $ _____

527238   Baby Speaking into Microphone
"Baby's First Word"

MM $40   B $30   S $25   SRD $25
GC $25   TRP $25   H $25

Comments: 1992; Original Retail $25.00
1992 Addition to _Baby's First Series_. Found with MM.

Personal Data: _____
___Want Mark ___ Mark ____ Purch. 19__ Pd $ _____

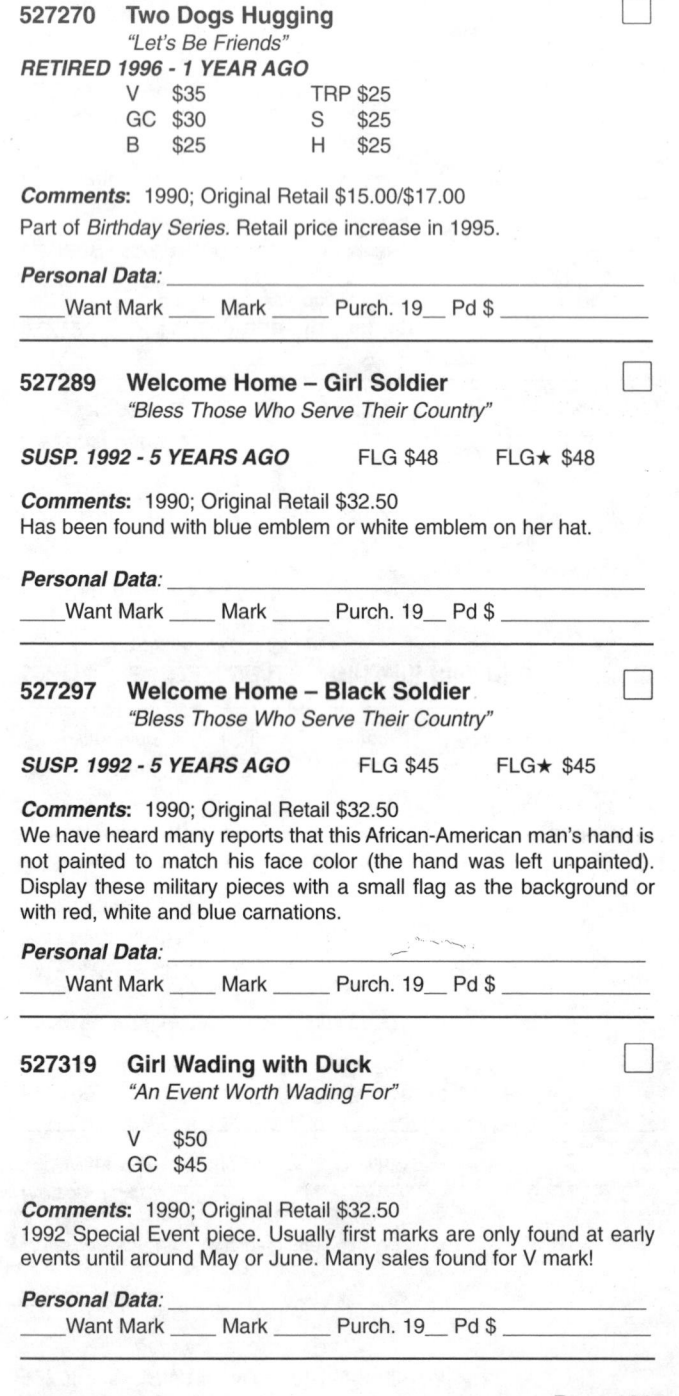

527270   Two Dogs Hugging
"Let's Be Friends"
RETIRED 1996 - 1 YEAR AGO
    V $35   TRP $25
   GC $30   S $25
    B $25   H $25

Comments: 1990; Original Retail $15.00/$17.00
Part of _Birthday Series_. Retail price increase in 1995.

Personal Data: _____
___Want Mark ___ Mark ____ Purch. 19__ Pd $ _____

527289   Welcome Home – Girl Soldier
"Bless Those Who Serve Their Country"

SUSP. 1992 - 5 YEARS AGO   FLG $48   FLG★ $48

Comments: 1990; Original Retail $32.50
Has been found with blue emblem or white emblem on her hat.

Personal Data: _____
___Want Mark ___ Mark ____ Purch. 19__ Pd $ _____

527297   Welcome Home – Black Soldier
"Bless Those Who Serve Their Country"

SUSP. 1992 - 5 YEARS AGO   FLG $45   FLG★ $45

Comments: 1990; Original Retail $32.50
We have heard many reports that this African-American man's hand is not painted to match his face color (the hand was left unpainted). Display these military pieces with a small flag as the background or with red, white and blue carnations.

Personal Data: _____
___Want Mark ___ Mark ____ Purch. 19__ Pd $ _____

527319   Girl Wading with Duck
"An Event Worth Wading For"

    V $50
   GC $45

Comments: 1990; Original Retail $32.50
1992 Special Event piece. Usually first marks are only found at early events until around May or June. Many sales found for V mark!

Personal Data: _____
___Want Mark ___ Mark ____ Purch. 19__ Pd $ _____

527327 ***ORNAMENT* – Soldier**
"Onward Christmas Soldiers"

TRP $20		H	$16
S $18		SRD	$16

Comments: 1993; Original Retail $16.00

Personal Data: _____
___Want Mark ___ Mark ___ Purch. 19__ Pd $ _____

527335 **Indian Girl with Tulip**
"Bless-um You"

GC	$45	TRP $35		H	$35
B	$42	S $35		SRD	$35

Comments: 1992; Original Retail $35.00
This piece has been found with a GC and a B mark, one on top of the other! Add $100 to GC mark. Another collector found that one of the hearts on the headband was not painted - add $25.

Personal Data: _____
___Want Mark ___ Mark ___ Purch. 19__ Pd $ _____

527343 **Chicken Blowing out Birthday Candle**
"Happy Birdie"
SUSP. 1996 - 1 YEAR AGO

GC	$28	TRP $20		H	$20
B	$25	S $20			

Comments: 1992; Original Retail $16.00/$17.50
1992 Addition to *Birthday Series*. Retail price increased in 1995 and 1996.

Personal Data: _____
___Want Mark ___ Mark ___ Purch. 19__ Pd $ _____

527378 **Girl Decorating Boy**
"You Are My Favorite Star"
RETIRED 1997

GC	$95	TRP $87		H	$85
B	$90	S $85			

Comments: 1992; Original Retail $60.00
A collector has this piece without the "PM" logo.

Personal Data: _____
___Want Mark ___ Mark ___ Purch. 19__ Pd $ _____

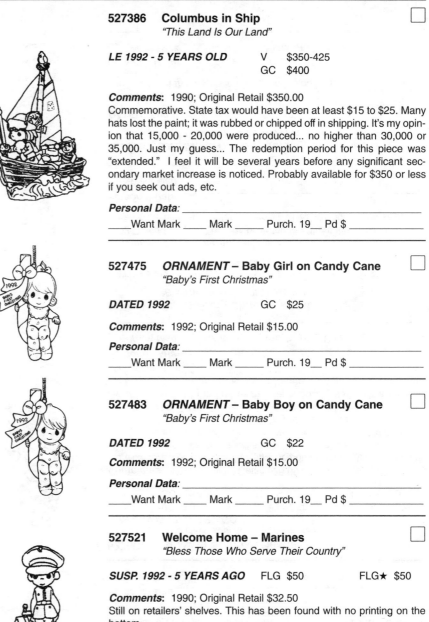

527386 **Columbus in Ship**
"This Land Is Our Land"

LE 1992 - 5 YEARS OLD		V	$350-425
		GC	$400

Comments: 1990; Original Retail $350.00
Commemorative. State tax would have been at least $15 to $25. Many hats lost the paint; it was rubbed or chipped off in shipping. It's my opinion that 15,000 - 20,000 were produced... no higher than 30,000 or 35,000. Just my guess... The redemption period for this piece was "extended." I feel it will be several years before any significant secondary market increase is noticed. Probably available for $350 or less if you seek out ads, etc.

Personal Data: _____
___Want Mark ___ Mark ___ Purch. 19__ Pd $ _____

527475 ***ORNAMENT* – Baby Girl on Candy Cane**
"Baby's First Christmas"

DATED 1992		GC	$25

Comments: 1992; Original Retail $15.00

Personal Data: _____
___Want Mark ___ Mark ___ Purch. 19__ Pd $ _____

527483 ***ORNAMENT* – Baby Boy on Candy Cane**
"Baby's First Christmas"

DATED 1992		GC	$22

Comments: 1992; Original Retail $15.00

Personal Data: _____
___Want Mark ___ Mark ___ Purch. 19__ Pd $ _____

527521 **Welcome Home – Marines**
"Bless Those Who Serve Their Country"

SUSP. 1992 - 5 YEARS AGO	FLG $50	FLG★	$50

Comments: 1990; Original Retail $32.50
Still on retailers' shelves. This has been found with no printing on the bottom.

Personal Data: _____
___Want Mark ___ Mark ___ Purch. 19__ Pd $ _____

527556 Girl Sharing Wordless Book with Two Children

"Bring The Little Ones To Jesus"

| V | $105 | B | $95 | S | $90 | SRD $90 |
| GC | $100 | TRP | $90 | H | $90 | |

Comments: 1990; Original Retail $90.00
First in a Series of figurines to benefit Child Evangelism Fellowship (CEF), an international, interdenominational group which works with children. See Vol. 9, #3, page 20 of *Precious Collectibles*™ for the story of this figurine. The Damien-Dutton figurine rose higher on the secondary market due to a special offering directly from the Society and was available for a limited production year. Bible accompanies this outstanding figurine.

Personal Data: _____

____Want Mark ____ Mark _____ Purch. 19__ Pd $ _____

527564 Uncle Sam Kneeling

"God Bless The USA"

LE 1992 - 5 YEARS OLD

| | V | $40-45 |
| | GC | $30-35 |

Comments: 1990; Original Retail $32.50
1992 National Day of Prayer Figurine. Display with military pieces. Sam presented President Bush with a similar figurine.

Personal Data: _____

____Want Mark ____ Mark _____ Purch. 19__ Pd $ _____

527580 Girl Wrapped with Ribbon

"Tied Up For The Holidays"

SUSP. 1996 - 1 YEAR AGO

| B | $55 | S | $45 |
| TRP | $45 | H | $45 |

Comments: 1992; Original Retail $40.00

Personal Data: _____

____Want Mark ____ Mark _____ Purch. 19__ Pd $ _____

527599 Boy on Sled with Turtle

"Bringing You A Merry Christmas"

RETIRED 1995 - 2 YEARS AGO

| B | $90 | S | $85 | TRP | $70 |

Comments: 1992; Original Retail $45.00

Personal Data: _____

____Want Mark ____ Mark _____ Purch. 19__ Pd $ _____

527629 Boy in Santa Suit

"Wishing You A Ho Ho Ho"

| GC | $48 | TRP | $40 | H | $40 |
| B | $45 | S | $40 | SRD $40 | |

Comments: 1992; Original Retail $40.00
Christmas pieces not found at shows, etc., as much as the regular line. Time for a suspension or retirement.

Personal Data _____

____Want Mark ____ Mark _____ Purch. 19__ Pd $ _____

527661 Girl with String of Hearts

"You Have Touched So Many Hearts"

SUSP. 1996 - 1 YEAR AGO

| V | $38 | B | $37.50 | S | $37.50 |
| GC | $37.50 | TRP | $37.50 | H | $37.50 |

Comments: 1991; Original Retail $35.00/$37.50
Identical to E-2821, except this figurine comes with letters to personalize the hearts. That piece will surely be suspended! The letters just did not produce quality results, in my opinion... at least not on my piece. ☺ (Looks almost as bad as "my painted" piece I painted in the Orient! Skill is definitely required to paint these li'l figurines! I probably would be fired the first day!) Reported in 1996 with a missing mark. We've seen price increases before suspension & retirement announcements.

Personal Data _____

____Want Mark ____ Mark _____ Purch. 19__ Pd $ _____

527688 Girl Holding Christmas List

"But The Greatest Of These Is Love"

DATED 1992

| | V | $ | GC | $30 |
| | MM | $35 | | |

Comments: 1992; Original Retail $27.50
1992 Dated Figurine. This has been found without the inspiration decal on the bottom; also found with a MM. Easily found at these prices.

Personal Data _____

____Want Mark ____ Mark _____ Purch. 19__ Pd $ _____

527696 ORNAMENT – Girl Holding Christmas List

"But The Greatest Of These Is Love"

DATED 1992

| | GC | $40 |

Comments: 1992; Original Retail $15.00
Found without the inspiration decal on the bottom.

Personal Data _____

____Want Mark ____ Mark _____ Purch. 19__ Pd $ _____

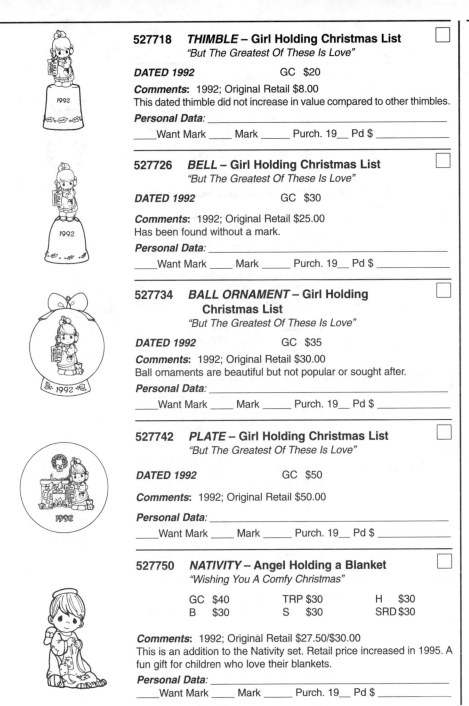

527718   ***THIMBLE* – Girl Holding Christmas List**
"But The Greatest Of These Is Love"

DATED 1992   GC $20

Comments: 1992; Original Retail $8.00
This dated thimble did not increase in value compared to other thimbles.

Personal Data: _____

____Want Mark ____ Mark _____ Purch. 19__ Pd $ _____

527726   ***BELL* – Girl Holding Christmas List**
"But The Greatest Of These Is Love"

DATED 1992   GC $30

Comments: 1992; Original Retail $25.00
Has been found without a mark.

Personal Data: _____

____Want Mark ____ Mark _____ Purch. 19__ Pd $ _____

527734   ***BALL ORNAMENT* – Girl Holding Christmas List**
"But The Greatest Of These Is Love"

DATED 1992   GC $35

Comments: 1992; Original Retail $30.00
Ball ornaments are beautiful but not popular or sought after.

Personal Data: _____

____Want Mark ____ Mark _____ Purch. 19__ Pd $ _____

527742   ***PLATE* – Girl Holding Christmas List**
"But The Greatest Of These Is Love"

DATED 1992   GC $50

Comments: 1992; Original Retail $50.00

Personal Data: _____

____Want Mark ____ Mark _____ Purch. 19__ Pd $ _____

527750   ***NATIVITY* – Angel Holding a Blanket**
"Wishing You A Comfy Christmas"

GC $40	TRP $30	H $30
B $30	S $30	SRD $30

Comments: 1992; Original Retail $27.50/$30.00
This is an addition to the Nativity set. Retail price increased in 1995. A fun gift for children who love their blankets.

Personal Data: _____

____Want Mark ____ Mark _____ Purch. 19__ Pd $ _____

527769   **Octopus Holding Fish**
"I Only Have Arms For You"

GC $20	TRP $17.50	H $17.50
B $17.50	S $17.50	SRD $17.50

Comments: 1992; Original Retail $15.00/$17.50
This is an addition to the *Birthday Series*. Retail price increased in 1995 and 1996.

Personal Data: _____

____Want Mark ____ Mark _____ Purch. 19__ Pd $ _____

527777   **Columbus with Flag and Bear**
"This Land Is Our Land"

LE 1992 - 5 YEARS OLD   GC $32

Comments: 1990; Original Retail $35.00
Seemed to be a slow seller. Commemorative pieces have always seemed to be overproduced, probably due to retailers' orders. Price fell below retail on many sales.

Personal Data: _____

____Want Mark ____ Mark _____ Purch. 19__ Pd $ _____

528021   ***CHAPEL EXCLUSIVE* – ORNAMENT**
Timmy at Chapel
"There's A Christian Welcome Here"

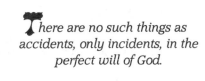

NM $35	TRP $22.50	H $22.50
B $25	S $22.50	SRD $22.50

Comments: 1992; Original Retail $22.50
Available only at the Chapel... very attractive ornament. I suggest you get one!

Personal Data: _____

____Want Mark ____ Mark _____ Purch. 19__ Pd $ _____

There are no such things as accidents, only incidents, in the perfect will of God.

528072 **_NATIVITY_ – Cart with Chicken**
"Nativity Cart"

TRP	$20	H	$18.50
S	$18.50	SRD	$18.50

Comments: 1993; Original Retail $18.50
Nativity Addition.

Personal Data: _____
____Want Mark ____ Mark _____ Purch. 19__ Pd $ _____

528080 **Girl with Signboard on Back**
"Follow Your Heart"

LE 1995 - 2 YEARS OLD	TRP	$50
	S	$38

Comments: 1994; Original Retail $30.00
1995 Special Event figurine. Collector reports decal on backwards.
Increase $100 for this error.

Personal Data: _____
____Want Mark ____ Mark _____ Purch. 19__ Pd $ _____

528137 **_MINI NATIVITY_ – African-American Boy/Scroll**
"Have I Got News For You"

TRP	$20	H	$17
S	$17	SRD	$17

Comments: 1994; Original Retail $16.00/$17.00
Mini Nativity addition. Retail price increased in 1995.
Collector reported decal on backwards; increase $100 for this error.

Personal Data: _____
____Want Mark ____ Mark _____ Purch. 19__ Pd $ _____

528218 **_ORNAMENT_ – Girl Angel with Basket**
"Sending You A White Christmas"

TRP	$20	H	$16
S	$16	SRD	$16

Comments: 1994; Original Retail $16.00

Personal Data: _____
____Want Mark ____ Mark _____ Purch. 19__ Pd $ _____

528226 **_ORNAMENT_ – Boy in Santa Suit**
"Bringing You A Merry Christmas"

TRP	$20	H	$16
S	$16	SRD	$16

Comments: 1993; Original Retail $16.00

Personal Data: _____
____Want Mark ____ Mark _____ Purch. 19__ Pd $ _____

528609 **Girl with Kite and Kitten**
"Sending My Love Your Way"

LE 1995 – 2 YEARS OLD	TRP	$50
	S	$45

Comments: 1994; Original Retail $40.00
Available only at DSR (Distinguished Service Retailers) shops for
Enesco special catalog promotion. Has been reported missing the kitten and kite strings, and the stripes not painted on the kite.

Personal Data: _____
____Want Mark ____ Mark _____ Purch. 19__ Pd $ _____

528617 **_EASTER EGG_ – Girl Looking at Goose**
"Make A Joyful Noise"

DATED 1993	GC $32	B	$28

Comments: 1992; Original Retail $27.50

Personal Data: _____
____Want Mark ____ Mark _____ Purch. 19__ Pd $ _____

528633 **Two Girls with Kittens and Gifts**
"To A Very Special Sister"

TRP	$70	H	$60
S	$65	SRD	$60

Comments: 1993; Original Retail $60.00

Personal Data: _____
____Want Mark ____ Mark _____ Purch. 19__ Pd $ _____

528846   ORNAMENT – Girl on Skis
"It's So Uplifting To Have A Friend Like You"

B	$22.50	S	$18	SRD $17
TRP	$18	H	$17	

Comments: 1992; Original Retail $16.00/$17.00
Perfect retirement candidate.

Personal Data: _____
____Want Mark ____ Mark _____ Purch. 19__ Pd $ _____

528862   Girl Holding Up a Torch
"America, You're Beautiful"

LE 1993 - 4 YEARS OLD   GC $50   B $45

Comments: 1992; Original Retail $35.00
1993 National Day of Prayer Figurine.

Personal Data: _____
____Want Mark ____ Mark _____ Purch. 19__ Pd $ _____

528870   ORNAMENT – Bride with Groom in Top Hat
"Our First Christmas Together"

DATED 1992   GC $25

Comments: 1992; Original Retail $17.50
Except for the date, this design is identical to the 1991 ornament.
See #28, page XIV.

Personal Data: _____
____Want Mark ____ Mark _____ Purch. 19__ Pd $ _____

529079   MEDALLION – Cruise 1993
"Friends Never Drift Apart"

DATED 1993 $450

Comments: 1993 , Special cruise medallion given as a gift.

Personal Data: _____
____Want Mark ____ Mark _____ Purch. 19__ Pd $ _____

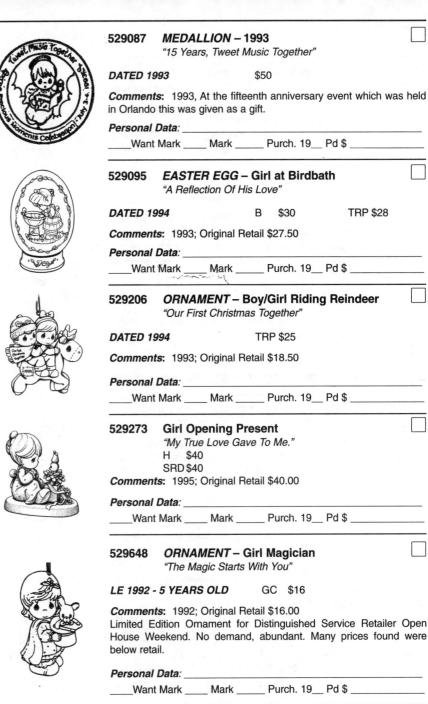

529087   MEDALLION – 1993
"15 Years, Tweet Music Together"

DATED 1993 $50

Comments: 1993, At the fifteenth anniversary event which was held in Orlando this was given as a gift.

Personal Data: _____
____Want Mark ____ Mark _____ Purch. 19__ Pd $ _____

529095   EASTER EGG – Girl at Birdbath
"A Reflection Of His Love"

DATED 1994   B $30   TRP $28

Comments: 1993; Original Retail $27.50

Personal Data: _____
____Want Mark ____ Mark _____ Purch. 19__ Pd $ _____

529206   ORNAMENT – Boy/Girl Riding Reindeer
"Our First Christmas Together"

DATED 1994   TRP $25

Comments: 1993; Original Retail $18.50

Personal Data: _____
____Want Mark ____ Mark _____ Purch. 19__ Pd $ _____

529273   Girl Opening Present
"My True Love Gave To Me."
    H $40
    SRD $40
Comments: 1995; Original Retail $40.00

Personal Data: _____
____Want Mark ____ Mark _____ Purch. 19__ Pd $ _____

529648   ORNAMENT – Girl Magician
"The Magic Starts With You"

LE 1992 - 5 YEARS OLD   GC $16

Comments: 1992; Original Retail $16.00
Limited Edition Ornament for Distinguished Service Retailer Open House Weekend. No demand, abundant. Many prices found were below retail.

Personal Data: _____
____Want Mark ____ Mark _____ Purch. 19__ Pd $ _____

529680 9" EASTER SEALS – Girl Holding Bunnies w/Dome
"Gather Your Dreams"

LE 1993 - 4 YEARS OLD   GC $575-600
                            B $550-575

Comments: 1992; Original Retail $500.
1993 9" Easter Seals Commemorative Figurine Limited to 2,000 on numbered pieces. This is shorter than other 9" pieces. Not many sales found.

Personal Data: _____
____Want Mark ____ Mark _____ Purch. 19__ Pd $ _____

529931 Girl Stretching to Touch a Butterfly
"Happiness Is At Our Fingertips"

LE 1993 - 4 YEARS OLD   GC $70   B $60

Comments: 1992; Original Retail $35.00.
It was originally planned that DSR shops could only order four figurines per every 500 catalogs ordered for a special promotion. (This proved to be untrue in several cases. Extras were ordered - sales were evident at department stores.) Two variations have been reported by a collector; the girl was looking forward and had the GC mark, and on another the girl was looking upward and had the B mark. Prices fell in '96-'97.

Personal Data: _____
____Want Mark ____ Mark _____ Purch. 19__ Pd $ _____

529966 Girl Ringing Bell
"Ring Out The Good News"

RETIRED 1997
                B $32   S $30
                TRP $30   H $30

Comments: 1992; Original Retail $27.50/$30.00

Personal Data: _____
____Want Mark ____ Mark _____ Purch. 19__ Pd $ _____

Luck is what enabled others to get where they are talent is what enabled us to get where we are.

529974 ORNAMENT – Girl in Raincoat with Puppy
"An Event For All Seasons"

LE 1993 - 4 YEARS OLD   B $15

Comments: 1993; Original Retail $16.00
This Second Annual Precious Moments Open House Weekend ornament was available on October 9 and 10, 1993, through local Distinguished Service Retailers. Secondary market folks tend to buy extra LEs, etc., and supply the market well. It takes 4 to 5 years to see a big jump on such pieces on the secondary market. Price fell in '96-'97!

Personal Data: _____
____Want Mark ____ Mark _____ Purch. 19__ Pd $ _____

529982 Girl Blowing Bubbles
"Memories Are Made Of This"

LE 1994 - 3 YEARS OLD   B $48   TRP $40

Comments: 1993; Original Retail $30.00
Available exclusively through Distinguished Service Retailers hosting Special Events in 1994. Looks similar to girl with blue bird. Collector reports having kitty with whiskers only on one side.

Personal Data: _____
____Want Mark ____ Mark _____ Purch. 19__ Pd $ _____

530026 EASTER SEALS – Girl Holding Trophy Cup
"You're My Number One Friend"

LE 1993 - 4 YEARS OLD   GC $55   . B $40

Comments: 1992; Original Retail $30.00
1993 Easter Seals Commemorative Figurine.
A collector found this piece with a TRP signed by Sam. Does anyone else have a TRP?

Personal Data: _____
____Want Mark ____ Mark _____ Purch. 19__ Pd $ _____

530042 NIGHT LIGHT – 3 pc. set Noah's Ark
"Two By Two"

GC	$135	TRP	$125	H	$125
B	$125	S	$125	SRD	$125

Comments: 1992; Original Retail $125.00
Two By Two Series. Three-piece set includes the Ark (a night light), Noah and his wife. Animals debut each year for this set. See complete listing in the descriptive index.

Personal Data: _____
____Want Mark ____ Mark _____ Purch. 19__ Pd $ _____

530077 **Noah's Ark**
"Sheep"

B	$18	S	$10	SRD $10
TRP	$14	H	$10	

Comments: 1992; Original Retail $10.00
Part of *Two By Two Series.*

Personal Data: _____
____Want Mark ____ Mark _____ Purch. 19__ Pd $ _____

530085 **Noah's Ark**
"Pigs"

B	$18	S	$12	SRD $12
TRP	$14	H	$12	

Comments: 1992; Original Retail $12.00
Part of *Two By Two Series.*

Personal Data: _____
____Want Mark ____ Mark _____ Purch. 19__ Pd $ _____

530115 **Noah's Ark**
"Giraffes"

B	$22	S	$16	SRD $16
TRP	$16	H	$16	

Comments: 1992; Original Retail $16.00
Part of *Two By Two Series.* Giraffes are collected by many.

Personal Data: _____
____Want Mark ____ Mark _____ Purch. 19__ Pd $ _____

530123 **Noah's Ark**
"Bunnies"

B	$18	S	$10	SRD $9
TRP	$10	H	$9	

Comments: 1992; Original Retail $9.00
Part of *Two By Two Series.*

Personal Data: _____
____Want Mark ____ Mark _____ Purch. 19__ Pd $ _____

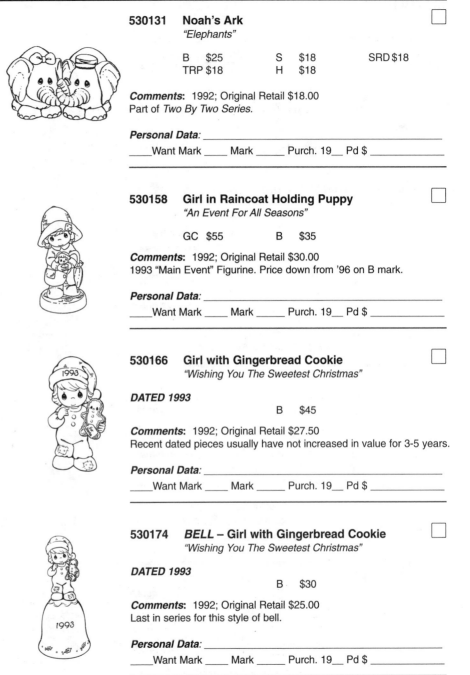

530131 **Noah's Ark**
"Elephants"

B	$25	S	$18	SRD $18
TRP	$18	H	$18	

Comments: 1992; Original Retail $18.00
Part of *Two By Two Series.*

Personal Data: _____
____Want Mark ____ Mark _____ Purch. 19__ Pd $ _____

530158 **Girl in Raincoat Holding Puppy**
"An Event For All Seasons"

GC	$55	B	$35

Comments: 1992; Original Retail $30.00
1993 "Main Event" Figurine. Price down from '96 on B mark.

Personal Data: _____
____Want Mark ____ Mark _____ Purch. 19__ Pd $ _____

530166 **Girl with Gingerbread Cookie**
"Wishing You The Sweetest Christmas"

DATED 1993

B	$45

Comments: 1992; Original Retail $27.50
Recent dated pieces usually have not increased in value for 3-5 years.

Personal Data: _____
____Want Mark ____ Mark _____ Purch. 19__ Pd $ _____

530174 ***BELL* – Girl with Gingerbread Cookie**
"Wishing You The Sweetest Christmas"

DATED 1993

B	$30

Comments: 1992; Original Retail $25.00
Last in series for this style of bell.

Personal Data: _____
____Want Mark ____ Mark _____ Purch. 19__ Pd $ _____

530182 *THIMBLE* – Girl with Gingerbread Cookie
"Wishing You The Sweetest Christmas"

DATED 1993   B $12

Comments: 1992; Original Retail $8.00
Last in series.

Personal Data: _____
____Want Mark ____ Mark _____ Purch. 19__ Pd $ _____

530190 *ORNAMENT* – Girl with Gingerbread Cookie
Round Porcelain Ball/Stand
"Wishing You The Sweetest Christmas"

DATED 1993   B $35

Comments: 1992; Original Retail $30.00
Bas Relief Ornament. Many sales found below original retail.

Personal Data: _____
____Want Mark ____ Mark _____ Purch. 19__ Pd $ _____

530204 *PLATE* – Girl with Gingerbread Cookie
"Wishing You The Sweetest Christmas"

DATED 1993   B $50

Comments: 1992; Original Retail $50.00
Somewhat more popular than other recent dated plates, but will not increase on secondary market any faster than others.

Personal Data: _____
____Want Mark ____ Mark _____ Purch. 19__ Pd $ _____

530212 *ORNAMENT* – Girl w/Gingerbread Cookie
"Wishing You The Sweetest Christmas"

DATED 1993   B $32.50

Comments: 1992; Original Retail $15.00
I predicted this could easily be a top retail seller. It received Ornament of the Year award in '94.

Personal Data: _____
____Want Mark ____ Mark _____ Purch. 19__ Pd $ _____

530255 *ORNAMENT* – Baby Girl with Doll
Riding Stick Horse
"Baby's First Christmas"

DATED 1994   TRP $20

Comments: 1992; Original Retail $16.00

Personal Data: _____
____Want Mark ____ Mark _____ Purch. 19__ Pd $ _____

530263 *ORNAMENT* – Baby Boy with Toy Bear
Riding Stick Horse
"Baby's First Christmas"

DATED 1994   TRP $20

Comments: 1993; Original Retail $16.00

Personal Data: _____
____Want Mark ____ Mark _____ Purch. 19__ Pd $ _____

530387 *ORNAMENT* – Round Porcelain Ball/Stand
Girl in Christmas Tree Dress
"You're As Pretty As A Christmas Tree"

DATED 1994   TRP $45

Comments: 1993; Original Retail $30.00

Personal Data: _____
____Want Mark ____ Mark _____ Purch. 19__ Pd $ _____

530395 *ORNAMENT* – Girl in Christmas Tree Dress
"You're As Pretty As A Christmas Tree"

DATED 1994   TRP $32

Comments: 1993; Original Retail $16.00
More scarce than some past years' dated ornaments.

Personal Data: _____
____Want Mark ____ Mark _____ Purch. 19__ Pd $ _____

530409 *PLATE* – Girl in Christmas Tree Dress
"You're As Pretty As A Christmas Tree"

DATED 1994   TRP $50

Comments: 1993; Original Retail $50.00

Personal Data: _____
____Want Mark ____ Mark _____ Purch. 19__ Pd $ _____

530425   **Girl in Christmas Tree Dress**
"You're As Pretty As A Christmas Tree"

DATED 1994   TRP $38

Comments: 1993; Original Retail $27.50
It is likely that she may be found without the year decal on her star. If so, add $50 for this error. ***See #15, page XIII.***

Personal Data: _____
____Want Mark ____ Mark _____ Purch. 19__ Pd $ _____

530492   **Elephant with Gift "To Jesus"**
"Happy Birthday Jesus"

B $25	S $20	SRD $20
TRP $22	H $20	

Comments: 1992; Original Retail $20.00

Personal Data: _____
____Want Mark ____ Mark _____ Purch. 19__ Pd $ _____

530506   *ORNAMENT* – Boy and Girl in Sleigh
"Our First Christmas Together"

DATED 1993   B $20

Comments: 1992; Original Retail $17.50
Report of missing decal on side of sleigh. Add $50 to secondary market value.

Personal Data: _____
____Want Mark ____ Mark _____ Purch. 19__ Pd $ _____

530697   **Girl Kneeling by Plaque**
"Serenity Prayer Girl"

B $40	S $37.50	SRD $37.50
TRP $37.50	H $37.50	

Comments: 1993; Original Retail $35.00/$37.50
Still "Plentiful!" Retailers report that girls have been shipped in boys' boxes. Reported PMI (Precious Moments® Incorporated) on base. Price increased in '96. Not a collectibles piece.

Personal Data: _____
____Want Mark ____ Mark _____ Purch. 19__ Pd $ _____

530700   **Boy Kneeling by Plaque**
"Serenity Prayer Boy"

B $40	S $37.50	SRD $37.50
TRP $37.50	H $37.50	

Comments: 1993; Original Retail $35.00/$37.50
Retail price increased in 1996. Not being sought after.

Personal Data: _____
____Want Mark ____ Mark _____ Purch. 19__ Pd $ _____

530786   **Angel Directing Choir of Bluebirds**
"15 Happy Years Together - What A Tweet!"

LE 1993 - 4 YEARS OLD   GC $150   B $125

Comments: 1992; Original Retail $100.00
1993 Commemorative Figurine - Limited to 1993 production year. Easily found at these prices for now. One per retailer was available with a walnut base display dome with brass plate and cloisonne 15 year logo Medallion. Add $100 to this figurine and medallion for the secondary market value for this figurine, walnut base dome, and cloisonne.
Personal Data: _____
____Want Mark ____ Mark _____ Purch. 19__ Pd $ _____

530840   *ORNAMENT* – Angel with Music and Bluebird
"15 Years - Tweet Music Together"

LE 1993 - 4 YEARS OLD   GC $20   B $15

Comments: 1992; Original Retail $15.00
1993 Commemorative Ornament - Limited to 1993 production year. Debuted in July 1993.

Personal Data: _____
____Want Mark ____ Mark _____ Purch. 19__ Pd $ _____

530859 ***ORNAMENT*** – **Baby Boy**
"Baby's First Christmas"

DATED 1993   B $22

Comments: 1992; Original Retail $15.00
Has been reported missing the decal.

Personal Data: _____
____Want Mark ____ Mark _____ Purch. 19__ Pd $ _____

530867 ***ORNAMENT*** – **Baby Girl**
"Baby's First Christmas"

DATED 1993   B $20

Comments: 1992; Original Retail $15.00

Personal Data: _____
____Want Mark ____ Mark _____ Purch. 19__ Pd $ _____

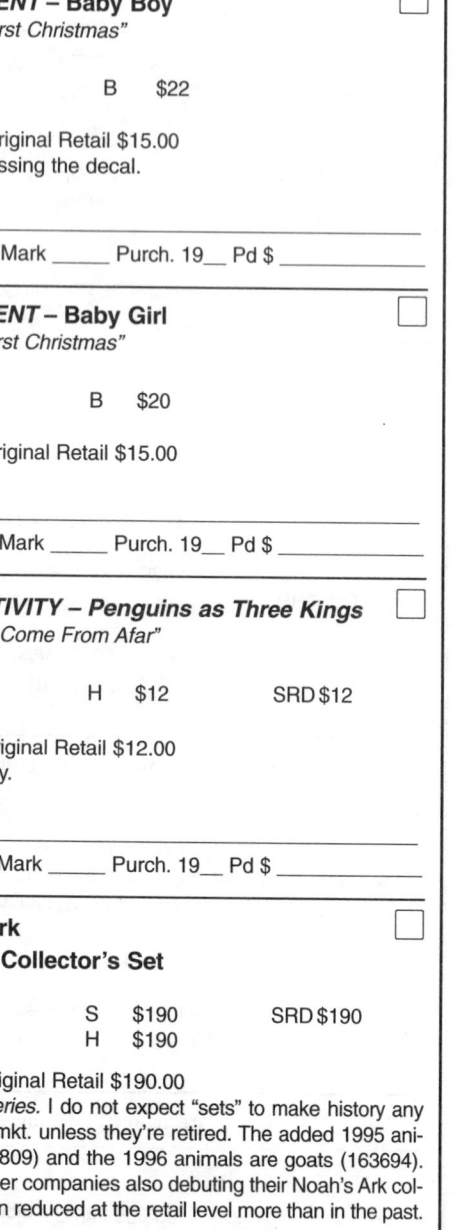

530913 ***MINI NATIVITY*** – **Penguins as Three Kings**
"We Have Come From Afar"

S $15   H $12   SRD $12

Comments: 1995; Original Retail $12.00
Addition to Mini Nativity.

Personal Data: _____
____Want Mark ____ Mark _____ Purch. 19__ Pd $ _____

530948 **Noah's Ark**
8 - Piece Collector's Set

B $200   S $190   SRD $190
TRP $190   H $190

Comments: 1992; Original Retail $190.00
Part of *Two By Two Series.* I do not expect "sets" to make history any time soon on the sec. mkt. unless they're retired. The added 1995 animals were zebras (127809) and the 1996 animals are goats (163694). 1995 and 1996 saw other companies also debuting their Noah's Ark collectibles. Sets have been reduced at the retail level more than in the past.

Personal Data: _____
____Want Mark ____ Mark _____ Purch. 19__ Pd $ _____

See Entries
530042-530131

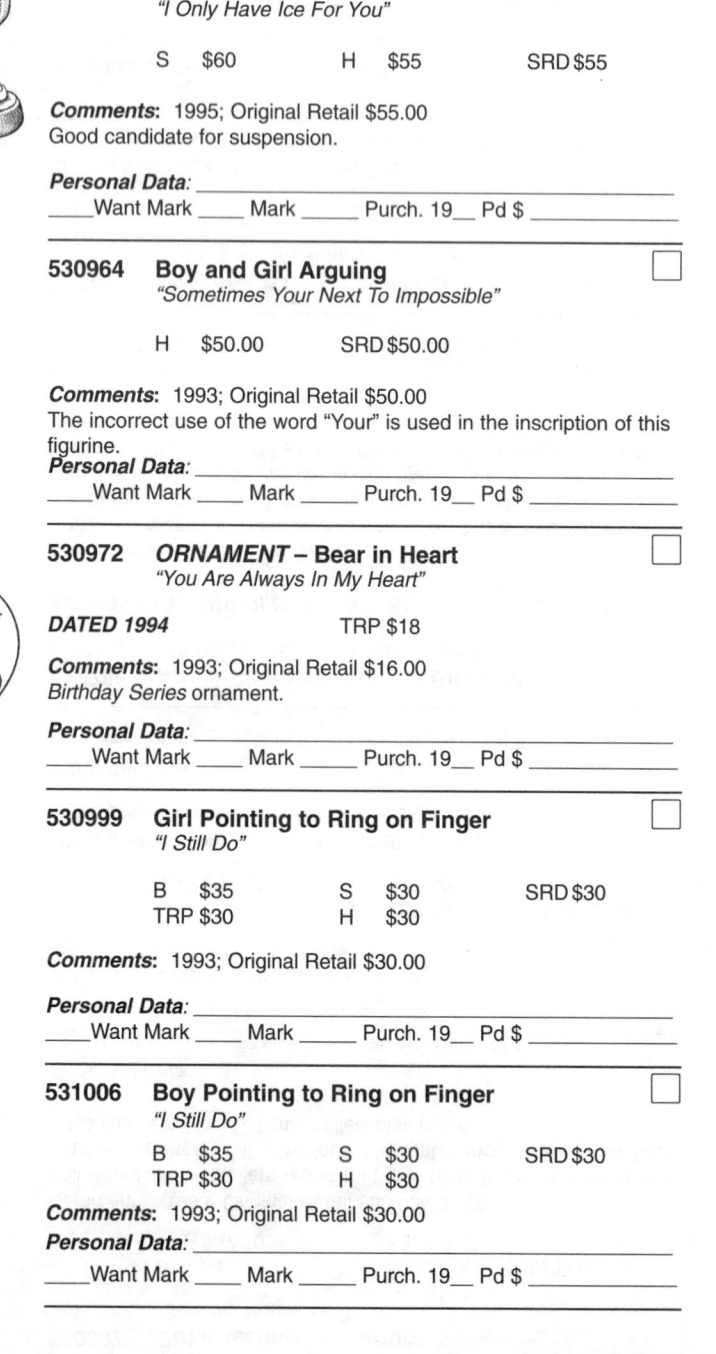

530956 **Boy and Girl Seated on Ice Block**
"I Only Have Ice For You"

S $60   H $55   SRD $55

Comments: 1995; Original Retail $55.00
Good candidate for suspension.

Personal Data: _____
____Want Mark ____ Mark _____ Purch. 19__ Pd $ _____

530964 **Boy and Girl Arguing**
"Sometimes Your Next To Impossible"

H $50.00   SRD $50.00

Comments: 1993; Original Retail $50.00
The incorrect use of the word "Your" is used in the inscription of this figurine.

Personal Data: _____
____Want Mark ____ Mark _____ Purch. 19__ Pd $ _____

530972 ***ORNAMENT*** – **Bear in Heart**
"You Are Always In My Heart"

DATED 1994   TRP $18

Comments: 1993; Original Retail $16.00
Birthday Series ornament.

Personal Data: _____
____Want Mark ____ Mark _____ Purch. 19__ Pd $ _____

530999 **Girl Pointing to Ring on Finger**
"I Still Do"

B $35   S $30   SRD $30
TRP $30   H $30

Comments: 1993; Original Retail $30.00

Personal Data: _____
____Want Mark ____ Mark _____ Purch. 19__ Pd $ _____

531006 **Boy Pointing to Ring on Finger**
"I Still Do"

B $35   S $30   SRD $30
TRP $30   H $30

Comments: 1993; Original Retail $30.00
Personal Data: _____
____Want Mark ____ Mark _____ Purch. 19__ Pd $ _____

531022 **Boy Sitting on Pot with Teddy Bear and Balloons**
"Potty Time"

H $25   SRD $25

Comments: 1996; Original Retail $25.00
Inspired by our own Mouse Reporter, Jeannie Jo, from Boston!

Personal Data: _____
____Want Mark ____ Mark _____ Purch. 19__ Pd $ _____

531057 **Dog with Hair Covering Eyes**
"I Haven't Seen Much of You Lately"

S $15   SRD $13.50
H $13.50

Comments: 1995; Original Retail $13.50
Birthday Series addition.

Personal Data: _____
____Want Mark ____ Mark _____ Purch. 19__ Pd $ _____

531065 **Angel Opening Up a Globe Full of Hearts**
"What The World Needs Is Love"

TRP $50   S $45
H $45   SRD $45

Comments: 1994; Original Retail $45.00

Personal Data: _____
____Want Mark ____ Mark _____ Purch. 19__ Pd $ _____

531073 **Boy Bandaging Tree**
"Money's Not The Only Green Thing Worth Saving"

RETIRED 1996 - 1 YEAR AGO
TRP $55   S $50   H $50

Comments: 1994; Original Retail $50.00
A collector from PA reported she bought this figurine with the cross patch missing on the right arm. Add $100 more when insuring. How about yours?

Personal Data: _____
____Want Mark ____ Mark _____ Purch. 19__ Pd $ _____

531111 ***EASTER SEALS* – Girl with Pail of Oysters**
"It Is No Secret What God Can Do"

LE 1994 - 3 YEARS OLD   B $40   TRP $35
Comments: 1993; Original Retail $30.00
1994 Easter Seals Commemorative Figurine.

Personal Data: _____
____Want Mark ____ Mark _____ Purch. 19__ Pd $ _____

531138 **Girl Painting Stripes on Rocking Horse**
"What A Difference You've Made In My Life"

S $50   H $50   SRD $50
Comments: 1995; Original Retail $50

Personal Data: _____
____Want Mark ____ Mark _____ Purch. 19__ Pd $ _____

531146 **Hispanic Girl Holding Rose**
"Vaya Con Dios (To Go With God)"

TRP $38   S $35   H $35   SRD $35

Comments: 1994; Original Retail $32.50/$35.00
This figurine commemorates a young girl's fifteenth birthday. In the Hispanic culture, on her fifteenth birthday, a young lady is honored at a Quinceañera where she wears a lovely dress and receives gifts. This señorita figurine can be compared to the Indian in Canoe figurines with variations of dark hair and grey hair. Retail increased in 1996.

Personal Data: _____
____Want Mark ____ Mark _____ Purch. 19__ Pd $ _____

531162 **Girl with Hole in Shoe**
"Bless Your Sole"
"Bless Your Soul" (error)

TRP $32   S $30   H $27.50   SRD $27.50

Comments: 1995; Original Retail $25.00/$27.50
Enesco introduced this as *"Bless Your Sole."* To date, only *"Bless Your Soul"* has been found.

Personal Data: _____
____Want Mark ____ Mark _____ Purch. 19__ Pd $ _____

531200 **Bear with Gift**
"Wishing You A Bear-ie Merry Christmas"

H $17   SRD $17

Comments: 1996; Original Retail $17.00
Holiday Preview Event piece available at Century Circle and Distinguished Service Retailers Nov. 1 and 2, 1996.

Personal Data: _____
____Want Mark ____ Mark _____ Purch. 19__ Pd $ _____

531243 **9" EASTER SEALS –**
Girl with Basket of Roses
"You Are The Rose Of His Creation"

LE 1994 - 3 YEARS OLD B $500-550
TRP $500

Comments: 1993; 1994 Easter Seals Commemorative "9 figurine. Limited to 2,000 Numbered Pieces. Very little trading found on this piece. *See #25, page XIV.*

Personal Data: _____
____Want Mark ____ Mark ____ Purch. 19__ Pd $ _____

531359 **PLATE – Girl Sharing Wordless Book**
"Bring The Little Ones To Jesus"

LE 1994 - 3 YEARS OLD B $45 TRP $40

Comments: 1993; Original Retail $50.00 Limited Edition. Limited to one year of production. Child Evangelism Fellowship plate. Price down from '96. *See #1, page XI.*

Personal Data: _____
____Want Mark ____ Mark ____ Purch. 19__ Pd $ _____

531375 **Noah's Ark**
"Llamas"

TRP $18 S $15
H $15 SRD $15

Comments: 1993; Original Retail $15.00 Part of *Two By Two Series.* *See #38, page XV.*

Personal Data: _____
____Want Mark ____ Mark ____ Purch. 19__ Pd $ _____

531634S Girl in High Heels
"Who's Gonna Fill Your Shoes"

H $40

Comments: 1995; Original Retail $37.50 Parade of Gifts catalog exclusive available at a limited number of select retail locations. Only 8,500 pieces have the special understamp, "1996 Catalog." The bows on her shoes were a flat white color and did not have stones in them.

Personal Data: _____
____Want Mark ____ Mark ____ Purch. 19__ Pd $ _____

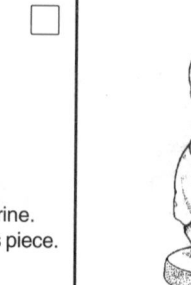

531634 **Girl in High Heels**
"Who's Gonna Fill Your Shoes"

SRD $37.50

Comments: 1996; Original Retail $37.50 Identical to 531634S which was produced in early '96 as a catalog syndicate exclusive. This piece was available from all Precious Moments retailers in the Spring of 1997. The bows on her pink shoes were white with red stones on them.

Personal Data: _____
____Want Mark ____ Mark ____ Purch. 19__ Pd $ _____

531677 **CHAPEL EXCLUSIVE – Girl with Wreath**
"Surrounded With Joy"

NM $40 S $30 SRD $30
TRP $35 H $30

Comments: 1993; Original Retail $30.00 Available exclusively at the Precious Moments® Chapel. Complements the "Boy with Wreath" figurine (E-0506).

Personal Data: _____
____Want Mark ____ Mark ____ Purch. 19__ Pd $ _____

531685 **CHAPEL EXCLUSIVE – ORNAMENT**
Girl with Wreath
"Surrounded With Joy"

NM $27 S $17.50 SRD $17.50
TRP $20 H $17.50

Comments: 1993; Original Retail $17.50 Available exclusively at the Precious Moments® Chapel. Complements the "Boy with Wreath" ornament (E-0513).

Personal Data: _____
____Want Mark ____ Mark ____ Purch. 19__ Pd $ _____

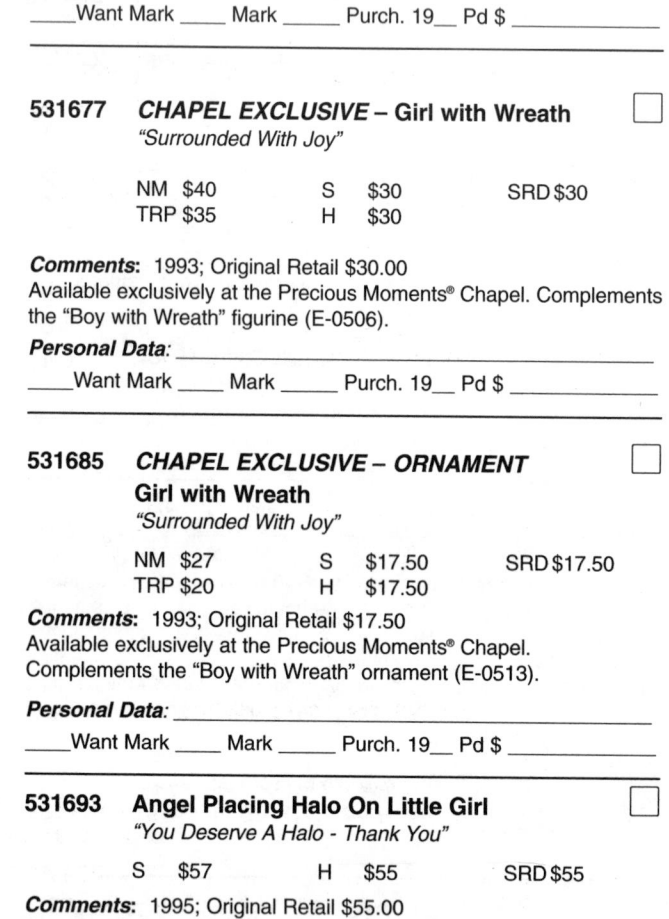

531693 **Angel Placing Halo On Little Girl**
"You Deserve A Halo - Thank You"

S $57 H $55 SRD $55

Comments: 1995; Original Retail $55.00 This reminds me of the new mural at the Chapel where the children are standing in line waiting to receive their halos.

Personal Data: _____
____Want Mark ____ Mark ____ Purch. 19__ Pd $ _____

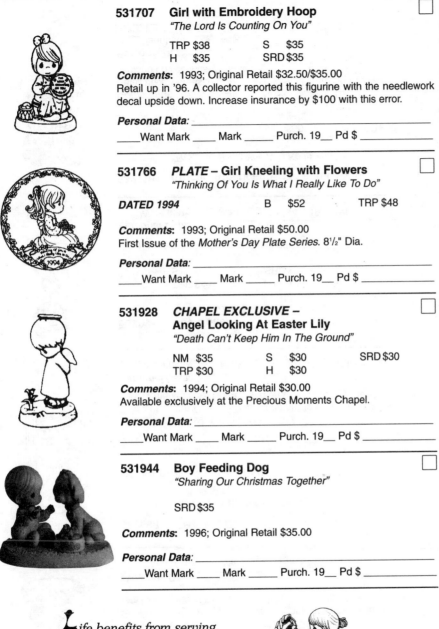

531707 Girl with Embroidery Hoop
"The Lord Is Counting On You"

TRP $38	S $35
H $35	SRD $35

Comments: 1993; Original Retail $32.50/$35.00
Retail up in '96. A collector reported this figurine with the needlework decal upside down. Increase insurance by $100 with this error.

Personal Data: _____
____Want Mark ____ Mark _____ Purch. 19__ Pd $ _____

531766 PLATE – Girl Kneeling with Flowers
"Thinking Of You Is What I Really Like To Do"

DATED 1994   B $52   TRP $48

Comments: 1993; Original Retail $50.00
First Issue of the *Mother's Day Plate Series.* 8½" Dia.

Personal Data: _____
____Want Mark ____ Mark _____ Purch. 19__ Pd $ _____

531928 CHAPEL EXCLUSIVE –
Angel Looking At Easter Lily
"Death Can't Keep Him In The Ground"

NM $35	S $30	SRD $30
TRP $30	H $30	

Comments: 1994; Original Retail $30.00
Available exclusively at the Precious Moments Chapel.

Personal Data: _____
____Want Mark ____ Mark _____ Purch. 19__ Pd $ _____

531944 Boy Feeding Dog
"Sharing Our Christmas Together"

SRD $35

Comments: 1996; Original Retail $35.00

Personal Data: _____
____Want Mark ____ Mark _____ Purch. 19__ Pd $ _____

*L*ife benefits from serving
others, for as it reaches out to
help, it gathers something for
itself – friendship.

531952 Angel In Eggnog Cup
"Dropping In For The Holidays"

TRP $45	H $40
S $40	SRD $40

Comments: 1994; Original Retail $40.00
Decal found upside down on some pieces. Add $100 to the secondary market value when insuring. Also found with a light pink cup and green lettering with a S mark.
See # 15, page XIII.

Personal Data: _____
____Want Mark ____ Mark _____ Purch. 19__ Pd $ _____

532002 Boy Holding Cross and Lily
"Hallelujah For The Cross"

TRP $35	H $35
S $35	SRD $35

Comments: 1994; Original Retail $35.00
Cross is yellow instead of gold as shown on prototype. (Gold paint can easily be removed.) Very little demand on secondary market to date.

Personal Data: _____
____Want Mark ____ Mark _____ Purch. 19__ Pd $ _____

532010 Boy Holding Bottle w/ Message
"Sending You Oceans Of Love"

RETIRED 1996 - 1 YEAR AGO

TRP $40	H $37.50
S $37.50	

Comments: 1994; Original Retail $35.00/$37.50
Retail raised in '96 then retired – no demand on secondary market found to date.

Personal Data: _____
____Want Mark ____ Mark _____ Purch. 19__ Pd $ _____

532037 Cowgirl and Bear
"I Can't Bear To Let You Go"

TRP $55	S $50
H $50	SRD $50

Comments: 1994; Original Retail $50.00

Personal Data: _____
____Want Mark ____ Mark _____ Purch. 19__ Pd $ _____

532061　Boy in Dad's Shoes
"Who's Gonna Fill Your Shoes"

SRD $37.50

Comments: 1996; Original Retail $37.50
Enesco spring catalog exclusive available at a limited number of select retail locations. Will have a special understamp, "1997 Catalog."

Personal Data: _____
____Want Mark ____ Mark _____ Purch. 19__ Pd $ _____

532088　*CHAPEL EXCLUSIVE – ORNAMENT*

Baby Jesus in Manger/Altar
"A King Is Born"

RETIRED 1995 - 2 YEARS AGO

NM　$27.50　　　TRP $22.50

Comments: 1994; Original Retail $17.50
Sold out at the Chapel. This ornament is only available on the secondary market now. No demand on the secondary market to date.

Personal Data: _____
____Want Mark ____ Mark _____ Purch. 19__ Pd $ _____

532096　Boy Golfer
"Lord Help Me To Stay On Course"

TRP	$40	H	$35
S	$38	SRD	$35

Comments: 1994; Original Retail $35.00

Personal Data: _____
____Want Mark ____ Mark _____ Purch. 19__ Pd $ _____

532118　African-American Bride and Groom

"The Lord Bless You And Keep You"

B	$50	S	$50	SRD $50
TRP	$50	H	$50	

Comments: 1993; Original Retail $40.00/$50.00
Retail price increased in 1995 and 1996! Up $10 in two years. No demand on secondary market.

Personal Data: _____
____Want Mark ____ Mark _____ Purch. 19__ Pd $ _____

532126　African-American Graduate Girl
"The Lord Bless You And Keep You"

B	$30	S	$30	SRD $30
TRP	$30	H	$30	

Comments: 1993; Original Retail $30.00/$35.00
Retail price increased in 1995 and 1996. Up nearly 17%. Not enough sales reported on the secondary market to notice any significant demand even for first mark. Price falling below retail.

Personal Data: _____
____Want Mark ____ Mark _____ Purch. 19__ Pd $ _____

532134　African-American Graduate Boy
"The Lord Bless You And Keep You"

B	$30	S	$30	SRD $35
TRP	$30	H	$30	

Comments: 1993; Original Retail $30.00/$35.00
Retail price increased in 1995 and 1996. Prices below retail.

Personal Data: _____
____Want Mark ____ Mark _____ Purch. 19__ Pd $ _____

532916　Shepherd Kneeling by Plaque with Lamb
"Luke 2:10-11"

TRP	$35	S	$35	H	$35	SRD $35

Comments: 1993; Original Retail $35.00

Personal Data: _____
____Want Mark ____ Mark _____ Purch. 19__ Pd $ _____

603171　Angel on Arch
"Ornament Enhancer"

TRP	$32	S	$30	H	$30	SRD $30

Comments: 1994; Original Retail $30.00

Personal Data: _____
____Want Mark ____ Mark _____ Purch. 19__ Pd $ _____

603503　*CHAPEL EXCLUSIVE –*

Two Angels with Chapel Poem Plaque
"On The Hill Overlooking The Quiet Blue Stream"

NM	$45	S	$45	SRD $45
TRP	$45	H	$45	

Comments: 1994; Original Retail $45.00
Available exclusively at the Precious Moments Chapel.

Personal Data: _____
____Want Mark ____ Mark _____ Purch. 19__ Pd $ _____

603864   Boy and Dog Filling Sandbag
"Nothing Can Dampen The Spirit Of Caring"

B $35	S $28	SRD $28
TRP $30	H $28	

Comments: 1993; Original Retail $35.00
First Issue in the *Good Samaritan Series*. Dedicated to those who aided Mississippi River flood victims in 1993. Enesco and Sam Butcher have made a donation to these agencies committed to assisting in the flood relief effort. Reportedly missing the turtle; add $100 to the secondary market value when insuring. Over production has effected the demand on the secondary market. Many dealers over bought on this piece. **See #32, page XIV.**

Personal Data: _____

____Want Mark ____ Mark _____ Purch. 19__ Pd $ _____

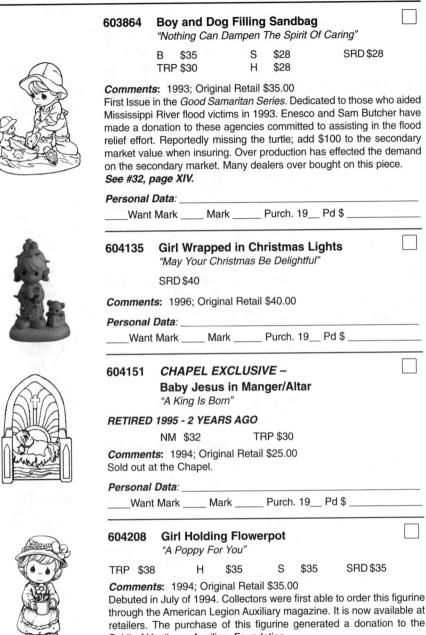

604135   Girl Wrapped in Christmas Lights
"May Your Christmas Be Delightful"

SRD $40

Comments: 1996; Original Retail $40.00

Personal Data: _____

____Want Mark ____ Mark _____ Purch. 19__ Pd $ _____

604151   *CHAPEL EXCLUSIVE –*
Baby Jesus in Manger/Altar
"A King Is Born"

RETIRED 1995 - 2 YEARS AGO

NM $32	TRP $30

Comments: 1994; Original Retail $25.00
Sold out at the Chapel.

Personal Data: _____

____Want Mark ____ Mark _____ Purch. 19__ Pd $ _____

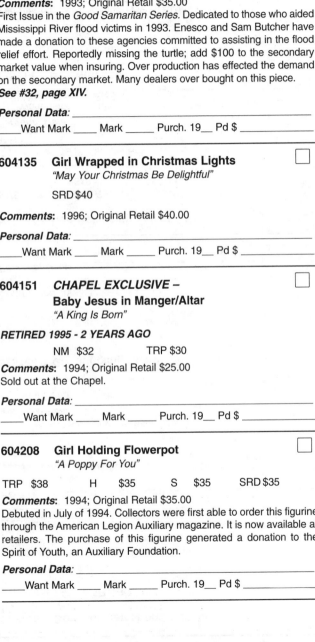

604208   Girl Holding Flowerpot
"A Poppy For You"

TRP $38	H $35	S $35	SRD $35

Comments: 1994; Original Retail $35.00
Debuted in July of 1994. Collectors were first able to order this figurine through the American Legion Auxiliary magazine. It is now available at retailers. The purchase of this figurine generated a donation to the Spirit of Youth, an Auxiliary Foundation.

Personal Data: _____

____Want Mark ____ Mark _____ Purch. 19__ Pd $ _____

604216   *BELL –* Girl in Christmas Tree Dress
"You're As Pretty As A Christmas Tree"

DATED 1994   TRP $28

Comments: 1993; Original Retail $27.50
It is likely that she may be found without the year decal on her star. If so, add $50 for this error.

Personal Data: _____

____Want Mark ____ Mark _____ Purch. 19__ Pd $ _____

617334 ♪ *ANIMATED MUSICAL*
ANGEL TREE TOPPER
"Rejoice O Earth"

RETIRED
FLM $115

Comments: 1989; Original Retail $125.00
Plays *Hark, The Herald Angels Sing.* Arms and wings move.

Personal Data: _____

____Want Mark ____ Mark _____ Purch. 19__ Pd $ _____

SAMMY'S CIRCUS

Sammy's Circus is a "backyard circus" inspired by Sam Butcher's grandchildren and their friends.

528099   Girl on Balance Beam
"Markie"
SUSP. 1996 - 1 YEAR AGO

B $25	S $18.50
TRP $21	H $18.50

Comments: 1993; Original Retail $18.50

Personal Data: _____

____Want Mark ____ Mark _____ Purch. 19__ Pd $ _____

528196   *NIGHT LIGHT*
"Circus Tent"
SUSP. 1996 - 1 YEAR AGO

B $105	S $90
TRP $95	H $90

Comments: 1993; Original Retail $90.00

Personal Data: _____

____Want Mark ____ Mark _____ Purch. 19__ Pd $ _____

529168   Boy Lion Tamer and Kitty Lion
"Jordan"

SUSP. 1996 - 1 YEAR AGO

B	$25	S	$20
TRP	$20	H	$20

Comments: 1994; Original Retail $20.00

Personal Data: _____

____Want Mark ____ Mark _____ Purch. 19__ Pd $ _____

529176   Boy Clown with Cannon
"Dusty"

SUSP. 1996 - 1 YEAR AGO

B	$25	S	$22.50
TRP	$25	H	$22.50

Comments: 1993; Original Retail $22.50

Personal Data: _____

____Want Mark ____ Mark _____ Purch. 19__ Pd $ _____

529184   Girl Juggling Hearts
"Katie"

SUSP. 1996 - 1 YEAR AGO

B	$25	S	$18
TRP	$22	H	$17

Comments: 1993; Original Retail $17.00
3-1/2" H.

Personal Data: _____

____Want Mark ____ Mark _____ Purch. 19__ Pd $ _____

529192   Dog Balancing Ball and Mouse
"Tippy"

SUSP. 1996 - 1 YEAR AGO

B	$18	S	$12
TRP	$15	H	$12

Comments: 1993; Original Retail $12.00
3" H.

Personal Data: _____

____Want Mark ____ Mark _____ Purch. 19__ Pd $ _____

529214   Boy with Drum
"Collin"

SUSP. 1996 - 1 YEAR AGO

B	$28	S	$22
TRP	$24	H	$20

Comments: 1993; Original Retail $20.00
4" H. Suspension has not effected demand for the Circus set to date.

Personal Data: _____

____Want Mark ____ Mark _____ Purch. 19__ Pd $ _____

529222   Boy Hanging Sign
"Sammy"

LE 1994 - 3 YEARS OLD   B $45   TRP $30

Comments: 1993; Original Retail $20.00
3" H.

Personal Data: _____

____Want Mark ____ Mark _____ Purch. 19__ Pd $ _____

163708   Girl Clown and Teddy Bear
"Jennifer"

SUSP. 1996 - 1 YEAR AGO

		S	$25
		H	$20

Comments: 1995; Original Retail $20.00

Personal Data: _____

____Want Mark ____ Mark _____ Purch. 19__ Pd $ _____

SUGAR TOWN

The complete 1992 Sugar Town set including the LE population sign in a GC mark has a secondary market value of $397 - $412.

1992

528684   Decorated Evergreen Tree
"Christmas Tree"

RETIRED 1994 - 3 YEARS AGO

GC $30   B $26   TRP $25

Comments: 1991; Original Retail $15.00
One of the original pieces for '92.

Personal Data: _____

____Want Mark _____ Mark _____ Purch. 19__ Pd $ _____

529486   Two Women Singing
"Aunt Ruth & Aunt Dorothy"

RETIRED 1994 - 3 YEARS AGO

GC $35   B $30   TRP $25

Comments: 1991; Original Retail $20.00

Personal Data: _____

____Want Mark _____ Mark _____ Purch. 19__ Pd $ _____

529494   Boy Singing
"Philip"

RETIRED 1994 - 3 YEARS AGO

GC $30   B $20   TRP $20

Comments: 1991; Original Retail $17.00

Personal Data: _____
____Want Mark ____ Mark _____ Purch. 19__ Pd $ _____

529508   NATIVITY Scene
"Nativity"

RETIRED 1994 - 3 YEARS AGO

GC $32   B $30   TRP $25

Comments: 1991; Original Retail $20.00

Personal Data: _____
____Want Mark ____ Mark _____ Purch. 19__ Pd $ _____

529516   Old Man Kneeling
"Grandfather"

RETIRED 1994 - 3 YEARS AGO

GC $30   B $20   TRP $20

Comments: 1991; Original Retail $15.00

Personal Data: _____
____Want Mark ____ Mark _____ Purch. 19__ Pd $ _____

529567   Sam Standing Next to Town Sign Painting
"Sam Butcher"

LE 1992 - 5 YEARS OLD
Population 5 and Growing!   GC $110-125

Comments: 1991; Original Retail $22.50
Limited Edition. Came with the first set which is now retired. Sign is changed each year to "new population" figure. Most sought after of the Sugar Town pieces. This was not retired; it was a one year LE production piece.

Personal Data: _____
____Want Mark ____ Mark _____ Purch. 19__ Pd $ _____

529621   NIGHT LIGHT – Chapel
"Chapel"

RETIRED 1994 - 3 YEARS AGO

GC $130   TRP $120
B $120

Comments: 1991; Original Retail $85.00
No change from '96.

Personal Data: _____
____Want Mark ____ Mark _____ Purch. 19__ Pd $ _____

1993

528668   Boy with Snowballs
"Sammy"

B $28   S $17   SRD $17
TRP $17   H $17

Comments: 1992; Original Retail $17.00
Sugar Town sets were not increasing on the secondary market until the first set was retired. Most sets purchased "to keep." Extra not bought up.

Personal Data: _____
____Want Mark ____ Mark _____ Purch. 19__ Pd $ _____

529435   Boy with Box of Christmas Decorations
"Dusty"

B $20   S $17   SRD $17
TRP $17   H $17

Comments: 1992; Original Retail $17.00

Personal Data: _____
____Want Mark ____ Mark _____ Purch. 19__ Pd $ _____

529443   Car with Tree on Top
"Sam's Car"

B $27   S $22.50   SRD $22.50
TRP $22.50   H $22.50

Comments: 1992; Original Retail $22.50

Personal Data: _____
____Want Mark ____ Mark _____ Purch. 19__ Pd $ _____

529524 Girl with Snowman
"Katy Lynne"

GC	$35	TRP $22	H $20
B	$30	S $20	SRD $20

Comments: 1992; Original Retail $20.00

Personal Data: _____

____Want Mark ____ Mark _____ Purch. 19__ Pd $ _____

529605 NIGHT LIGHT – House
"Sam's House"

B	$98	S $85	SRD $85
TRP	$85	H $85	

Comments: 1992; Original Retail $80.00/$85.00
Retail price increased last in 1995.

Personal Data: _____

____Want Mark ____ Mark _____ Purch. 19__ Pd $ _____

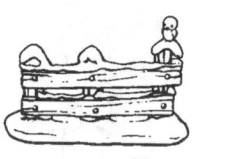

529796 Fence

B	$15	S $10	SRD $10
TRP	$10	H $10	

Comments: 1992; Original Retail $10.00
We'd love to receive photos of your displays of the Sugar Town set.

Personal Data: _____

____Want Mark ____ Mark _____ Purch. 19__ Pd $ _____

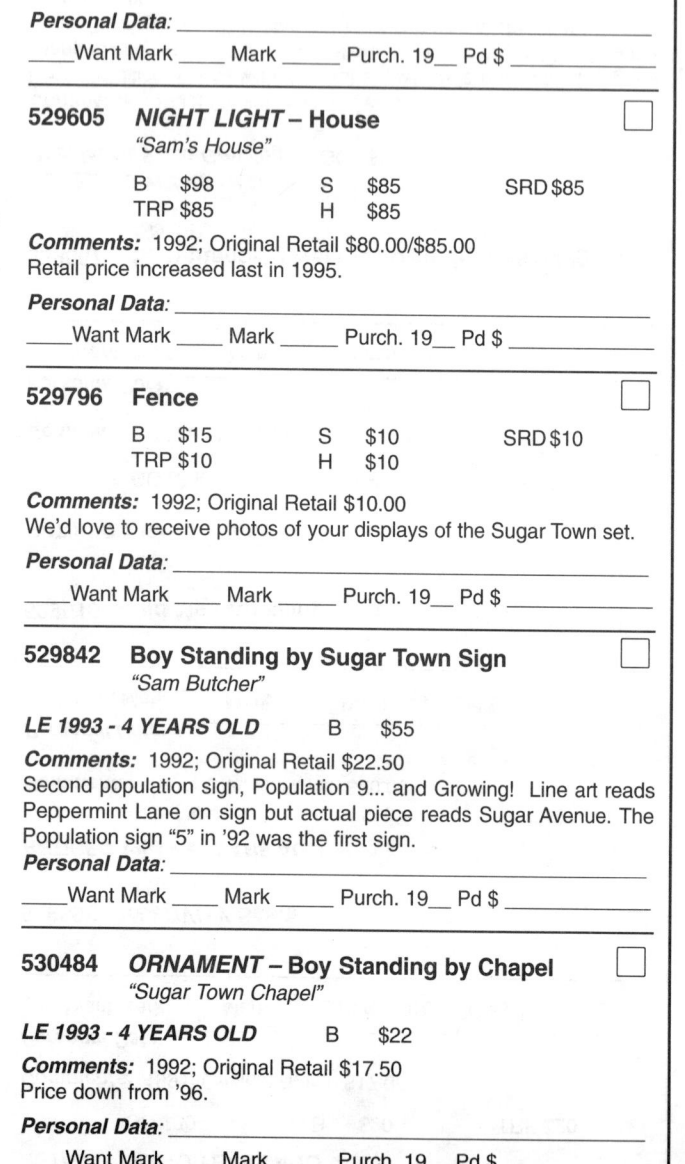

529842 Boy Standing by Sugar Town Sign
"Sam Butcher"

LE 1993 - 4 YEARS OLD   B $55

Comments: 1992; Original Retail $22.50
Second population sign, Population 9... and Growing! Line art reads Peppermint Lane on sign but actual piece reads Sugar Avenue. The Population sign "5" in '92 was the first sign.

Personal Data: _____

____Want Mark ____ Mark _____ Purch. 19__ Pd $ _____

530484 ORNAMENT – Boy Standing by Chapel
"Sugar Town Chapel"

LE 1993 - 4 YEARS OLD   B $22

Comments: 1992; Original Retail $17.50
Price down from '96.

Personal Data: _____

____Want Mark ____ Mark _____ Purch. 19__ Pd $ _____

See Individual Listings.

531774 1993 Sugar Town House Collector's Set

B $273

Comments: 1992; Original Retail $189.00
7-piece set. Includes: 528668, 529435, 529443, 529524, 529605, 529796, 529842

Personal Data: _____

____Want Mark ____ Mark _____ Purch. 19__ Pd $ _____

1994

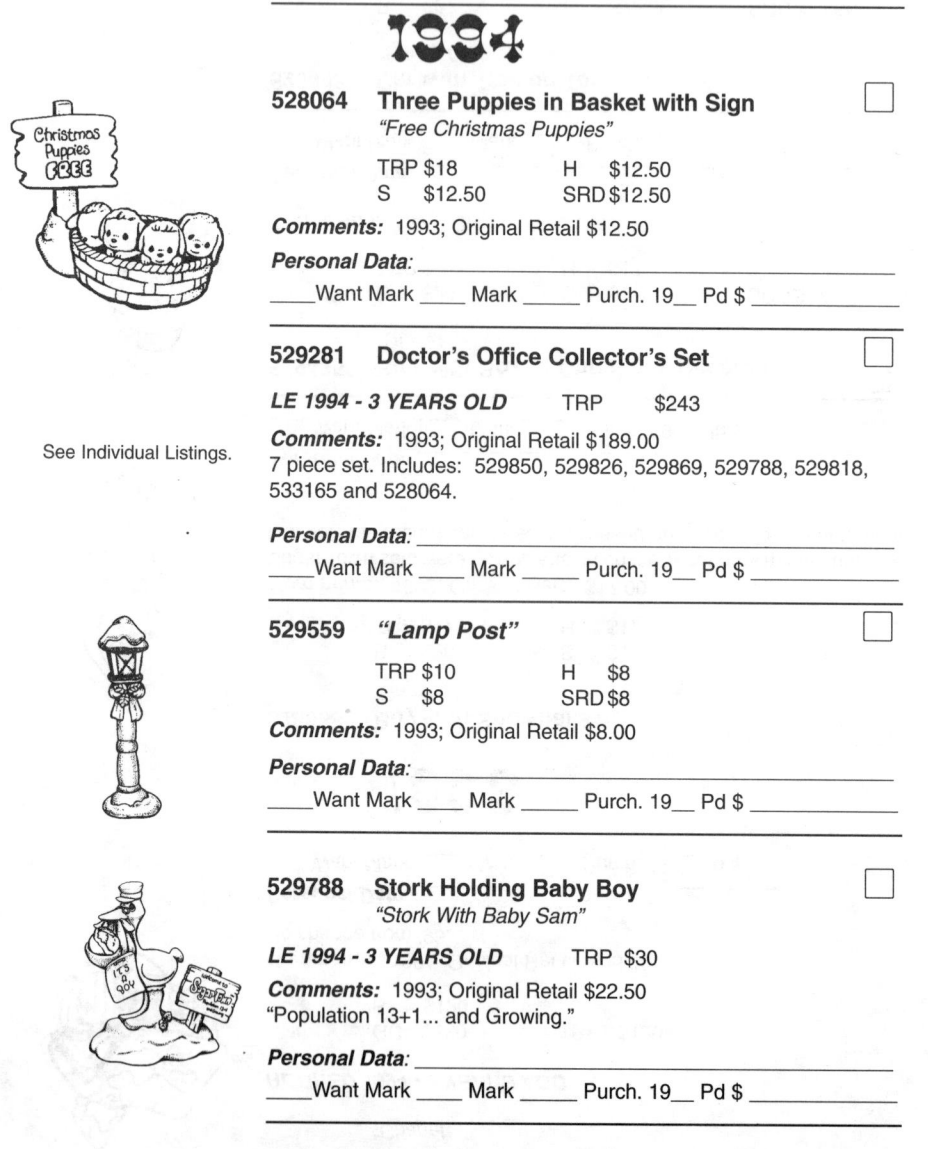

528064 Three Puppies in Basket with Sign
"Free Christmas Puppies"

TRP	$18	H $12.50	
S	$12.50	SRD $12.50	

Comments: 1993; Original Retail $12.50

Personal Data: _____

____Want Mark ____ Mark _____ Purch. 19__ Pd $ _____

529281 Doctor's Office Collector's Set

LE 1994 - 3 YEARS OLD   TRP $243

Comments: 1993; Original Retail $189.00
7 piece set. Includes: 529850, 529826, 529869, 529788, 529818, 533165 and 528064.

Personal Data: _____

____Want Mark ____ Mark _____ Purch. 19__ Pd $ _____

See Individual Listings.

529559 "Lamp Post"

TRP	$10	H $8	
S	$8	SRD $8	

Comments: 1993; Original Retail $8.00

Personal Data: _____

____Want Mark ____ Mark _____ Purch. 19__ Pd $ _____

529788 Stork Holding Baby Boy
"Stork With Baby Sam"

LE 1994 - 3 YEARS OLD   TRP $30

Comments: 1993; Original Retail $22.50
"Population 13+1... and Growing."

Personal Data: _____

____Want Mark ____ Mark _____ Purch. 19__ Pd $ _____

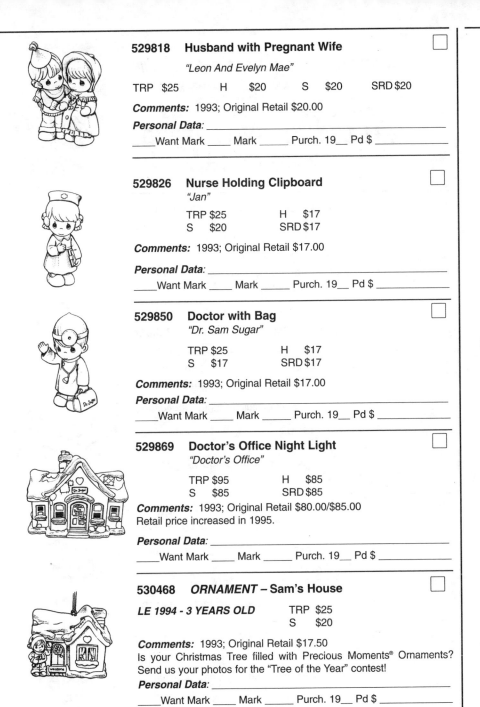

529818   Husband with Pregnant Wife
"Leon And Evelyn Mae"

TRP $25   H $20   S $20   SRD $20

Comments: 1993; Original Retail $20.00

Personal Data: _____
____Want Mark ____ Mark _____ Purch. 19__ Pd $ _____

529826   Nurse Holding Clipboard
"Jan"

TRP $25   H $17
S $20   SRD $17

Comments: 1993; Original Retail $17.00

Personal Data: _____
____Want Mark ____ Mark _____ Purch. 19__ Pd $ _____

529850   Doctor with Bag
"Dr. Sam Sugar"

TRP $25   H $17
S $17   SRD $17

Comments: 1993; Original Retail $17.00

Personal Data: _____
____Want Mark ____ Mark _____ Purch. 19__ Pd $ _____

529869   Doctor's Office Night Light
"Doctor's Office"

TRP $95   H $85
S $85   SRD $85

Comments: 1993; Original Retail $80.00/$85.00
Retail price increased in 1995.

Personal Data: _____
____Want Mark ____ Mark _____ Purch. 19__ Pd $ _____

530468   *ORNAMENT* – Sam's House

LE 1994 - 3 YEARS OLD   TRP $25
S $20

Comments: 1993; Original Retail $17.50
Is your Christmas Tree filled with Precious Moments® Ornaments?
Send us your photos for the "Tree of the Year" contest!

Personal Data: _____
____Want Mark ____ Mark _____ Purch. 19__ Pd $ _____

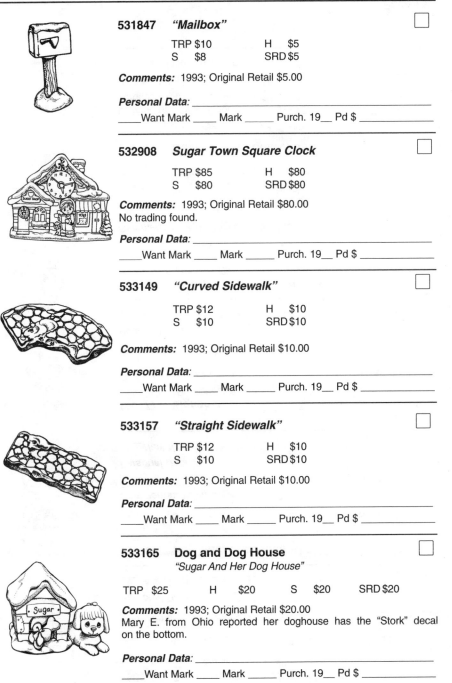

531847   *"Mailbox"*

TRP $10   H $5
S $8   SRD $5

Comments: 1993; Original Retail $5.00

Personal Data: _____
____Want Mark ____ Mark _____ Purch. 19__ Pd $ _____

532908   *Sugar Town Square Clock*

TRP $85   H $80
S $80   SRD $80

Comments: 1993; Original Retail $80.00
No trading found.

Personal Data: _____
____Want Mark ____ Mark _____ Purch. 19__ Pd $ _____

533149   *"Curved Sidewalk"*

TRP $12   H $10
S $10   SRD $10

Comments: 1993; Original Retail $10.00

Personal Data: _____
____Want Mark ____ Mark _____ Purch. 19__ Pd $ _____

533157   *"Straight Sidewalk"*

TRP $12   H $10
S $10   SRD $10

Comments: 1993; Original Retail $10.00

Personal Data: _____
____Want Mark ____ Mark _____ Purch. 19__ Pd $ _____

533165   Dog and Dog House
"Sugar And Her Dog House"

TRP $25   H $20   S $20   SRD $20

Comments: 1993; Original Retail $20.00
Mary E. from Ohio reported her doghouse has the "Stork" decal
on the bottom.

Personal Data: _____
____Want Mark ____ Mark _____ Purch. 19__ Pd $ _____

533173 *"Single Tree"*

TRP $16	H $10
S $10	SRD $10

Comments: 1993; Original Retail $10.00

Personal Data: _____

___Want Mark ___ Mark ___ Purch. 19__ Pd $ _____

533181 *"Double Tree"*

TRP $15	H $10
S $10	SRD $10

Comments: 1993; Original Retail $10.00

Personal Data: _____

___Want Mark ___ Mark ___ Purch. 19__ Pd $ _____

533203 *"Cobblestone Bridge"*

TRP $22	H $17
S $17	SRD $17

Comments: 1993; Original Retail $17.00

Personal Data: _____

___Want Mark ___ Mark ___ Purch. 19__ Pd $ _____

770272 *"Sugar Town Enhancement"*

TRP $97	S $73	H $70	SRD $70

Comments: 1993; Original Retail $70.00
Seven piece set. Includes: 529559, 531847, 533149, 533157, 533173, 533181, 533203. Send photos of your display...We may just publish them!

Personal Data: _____

___Want Mark ___ Mark ___ Purch. 19__ Pd $ _____

See Individual Listings.

1995

150150 **Ticket Booth and Waiting Room**
"Train Station Night Light"

S $105	H $100	SRD $100

Comments: 1994; Original Retail $100.00

Personal Data: _____

___Want Mark ___ Mark ___ Purch. 19__ Pd $ _____

150169 **Boy Train Conductor with Sign Population**
"Sam"

S $22	H $20	SRD $20

Comments: 1994; Original Retail $20.00
Population total = 18.

Personal Data: _____

___Want Mark ___ Mark ___ Purch. 19__ Pd $ _____

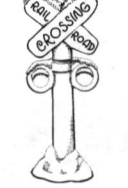

150177 **Signpost**
"Railroad Crossing Sign"

S $15	H $12	SRD $12

Comments: 1994; Original Retail $12.00

Personal Data: _____

___Want Mark ___ Mark ___ Purch. 19__ Pd $ _____

150185 **Cart with Suitcase and Kitten**
"Luggage Cart"

S $15	H $13	SRD $13

Comments: 1994; Original Retail $13.00

Personal Data: _____

___Want Mark ___ Mark ___ Purch. 19__ Pd $ _____

See Individual Listings.

150193 **Train Station - Collectors' 6 piece set**

S $202	H $190	SRD $190

Comments: 1994; Original Retail $190.00
Includes: 150150, 150169, 150177, 150185, 531812, 531871

Personal Data: _____

___Want Mark ___ Mark ___ Purch. 19__ Pd $ _____

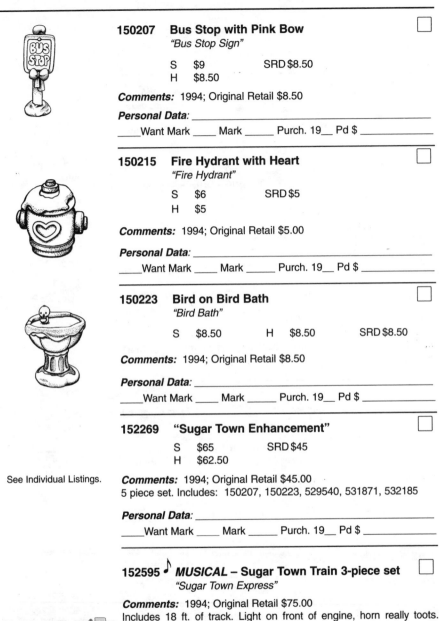

150207   **Bus Stop with Pink Bow**
"Bus Stop Sign"

S $9   SRD $8.50
H $8.50

Comments: 1994; Original Retail $8.50

Personal Data: _____
____Want Mark ____ Mark ____ Purch. 19__ Pd $ _____

150215   **Fire Hydrant with Heart**
"Fire Hydrant"

S $6   SRD $5
H $5

Comments: 1994; Original Retail $5.00

Personal Data: _____
____Want Mark ____ Mark ____ Purch. 19__ Pd $ _____

150223   **Bird on Bird Bath**
"Bird Bath"

S $8.50   H $8.50   SRD $8.50

Comments: 1994; Original Retail $8.50

Personal Data: _____
____Want Mark ____ Mark ____ Purch. 19__ Pd $ _____

152269   **"Sugar Town Enhancement"**

S $65   SRD $45
H $62.50

See Individual Listings.

Comments: 1994; Original Retail $45.00
5 piece set. Includes: 150207, 150223, 529540, 531871, 532185

Personal Data: _____
____Want Mark ____ Mark ____ Purch. 19__ Pd $ _____

152595 ♪ *MUSICAL* – **Sugar Town Train 3-piece set**
"Sugar Town Express"

Comments: 1994; Original Retail $75.00
Includes 18 ft. of track. Light on front of engine, horn really toots. Operates forward and reverse. Plays three tunes: *Jingle Bells, Santa Claus Is Coming To Town* and *We Wish You A Merry Christmas.*

Personal Data: _____
____Want Mark ____ Mark ____ Purch. 19__ Pd $ _____

529540   **Dog and Cat on Bench**
"Park Bench"

S $15   SRD $13
H $13

Comments: 1994; Original Retail $13.00

Personal Data: _____
____Want Mark ____ Mark ____ Purch. 19__ Pd $ _____

530441   *ORNAMENT* – **Doctor's Office**
"Dr. Sugar's Office Ornament"

S $20   H $17.50   SRD $17.50

Comments: 1994; Original Retail $17.50

Personal Data: _____
____Want Mark ____ Mark ____ Purch. 19__ Pd $ _____

531812   **Girls with Gifts**
"Tammy And Debbie"

S $22.50   H $22.50   SRD $22.50

Comments: 1994; Original Retail $22.50

Personal Data: _____
____Want Mark ____ Mark ____ Purch. 19__ Pd $ _____

531871   **Boy with Sled/Logs**
"Donny"

S $22.50   H $22.50   SRD $22.50

Comments: 1994; Original Retail $22.50
No trading found.

Personal Data: _____
____Want Mark ____ Mark ____ Purch. 19__ Pd $ _____

532185   **Signpost with Street Names**
"Street Sign"

S $10   H $10   SRD $10

Comments: 1994; Original Retail $10.00

Personal Data: _____
____Want Mark ____ Mark ____ Purch. 19__ Pd $ _____

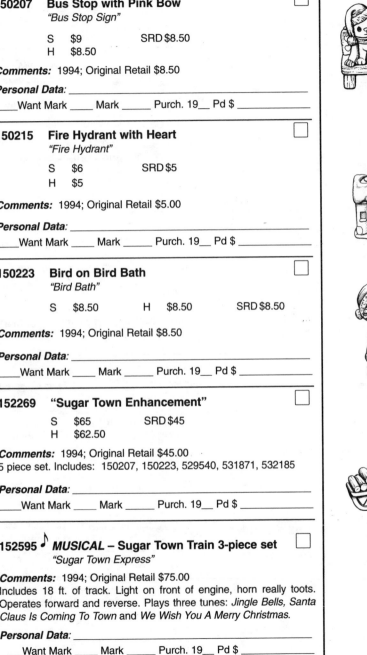

150304 *PLATE* – **Chapel Lighted Plate**
"Sugar Town Chapel"

H $90   SRD $90

Comments: 1995; Original Retail $90.00
1996 Limited Edition. This lighted plate depicts three carolers and a nativity scene in front of a chapel. No trading found.

Personal Data: _____
____Want Mark ____ Mark _____ Purch. 19__ Pd $ _____

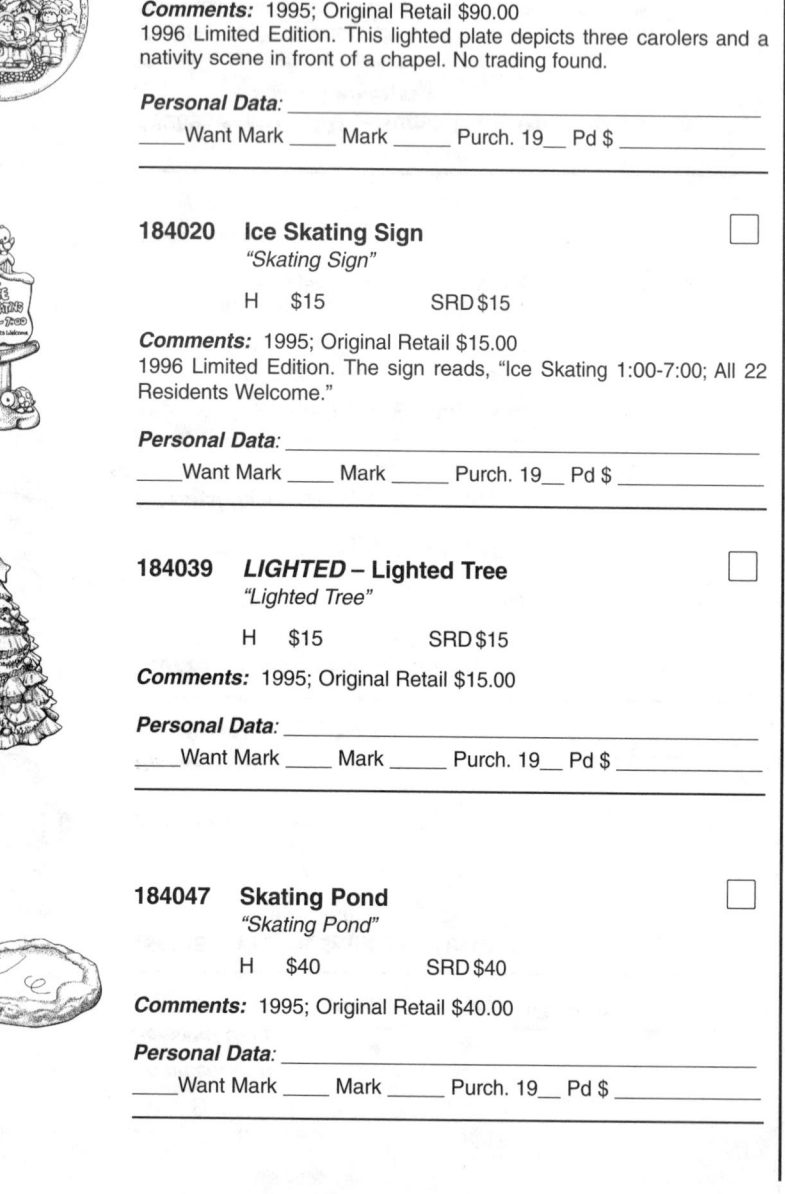

184020 **Ice Skating Sign**
"Skating Sign"

H $15   SRD $15

Comments: 1995; Original Retail $15.00
1996 Limited Edition. The sign reads, "Ice Skating 1:00-7:00; All 22 Residents Welcome."

Personal Data: _____
____Want Mark ____ Mark _____ Purch. 19__ Pd $ _____

184039 *LIGHTED* – **Lighted Tree**
"Lighted Tree"

H $15   SRD $15

Comments: 1995; Original Retail $15.00

Personal Data: _____
____Want Mark ____ Mark _____ Purch. 19__ Pd $ _____

184047 **Skating Pond**
"Skating Pond"

H $40   SRD $40

Comments: 1995; Original Retail $40.00

Personal Data: _____
____Want Mark ____ Mark _____ Purch. 19__ Pd $ _____

184055 **Girl on Ice Skates**
"Mazie"

H $18.50   SRD $18.50

Comments: 1995; Original Retail $18.50

Personal Data: _____
____Want Mark ____ Mark _____ Purch. 19__ Pd $ _____

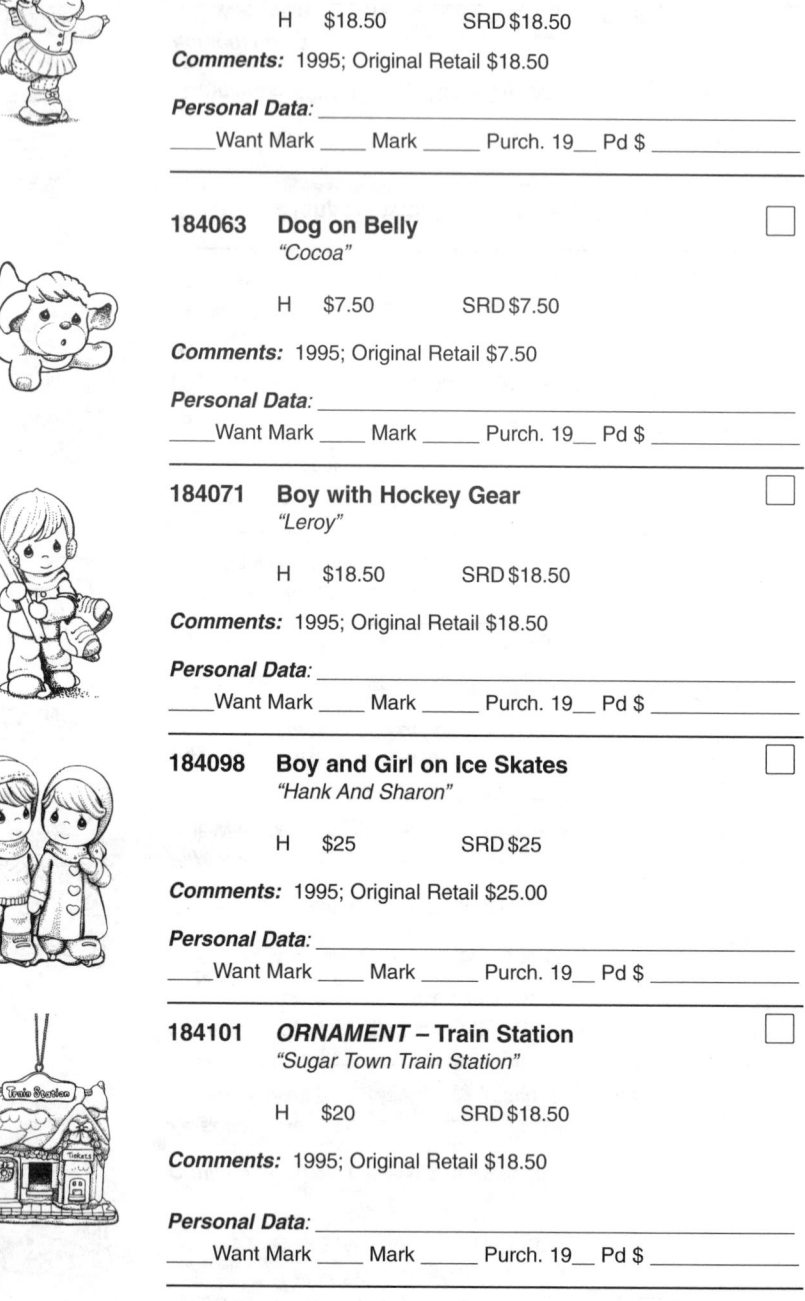

184063 **Dog on Belly**
"Cocoa"

H $7.50   SRD $7.50

Comments: 1995; Original Retail $7.50

Personal Data: _____
____Want Mark ____ Mark _____ Purch. 19__ Pd $ _____

184071 **Boy with Hockey Gear**
"Leroy"

H $18.50   SRD $18.50

Comments: 1995; Original Retail $18.50

Personal Data: _____
____Want Mark ____ Mark _____ Purch. 19__ Pd $ _____

184098 **Boy and Girl on Ice Skates**
"Hank And Sharon"

H $25   SRD $25

Comments: 1995; Original Retail $25.00

Personal Data: _____
____Want Mark ____ Mark _____ Purch. 19__ Pd $ _____

184101 *ORNAMENT* – **Train Station**
"Sugar Town Train Station"

H $20   SRD $18.50

Comments: 1995; Original Retail $18.50

Personal Data: _____
____Want Mark ____ Mark _____ Purch. 19__ Pd $ _____

184128 Skating Pond (Collectors' 7-Piece Set) ☐

See Individual Listings.

H $184.50   SRD $184.50

Comments: 1995; Original Retail $184.50
Includes: 184020, 184047, 184055, 184063, 184071, 184098, 192341.

Personal Data: _____
____Want Mark ____ Mark _____ Purch. 19__ Pd $ _____

184136 Flag Pole with Kitten on Fence ☐
"Flag Pole"

H $15   SRD $15

Comments: 1995; Original Retail $15.00

Personal Data: _____
____Want Mark ____ Mark _____ Purch. 19__ Pd $ _____

184144 Barrel with Cookies and Cocoa ☐
"Hot Cocoa Stand"

H $15   SRD $15

Comments: 1995; Original Retail $15.00

Personal Data: _____
____Want Mark ____ Mark _____ Purch. 19__ Pd $ _____

184152 Bunnies by Fire ☐
"Bonfire"

H $10   SRD $10

Comments: 1995; Original Retail $10.00

Personal Data: _____
____Want Mark ____ Mark _____ Purch. 19__ Pd $ _____

184160 Enhancement 3-Piece Prepack ☐

See Individual Listings.

H $40   SRD $40

Comments: 1995; Original Retail $40.00
Includes: 184136, 184144, 184152.

Personal Data: _____
____Want Mark ____ Mark _____ Purch. 19__ Pd $ _____

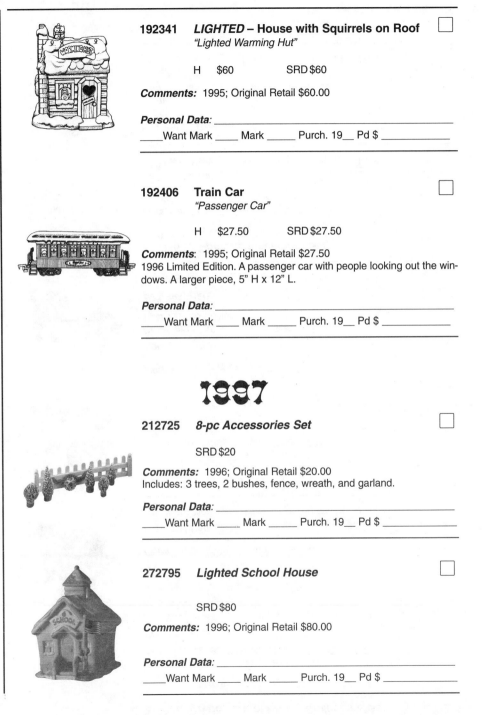

192341 *LIGHTED* – House with Squirrels on Roof ☐
"Lighted Warming Hut"

H $60   SRD $60

Comments: 1995; Original Retail $60.00

Personal Data: _____
____Want Mark ____ Mark _____ Purch. 19__ Pd $ _____

192406 Train Car ☐
"Passenger Car"

H $27.50   SRD $27.50

Comments: 1995; Original Retail $27.50
1996 Limited Edition. A passenger car with people looking out the windows. A larger piece, 5" H x 12" L.

Personal Data: _____
____Want Mark ____ Mark _____ Purch. 19__ Pd $ _____

1997

212725 *8-pc Accessories Set* ☐

SRD $20

Comments: 1996; Original Retail $20.00
Includes: 3 trees, 2 bushes, fence, wreath, and garland.

Personal Data: _____
____Want Mark ____ Mark _____ Purch. 19__ Pd $ _____

272795 *Lighted School House* ☐

SRD $80

Comments: 1996; Original Retail $80.00

Personal Data: _____
____Want Mark ____ Mark _____ Purch. 19__ Pd $ _____

272809　Boy with School Sign
"Chuck"

LE 1997　SRD $22.50

Comments: 1996; Original Retail $22.50
1997 Limited Edition.

Personal Data: _____
____Want Mark ____ Mark _____ Purch. 19__ Pd $ _____

272817　Woman with Books
"Aunt Cleo"

SRD $18.50

Comments: 1996; Original Retail $18.50

Personal Data: _____
____Want Mark ____ Mark _____ Purch. 19__ Pd $ _____

272825　Man and Woman with Pie
"Aunt Bulah And Uncle Sam"

SRD $22.50

Comments: 1996; Original Retail $22.50

Personal Data: _____
____Want Mark ____ Mark _____ Purch. 19__ Pd $ _____

272833　Girl Sitting on Bench with Books
"Heather"

SRD $20

Comments: 1996; Original Retail $20.00

Personal Data: _____
____Want Mark ____ Mark _____ Purch. 19__ Pd $ _____

272841　*Merry Go Round*

SRD $20

Comments: 1996; Original Retail $20.00

Personal Data: _____
____Want Mark ____ Mark _____ Purch. 19__ Pd $ _____

272876　*6-pc School House Collector's Set*

SRD $183.50

Comments: 1996; Original Retail $183.50
Includes: 272795; 272809; 272817; 272825; 272833; 272841.

Personal Data: _____
____Want Mark ____ Mark _____ Purch. 19__ Pd $ _____

See Individual Listings.

272906　*Bike Rack*

SRD $15

Comments: 1996; Original Retail $15.00

Personal Data: _____
____Want Mark ____ Mark _____ Purch. 19__ Pd $ _____

272914　*Garbage Can*

SRD $20

Comments: 1996; Original Retail $20.00

Personal Data: _____
____Want Mark ____ Mark _____ Purch. 19__ Pd $ _____

273007　*Train Cargo Car*

SRD $27.50

Comments: 1996; Original Retail $27.50
1997 Limited Edition.

Personal Data: _____
____Want Mark ____ Mark _____ Purch. 19__ Pd $ _____

273015　*3-pc Enchancement Set*

SRD $43.50

Comments: 1996; Original Retail $43.50
Includes: 272906; 531804; 272914.

Personal Data: _____
____Want Mark ____ Mark _____ Purch. 19__ Pd $ _____

See Individual Listings.

531804　*Bunnies*

SRD $10

Comments: 1996; Original Retail $10.00
Personal Data: _____
____Want Mark ____ Mark _____ Purch. 19__ Pd $ _____

PRECIOUS MOMENTS®
COLLECTORS' CLUB
MEMBERSHIP PIECES

Charter Membership pieces have "1981 Charter Member" written on them. There are less Charter membership pieces than new member pieces will become less and less as years pass. Charter members pieces 99% of the time will be worth a fraction more.

E-0001   1981 SPECIAL CLUB WELCOME GIFT
Boy/Girl Angels on Cloud
"But Love Goes On Forever"

NM $175-185   T $150-165   HG $150-160

Comments: 1979; Club Membership fee was $15.00
Figurine came with NM, T and HG. Less of HG mark. Charter Members' Club pieces have "Charter Member" on all subsequent years' pieces. Generally valued $5 more per mark. It's my opinion fewer "Charter pieces" are being produced due to dropped memberships. These memberships have been passed on with original name remaining and a changed address. Memberships have sold as high as $100. Charter Members would "love" to see a different look to the Charter Member piece to distinguish it from the New Member piece.

Personal Data: _____
____Want Mark ____ Mark _____ Purch. 19__ Pd $ _____

E-0102   CHARTER MEMBER –
1982 Membership Plaque
Boy/Girl Angels on Cloud
"But Love Goes On Forever"

MM $90   T $85   HG $65

Comments: 1981; Club Membership Renewal fee was $13.50
T mark scarce. The inspiration (title) is different than the saying on the front of the plaque (*Precious Moments Last Forever*). If a MM is found it's because the mark was left off the mold. At one time, a mold produced approximately 75 figurines.
See #40, page XV.

Personal Data: _____
____Want Mark ____ Mark _____ Purch. 19__ Pd $ _____

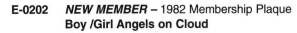

E-0202   NEW MEMBER – 1982 Membership Plaque
Boy /Girl Angels on Cloud
"But Love Goes On Forever"

MM $90   T $80   HG $65
Canadian Error D $110-120

Comments: 1981; New Club Membership fee was $15.00
The inspiration (title) is different than the saying on the front of the plaque (*Precious Moments Last Forever*). This piece was produced by mistake in **1985** with a D mark and sent to Canada. A mad rush of collectors headed to Canada! *Precious Collectibles®* was the first to alert the collectors of this error and we were the first to alert Enesco. Very little notice of a price increase impact with no box one may find for under $50 (HG mark)!

Personal Data: _____
____Want Mark ____ Mark _____ Purch. 19__ Pd $ _____

E-0103   CHARTER MEMBER – 1983 Membership
Boy Conducting Meeting
"Let Us Call The Club To Order"

HG $65   F $55   C $65

Comments: 1982; Renewal Club Membership fee was $13.50
Few C marks.

Personal Data: _____
____Want Mark ____ Mark _____ Purch. 19__ Pd $ _____

E-0303   NEW MEMBER – 1983 Membership
Boy Conducting Meeting
"Let Us Call The Club To Order"

HG $60   F $50   C $60

Comments: 1982; Club Membership fee was $15.00
Only a few C marks.

Personal Data: _____
____Want Mark ____ Mark _____ Purch. 19__ Pd $ _____

 good way to forget your troubles is to help others to forget theirs.

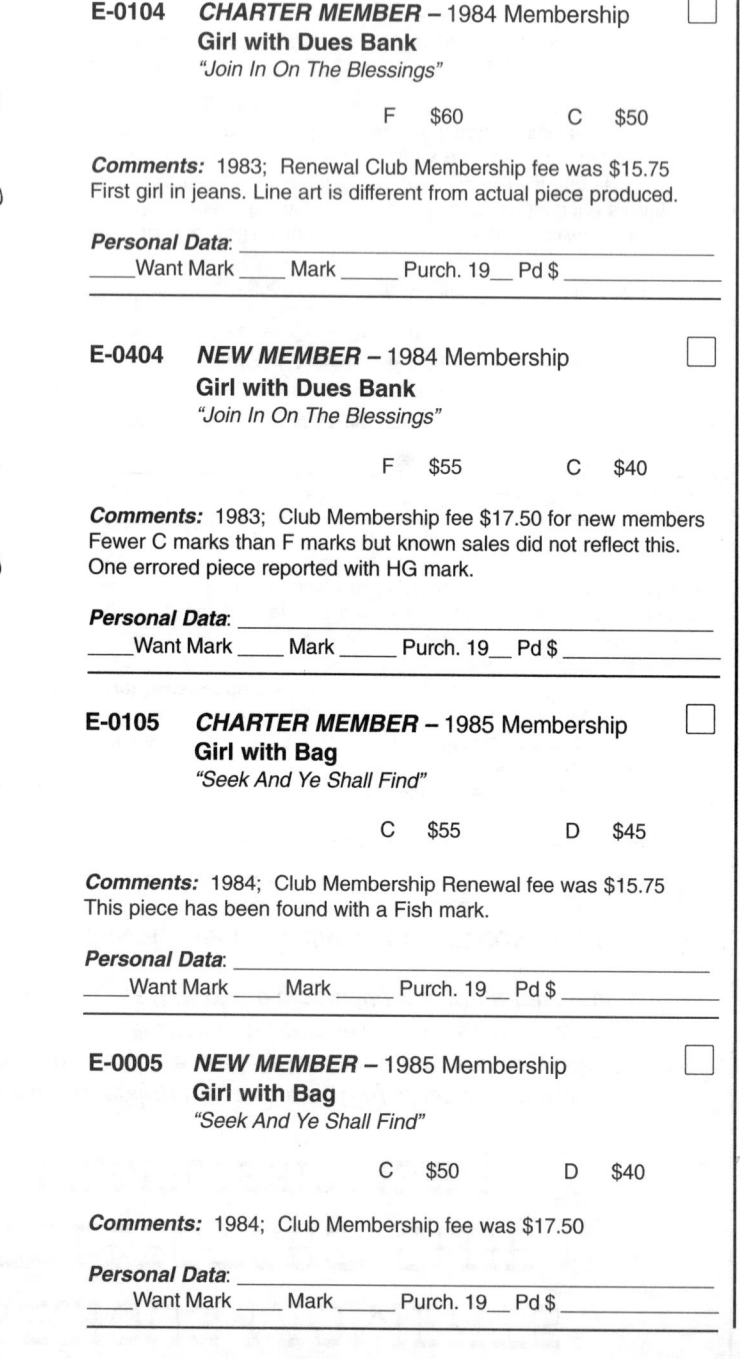

E-0104   *CHARTER MEMBER* – 1984 Membership
Girl with Dues Bank
"Join In On The Blessings"

F $60   C $50

Comments: 1983; Renewal Club Membership fee was $15.75
First girl in jeans. Line art is different from actual piece produced.

Personal Data: _____
____Want Mark ____ Mark _____ Purch. 19__ Pd $ _____

E-0404   *NEW MEMBER* – 1984 Membership
Girl with Dues Bank
"Join In On The Blessings"

F $55   C $40

Comments: 1983; Club Membership fee $17.50 for new members
Fewer C marks than F marks but known sales did not reflect this.
One errored piece reported with HG mark.

Personal Data: _____
____Want Mark ____ Mark _____ Purch. 19__ Pd $ _____

E-0105   *CHARTER MEMBER* – 1985 Membership
Girl with Bag
"Seek And Ye Shall Find"

C $55   D $45

Comments: 1984; Club Membership Renewal fee was $15.75
This piece has been found with a Fish mark.

Personal Data: _____
____Want Mark ____ Mark _____ Purch. 19__ Pd $ _____

E-0005   *NEW MEMBER* – 1985 Membership
Girl with Bag
"Seek And Ye Shall Find"

C $50   D $40

Comments: 1984; Club Membership fee was $17.50

Personal Data: _____
____Want Mark ____ Mark _____ Purch. 19__ Pd $ _____

E-0106   *CHARTER MEMBER* – 1986 Membership
Girl with Needlepoint
"Birds Of A Feather Collect Together"

D $50   OB $45

Comments: 1985; Club Membership renewal fee was $15.75

Personal Data: _____
____Want Mark ____ Mark _____ Purch. 19__ Pd $ _____

E-0006   *NEW MEMBER* – 1986 Membership
Girl with Needlepoint
"Birds Of A Feather Collect Together"

D $45   OB $38

Comments: 1985; Club Membership fee was $17.50
A no box is down to $25.

Personal Data: _____
____Want Mark ____ Mark _____ Purch. 19__ Pd $ _____

E-0107   *CHARTER MEMBER* – 1987 Membership
Girl with Wrapped Package
"Sharing Is Universal"

OB $48   CT $45

Comments: 1987; Club Membership renewal fee was $17.50

Personal Data: _____
____Want Mark ____ Mark _____ Purch. 19__ Pd $ _____

E-0007   *NEW MEMBER* – 1987 Membership
Girl with Wrapped Package
"Sharing Is Universal"

OB $40   CT $35

Comments: 1987; Club Membership fee was $17.50
CT mark easily found.

Personal Data: _____
____Want Mark ____ Mark _____ Purch. 19__ Pd $ _____

Sharing, whether good or bad, usually produces happiness.

E-0108 *CHARTER MEMBER* – 1988 Membership
Girl with Sunflower
"A Growing Love"

	CT $50	FL $40

Comments: 1987; Club Membership renewal fee was $17.50
A girl with a string of sunflowers appears as a PMC doll and on '95 Regional Ball ornaments.

Personal Data: _____
____Want Mark ____ Mark _____ Purch. 19__ Pd $ _____

E-0008 *NEW MEMBER* – 1988 Membership
Girl with Sunflower
"A Growing Love"

	CT $40	FL $35

Comments: 1987; Club Membership fee was $18.50
Many reported that the "flat" look of the flower was a disappointment. Has for this reason been a slow seller.

Personal Data: _____
____Want Mark ____ Mark _____ Purch. 19__ Pd $ _____

C-0109 *CHARTER MEMBER* – 1989 Membership
Girl Putting Puppy in Box
"Always Room For One More"

	FL $47	BA $45

Comments: 1988; Club Membership renewal fee was $18.25
Most trading found on BA mark only.

Personal Data: _____
____Want Mark ____ Mark _____ Purch. 19__ Pd $ _____

C-0009 *NEW MEMBER* – 1989 Membership
Girl Putting Puppy in Box
"Always Room For One More"

FL $40	BA $38	FLM $35

Comments: 1988; Club Membership fee was $19.50

Personal Data: _____
____Want Mark ____ Mark _____ Purch. 19__ Pd $ _____

C-0110 *CHARTER MEMBER* – 1990 Membership
Girl at Table with Figurine
"My Happiness"

	BA $48	FLM $42.50

Comments: 1989; Club Membership renewal fee $21.00

Personal Data: _____
____Want Mark ____ Mark _____ Purch. 19__ Pd $ _____

C-0010 *NEW MEMBER* – 1990 Membership
Girl at Table with Figurine
"My Happiness"

	BA $40	FLM $28

Comments: 1989; Club Membership fee $21.00
The 1990 Sharing Season Ornament (PM904) is similar to this figurine.

Personal Data: _____
____Want Mark ____ Mark _____ Purch. 19__ Pd $ _____

C-0111 Charter Member – 1991 Membership
Girl at Mailbox
"Sharing The Good News Together"

BA $50	FLM $42	V $40

Comments: 1990; Club Membership renewal fee $21.00
"Flat" mailbox was not popular.

Personal Data: _____
____Want Mark ____ Mark _____ Purch. 19__ Pd $ _____

C-0011 *NEW MEMBER* – 1991 Membership
Girl at Mailbox
"Sharing The Good News Together"

	FLM $35	V $25

Comments: 1990; Club Membership fee $21.50
Found with only one eye painted - add $35 to secondary market value. Slow on secondary market for several years. Membership pieces have not continued to rise in value compared to many regular line pieces. Even most regular line pieces have been slow to rise in price since approximately 1986 except for first marks, suspended or retired pieces.

Personal Data: _____
____Want Mark ____ Mark _____ Purch. 19__ Pd $ _____

C-0112 **CHARTER MEMBER** – 1992 Membership
Girl in Space Suit
"The Club That's Out Of This World"

V $42   GC $40

Comments: 1990; Club Membership renewal fee $25.00
Came with a matching patch. Collectors received the astronaut ornament in 1992 when signing up two new members to the National Club.

Personal Data: _____
____Want Mark ____ Mark _____ Purch. 19__ Pd $ _____

Colonel Steven R. Nagle
100th Astronaut in Space

Rosie presented Steve with the Astronaut Girl Precious Moments Membership Figurine and Membership in the National Club. Steve and Rosie both claim Canton, Illinois, as their hometown. Rosie also sent the same figurine to Steve's mother.

C-0012 **NEW MEMBER** – 1992 Membership
Girl in Space Suit
"The Club That's Out Of This World"

V $38   GC $35

Comments: 1990; Club Membership fee $25.00
Came with a matching patch. I presented this piece to the 100th astronaut of the United States, Col. Steve Nagel. He is from my hometown, Canton, Illinois. Most trading found was on GC mark.

Personal Data: _____
____Want Mark ____ Mark _____ Purch. 19__ Pd $ _____

C-0113 **CHARTER MEMBER** – 1993 Membership
Girl with Satchel by Signs
"Loving, Caring And Sharing Along The Way"

GC $45   B $35

Comments: 1992; Club Membership renewal fee $25.00

Personal Data: _____
____Want Mark ____ Mark _____ Purch. 19__ Pd $ _____

C-0013 **NEW MEMBER** – 1993 Membership
Girl with Satchel by Signs
"Loving, Caring And Sharing Along The Way"

GC $35   B $30

Comments: 1993; Club Membership fee $25.00

Personal Data: _____
____Want Mark ____ Mark _____ Purch. 19__ Pd $ _____

C-0114 **CHARTER MEMBER** – 1994 Membership
Girl Sitting in Pot of Gold
"You're The End Of My Rainbow"

B $38   TRP $32

Comments: 1993; Club Membership renewal fee $25.00
Cute!

Personal Data: _____
____Want Mark ____ Mark _____ Purch. 19__ Pd $ _____

C-0014   *NEW MEMBER* – 1994 Membership
Girl Sitting in Pot of Gold
"You're The End Of My Rainbow"

B $35   TRP $20   S $20

Comments: 1993; Club Membership fee $25.00
Price dropped on TRP mark.

Personal Data: _____
____Want Mark ____ Mark _____ Purch. 19__ Pd $ _____

C-0115   *CHARTER MEMBER* – 1995 Membership
Girl w/ Heart Shaped Cookies on Tray
"You're The Sweetest Cookie In The Batch"

TRP $30   S $22

Comments: 1994; Club Membership renewal fee $25.00
Cute!

Personal Data: _____
____Want Mark ____ Mark _____ Purch. 19__ Pd $ _____

C-0015   *NEW MEMBER* – 1995 Membership
Girl w/Heart Shaped Cookies on Tray
"You're The Sweetest Cookie In The Batch"

TRP $30   S $22

Comments: 1994; Club Membership fee $27.00

Personal Data: _____
____Want Mark ____ Mark _____ Purch. 19__ Pd $ _____

C-0116   *CHARTER MEMBER* – 1996 Membership
Girl Holding Picture Frame
"You're As Pretty As A Picture"

S $32   H $22

Comments: 1995; Club Membership renewal fee $25.00

Personal Data: _____
____Want Mark ____ Mark _____ Purch. 19__ Pd $ _____

C-0016   *NEW MEMBER* – 1996 Membership
Girl Holding Picture Frame
"You're As Pretty As A Picture"

S $30   H $27

Comments: 1995; Club Membership fee $27.00
Personal Data: _____
____Want Mark ____ Mark _____ Purch. 19__ Pd $ _____

C-0117   *CHARTER MEMBER* – 1997 Membership
Girl with Toaster
"A Special Toast To Precious Moments"

H $27   SRD $27

Comments: 1996; Club Membership fee $27.00
Personal Data: _____
____Want Mark ____ Mark _____ Purch. 19__ Pd $ _____

C-0017   *NEW MEMBER* – 1997 Membership
Girl with Toaster
"A Special Toast To Precious Moments"

H $27   SRD $27

Comments: 1996; Club Membership fee $27.00
Personal Data: _____
____Want Mark ____ Mark _____ Purch. 19__ Pd $ _____

PRECIOUS MOMENTS®
COLLECTORS' CLUB
CLUB PIECES

PC112   **CLOISONNÉ Medallions**
"Loving, Caring And Sharing"

$25

Comments: 1993; Original Retail $22.50
Set of three medallions in special gift box.

Personal Data: _____
____Want Mark ____ Mark _____ Purch. 19__ Pd $ _____

PM034   **Club Member Desk Flag**

$1.00

Comments: 1990; Original Retail $4.00
Accessory to be placed with PM901, 1990 Club piece.

Personal Data: _____
____Want Mark ____ Mark _____ Purch. 19__ Pd $ _____

PM040   ORNAMENT – Girl At Signpost with Satchel ☐
"Loving, Caring And Sharing Along The Way"

B $30

Comments: 1992; Original Retail $12.50
1993 Club Member Appreciation ornament. This took the place of the Sharing Season ornament for 1993.

Personal Data: _____
____Want Mark ____ Mark _____ Purch. 19__ Pd $ _____

PM041   ORNAMENT – Girl with Rainbow ☐
"You Are The End Of My Rainbow"

TRP $35

Comments: 1994; Original Retail $15.00
1994 Club Member Appreciation ornament. Price up from last year!

Personal Data: _____
____Want Mark ____ Mark _____ Purch. 19__ Pd $ _____

Testing, Testing – Precious Moments, Sam Retired, Suspended, Club pieces...

CHAPEL WINDOW ORNAMENTS

Insignificant amount of sales reported to establish a price.

Comments: 1990; Original Retail $15.00 $18-$20

PM190	*"Blessed Are The Poor In Spirit, For Theirs Is The Kingdom Of God"*	☐
PM290	*"Blessed Are They That Mourn, For They Shall Be Comforted"*	☐
PM390	*"Blessed Are The Meek, For They Shall Inherit The Earth"*	☐
PM490	*"Blessed Are They That Hunger And Thirst For Righteousness, For They Shall Be Filled"*	☐
PM590	*"Blessed Are The Merciful, For They Shall Obtain Mercy"*	☐
PM690	*"Blessed Are The Pure In Heart, For They Shall See God"*	☐
PM790	*"Blessed Are The Peacemakers, For They Shall Be Called Sons Of God"*	☐
PM890	7 Piece Assortment	☐

Comments: 1990; Original Retail $105.00 set.
Try several as wind chimes! Available to Club Members Only. Do not look for a secondary market on these for another year or more. No trading found. Precious Moments collectors collect mainly the figurines.

Personal Data: _____
____Want Mark ____ Mark _____ Purch. 19__ Pd $ _____

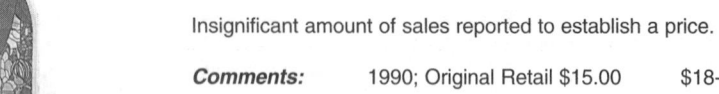

PM811   Boy On Telephone ☐
"Hello, Lord, It's Me Again"

T $400   HG $460

Comments: 1981; Original Retail $25.00
1981 Club piece. A popular Club piece. **More T than HG marks.** Excellent to display with Girl on Telephone (521477). Sam designed this for his son, Jon, who received a "Dear Jon" note. As old as this piece is new collectors will pay the same to own. Insure T mark at $450.

Personal Data: _____
____Want Mark ____ Mark _____ Purch. 19__ Pd $ _____

PM821 Girl in Curlers with Mirror
"Smile, God Loves You"

HG $195 F $175

Comments: 1982; Original Retail $25.00
1982 Club piece. HG mark can easily be found at above price of $195 or less. Do not over insure! 1981 and 1982 Club pieces are high in value mainly because members never thought to get extra memberships.

Personal Data: _____
____Want Mark ____ Mark ____ Purch. 19__ Pd $ _____

PM822 Clown with Mask
"Put On A Happy Face"

HG $195 F $165 C $175

Comments: 1981; Original Retail $25.00
1983 Club piece. Bottoms of bases had differences also; no real significance on the secondary market. This piece has been found with color variations in the clown's outfit. First two Club pieces higher on secondary market due to "popular pieces" as well as less production until 1983. 1983-1984 were the "over produced" years. Have seen gray hearts instead of pink on this piece.

Personal Data: _____
____Want Mark ____ Mark ____ Purch. 19__ Pd $ _____

PM831 Girl Looking Under Blanket
"Dawn's Early Light"

F $65 C $60

Comments: 1983; Original Retail $27.50
1983 Club piece. "Dawn" is Sam's sister.

Personal Data: _____
____Want Mark ____ Mark ____ Purch. 19__ Pd $ _____

PM841 Boy with Flashlight
"God's Ray Of Mercy"

F $75 C $50 D $40

Comments: 1983; Original Retail $25.00
1984 Special Edition. Sam's tribute to his brother, Ray Butcher. Cute piece!

Personal Data: _____
____Want Mark ____ Mark ____ Purch. 19__ Pd $ _____

PM842 Race Car Driver
"Trust In The Lord To The Finish"

C $60 D $55

Comments: 1984; Original Retail $25.00
1984 Club piece. Sam's tribute to his younger brother, Hank Butcher. Most club pieces can be found at *Precious Collectibles*® swap meets. Remember our shows on March 16 and October 26, 1996, in Westmont IL. Usually 150 to 200 tables of collectibles. A great time to meet other collectors represented from over 16 states.

Personal Data: _____
____Want Mark ____ Mark ____ Purch. 19__ Pd $ _____

PM843 *NEEDLECRAFT* - Race Car Driver
"Trust In The Lord To The Finish"

$12.50

Comments: 1984; Original Retail $11.00

Personal Data: _____
____Want Mark ____ Mark ____ Purch. 19__ Pd $ _____

PM851 Girl with Lambs
"The Lord Is My Shepherd"

NM $90 C $75 D $70
OB $80

Comments: 1984; Original Retail $25.00.
1985 Club piece. (We've heard two reports of MM pieces.) Occurs on most pieces. OB mark is scarce. This is one of the more popular ones. Club pieces tend to be slow in trading the last five years!

Personal Data: _____
____Want Mark ____ Mark ____ Purch. 19__ Pd $ _____

PM852 Boy Lying on Stomach with Lamb
"I Love To Tell The Story"

D $65 OB $60

Comments: 1984; Original Retail $27.50.
1985 Club piece. A popular piece. This figurine was a tribute to Pastor Blue who led Sam to the Lord. He is a man in whom we can see Jesus. Pastor Blue writes an article in each issue of *Precious Collectibles.*® This is a very special piece; a favorite of many.

Personal Data: _____
____Want Mark ____ Mark ____ Purch. 19__ Pd $ _____

PM853 Needlecraft - Girl with Lambs
"The Lord Is My Shepherd"

$15

Comments: 1984; Original Retail $11.00.

Personal Data: _____
___Want Mark ___ Mark ___ Purch. 19__ Pd $ _____

PM861 Grandma Praying
"Grandma's Prayer"

D $80   OB $70   CT $80

Comments: 1986; Original Retail $25.00.
1986 Club piece. Less of CT mark than other marks. More OB than others.

Personal Data: _____
___Want Mark ___ Mark ___ Purch. 19__ Pd $ _____

PM862 Boy in Car
"I'm Following Jesus"

D $100   CT $80
OB $90   FL $80

Comments: 1986; Original Retail $25.00
1986 Club piece. Our research indicates this 1986 piece was produced with the CT mark and the FL mark. May eventually prove to be scarce marks. OB mark continues to be the most traded of the marks. Also, several D marks recently reported in '96!

Personal Data: _____
___Want Mark ___ Mark ___ Purch. 19__ Pd $ _____

PM863 Mugs - Boy in Car
"I'm Following Jesus"

$20

Comments: 1986; Original Retail $17.50
Set of four mugs.

Personal Data: _____
___Want Mark ___ Mark ___ Purch. 19__ Pd $ _____

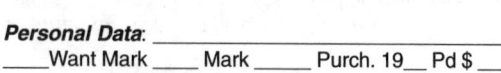

*P*eople take your example far more
seriously than your advice.

PM871 Girl with Lamb
"Feed My Sheep"

OB $85   CT $65   FL $50

Comments: 1986; Original Retail $25.00
1987 Club piece. A very popular piece! This piece is becoming harder to find on the secondary market. Collectors are saying that "Club" pieces should be "different" from the regular line. Most trading foundd on CT mark in '95 & '96. Reported OB mark found.

Personal Data: _____
___Want Mark ___ Mark ___ Purch. 19__ Pd $ _____

PM872 Boy Watching Seeds
"In His Time"

OB $50   CT $50   FL $37.50

Comments: 1987; Original Retail $25.00
1987 Club piece. 1986 license date on box; 1987 on figurines.
Two other figurines in the regular line are very similar. Notice price compared to other Club pieces because of this similarity. Most sales reported being sold were the CT mark.

Personal Data: _____
___Want Mark ___ Mark ___ Purch. 19__ Pd $ _____

PM873 Boy Drawing Valentine
"Loving You Dear Valentine"

OB $40   CT $40   FL $35

Comments: 1986; Original Retail $25.00
1987 Club piece. Most marks found being sold in '96 was the OB mark.

Personal Data: _____
___Want Mark ___ Mark ___ Purch. 19__ Pd $ _____

PM874 Girl Drawing Valentine
"Loving You Dear Valentine"

OB $45   CT $40   FL $35

Comments: 1986; Original Retail $25.00
1987 Club piece. Many sales found on OB mark!

Personal Data: _____
___Want Mark ___ Mark ___ Purch. 19__ Pd $ _____

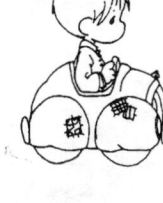

PM821   Girl in Curlers with Mirror
"Smile, God Loves You"

HG $195   F $175

Comments: 1982; Original Retail $25.00
1982 Club piece. HG mark can easily be found at above price of $195 or less. Do not over insure! 1981 and 1982 Club pieces are high in value mainly because members never thought to get extra memberships.

Personal Data: _____
____Want Mark ____ Mark _____ Purch. 19__ Pd $ _____

PM822   Clown with Mask
"Put On A Happy Face"

HG $195   F $165   C $175

Comments: 1981; Original Retail $25.00
1983 Club piece. Bottoms of bases had differences also; no real significance on the secondary market. This piece has been found with color variations in the clown's outfit. First two Club pieces higher on secondary market due to "popular pieces" as well as less production until 1983. 1983-1984 were the "over produced" years. Have seen gray hearts instead of pink on this piece.

Personal Data: _____
____Want Mark ____ Mark _____ Purch. 19__ Pd $ _____

PM831   Girl Looking Under Blanket
"Dawn's Early Light"

F $65   C $60

Comments: 1983; Original Retail $27.50
1983 Club piece. "Dawn" is Sam's sister.

Personal Data: _____
____Want Mark ____ Mark _____ Purch. 19__ Pd $ _____

PM841   Boy with Flashlight
"God's Ray Of Mercy"

F $75   C $50   D $40

Comments: 1983; Original Retail $25.00
1984 Special Edition. Sam's tribute to his brother, Ray Butcher. Cute piece!

Personal Data: _____
____Want Mark ____ Mark _____ Purch. 19__ Pd $ _____

PM842   Race Car Driver
"Trust In The Lord To The Finish"

C $60   D $55

Comments: 1984; Original Retail $25.00
1984 Club piece. Sam's tribute to his younger brother, Hank Butcher. Most club pieces can be found at *Precious Collectibles*® swap meets. Remember our shows on March 16 and October 26, 1996, in Westmont IL. Usually 150 to 200 tables of collectibles. A great time to meet other collectors represented from over 16 states.

Personal Data: _____
____Want Mark ____ Mark _____ Purch. 19__ Pd $ _____

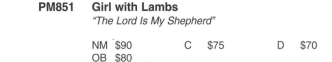

PM843   *NEEDLECRAFT* - Race Car Driver
"Trust In The Lord To The Finish"

$12.50

Comments: 1984; Original Retail $11.00

Personal Data: _____
____Want Mark ____ Mark _____ Purch. 19__ Pd $ _____

PM851   Girl with Lambs
"The Lord Is My Shepherd"

NM $90   C $75   D $70
OB $80

Comments: 1984; Original Retail $25.00.
1985 Club piece. (We've heard two reports of MM pieces.) Occurs on most pieces. OB mark is scarce. This is one of the more popular ones. Club pieces tend to be slow in trading the last five years!
Personal Data: _____
____Want Mark ____ Mark _____ Purch. 19__ Pd $ _____

PM852   Boy Lying on Stomach with Lamb
"I Love To Tell The Story"

D $65   OB $60

Comments: 1984; Original Retail $27.50.
1985 Club piece. A popular piece. This figurine was a tribute to Pastor Blue who led Sam to the Lord. He is a man in whom we can see Jesus.   Pastor Blue writes an article in each issue of *Precious Collectibles*.® This is a very special piece; a favorite of many.

Personal Data: _____
____Want Mark ____ Mark _____ Purch. 19__ Pd $ _____

PM853 **Needlecraft - Girl with Lambs**
"The Lord Is My Shepherd"

$15

Comments: 1984; Original Retail $11.00.

Personal Data: _____
____Want Mark ____ Mark ____ Purch. 19__ Pd $ _____

PM861 **Grandma Praying**
"Grandma's Prayer"

D $80   OB $70   CT $80

Comments: 1986; Original Retail $25.00.
1986 Club piece. Less of CT mark than other marks. More OB than others.

Personal Data: _____
____Want Mark ____ Mark ____ Purch. 19__ Pd $ _____

PM862 **Boy in Car**
"I'm Following Jesus"

D $100   CT $80
OB $90   FL $80

Comments: 1986; Original Retail $25.00
1986 Club piece. Our research indicates this 1986 piece was produced with the CT mark and the FL mark. May eventually prove to be scarce marks. OB mark continues to be the most traded of the marks. Also, several D marks recently reported in '96!

Personal Data: _____
____Want Mark ____ Mark ____ Purch. 19__ Pd $ _____

PM863 **Mugs - Boy in Car**
"I'm Following Jesus"

$20

Comments: 1986; Original Retail $17.50
Set of four mugs.

Personal Data: _____
____Want Mark ____ Mark ____ Purch. 19__ Pd $ _____

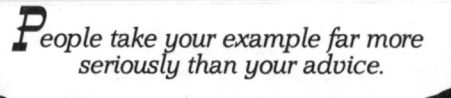

PM871 **Girl with Lamb**
"Feed My Sheep"

OB $85   CT $65   FL $50

Comments: 1986; Original Retail $25.00
1987 Club piece. A very popular piece! This piece is becoming harder to find on the secondary market. Collectors are saying that "Club" pieces should be "different" from the regular line. Most trading found on CT mark in '95 & '96. Reported OB mark found.

Personal Data: _____
____Want Mark ____ Mark ____ Purch. 19__ Pd $ _____

PM872 **Boy Watching Seeds**
"In His Time"

OB $50   CT $50   FL $37.50

Comments: 1987; Original Retail $25.00
1987 Club piece. 1986 license date on box; 1987 on figurines. Two other figurines in the regular line are very similar. Notice price compared to other Club pieces because of this similarity. Most sales reported being sold were the CT mark.

Personal Data: _____
____Want Mark ____ Mark ____ Purch. 19__ Pd $ _____

PM873 **Boy Drawing Valentine**
"Loving You Dear Valentine"

OB $40   CT $40   FL $35

Comments: 1986; Original Retail $25.00
1987 Club piece. Most marks found being sold in '96 was the OB mark.

Personal Data: _____
____Want Mark ____ Mark ____ Purch. 19__ Pd $ _____

PM874 **Girl Drawing Valentine**
"Loving You Dear Valentine"

OB $45   CT $40   FL $35

Comments: 1986; Original Retail $25.00
1987 Club piece. Many sales found on OB mark!

Personal Data: _____
____Want Mark ____ Mark ____ Purch. 19__ Pd $ _____

PM881 **Girl Painting Butterfly**
"God Bless You For Touching My Life"

CT $60   FL $50   BA $45

Comments: 1988; Original Retail $27.50
1988 Club piece. This is a pretty piece. Many sales found on FL mark!

Personal Data: _____
____Want Mark ____ Mark _____ Purch. 19__ Pd $ _____

PM901 **Girl in Race Car**
"Ten Years And Still Going Strong"

FLM $50   V $45

Comments: 1990; Original Retail $30.00
1990 Club piece. A *"desk flag"* (PM034) was sold separately to be displayed with this piece. This is a popular figurine! Most sales found were for the FLM mark.

Personal Data: _____
____Want Mark ____ Mark _____ Purch. 19__ Pd $ _____

PM882 **Boy with Dog in Trash Can**
"You Just Cannot Chuck A Good Friendship"

FL $50   BA $40

Comments: 1988; Original Retail $27.50
1988 Club piece. A tribute to "Chuck," Sam's brother.

Personal Data: _____
____Want Mark ____ Mark _____ Purch. 19__ Pd $ _____

PM902 **Girl Patching Teddy Bear**
"You Are A Blessing To Me"

FLM $50   V $45

Comments: 1990; Original Retail $27.50
1990 Club piece. Fewer V marks. Teddy bear lovers want this piece! Many sales foun on FLM!

Personal Data: _____
____Want Mark ____ Mark _____ Purch. 19__ Pd $ _____

PM891 **Girl at Ballot Box**
"You Will Always Be My Choice"

BA $42   FLM $35

Comments: 1989; Original Retail $27.50
1989 Club piece.

Personal Data: _____
____Want Mark ____ Mark _____ Purch. 19__ Pd $ _____

PM911 **Girl Helping Baby Walk**
"One Step At A Time"

V $52.50   GC $40

Comments: 1990; Original Retail $33.00
1991 Club piece. Was not popular for a Club piece. Collectors voiced their opinion – "Resembles *Baby's First Series.*" So why not display this piece with that series?

Personal Data: _____
____Want Mark ____ Mark _____ Purch. 19__ Pd $ _____

PM892 **Boy with Push Mower**
"Mow Power To Ya!"

BA $52.50   FLM $47.50

Comments: 1989; Original Retail $27.50
1989 Club piece. Cute piece!

Personal Data: _____
____Want Mark ____ Mark _____ Purch. 19__ Pd $ _____

PM912 **Indian Boy Eating Spinach**
"Lord Keep Me In TeePee-Top Shape"

V $60   GC $50

Comments: 1990; Original Retail $27.50
1991 Club piece.

Personal Data: _____
____Want Mark ____ Mark _____ Purch. 19__ Pd $ _____

*A*ll things come to him who waits. Sometimes, though, it's just the leftovers from the fellow who got there first.

PM921   Mr. Webb Building a Bird House
"Only Love Can Make A Home"

GC $60   B $50

Comments: 1992; Original Retail $30.00
Dedicated to Mr. Webb, a friend of Sam's, who made homes for blue birds in Missouri.

Personal Data: _____
____Want Mark ____ Mark _____ Purch. 19__ Pd $ _____

PM922   Girl Kneeling in Garden
"Sowing The Seeds Of Love"

GC $35   B $35

Comments: 1992; Original Retail $30.00
1992 Club piece.

Personal Data: _____
____Want Mark ____ Mark _____ Purch. 19__ Pd $ _____

PM931   Girl Kneeling by Sand Pail
"His Little Treasure"

B $40   TRP $35

Comments: 1992; Original Retail $30.00
1993 Club piece. Many sales found on B mark.

Personal Data: _____
____Want Mark ____ Mark _____ Purch. 19__ Pd $ _____

PM932   Girl Holding Teddy Bear
"Loving"

B $70   TRP $45

Comments: 1992; Original Retail $30.00
1993 Club piece. Great for Precious Moments® collectors as well as teddy bear collectors.

Personal Data: _____
____Want Mark ____ Mark _____ Purch. 19__ Pd $ _____

*T*his world would be a fine place if people were always as patient as they are when they are waiting for a fish to bite.

PM941   Girl Bandaging Teddy Bear
"Caring"

TRP $55   S $50

Comments: 1992; Original Retail $35.00
1994 Club piece.

Personal Data: _____
____Want Mark ____ Mark _____ Purch. 19__ Pd $ _____

PM942   Girl Feeding Teddy Bear
"Sharing"

TRP $55   S $40

Comments: 1992; Original Retail $35.00
1994 Club piece. PM932, PM941 and PM942, together, form the theme of the Precious Moments® collection - *Loving, Caring and Sharing.*

Personal Data: _____
____Want Mark ____ Mark _____ Purch. 19__ Pd $ _____

PMB034   Girl with Book
"You Fill The Pages Of My Life"
LE 1994
Error – *You Fill The Page Of My Life*   TRP $75
Corrected   TRP $70

Comments: 1994; Original Retail $67.50
Available in the Members Only package containing the Club edition of the hardcover book *Precious Moments Last Forever* and figurine (530980). This figurine's earliest production pieces have been known to contain an error which has since been corrected. The inscription was incorrectly printed as *You Fill The Page Of My Life.* Price plummeted in '96-'97.

Personal Data: _____
____Want Mark ____ Mark _____ Purch. 19__ Pd $ _____

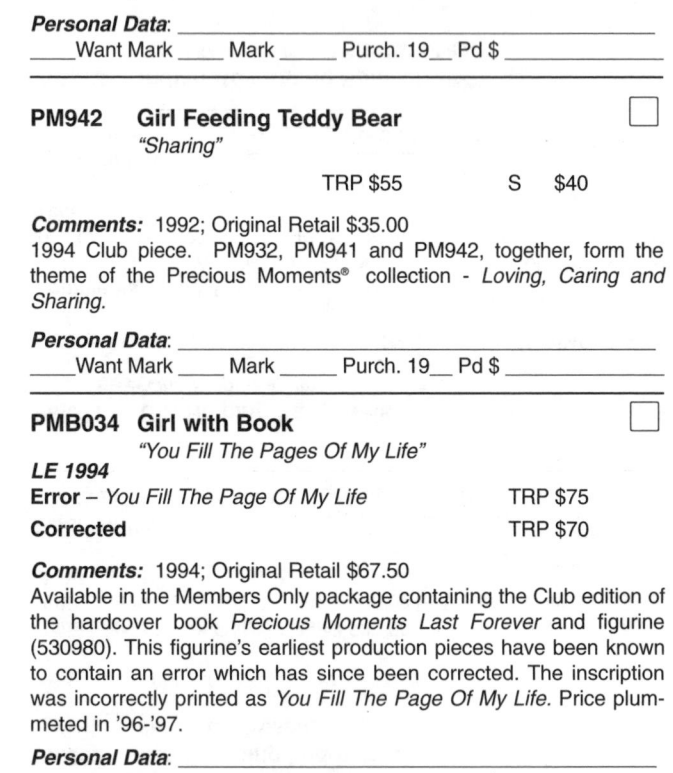

PM951   Girl Panning for Gold
"You're One In A Million To Me"

S $40

Comments: 1994; Original Retail $35.00
1995 Club piece. I always wanted to pan for gold and got to do it in Alaska in 1996. I did not start another gold rush, sorry to say.

Personal Data: _____
____Want Mark ____ Mark _____ Purch. 19__ Pd $ _____

PM952   Girl Peeling Potatoes
"Always Take Time To Pray"

S $40

Comments: 1995; Original Retail $35.00
1995 Club piece.

Personal Data: _____
____Want Mark ____ Mark _____ Purch. 19__ Pd $ _____

PM961   Girl Standing at Blackboard
"Teach Us To Love One Another"

S $50   H $45

Comments: 1995; Original Retail $40.00
1996 Club piece. This figurine was found with a Ship mark. Has been found with decal upside down. This teacher is a red head! *See #33, page XIV.*

Personal Data: _____
____Want Mark ____ Mark _____ Purch. 19__ Pd $ _____

PM962   Girl in Poodle Skirt with Soda
"Our Club Is Soda-licious"

H $38

Comments: 1995; Original Retail $35.00
1996 Club piece.

Personal Data: _____
____Want Mark ____ Mark _____ Purch. 19__ Pd $ _____

PM971   Boy with Trunk of Figurines
"You Will Always Be A Treasure To Me"

SRD $50

Comments: 1996; Original Retail $50.00
1997 Club piece.

Personal Data: _____
____Want Mark ____ Mark _____ Purch. 19__ Pd $ _____

PM972   Girl Bandaging Mouse's Tail
"Blessed Are The Merciful"

SRD $40

Comments: 1996; Original Retail $40.00
1997 Club piece.

Personal Data: _____
____Want Mark ____ Mark _____ Purch. 19__ Pd $ _____

12440   Commemorative Edition 5th Anniversary
"God Bless Our Years Together"

D $260

Comments: 1984; Original Retail $175.00
Extra large pieces haven't risen on the secondary market proportionately to regular pieces.

Personal Data: _____
____Want Mark ____ Mark _____ Purch. 19__ Pd $ _____

127817   Girl Standing by Curio Cabinet
"A Perfect Display Of Fifteen Happy Years"

S $115

Comments: 1994; Original Retail $100.00
Special commemorative figurine of the Fifteenth Anniversary of the Enesco Precious Moments Collectors' Club.

Personal Data: _____
____Want Mark ____ Mark _____ Purch. 19__ Pd $ _____

227986   ORNAMENT
"Celebrating A Decade Of Loving, Caring And Sharing"

DATED 1990 $10

Comments: 1984; Original Retail $7.00
Special Ten-Year Anniversary Ornament. Flat porcelain ornament.

Personal Data: _____
____Want Mark ____ Mark _____ Purch. 19__ Pd $ _____

527386 Columbus in Large Ship
"This Land Is Our Land"

LE 1992 - 5 YEARS OLD   V $350-425   GC $350-400

Comments: 1991; Original Retail $350.00
1992 Limited Edition Commemorative available to Club Members only.
Production problems with paint chipping off of Columbus' hat.

Personal Data: _____
____Want Mark ____ Mark _____ Purch. 19__ Pd $ _____

SHARING SEASON GIFTS

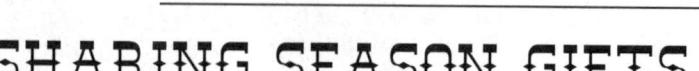

Gift from Enesco for signing up new Club Members

12246   MEDALLION – 1984
"Precious Moments Last Forever"

C $120

Comments: 1984 Sharing Season Gift

Personal Data: _____
____Want Mark ____ Mark _____ Purch. 19__ Pd $ _____

MAGNET – 1985
B/G on Cloud Precious Moments Logo

$25

Comments: 1985 Sharing Season Gift

Personal Data: _____
____Want Mark ____ Mark _____ Purch. 19__ Pd $ _____

PM864   ORNAMENT – 1986
"Birds Of A Feather Collect Together"

OB $155-165

Comments: 1986 Sharing Season Gift
Very little trading found on this ornament in research the past few
years. No increase reported or found from last year.

Personal Data: _____
____Want Mark ____ Mark _____ Purch. 19__ Pd $ _____

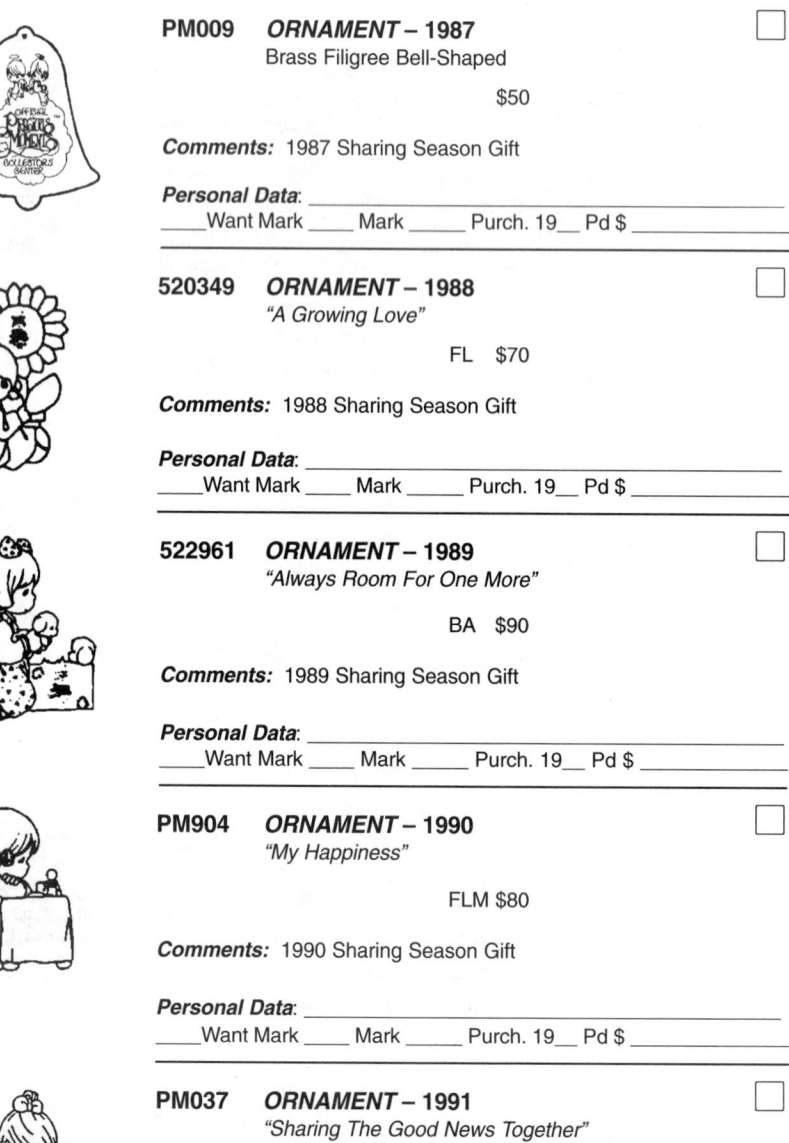

PM009   ORNAMENT – 1987
Brass Filigree Bell-Shaped

$50

Comments: 1987 Sharing Season Gift

Personal Data: _____
____Want Mark ____ Mark _____ Purch. 19__ Pd $ _____

520349   ORNAMENT – 1988
"A Growing Love"

FL $70

Comments: 1988 Sharing Season Gift

Personal Data: _____
____Want Mark ____ Mark _____ Purch. 19__ Pd $ _____

522961   ORNAMENT – 1989
"Always Room For One More"

BA $90

Comments: 1989 Sharing Season Gift

Personal Data: _____
____Want Mark ____ Mark _____ Purch. 19__ Pd $ _____

PM904   ORNAMENT – 1990
"My Happiness"

FLM $80

Comments: 1990 Sharing Season Gift

Personal Data: _____
____Want Mark ____ Mark _____ Purch. 19__ Pd $ _____

PM037   ORNAMENT – 1991
"Sharing The Good News Together"

V $70

Comments: 1991 Sharing Season Gift
Personal Data: _____
____Want Mark ____ Mark _____ Purch. 19__ Pd $ _____

PM038 *ORNAMENT – 1992*
"The Club That's Out Of This World"

GC $70

Comments: 1992 Sharing Season Gift

Personal Data: _____
___Want Mark ____ Mark _____ Purch. 19__ Pd $ _____

PM030 *MEDALLION*
Goose Girl

$375

Comments: Gift by the factory to those who went on the Annual Tour of The Orient and visited the factory. Less than 150 are in the hands of collectors now. Around 25 per year were given to the group of visitors who traveled on the Enesco Orient Tour. If more have been given I am not aware of them. A great trip! You're treated like royalty! Go if you can should this trip be offered again by Enesco. Plan to shop in Hong Kong! Don't plan on sleeping or eating foods with sugar! Walk and exercise before you go! Jet lag will be something else! Memories will last forever. If this medallion has only a $375 value, then don't insure the Enesco Cruise medallions for any more! There are approximately 800 of those and they can be found on the secondary market.

Personal Data: _____
___Want Mark ____ Mark _____ Purch. 19__ Pd $ _____

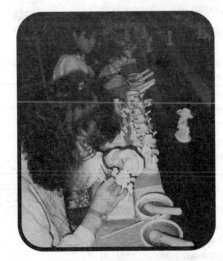

The Precious Moments® line of porcelain collectibles are molded and hand painted in the Orient. At left, Hallelujah Country, the cute l'il guy from our cover, is being painted by employees on an assembly line.

Birthday Club
Membership Pieces

The following membership pieces came with the purchase of the Birthday Club Membership Kit. Club pieces are purchased using redemption forms after you receive the Membership Kit.
Hint: Join on January 1 in order to get the prior year's mark on your Club pieces!

B-0001 **1986 Charter Membership**
Clown Beating Drum
"Our Club Can't Be Beat"

HG	$100	OB	$70
D	$85	CT	$65

Comments: 1985; Club Membership fee was $10.00.
Has "Charter Member" on base. New in 1986. HG very rare but it is out there! Lots of trading found on this piece.

Personal Data: _____
___Want Mark ____ Mark _____ Purch. 19__ Pd $ _____

B-0102 *1987 Charter Membership*
Clown with Cymbals
"A Smile's The Cymbal Of Joy"

A Smile's The Symbol Of Joy (error)	OB	$80
	CT	$75
A Smile's The Cymbal Of Joy (corrected)	OB	$70
	CT	$65
	FL	$60

Comments: 1987; Club Membership fee was $10.00
Has "Charter Member" on base.

Personal Data: _____
___Want Mark ____ Mark _____ Purch. 19__ Pd $ _____

B-0002   *1987 New Member*

Clown with Cymbals
"A Smile's The Cymbal Of Joy"

A Smile's The Symbol Of Joy (error)   OB $70
                                               CT $60

A Smile's The Cymbal Of Joy (corrected)   FL $50

Comments: 1987; Club Membership fee was $10.00
No "Charter Member" on base.

Personal Data: _____
____Want Mark ____ Mark _____ Purch. 19__ Pd $ _____

B-0103   *1988 Charter Membership*

Clown with Birthday Cake
"The Sweetest Club Around"

                        FL $45   BA $40

Comments: 1988; Club Membership fee was $11.50
Has "Charter Member" on base. Those who signed up in 1986 were
"Charter Members," first in the club. Each year's Charter Member
piece will state "Charter Member" on it (omitted in 1990). Notice two
different numerals for the same piece; one for Charter Members, one
for Club Members who did not join the first year.

Personal Data: _____
____Want Mark ____ Mark _____ Purch. 19__ Pd $ _____

B-0003   *1988 New Member*

Clown with Birthday Cake
"The Sweetest Club Around"

                        FL $45   BA $40

Comments: 1988; Club Membership fee was $11.50
1988 Membership Renewal Gift.

Personal Data: _____
____Want Mark ____ Mark _____ Purch. 19__ Pd $ _____

B-0104   *1989 Charter Membership*

Bear Holding Balloons
"Have A Beary Special Birthday"

FL $40   BA $35   FLM $25

Comments: 1988; Club Membership fee was $11.50
Prices fell from '96.

Personal Data: _____
____Want Mark ____ Mark _____ Purch. 19__ Pd $ _____

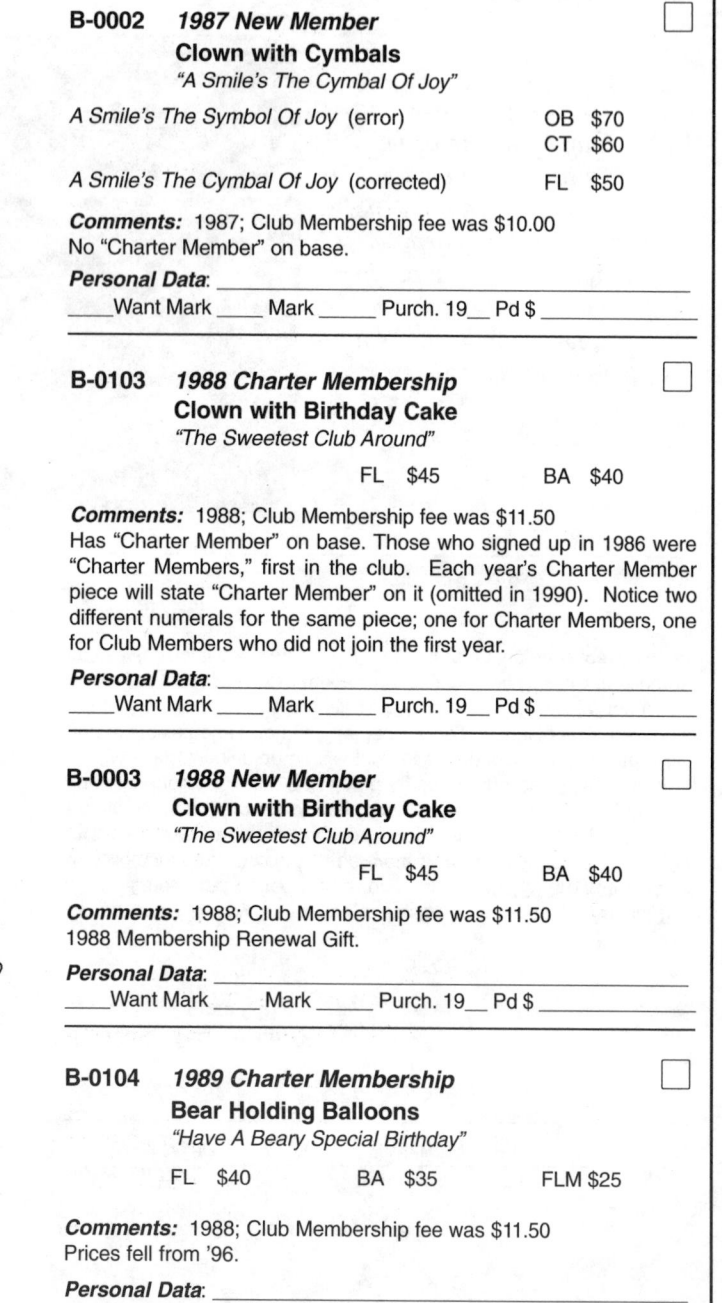

B-0004   *1989 New Member*

Bear Holding Balloons
"Have A Beary Special Birthday"

                BA $28   FLM $25

Comments: 1988; Club Membership fee was $11.50
Very little trading found on this piece in the past few years.

Personal Data: _____
____Want Mark ____ Mark _____ Purch. 19__ Pd $ _____

B-0105   *1990 Charter Member*

Clown with Dog Jumping Through Hoop
"Our Club Is A Tough Act To Follow"

                BA $35   V $25
                FLM $32

Comments: 1988; Club Membership fee was $13.50.

Personal Data: _____
____Want Mark ____ Mark _____ Purch. 19__ Pd $ _____

B-0005   *1990 New Member*

Clown with Dog Jumping Through Hoop
"Our Club Is A Tough Act To Follow"

                BA $30   V $25
                FLM $25

Comments: 1988; Club Membership fee was $13.50
One collector has reported no white dots in the eyes of the clown and
the dog... add $25 to the secondary market value.

Personal Data: _____
____Want Mark ____ Mark _____ Purch. 19__ Pd $ _____

B-0106   *1991 Charter Member*

Clown Jack-in-the-Box
"Jest To Let You Know You're Tops"

                V $28   GC $22

Comments: 1990; Club Renewal fee was $13.50

Personal Data: _____
____Want Mark ____ Mark _____ Purch. 19__ Pd $ _____

B-0006 *1991 New Member*
Clown Jack-in-the-Box
"Jest To Let You Know You're Tops"

V $25   GC $22

Comments: 1990; Club Membership fee was $15.00
Very little trading reported.

Personal Data: _____
____Want Mark ____ Mark _____ Purch. 19__ Pd $ _____

B-0107 **1992 Charter Member**
Clown Riding a Train
"All Aboard For Birthday Club Fun"

GC $35   B $28

Comments: 1992; Club Renewal fee was $16.00
Wow! Don't you just love this piece!? Has not been traded a lot...

Personal Data: _____
____Want Mark ____ Mark _____ Purch. 19__ Pd $ _____

B-0007 **1992 New Member**
Clown Riding a Train
"All Aboard For Birthday Club Fun"

GC $28   B $25

Comments: 1992; Club Membership fee was $16.00

Personal Data: _____
____Want Mark ____ Mark _____ Purch. 19__ Pd $ _____

B-0108 **1993 Charter Member**
Clown with Heart-Shaped Balloon
"Happiness Is Belonging"

B $28   TRP $25

Comments: 1992; Club Renewal fee was $16.00

Personal Data: _____
____Want Mark ____ Mark _____ Purch. 19__ Pd $ _____

B-0008 **1993 New Member**
Clown with Heart-Shaped Balloon
"Happiness Is Belonging"

B $22   TRP $20

Comments: 1992; Club Membership fee $16.00
Personal Data: _____
____Want Mark ____ Mark _____ Purch. 19__ Pd $ _____

B-0109 **1994 Charter Member**
Girl Clown Feeding Doll
"Can't Get Enough Of Our Club"

TRP $28   S $25

Comments: 1994; Club Renewal fee was $19.00

Personal Data: _____
____Want Mark ____ Mark _____ Purch. 19__ Pd $ _____

B-0009 **1994 New Member**
Girl Clown Feeding Doll
"Can't Get Enough Of Our Club"

TRP $30   S $22

Comments: 1994; Club Membership fee $19.00

Personal Data: _____
____Want Mark ____ Mark _____ Purch. 19__ Pd $ _____

B-0110 **1995 Charter Member**
Frog on Birthday Cake
"Hoppy Birthday"

S $25   H $22

Comments: 1995, Club Renewal fee was $20.00

Personal Data: _____
____Want Mark ____ Mark _____ Purch. 19__ Pd $ _____

B-0010 **1995 New Member**
Frog on Birthday Cake
"Hoppy Birthday"

S $22   H $20

Comments: 1995, Club Membership fee was $20.00

Personal Data: _____
____Want Mark ____ Mark _____ Purch. 19__ Pd $ _____

B-0111 **1996/97 Charter Member**
Clown on Scooter
"Scootin' By Just To Say Hi"

H $21

Comments: 1996, Club Membership fee was $21.00

Personal Data: _____
___Want Mark ____ Mark _____ Purch. 19__ Pd $ _____

B-0011 **1996/97 New Member**
Clown on Scooter
"Scootin' By Just To Say Hi"

H $21

Comments: 1996, Club Membership fee was $21.00

Personal Data: _____
___Want Mark ____ Mark _____ Purch. 19__ Pd $ _____

Birthday Club
Club Pieces

Birthday Club Pieces are available only to Birthday Club Members.
Also known as "Members Only" pieces, these are purchased
with a redemption certificate included in the Membership Kit.
Membership pieces may carry marks for several years.

BC861 **1986 Members Only**
Raccoon
"Fishing For Friends"

D $160   OB $135   CT $120

Comments: 1986; Original Retail $10.00
Miniature figurine. First Club Piece, 1986. Many reported the "fish" had been broken from this piece (watch for "glued on" fish). Sellers, be sure to tell your buyer that a piece is *"glued."* Although Club pieces are designated for a specific year, earlier years' marks and following years' marks have also appeared on pieces. Easily found at OB prices. Most trading has been on the OB mark for several years.

Personal Data: _____
___Want Mark ____ Mark _____ Purch. 19__ Pd $ _____

BC871 **1987 Members Only**
Mouse in Sugar Bowl
"Hi, Sugar"

CT $100   FL $95   BA $85

Comments: 1987; Original Retail $11.00
Second Club Piece, 1987. A great little collectible. He's special!

Personal Data: _____
___Want Mark ____ Mark _____ Purch. 19__ Pd $ _____

BC881 **1988 Members Only**
Baby Bunny with Patched Carrot
"Somebunny Cares"

FL $60   BA $50

Comments: 1988; Original Retail $13.50
Third Club Piece, 1988.

Personal Data: _____
___Want Mark ____ Mark _____ Purch. 19__ Pd $ _____

BC891 **1989 Members Only**
Bear with Bee Hive
"Can't Bee Hive Myself Without You"

BA $50   FLM $45   V $40

Comments: 1989; Original Retail $13.50
Fourth Club Piece, 1989. Cute piece! Found prices even lower. Insure at these prices.

Personal Data: _____
___Want Mark ____ Mark _____ Purch. 19__ Pd $ _____

BC901 **1990 Members Only**
Skunk with Bouquet of Flowers
"Collecting Makes Good Scents"

FLM $35   V $30

Comments: 1990; Original Retail $15.00
Fifth Club Piece, 1990. He's precious! I hear he's still the club mascot in Utah and stays with Diane.

Personal Data: _____
___Want Mark ____ Mark _____ Purch. 19__ Pd $ _____

BC902   1990 Members Only
Squirrel with Bag of Nuts
"I'm Nuts Over My Collection"

FLM $40   V $35

Comments: 1990; Original Retail $15.00
Sixth Club Piece, 1990. These Club Pieces get sweeter every year!

Personal Data: _____
____Want Mark ____ Mark _____ Purch. 19__ Pd $ _____

BC911   1991 Members Only
Girl Monkey with Pacifier
"Love Pacifies"

V $38   GC $32

Comments: 1990; Original Retail $15.00
Seventh Club Piece, 1991. A favorite for many! V sales more abundant.

Personal Data: _____
____Want Mark ____ Mark _____ Purch. 19__ Pd $ _____

BC912   1991 Members Only
Cat and Dog Holding a Paint Brush
"True Blue Friends"

V $40   GC $35

Comments: 1990; Original Retail $15.00
Eighth Club Piece, 1991.

Personal Data: _____
____Want Mark ____ Mark _____ Purch. 19__ Pd $ _____

BC921   1992 Members Only
Beaver Building House From Twigs
"Every Man's House Is His Castle"

GC $35   B $30

Comments: 1991; Original Retail $16.50
Ninth Club Piece, 1992. Popular! We have received one report of this piece having a TRP. Mm, very unusual.

Personal Data: _____
____Want Mark ____ Mark _____ Purch. 19__ Pd $ _____

BC922   1992 Members Only
Dog with Sheep Skin
"I've Got You Under My Skin"

GC $30   B $28

Comments: 1991; Original Retail $16.50
Tenth Club Piece, 1992. The actual figurine shows a sheep's "face."

Personal Data: _____
____Want Mark ____ Mark _____ Purch. 19__ Pd $ _____

BC931   1993 Members Only
Kangaroo with Boxing Gloves
"Put A Little Punch In Your Birthday"

B $22   TRP $20

Comments: 1991; Original Retail $16.00
Eleventh Club Piece, 1993. Very little trading reported over these prices.

Personal Data: _____
____Want Mark ____ Mark _____ Purch. 19__ Pd $ _____

BC932   1993 Members Only
Owls Sitting on Branch
"Owl Always Be Your Friend"

B $22   TRP $20

Comments: 1991; Original Retail $16.00
Twelfth Club Piece, 1993.

Personal Data: _____
____Want Mark ____ Mark _____ Purch. 19__ Pd $ _____

BC941   1994 Members Only
Turtle with Mouse On Back
"God Bless Our Home"

TRP $25   S $20

Comments: 1993; Original Retail $16.00
Thirteenth Club Piece, 1994.

Personal Data: _____
____Want Mark ____ Mark _____ Purch. 19__ Pd $ _____

BC942   **1994 Members Only**
Penguin and Pelican
"You're A Pel-I-Can Count On"

TRP $22   S $18

Comments: 1994; Original Retail $16.00
Fourteenth Club Piece, 1994-95.

Personal Data: _____
____Want Mark _____ Mark _____ Purch. 19__ Pd $ _____

BC951   **1995 Members Only**
Porcupine
"Making A Point To Say You're Special"

S $25

Comments: 1994; Original Retail $15.00
Fifteenth Club Piece, 1995.

Personal Data: _____
____Want Mark _____ Mark _____ Purch. 19__ Pd $ _____

BC952   **1995 Members Only**
Clown with Birthday Cake
"10 Wonderful Years Of Wishes"

S $55

Comments: 1995; Original Retail $50.00
Sixteenth Club Piece, 1995. Very little trading found.

Personal Data: _____
____Want Mark _____ Mark _____ Purch. 19__ Pd $ _____

BC961   **1996 Members Only**
Dalmatian Pup in Gift Box
"There's A Spot In My Heart For You"

SWD $15

Comments: 1996; Original Retail $15.00
1997 Birthday Club piece.

Personal Data: _____
____Want Mark _____ Mark _____ Purch. 19__ Pd $ _____

BC962   **1996 Members Only**
Panda with #1 Medallion Around Neck
"You're First In My Heart"

SWD $15

Comments: 1996; Original Retail $15.00
1997 Birthday Club piece.

Personal Data: _____
____Want Mark _____ Mark _____ Purch. 19__ Pd $ _____

PRECIOUS MOMENTS®
CLUB HAPPENINGS

Friendship Hits The Spot
Tippy spends the day at a local
daycare center with the children.

My Favorite Fan
Precious Moments Club
A club Meet and Mingle Fund raiser was
held and a few of the Chicago Bears attended.
Pictured here is Glen Kozlowski #88 and Tippy.

Precious Moments,
Precious Memories
Sam signed many
collectors pieces after the
Hallelujah Hoedown event.

PRECIOUS COLLECTORS

PRECIOUS COLLECTIONS *and their*

GEENA MARIE NICOLICH

Geena is pictured with her older brother, Mario, in front of their Precious Moments collection.

PRECIOUS ANN CALAMUSA

Little Precious Ann (20 months old) has a special collection which will only grow as she does. Precious has an older sister, Cherish, who collects Cherished Teddies.

BIRTHDAY TRAIN

It is not necessary to join the Birthday Club in order to get "Birthday Train" pieces. The animals with numerals may be purchased from retailers; no redemption forms are necessary. Ages Nine and Ten debuted in the Spring of 1992. Collectors are hoping these will go to age sixteen in years to come, but today retailers are happy just to get delivery on pieces one through ten. This is especially so for ages one, two, three and four due to their popularity for young children. The Birthday Train cars are designed to hook together starting with the Clown, then Age 10, Age 9, etc., ending with the Baby Teddy on the Caboose.

16004
Clown Pulling Train
See page 56

521825
Age 10 - Whale
See page 111

521833
Age 9 - Horse
See page 112

109460
Age 8 - Ostrich
See page 71

109479
Age 7 - Leopard
See page 71

15997
Age 6 - Giraffe
See page 56

15989
Age 5 - Lion
See page 56

15970
Age 4 - Elephant
See page 55

15954
Age 3 - Pig
See page 55

15962
Age 2 -Seal
See page 55

15946
Age 1 - Lamb
See page 55

15938
Baby - Teddy/
Caboose
See page 55

Numerals one through four are the hardest to find at retailers as these are the most popular for "gift" buyers. This set is planned to go only to age ten until further notice. Numeral decals have been found to be missing on each of these pieces. Add $50-75 to the regular secondary market value of these "missing numeral" pieces.

BIRTHDAY SERIES FIGURINES

The Birthday Series, a unique collection of charming little animals, is a delightful way to celebrate a child's special day (many adults are also captivated by this collection). It is not required that you be a Birthday Club member to acquire these figurines and ornaments.

524506
Pig with Gift
See page 126

527769
Octopus
See page 135

526924
Elephant with
String Around Trunk
See page 131

105953
Skunk and Mouse
See page 69

522260
Giraffe with
Baby in Mouth
See page 115

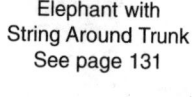

521671
Camel with Monkey
on Back
See page 111

105945
Elephant
Showering Mouse
See page 69

527343
Chick with
Birthday Cake
See page 133

527270
Two Dogs
Hugging
See page 132

521175
Kangaroo with
Baby in Pouch
See page 108

524492
Cat with Bird
in Cage
See page 126

521043
Gorilla with Fan
See page 108

104418
Rhino with Bird
See page 68

520659
Bear with Cake
See page 105

128686
Rabbits with Cake
See page 79

183792
Bunny on Snowball
See page 89

531057
Dog with
Hair in Eyes
See page 143

~R.STUBLER~

You're right! That figurine does have a double stamp.

BIRTHDAY SERIES ORNAMENTS

1986
102466
ORNAMENT
Reindeer
See page 65

1987
104515
ORNAMENT
Bear in Tub/Skis
See page 68

1988
520292
ORNAMENT
Kitten on Wreath
See page 102

1989
520462
ORNAMENT
Dog/Gift Box
See page 103

1990
520497
ORNAMENT
Kitten with Ornament
See page 104

1991
520438
ORNAMENT
Bunny with Ice
Skates
See page 103

1992
520411
ORNAMENT
Squirrel on
Dated Log
See page 103

1993
520489
ORNAMENT
Turtle with Gift
See page 103

1994
530972
ORNAMENT
Bear in Heart
See page 142

1995
520403
ORNAMENT
Hippo
See page 103

1996
128708
ORNAMENT
Owl
See page 80

1997
272760
ORNAMENT
Snail
See page 98

EVENT FIGURINES

1988
115231
Girl Carrying
Bag/Balloons
See page 78

1989
520861
Girl with Slate
See page 107

1990
523526
Girl with Fan
See page 120

1991
527122
Girl with Puppy
in Blanket
See page 131

1992
527319
Girl Wading
with Duck
See page 132

1993
530158
Girl in Raincoat
with Dog
See page 139

1994
529982
Girl Blowing
Bubbles
See page 138

1995
528080
Girl with
Signboard
See page 136

1996
163864
Girl with Guitar
See page 87

OPEN HOUSE ORNAMENTS

1990
525057
Bundles Of Joy
See page 128

1992
529648
*The Magic Starts
With You*
See page 137

1993
529974
*An Event For
All Seasons*
See page 138

1994
520470
*Take A Bow
Cuz You're My
Christmas Star*
See page 103

1995
150134
*Merry
Chrismoose*
See page 84

EASTER SEALS FIGURINES

1987
107999
Girl on Crutches
See page 71

1988
115479
Boy with
Arm Braces/Dog
See page 79

1989
522376
Girl with Easter
Lily in Hands
See page 115

1990
524522
Girl with Chick
in Egg
See page 127

1991
527114
Girl with
Bluebird
See page 131

1992
527173
Girl Hand-Signing
"I Love You"
See page 132

1993
530026
Girl with
Trophy Cup
See page 138

1994
531111
Girl with Pail
of Oysters
See page 143

1995
524387
Girl with Roses
See page 125

1996
526827
Girl with
Piggy Bank
See page 130

1997
192368
Boy with basketball in
wheelchair
See page 91

1998
522325
Clown with Monkey
See page 115

9" EASTER SEALS FIGURINES

"ANNOUNCED EACH JULY"

1988
104531
Girl with Bunny
See page 68

1989
520322
Girl with
Goose
See page 102

1990
523283
Girl with
String of Hearts
See page 119

1991
523879
Girl with Butterfly
See page 123

1992
526010
Girl Holding
Kitten
See page 129

1993
529680
Girl Kneeling with
Bunnies in Lap
See page 138

1994
531243
Girl with Basket
of Roses
See page 144

1995
526886
Angel with
World in Hands
See page 130

1996
152277
Girl with Daisy
See page 85

1997
192376
Girl Signing
See page 91

EASTER SEALS ORNAMENTS

1990
225290
ORNAMENT
Girl with
Chick in Egg
See page 92

1991
233196
ORNAMENT
Girl with Dove
See page 93

1992
238899
ORNAMENT
Girl Signing
"I Love You"
See page 93

1993
250112
ORNAMENT
Girl with
Trophy Cup
See page 93

1994
244570
ORNAMENT
Girl with Pail
of Oysters
See page 93

1995
128899
ORNAMENT
Girl with Roses
See page 80

1996
152579
ORNAMENT
Girl with
Piggy Bank
See page 85

1997
192384
ORNAMENT
Boy with basketball in
wheelchair
See page 91

1998
272922
ORNAMENT
Clown with Monkey
See page 98

WREATHS

Bea Butler's Christmas Wreaths

See Photo Above.

111465   1987 Christmas Wreath w/8 Ornaments   ☐

With "Heaven Bound" error upside down
on plane ornament. $245-250

                                        CT $195-200

Comments: 1986; Original Retail $150.00

Personal Data: _____
____Want Mark ____ Mark _____ Purch. 19__ Pd $ _____

**112348   Porcelain Bell
            from the '87 Christmas Wreath**   ☐

Photo Not Available.

With Hook   CT $75-80
Without Hook   CT $60-62

Comments: 1986 Many bells were broken off the wreath, leaving no
hook on the bell. Most bells for sale by collectors have a broken hook.

Personal Data: _____
____Want Mark ____ Mark _____ Purch. 19__ Pd $ _____

1988 Christmas Wreath with Ornaments   ☐

                               FL $115-120
Bell alone   FL $50-55

See Photo Above.

Comments: 1987; Original Retail $100.00

Personal Data: _____
____Want Mark ____ Mark _____ Purch. 19__ Pd $ _____

CHAPEL LITHOGRAPHS

THE LIFE OF CHRIST

Chapel Masterpieces, Volume One

A Collector's Set of Seven
16" x 20"
Limited Edition Lithographs
750 Numbered Sets,
75 Artist Proof Sets.
Original Retail $420

HEROES OF THE OLD TESTAMENT

Chapel Masterpieces, Volume Two

A Collector's Set of Seven 16" x 20"
Limited Edition Lithographs - 1990
1,950 Numbered Sets,
150 Artist Proof Sets.
Original Retail $550

RETIRED 12/31/93

All lithos unsold as of 12/31/93 were burned at the Chapel in February, 1994. See the May '94 issue of *Precious Collectibles®* for press coverage. Rosie and Dave were personally invited to attend this special event.

Samuel and his mother stand before the Temple of Shiloh.

Esther pleas to the King for her people, Israel.

Artist Proof Sets are signed by Sam and are "hand picked" as to the "best productions" from the presses.

THE SEVEN DAYS OF THE CREATION

Chapel Masterpieces, Volume Four

A Collector's Set of Seven
Limited Edition Lithographs
Each lithograph has
an image area of
10" x 18½" on a 13" x 21½"
sheet.
RETIRED 12/31/93
All unsold lithos were burned at the Chapel in February, 1994. Each print includes a certificate of authenticity signed by Sam and his son Jon Butcher, which were handnumbered and embossed with the artist's signature.
**3,000 Numbered Sets,
250 Artist Proof Sets.
Original Retail
$295 per set of 7**

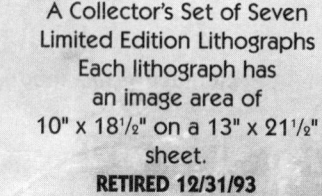

HALLELUJAH SQUARE

Chapel Masterpieces, Volume Three

An Exclusive 22" x 28"
Limited Edition Lithograph -1991
2,500 Numbered Sets,
200 Artist Proof Sets.
Original Retail $150

PHIL'S MURAL

Chapel Masterpieces, Volume Five

This print is 23" x 23," signed by Sam Butcher, and presented in a white leatherportfolio.

RETIRED 12/31/93.
All unsold lithos were burned at the Chapel in February, 1994.

Each print includes a certificate of authenticity signed by Jon Butcher. Limited to 2,250 prints. Original Retail $175

JONATHAN & DAVID MURAL

Chapel Masterpieces, Volume Six

Size: 25" x 15"
Each print includes a Certificate of Authenticity
Exclusively Limited to 1,000 prints
875 numbered prints, 125 Artist Proofs.
Original Retail $175

THE PARABLES

Chapel Masterpieces, Volume Seven

• Set of seven prints   • Each signed by the artist   • Limited to 825 sets   • Original Retail $425

Precious Moments® Paraphernalia

Dealers' Plaque - Girl/Boy on Stump - Shiny Glass.....................$120
Dealers' Plaque - Girl At Oven $100
Crewel Pictures on Brown Velvet ....$45 ea.
Avon Figs. (5) w/Precious Moments® inscription, see pg.XV $95
Old J&D Buttons..$50 ea.
Christmas Embroidered Stockings $10
Cardboard Display Cards:
    "Hello Lord" $40
    "Curler Girl" $40
    "Five Year Piece" $20
    Others $10
Old J&D Cards $10
British PM Cards $10
J&D Puzzles $20
Cloisonné pin – Enesco gift pin (tie-tack back) $25
Dear Customer – J&D Retailer Poster – mint in frame $200
Spanish Posters $75
5 year Enesco Pin $18
7 year Enesco Tac-pin $10
Magnet Gift from Enesco for signing up new Members.................$2
Keychain...$1
J&D Posters $25-40
1983 Enesco Round Blue Angel Pin $50
J&D Cloisonné Pins ....$25 ea.
J&D Bicentennial Greeting Cards...$20-25
Reg. Capiz Ornaments (Many appear to be coming apart) $25
Capiz Plaque Displays $45
Enesco's Birthday Club Animal Cloisonné Pin $15
Cheerleader Pin for collection of 200 or more $5
J&D Clown Dolls...$60
1990 Porcelain Egg (NM; more orders than production) $35
Medallion received from 1993 Convention....................................$50
Medallion received from 1993 Enesco Cruise ....$200 up
PM008 - 1987 Wreath Filigree Medallion.....................................$50
PM030 - Goose Girl Medallion
    (Received from Orient Tour)..$350 up

I received the Orient medallion, #495301, in a lavender gift box when I took the Orient Tour. The inscription was "A Special Gift Commemorating My Trip to the Precious Moments® Facility, April 1990." Several feel this medallion should be insured for at least $500. (I received one offer of $350 from an ad in 1993.) Has anyone sold theirs? How much did you receive?

J & D Pewter

Until 1990 the J&D pewter was rising steadily on the secondary market as it was no longer available on the retail market. Collectors were disappointed to see it reissued and once again available in the summer of 1990. It is now being produced by the Fort Company for Precious Moments Company. It appears the "same molds" are being used. Prices seem to remain stable, but there's much less trading now on the J&D Pewter than in previous years. Let us know if you are buying or selling the pewter in 1994. It's my opinion less than 20 avid Precious Moments collectors have "all" the pewter... if that many. Not being traded as in the mid '80s!

(Painted pewter by Enesco NOT being sought after as a collectible on the secondary market to date.)

Pewter By The Jonathan & David Company

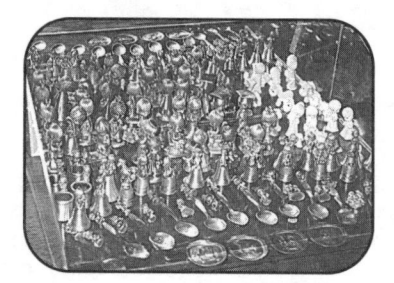

Insure for replacement cost

BABY CUPS

JY227	'82 Dated Angel/Boy	$20	$45.00
JY228	'82 Dated Angel/Girl	$20	$40.00
JY237	'83 Dated Angel/Girl	$20	$40.00
JY238	'83 Dated Angel/Boy	$20	$40.00

BELLS

JY202	Jesus Loves Me/Girl	$15	$50.00
JY203	Jesus Loves Me/Boy	$15	$50.00
JY205	Graduate Boy	$15	$50.00
JY206	Graduate Girl	$15	$50.00
JY208	Angels On a Cloud	$15	$50.00
JY219	'82 Dated Drummer Boy	$15	$50.00
JY225	Angel/Trumpet	$15	$40.00
JY239	'83 Dated Boy/Wreath	$15	$50.00
JY402	'84 Dated Choir Girl	$15	$45.00
JY405	'83 Dated Angel/Heart (Hardest to find)	$15	$65.00

BRACELETS

JY119	Jesus Loves Me/Girl	$13	$25.00
JY120	Jesus Loves Me/Boy	$13	$25.00
JY121	Girl/Goose	$13	$38.00
JY122	Graduate Girl	$13	$25.00
JY123	Graduate Boy	$13	$25.00
JY124	Girl/Candle and Doll	$13	$28.00

CHARMS

JY101	Jesus Loves Me/Girl	$10	$25.00
JY102	Jesus Loves Me/Boy	$10	$25.00
JY103	Girl/Goose	$10	$30.00
JY104	Graduate Girl	$10	$35.00
	(The Girl Graduate is hardest to find, probably because it was given as gift.)		
JY105	Graduate Boy	$10	$25.00
JY106	Girl/Candle and Doll	$10	$25.00
JY151	Bride and Groom	$14	$28.00
JY152	Boy and Girl On Cloud	$14	$35.00
JY153	Boy and Girl on Tree Stump	$14	$40.00
JY154	Boy and Girl/Baby	$14	$25.00

FIGURINES

JY200	Nativity Set	$100	$200.00
JY231	Graduate Girl	$30	$110.00
JY232	Graduate Boy	$30	$100.00
JY233	Girl/Candle and Doll	$30	$90.00
JY234	Girl/Goose	$30	$130.00
JY235	Jesus Loves Me/Girl	$30	$100.00
JY236	Jesus Loves Me/Boy	$30	$100.00
JY243	Drummer Boy	$30	$130.00
JY244	Angel/Trumpet	$30	$150.00
JY245	Wise Men (set of 3)	$90	$350.00
JY303	Boy/Ice Cream Cone	$40	$90.00
JY304	Girl/Puppies	$40	$150.00
JY305	Grandma in Rocker	$40	$90.00
JY306	Mother Sew Dear	$40	$90.00
JY307	Bride and Groom	$45	$100.00

KEY CHAINS

JY125	Bride and Groom	$17	$40.00
JY126	Boy and Girl on Cloud	$17	$40.00
JY127	Boy and Girl on Tree Stump	$17	$35.00
JY128	Boy and Girl/Baby	$17	$35.00

NECKLACES

JY113	Jesus Loves Me/Girl	$12	$40.00
JY114	Jesus Loves Me/Boy	$12	$40.00
JY115	Girl/Goose	$12	$40.00
JY116	Graduate Girl	$12	$30.00
JY117	Graduate Boy	$12	$28.00
JY118	Girl/Candle and Doll	$12	$30.00

PLATES

JY230	Nativity	$15	$38.00
JY242	Two Boys at Manger	$15	$35.00
JY300	Mother Sew Dear	$15	$40.00
JY404	Boy at Manger/Butterfly	$15	$40.00

SPOONS

JY212	Jesus Loves Me/Boy	$12	$40.00
JY213	Jesus Loves Me/Girl	$12	$40.00
JY214	Girl/Goose	$12	$40.00
JY215	Graduate Boy	$12	$40.00
JY216	Graduate Girl	$12	$40.00
JY217	Girl/Candle and Doll	$12	$40.00
JY220	'82 Dated Drummer Boy	$12	$60.00
JY226	Angel/Trumpet	$12	$40.00
JY240	'83 Dated Boy/Wreath	$12	$50.00
JY301	Mother Sew Dear	$12	$60.00
JY401	'84 Dated Choir Girl	$12	$38.00
JY407	'85 Dated Angel/Heart (Hard to Find)	$12	$ 70.00

If Sold Individually	$558
If Sold as a Complete Set	$465-510

THIMBLES

JY201	Mother Sew Dear	$16	$40.00
JY218	'82 Dated Drummer Boy	$16	$55.00
JY224	Angel/Trumpet	$16	$45.00
JY241	'83 Dated Boy/Wreath	$16	$45.00
JY246	Girl/Pie	$16	$55.00
JY302	Grandma	$16	$45.00
JY403	'84 Dated Choir Girl	$16	$45.00
JY406	'85 Dated Angel/Heart (Hard to Find)	$16	$60.00

**Painted Pewter Licensed By Samuel J. Butcher Company
Produced By Enesco Imports Corp.**

Because there is no secondary market increase on painted pewter and the numerous new productions by Precious Moments Company, we do not list this category. Should these pieces enter the secondary market, then we will once again include painted pewter in this guide as well as the Precious Moments

THE STORIES...

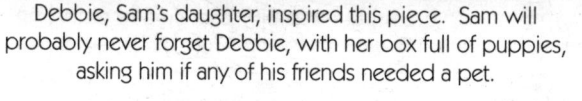

I'M SENDING YOU A WHITE CHRISTMAS

Sam's mother was born in Michigan, but was moved to Florida at an early age. After the death of her father, her mother moved the family back to Michigan. Sam's mother was only five years old and had never seen snow. Upon the first snow his mother was found packing snowballs in a box to be mailed to her relatives in Florida.

E-2829   p. 17

NO TEARS PAST THE GATE

This was painted for Sam's assistant, Levi, in the Philippines. Levi's sister was only eighteen when she died.

101826   p. 62

HELLO, LORD, IT'S ME AGAIN

Jon, Sam's oldest son, inspired this figurine after a romantic setback.

PM-811   p. 164

GRANDMA'S PRAYER

This figurine is a loving tribute to Sam's grandmother, who reminded Sam often that she was praying for him.

PM-861   p. 164

THE LORD GIVETH AND THE LORD TAKETH AWAY

After returning home from the Philippines, Sam found the house in total chaos. When he saw the empty, tipped-over canary cage, Sam realized that the family cat had eaten the canary.

100226   p. 59

GOD LOVETH A CHEERFUL GIVER

Debbie, Sam's daughter, inspired this piece. Sam will probably never forget Debbie, with her box full of puppies, asking him if any of his friends needed a pet.

E-1378   p. 7

MERRY CHRISTMAS DEER

A five year old girl newly adopted from an orphanage asked her parents to take all her Christmas presents except one, a stuffed reindeer, to her friends at the orphanage. On the way home, when she and her father left the subway train, her stuffed reindeer got stuck in the doors and the train took off. A few years ago, this lady wrote to Sam telling her story and asking him to help her locate the ornament of a little reindeer with a teddy bear on his back. Sam sent her the ornament from his personal collection. Her story inspired Sam to create the figurine of a little girl hanging ornaments on the antlers of a reindeer, called *Merry Christmas Deer*.

522317   p. 115

TO GOD BE THE GLORY

The figurine depicts Sam's life. Sam feels that the Lord has blessed him with the ability to draw children, but believes it is not his gift but the Lord's. The gift is only on loan to him. This may be Sam's favorite piece.

E-2823   p. 16

TRUST IN THE LORD TO THE FINISH

Sam began the painting for this figurine on his way to the Philippines. His youngest brother Hank always loved driving race cars. After a successful racing career the crowds' roar eventually died down. Sam realized that trust in the Lord would lead to the finish line.

PM - 842   p. 163

LORD, I'M COMING HOME

This design was inspired by a collector who was an Idea Contest winner. Her brother, who loved to play ball, died at the young age of 19. Sam was moved by the collector's story and her idea for a figurine, so he created this piece.

100110   **p. 58**

LOVE ONE ANOTHER

This was the first Precious Moments art. Tammy sat by "Uncle Bill" on a stool back to back and the love she portrayed for Uncle Bill was the inspiration for the first Precious Moments figurine. The original art was stolen from the Jonathan & David Company.

E-1376   **p. 7**

I LOVE TO TELL THE STORY

Inspired by the old Christian song, this piece was dedicated to Pastor Royal Blue. Pastor Blue led Sam to the Lord Jesus. "The child is speaking to a lamb, which symbolizes a pastor feeding God's flock with the bread of life, which is the word of God."

PM-852   **p. 163**

I'M FOLLOWING JESUS

After encountering a jobless Filipino friend, Carlito, Sam was inspired to create this figurine. Carlito and his family trusted the Lord to take care of their needs. Eventually, Carlito got his own cab which has a sign in the window which reads, "I'm Following Jesus."

PM-862   **p. 164**

HIS EYE IS ON THE SPARROW

This was first done as a card for a man who Sam had met. It was later made into a figurine. The man's son had committed suicide after returning home from war. The family was sent many cards at the death of their son, but Sam's card really touched them. The painting helped the family know the God had it in His hands from the very beginning.

E-0530   **p. 4**

GOD SENDS THE GIFT OF HIS LOVE

Sam's grandniece inspired him to create this piece. She looked precious in her frilly Christmas dress her mom had made for her. Sam felt the little child was God's special gift to her parents.

E-6613   **p. 35**

I BELIEVE IN MIRACLES

Sam's former partner, Bill, was given no hope for his eyesight, but through prayer Bill's sight was restored. This figurine also became the official gift of Child's Wish, an organization for terminally ill children.

E-7156   **p.36**

SMILE, GOD LOVES YOU

Sam believes that outward appearances don't matter and that "you can't judge a book by its cover."

PM-821   **p. 163**

PRAISE THE LORD ANYHOW

Philip, Sam's second son, was the inspiration for this figurine. Sam said you couldn't spend much time with him before you threw up your hands lovingly and said, Praise The Lord Anyhow!

E-1374B   **p. 6**

ONWARD CHRISTIAN SOLDIERS

This little soldier carried the message to Sam to keep going when things got tough. Sam could hardly wait to paint this idea.

E-0523   **p. 3**

LOVE IS KIND

Sam's son, Timmy, was the subject for this figurine. Timmy is the nature boy who liked to spend a lot of his time alone when he was small. He also enjoys painting and music. If he is like my son...he probably wants to be called Tim.

E-1379A   **p. 7**

SAMUEL J. BUTCHER......

UNTO US A CHILD IS BORN

Samuel John Butcher, born on January 1, 1939, in Jackson, Michigan, was the third child born to Leon Donald Butcher, a mechanic of English-Irish descent, and Evelyn Mae (Curry) Butcher, of Lebanese and Syrian ancestry.

SAFE IN THE ARMS OF JESUS

Sam received many *Blessings From Above.* He was described as being a different child, alone most of the time, and would spend hours under the kitchen table, writing and illustrating his own stories. His parents recognized his gift at an early age. *Have I Got News For You,* by the time he was in kindergarten, Sam knew he would be an artist. His teachers recognized his gift and gave him much encouragement. While in kindergarten Sam illustrated "Little Black Sambo."

When he was 10 years old, Sam's family moved to a small, mountainous community in Northern California. Sam spent many hours by himself, drawing and painting the scenery around him. It may have been there that he learned *We Are God's Workmanship.*

LORD HELP ME MAKE THE GRADE

Sam loved music and played the accordion and piano. He was popular in high school; he drew pictures and gave of his talents freely to *Brighten Someone's Day.* Sam was elected president of the sophomore class and vice-president of the student body. He worked on the school yearbook staff and the track team but, as *It's What's Inside That Counts,* nothing could take the place of art.

Sam's art teacher, Mr. Moravec, is the person he credits with teaching him how to put life into his paintings. Because of Mr. Moravec's instruction, Sam was awarded a scholarship to one of the finest private art schools in the country, the College of Arts and Crafts in Berkeley, California.

WITH THIS RING I

Sam and Katie Cushman were married in 1959. After Jon and Philip were born, Sam and Katie began attending North Valley Baptist Church in Redding, California, near their home to *Worship The Lord.* Pastor Royal Blue was God's instrument to lead Sam to the Lord. After Sam became a Christian the Lord was able to give him direction and a place to channel his ability, *To God Be The Glory!* Sam painted "his tallest picture ever" on the baptismal wall at the North Valley Baptist church. Sam worked and studied the Bible with fervor. Shortly after becoming a Christian he was offered a job in the shipping department at the international office of Child Evangelism Fellowship (CEF) in Grand Rapids, Michigan. *Walking By Faith,* Sam moved his family to Michigan and was quickly promoted to the art department.

As Sam's talent and ability grew, so did his family. More *Bundles Of Joy,* Tammy, Debbie and Timmy, followed Philip. When the work load for CEF grew to be too much, a new artist, Bill Biel, was brought in to work with Sam. Bill and Sam became *Friends To The End.* When Katie became ill, Sam and his young family returned to California to be near her parents.

BRINGING GOD'S BLESSING TO YOU

After Donny was born, Sam received a phone call from CEF asking him to come back to Grand Rapids. About one year after his return to Michigan, Sam became the storyteller for the CEF national television program, "The Tree House Club," first telling *The Story Of God's Love,* then illustrating it. While watching a film one day, Bill and Sam realized the need for visual aids in the Christian teaching field. With a bit of poster paint and God-given talent, they began the Jonathan & David Company.

The J&D Company first designed buttons and Bible flannelgraph backgrounds for Sunday schools and did free lance work for other companies. Mott Media persuaded Sam and Bill to attend the Christian Booksellers Convention in California. When they were told they could have a booth of their own, Sam quickly began preparing greeting cards; Bill thought of the name Precious Moments® for these products.

Guess who?
It's Sam!

BELIEVE THE IMPOSSIBLE

The Lord's hand in Sam's life and work is evident. Eugene Freedman (president and chief executive of Enesco Imports Corp.) wanted to produce Sam's art work in three-dimensional figurines. Master sculptor Yasuhei Fujioka of Nagoya, Japan, was sensitive in soul and could comprehend what Sam wanted to accomplish even though they didn't speak the same language. With unequaled skill he recreated Sam's work, with all of its intricate detail, in figural form.

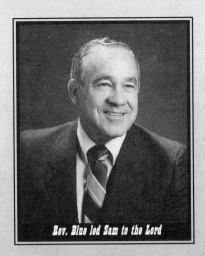

Rev. Blue led Sam to the Lord

I LOVE TO TELL THE STORY

Today, Sam travels throughout the world spreading the message of Precious Moments® but his message doesn't stop with the drawings he has created. He tells collectors everywhere that God is waiting to help us in every part of our lives and that *There Is Joy In Serving Jesus*. Sam cares deeply about those who have been wounded in life and he shares the hope we have in Christ.

MAKE ME A BLESSING

Another avenue through which Sam proclaims that *God Is Love* is the Precious Moments Chapel located near Carthage, Missouri. "The Chapel is my gift of thanksgiving to the Lord for all that He has given me," said Sam. "It also is my gift to all the people who appreciate Precious Moments, so that they might come and see my expression of love for the Lord."

Sam is currently working on an exciting "angelic" fountain which, when completed, will be a spectacular addition to the Chapel grounds. This Fountain of the Angels will feature dozens of sculpted bronze angels in many different poses. You will want to take a trip to the Chapel when this projected is completed and *Join In On The Blessings*.

BLESSED ARE THE HUMBLE

The work of this humble, talented man speaks for itself. Sam has been blessed by God, not only with his artistry, but with the message of Christ which he so readily and naturally shares with everyone he meets all over the world as *Sharing Is Universal*. Through his special gift, Sam offers a continual witness of the love and the Glory of God. *Precious Moments Last Forever!*

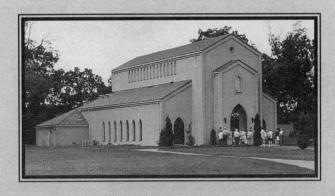

... A LIFETIME OF LOVING, CARING, AND SHARING ALONG THE WAY

PLATE SERIES

LIMITED EDITION PLATES

Inspired Thoughts
1 ......E-5215 ......1981 ....*Love One Another*
2 ......E-7174 ......1982 ....*Make A Joyful Noise*
3 ......E-9257 ......1983 ....*I Believe In Miracles*
4 ......E-2847 ......1984 ....*Love Is Kind*

Mother's Love
1 ......E-5217 ......1981 ....*Mother Sew Dear*
2 ......E-7173 ......1982 ....*The Purr-fect Grandma*
3 ......E-9256 ......1983 ....*The Hand That Rocks The Future*
4 ......E-2848 ......1984 ....*Loving Thy Neighbor*

Christmas Collection
1 ......E-5646 ......1981 ....*Come Let Us Adore Him*
2 ......E-2347 ......1982 ....*Let Heaven And Nature Sing*
3 ......E-0538 ......1983 ....*Wee Three Kings*
4 ......E-5395 ......1984 ....*Unto Us A Child Is Born*

LIMITED EDITION PLATES

Mother's Day
1 ......531766 ......1994 ....*Thinking Of You Is What I Really Like To Do*
2 ......129151 ......1995 ....*He Hath Made Everything Beautiful In His Time*
3 .....163716 .....1996 ....*Of All The Mothers I Have Known, There's None as Precious As My Own*

ANNUAL DATED PLATES

Joy Of Christmas
1 ......E-2357 ......1982 ....*I'll Play My Drum For Him*
2 ......E-0505 ......1983 ....*Christmastime Is For Sharing*
3 ......E-5396 ......1984 ....*The Wonder Of Christmas*
4 ......15237 ....1985 ....*Tell Me The Story Of Jesus*

Christmas Love
1 ......101834 ......1986 ....*I'm Sending You A White Christmas*
2 ......102954 ......1987 ....*My Peace I Give Unto Thee*
3 ......520284 ......1988 ....*Merry Christmas Deer*
4 ......523003 ......1989 ....*May Your Christmas Be A Happy Home*

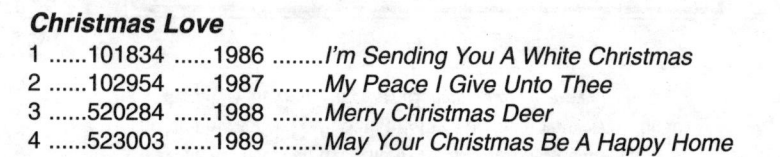

Christmas Blessing

1 ......523801 ......1990 ....*Wishing You A Yummy Christmas*
2 ......523860 ......1991 ....*Blessings From Me To Thee*
3 ......527742 ......1992 ....*But The Greatest Of These Is Love*
4 ......530204 ......1993 ....*Wishing You The Sweetest Christmas*

The Beauty of Christmas

1 ......530409 ......1994 ....*You're As Pretty As A Christmas Tree*
2 ......142670 ......1995 ....*He Covers The Earth With His Beauty*

♪ FIGURINE SERIES ♪

Baby's First

1 ...E-2840..........*Baby's First Step*
2 ...E-2841..........*Baby's First Picture*
3 .... 12211..........*Baby's First Haircut*
4 .... 16012 ....*Baby's First Trip*
5 ....520705 ......*Baby's First Pet*
6 ....524077 ....*Baby's First Meal*
7 ....527238 ....*Baby's First Word*
8 ....524069 ....*Baby's First Birthday*

Bridal Party

1 ....E-2831 ....*Bridesmaid*
2 ....E-2836 ....*Groomsman*
3 ....E-2835 ....*Flower Girl*
4 ....E-2833 ....*Ringbearer*
5 ....E-2845 ....*Junior Bridesmaid*
6 ....E-2837 ....*Groom*
7 ....E-2846 ....*Bride*
8 ....E-2838 ....*This Is The Day Which The Lord Hath Made*

Calendar Girl

1 ....109983 ....January
2 ....109991 ....February
3 ....110019..........March
4 ....110027..........April
5 ....110035..........May
6 ....110043..........June
7 ....110051 ....July
8 ....110078 ....August
9....110086 ....September
10 .110094 ....October
11 ..110108 ....November
12 ..110116 ....December

Clown

1 .... 12262 ......*I Get A Bang Out Of You*
2 .... 12459 ......*Waddle I Do Without You*
3 .... 12467 ......*The Lord Will Carry You Through*
4 .... 12270 ......*Lord, Keep Me On The Ball*
5 ....520632 ....*A Friend Is Someone Who Cares*

(For more clowns not in series see Alphabetical Listing by Description)

Family Christmas Scene All Suspended 1992

1 .... 15776 ....*May You Have The Sweetest Christmas*
2 .... 15784 ....*The Story Of God's Love*
3 .... 15792 ....*Tell Me A Story*
4 .... 15806 ....*God Gave His Best*
5 .... 15814 ....*Silent Night*
6 ....522856 ....*Have A Beary Merry Christmas*
7 ....524883 ....*Christmas Fireplace*

Growing In Grace Series

136204 ....Infant Angel with Newspaper
136190 ....Age 1 - Baby with Cake
136212 ....Age 2 - Girl with Blocks
136220 ....Age 3 - Girl with Flowers
136239 ....Age 4 - Girl with Doll
136247 ....Age 5 - Girl with Lunch Box
136255 ....Age 6 - Girl on Bicycle
163740 ....Age 7 - Girl Nursing Sick Kitten
163759....Age 8 - Girl Puppies/Marbles
183865....Age 9 - Girl with Bird
183873....Age 10 - Girl with Bowling Ball
260924....Age 11 - Girl with Dog and Sign
260932....Age 12 - Girl with Dog Holding Alarm Clock
272647....Age 13 - Girl Praying at Turtle Race
272655....Age 14 - Girl Holding Diary
272663....Age 15 - Girlwith Puppy Holding List
136263....Sweet Sixteen - Girl Holding Sixteen Roses

Rejoice In The Lord Band Series

12165 ....*Lord, Keep My Life In Tune*
12173 ....*There's A Song In My Heart*
12378 ....*Happiness Is The Lord*
12386 ....*Lord Give Me A Song*
12394 ....*He Is My Song*
12580 ....*Lord, Keep My Life In Tune*

Heavenly Halo Angel Series

This *Series* was so named by collectors who had seen the "Heavenly Halo" Angel Cards. Enesco does not show a *Series* by this name.

- E-9260 ...... *God's Promises Are Sure*
- E-9274 ...... *Taste And See That The Lord Is Good*
- E-9288 ...... *Sending You A Rainbow*
- E-9289 ...... *Trust In The Lord*

ANNUAL ISSUES

Child Evangelism Fellowship Figurines

- 1992 .... 527556 .... *Bring The Little Ones To Jesus*
- 1993 .... 521922 .... *Safe In The Arms Of Jesus*
- 1994 .... 531359 .... *Bring The Little Ones To Jesus*

National Day of Prayer Figurines

- 1992 .... 527564 .... *God Bless The USA*
- 1993 .... 528862 .... *America, You're Beautiful*
- 1994 .... 524158 .... *Lord Teach Us To Pray*

Dated Porcelain Easter Eggs

- 1991 .... 523534 .... *I Will Cherish The Old Rugged Cross*
- 1992 .... 525960 .... *We Are God's Workmanship*
- 1993 .... 528617 .... *Make A Joyful Noise*
- 1994 .... 529095 .... *A Reflection Of His Love*

Cross Series Figurines

- 1995 .... 127019 .... *Love Blooms Eternal*
- 1996 .... 163732 .... *Standing In The Presence Of The Lord*

MASTERPIECE SERIES

Porcelain Ball Ornaments

1	523062	1989	*Peace on Earth*
2	523704	1990	*May Your Christmas Be A Happy Home*
3	526940	1991	*May Your Christmas Be Merry*
4	527734	1992	*But The Greatest Of These Is Love*
5	530190	1993	*Wishing You The Sweetest Christmas*
6	530387	1994	*You're As Pretty As A Christmas Tree*
7	142689	1995	*He Covers The Earth With His Beauty*
8	183350	1996	*Peace On Earth... Anyway*
9	272728	1997	*Cane You Join Us For A Merry Christmas*

Only the first four Porcelain Ball Ornaments are listed as Masterpiece Series, however, we have included the 1993 through 1997 ball ornaments with this listing.

 # FOUR SEASONS SERIES

FIGURINES

1	12068	1985	*The Voice Of Spring* (most sought after)
2	12076	1985	*Summer's Joy*
3	12084	1986	*Autumn's Praise*
4	12092	1986	*Winter's Song*

PLATES

1	12106	1985	*The Voice Of Spring*
2	12114	1985	*Summer's Joy*
3	12122	1986	*Autumn's Praise*
4	12130	1986	*Winter's Song*

THIMBLES

- 100641 .... Set of Four/Four Seasons

DOLLS

Limited to Two Years Production 1990-1991

- 1 ..... 408786 .... *The Voice Of Spring*
- 2 ..... 408743 .... *Summer's Joy*
- 3 .... 408808 .... *Autumn's Praise*
- 4 ..... 408816 .... *Winter's Song*

JACK-IN-THE BOX

Limited to Two Years Production 1990-1991

- 1 ..... 408735 .... *The Voice Of Spring*
- 2 ..... 408743 .... *Summer's Joy*
- 3 ..... 408751 .... *Autumn's Praise*
- 4 ..... 408778 .... *Winter's Song*

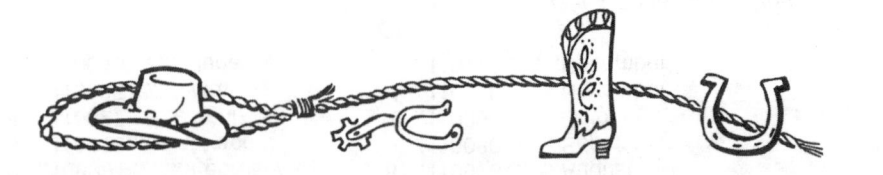

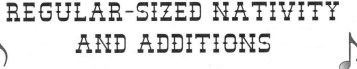

REGULAR-SIZED NATIVITY AND ADDITIONS

104000 ...*O Come Let Us Adore Him*
................*9-pc w/Cassette* (form. E2800)
E-0511 ....*Tubby's First Christmas*
E-0512....*It's A Perfect Boy*
E-2360....*I'll Play My Drum For Him*
E-2363....*Camel*
E-2364....*Goat*
E-2365....*The First Noel* (boy)
E-2366....*The First Noel* (girl)
E-2800....*Come Let Us Adore Him* (9-Pc Set)
E-5378....*Joy To The World*
E-5379....*Isn't He Precious*
E-5621....*Donkey*
E-5624....*They Followed The Star* (3-Pc Set)
E-5635....*Wee Three Kings* (2-Pc Set)
E-5636....*Rejoice O Earth*
E-5637....*The Heavenly Light*
E-5638....*Cow*
E-5639....*Isn't He Wonderful* (boy)
E-5640....*Isn't He Wonderful* (girl)

E-5644 ....*Nativity Walls* (2-Pc Set)
15490 .....*Honk If You Love Jesus*
102962 ...*It's The Birthday Of A King*
105635 ...*Have I Got News For You*
111333 ....*Come Let Us Adore Him* (4-Pc Set)
115274....*Some Bunny's Sleeping*
142751 ...*Making A Trail To Bethlehem*
183954 ...*Shepherd With Lambs*
183962 ...*Shepherd With Lambs*
272582 ...*Palm Trees, Hay Bail and Baby Food*
272787 ...*Boy with Halo Wearing Star*
283428 ...*Lighted Inn*
292753 ...*Wishing Well*
520357 ...*Jesus The Savior Is Born*
523097 ...*Jesus Is The Sweetest Name I Know*
524875 ...*Happy Birthday Dear Jesus*
526959 ...*We Have Come From Afar*
527750 ...*Wishing You A Comfy Christmas*
528072 ...*Nativity Cart*
529966 ...*Ring Out The Good News*

MINIATURE NATIVITY AND ADDITIONS

E-2395 ...*Come Let Us Adore Him*
..............*11-Pc Set*
E-2387 ...*Three Houses and Palm Tree*
..............*4-Pc Set*
E-5384 ...*I'll Play My Drum For Him*
E-5385 ...*Oh Worship The Lord* (boy)
E-5386 ...*Oh Worship The Lord* (girl)
102261 ..*Shepherd Of Love*
102296 ..*Turtle, Rabbit & Lamb*
108243 ..*They Followed The Star*
184004 .....*Making A Trail To Bethlehem*
213616 ..*Shepherd with Sheep*

216624 ..*Wee Three Kings*
279323 ..*Camel, Cow and Donkey*
283436 ..*Wall*
283444 ..*Girl Angel Sitting*
291293 ..*Cats with Kitten*
520268 ..*Rejoice O Earth*
522988 ..*Isn't He Precious*
522996 ..*Some Bunny's Sleeping*
525278 ..*Tubby's First Christmas*
525286 ..*It's A Perfect Boy*
528137 ..*Have I Got News For You*
530492 ..*Happy Birthday Jesus*
530913 ..*We Have Come From Afar*

BELLS

E-5620
Shepherd/Lamb
See page 31

E-7179
Bride/Groom
See page 39

E-7175
Boy Graduate
See page 39

E-7176
Girl Graduate
See page 39

E-7181
Mother Sew Dear
See page 39

E-5623
Shepherd
See page 32

E-7183
Grandma
See page 40

E-5208
Boy w/Teddy
See page 26

E-5209
Girl w/Bunny
See page 26

E-5211
Boy/Report Card
See page 27

E-5210
Praying Girl
See page 26

DATED ANNUAL BELLS

E-5622
1981Annual
See page 32

E-2358
1982 Annual
See page 11

E-0522
1983 Annual
See page 3

E-5393
1984 Annual
See page 30

E-15873
1984 Annual
See page 54

102318
1986 Annual
See page 63

109835
1987 Annual
See page 73

115304
1988 Annual
See page 78

522821
1989 Annual
See page 116

523828
1990 Annual
See page 122

524182
1982 Annual
See page 124

527726
1983 Annual
See page 135

530174
1984 Annual
See page139

604216
Girl/Christmas
Tree Skirt
See page 147

DATED ANNUAL ORNAMENTS

E-5629
1981 Annual
See page 32

E-2359
1982 Annual
See page 11

E-0513
1983 Annual
See page 2

E-5387
1984 Annual
See page 29

15768
1985 Annual
See page 53

102326
1986 Annual
See page 63

109770
1987 Annual
See page 72

115320
1988 Annual
See page 78

522848
1989 Annual
See page 116

523852
1990 Annual
See page 122

524174
1991 Annual
See page 124

527696
1992 Annual
See page 134

530212
1993 Annual
See page 140

530395
1994 Annual
See page 140

142662
1995 Annual
See page 83

183369
1996 Annual
See page 89

272671
1997 Annual
See page 97

RETIRED PIECES

RETIRED 1993

E-1375A	LOVE LIFTED ME	FIGURINE	5/1993
E-3110B	LOVING IS SHARING	FIGURINE	5/1993
105945	SHOWERS OF BLESSINGS	FIGURINE	5/1993
521396	FAITH IS A VICTORY	FIGURINE	5/1993
E-2374	BUNDLES OF JOY	FIGURINE	10/1993
100188	I'M A POSSIBILITY	FIGURINE	10/1993
112402	I'M SENDING YOU A WHITE CHRISTMAS	MUSICAL	10/1993
522112	DON'T LET THE HOLIDAYS GET YOU DOWN	FIGURINE	10/1993

RETIRED 1994

E-3116	THEE I LOVE	FIGURINE	6/1994
E-9254	PRAISE THE LORD ANYHOW	FIGURINE	6/1994
521590	DON'T LET THE HOLIDAYS GET YOU DOWN	ORNAMENT	6/1994
522260	TO BE WITH YOU IS UPLIFTING	FIGURINE	6/1994
523747	BLESSINGS FROM ABOVE	FIGURINE	6/1994
524271	FRIENDSHIP GROWS WHEN YOU PLANT A SEED	FIGURINE	6/1994
528684	EVERGREEN TREE	FIGURINE	11/1994
529486	AUNT RUTH AND AUNT DOROTHY	FIGURINE	11/1994
529494	PHILIP	FIGURINE	11/1994
529508	NATIVITY	FIGURINE	11/1994
529516	GRANDFATHER	FIGURINE	11/1994
529621	LIGHTED CHAPEL	FIGURINE	11/1994

RETIRED 1995

100226	THE LORD GIVETH AND THE LORD TAKETH AWAY	FIGURINE	6/1995
106798	PUPPY LOVE IS FROM ABOVE	FIGURINE	6/1995
520632	A FRIEND IS SOMEONE WHO CARES	FIGURINE	6/1995
523623	I'M SO GLAD THAT GOD BLESSED ME WITH A FRIEND LIKE YOU	FIGURINE	6/1995
109762	WE GATHER TOGETHER TO ASK THE LORD'S BLESSING	FIGURINE	11/1995
521299	HUG ONE ANOTHER	FIGURINE	11/1995
522937	FRIENDS NEVER DRIFT APART	ORNAMENT	11/1995
527599	BRINGING YOU A MERRY CHRISTMAS	FIGURINE	11/1995

RETIRED 1996

E-1381R	JESUS IS THE ANSWER	FIGURINE	10/1996
521418	I'LL NEVER STOP LOVING YOU	FIGURINE	10/1996
521779	SWEEP ALL YOUR WORRIES AWAY	FIGURINE	10/1996
523631	I WILL ALWAYS BE THINKING OF YOU	FIGURINE	10/1996
524085	MY WARMEST THOUGHTS ARE YOU	FIGURINE	10/1996
524441	SEALED WITH A KISS	FIGURINE	10/1996
524476	GOD CARED ENOUGH TO SEND HIS BEST	FIGURINE	10/1996
524921	ANGELS WE HAVE HEARD ON HIGH	FIGURINE	10/1996
525898	RING THOSE CHRISTMAS BELLS	FIGURINE	10/1996
527270	LET'S BE FRIENDS	FIGURINE	10/1996
531073	MONEY'S NOT THE ONLY GREEN THING WORTH SAVING	FIGURINE	10/1996
532010	SENDING YOU OCEANS OF LOVE	FIGURINE	10/1996

RETIRED 1997

12262	I GET A BANG OUT OF YOU	FIGURINE	2/1997
104035	CHEERS TO THE LEADER	FIGURINE	2/1997
106844	SEW IN LOVE	FIGURINE	2/1997
112356	YOU HAVE TOUCHED SO MANY HEARTS	ORNAMENT	2/1997
521450	LORD, HELP ME STICK TO MY JOB	FIGURINE	2/1997
522058	NOW I LAY ME DOWN TO SLEEP	FIGURINE	2/1997
522317	MERRY CHRISTMAS DEER	FIGURINE	2/1997
524131	GOOD FRIENDS ARE FOR ALWAYS	ORNAMENT	2/1997
524352	WHAT THE WORLD NEEDS NOW	FIGURINE	2/1997
524468	A SPECIAL CHIME FOR JESUS	FIGURINE	2/1997
526150	FRIENDS TO THE VERY END	FIGURINE	2/1997
527378	YOU ARE MY FAVORITE STAR	FIGURINE	2/1997
529966	RING OUT THE GOOD NEWS	FIGURINE	2/1997

CHAPEL ONLY

RETIRED 1995:

532088	A KING IS BORN	ORNAMENT	11/1995
604151	A KING IS BORN	FIGURINE	11/1995

SUSPENDED 1995:

523011	THERE'S A CHRISTIAN WELCOME HERE (CHAPEL)	FIGURINE	11/1995

HAPPY 15TH ANNIVERSARY PRECIOUS COLLECTIBLES®

SUSPENDED PIECES

SUSPENDED 1984

ITEM #	NAME	STYLE
E-1375B	PRAYER CHANGES THINGS	FIGURINE
E-1377A	HE LEADETH ME	FIGURINE
E-1377B	HE CARETH FOR YOU	FIGURINE
E-1379A	LOVE IS KIND	FIGURINE
E-1379B	GOD UNDERSTANDS	FIGURINE
E-1381	JESUS IS THE ANSWER	FIGURINE
E-2010	WE HAVE SEEN HIS STAR	FIGURINE
E-2012	JESUS IS BORN	FIGURINE
E-2013	UNTO US A CHILD IS BORN	FIGURINE
E-2345	MAY YOUR CHRISTMAS BE COZY	FIGURINE
E-2350	DROPPING IN FOR CHRISTMAS	FIGURINE
E-2352	O COME ALL YE FAITHFUL	MUSICAL
E-2355	I'LL PLAY MY DRUM FOR HIM	MUSICAL
E-2365	THE FIRST NOEL	FIGURINE
E-2366	THE FIRST NOEL	FIGURINE
E-2367	THE FIRST NOEL	ORNAMENT
E-2381	MOUSE WITH CHEESE	ORNAMENT
E-2386	CAMEL, DONKEY, COW	ORNAMENT
E-2801	JESUS IS BORN	FIGURINE
E-2802	CHRISTMAS IS A TIME TO SHARE	FIGURINE
E-2803	CROWN HIM LORD OF ALL	FIGURINE
E-2804	PEACE ON EARTH	FIGURINE
E-2807	CROWN HIM LORD OF ALL	MUSICAL
E-2808	UNTO US A CHILD IS BORN	MUSICAL
E-3105	HE WATCHES OVER US ALL	FIGURINE
E-3108	THE HAND THAT ROCKS THE FUTURE	FIGURINE
E-3119	IT'S WHAT'S INSIDE THAT COUNTS	FIGURINE
E-4723	PEACE AMID THE STORM	FIGURINE
E-4725	PEACE ON EARTH	FIGURINE
E-4726	PEACE ON EARTH	MUSICAL
E-5200	BEAR YE ONE ANOTHER'S BURDENS	FIGURINE
E-5201	LOVE LIFTED ME	FIGURINE
E-5202	THANK YOU FOR COMING TO MY ADE	FIGURINE
E-5203	LET NOT THE SUN GO DOWN UPON YOUR WRATH	FIGURINE
E-5207	MY GUARDIAN ANGEL	NIGHT LIGHT
E-5210	PRAYER CHANGES THINGS	BELL
E-5214	PRAYER CHANGES THINGS	FIGURINE
E-5623	JESUS IS BORN	BELL
E-5633	COME LET US ADORE HIM	ORNAMENT
E-5634	WEE THREE KINGS	ORNAMENT
E-7155	THANKING HIM FOR YOU	FIGURINE
E-7161	HIS SHEEP AM I	FIGURINE
E-7162	LOVE IS SHARING	FIGURINE
E-7163	GOD IS WATCHING OVER YOU	FIGURINE
E-7164	BLESS THIS HOUSE	FIGURINE

E-7168	MY GUARDIAN ANGEL	FRAME
E-7169	MY GUARDIAN ANGEL	FRAME
E-9283	FOREVER FRIENDS	CONTAINER

SUSPENDED 1985

ITEM #	NAME	STYLE
E-0526	HE UPHOLDETH THOSE WHO CALL	FIGURINE
E-0537	JESUS IS THE LIGHT THAT SHINES	ORNAMENT
E-2344	JOY TO THE WORLD	CANDLE CLIMBERS
E-2349	TELL ME THE STORY OF JESUS	FIGURINE
E-2356	I'LL PLAY MY DRUM FOR HIM	FIGURINE
E-2372	BABY'S FIRST CHRISTMAS	ORNAMENT
E-2377	OUR FIRST CHRISTMAS TOGETHER	FIGURINE
E-2378	OUR FIRST CHRISTMAS TOGETHER	PLATE
E-2809	JESUS IS BORN	MUSICAL
E-4722	LOVE CANNOT BREAK A TRUE FRIENDSHIP	FIGURINE
E-5205	MY GUARDIAN ANGEL	MUSICAL
E-5208	JESUS LOVES ME	BELL
E-5209	JESUS LOVES ME	BELL
E-5619	COME LET US ADORE HIM	FIGURINE
E-5620	WE HAVE SEEN HIS STAR	BELL
E-5627	BUT LOVE GOES ON FOREVER	ORNAMENT
E-5628	BUT LOVE GOES ON FOREVER	ORNAMENT
E-5630	UNTO US A CHILD IS BORN	ORNAMENT
E-5631	BABY'S FIRST CHRISTMAS	ORNAMENT
E-5632	BABY'S FIRST CHRISTMAS	ORNAMENT
E-5639	ISN'T HE WONDERFUL?	FIGURINE
E-5640	ISN'T HE WONDERFUL?	FIGURINE
E-5641	THEY FOLLOWED THE STAR	FIGURINE
E-5642	SILENT KNIGHT	MUSICAL
E-6214B	MIKEY	DOLL
E-6214G	DEBBIE	DOLL
E-7156	I BELIEVE IN MIRACLES	FIGURINE
E-7159	LORD GIVE ME PATIENCE	FIGURINE
E-7167	THE LORD BLESS YOU AND KEEP YOU	CONTAINER
E-7170	JESUS LOVES ME	FRAME
E-7171	JESUS LOVES ME	FRAME
E-7172	REJOICING WITH YOU	PLATE
E-7175	THE LORD BLESS YOU AND KEEP YOU	BELL
E-7176	THE LORD BLESS YOU AND KEEP YOU	BELL
E-9251	LOVE IS PATIENT	FIGURINE
E-9253	THE END IS IN SIGHT	FIGURINE
E-9263	HOW CAN TWO WALK TOGETHER EXCEPT THEY AGREE	FIGURINE
E-9275	JESUS LOVES ME	PLATE
E-9276	JESUS LOVES ME	PLATE
E-9280	JESUS LOVES ME	CONTAINER
E-9281	JESUS LOVES ME	CONTAINER
E-9285	IF GOD BE FOR US, WHO CAN BE AGAINST US	FIGURINE

SUSPENDED 1986

ITEM #	NAME	STYLE
E-0501	SHARING OUR SEASON TOGETHER	FIGURINE
E-0502	JESUS IS THE LIGHT THAT SHINES	FIGURINE
E-0503	BLESSINGS FROM MY HOUSE TO YOURS	FIGURINE
E-0508	PREPARE YE THE WAY OF THE LORD	FIGURINE
E-0520	WEE THREE KINGS	MUSICAL
E-0531	O COME ALL YE FAITHFUL	ORNAMENT
E-0535	LOVE IS PATIENT	ORNAMENT
E-0536	LOVE IS PATIENT	ORNAMENT
E-2361	CHRISTMAS JOY FROM HEAD TO TOE	FIGURINE
E-2826	MAY YOUR BIRTHDAY BE A BLESSING	FIGURINE
E-2827	I GET A KICK OUT OF YOU	FIGURINE
E-3120	TO THEE WITH LOVE	FIGURINE
E-5376	MAY YOUR CHRISTMAS BE BLESSED	FIGURINE
E-5380	A MONARCH IS BORN	FIGURINE
E-5382	FOR GOD SO LOVED THE WORLD	FIGURINE
E-5385	O WORSHIP THE LORD	FIGURINE
E-5386	O WORSHIP THE LORD	FIGURINE
E-5389	PEACE ON EARTH	ORNAMENT
E-5394	WISHING YOU A MERRY CHRISTMAS	MUSICAL
E-6901	PRECIOUS MOMENTS LAST FOREVER	PLAQUE
E-7153	GOD IS LOVE, DEAR VALENTINE	FIGURINE
E-7154	GOD IS LOVE, DEAR VALENTINE	FIGURINE
E-7160	THE PERFECT GRANDPA	FIGURINE
E-7186	LET THE WHOLE WORLD KNOW	MUSICAL
E-7241	MOTHER SEW DEAR	FRAME
E-9261	SEEK YE THE LORD	FIGURINE
E-9262	SEEK YE THE LORD	FIGURINE
E-9287	PEACE ON EARTH	FIGURINE
E-9288	SENDING YOU A RAINBOW	FIGURINE
12203	GET INTO THE HABIT OF PRAYER	FIGURINE
12343	JESUS IS COMING SOON	FIGURINE
12424	AARON	DOLL
12432	BETHANY	DOLL
12475	P.D	DOLL
12483	TRISH	DOLL

Some folks we click with. Some folks we cross with. Love is manifested when we love those we cross with.

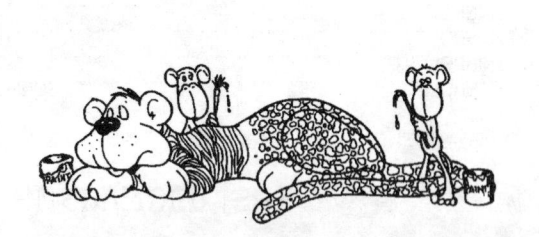

SUSPENDED 1987

ITEM #	NAME	STYLE
E-0507	GOD SENT HIS SON	FIGURINE
E-0509	BRINGING GOD'S BLESSING TO YOU	FIGURINE
E-0521	BLESSED ARE THE PURE IN HEART	FRAME
E-2823	TO GOD BE THE GLORY	FIGURINE
E-4720	THE LORD BLESS YOU AND KEEP YOU	FIGURINE
E-5216	THE LORD BLESS YOU AND KEEP YOU	PLATE
E-5381	HIS NAME IS JESUS	FIGURINE
E-6613	GOD SENDS THE GIFT OF HIS LOVE	FIGURINE
E-7165	LET THE WHOLE WORLD KNOW	FIGURINE
E-7177	THE LORD BLESS YOU AND KEEP YOU	FRAME
E-7178	THE LORD BLESS YOU AND KEEP YOU	FRAME
E-9260	GOD'S PROMISES ARE SURE	FIGURINE
E-9289	TRUST IN THE LORD	FIGURINE
12017	LOVING YOU	FRAME
12025	LOVING YOU	FRAME
12033	GOD'S PRECIOUS GIFT	FRAME
12211	BABY'S FIRST HAIRCUT	FIGURINE
12297	IT IS BETTER TO GIVE THAN TO RECEIVE	FIGURINE
12408	WE SAW A STAR	MUSICAL

SUSPENDED 1988

ITEM #	NAME	STYLE
E-0515	TO A SPECIAL DAD	ORNAMENT
E-0533	TELL ME THE STORY OF JESUS	ORNAMENT
E-0539	KATIE LYNNE	DOLL
E-2343	JOY TO THE WORLD	ORNAMENT
E-2348	MAY YOUR CHRISTMAS BE WARM	FIGURINE
E-2362	BABY'S FIRST CHRISTMAS	ORNAMENT
E-2840	BABY'S FIRST STEP	FIGURINE
E-5206	MY GUARDIAN ANGEL	MUSICAL
E-6118	BUT LOVE GOES ON FOREVER	CANDLE CLIMBERS
E-7181	MOTHER SEW DEAR	BELL
E-7183	THE PURR-FECT GRANDMA	BELL
E-7242	THE PURR-FECT GRANDMA	FRAME
E-9266	OUR LOVE IS HEAVEN SCENT	CONTAINER
	I'M FALLING FOR SOME BUNNY AND IT HAPPENS TO BE YOU	CONTAINER
12335	YOU CAN FLY	FIGURINE
12351	HALO, AND MERRY CHRISTMAS	FIGURINE
100021	TO MY FAVORITE PAW	FIGURINE
100668	THIMBLES -- CLOWNS	THIMBLES
102431	SERVE WITH A SMILE	ORNAMENT
102458	SERVE WITH A SMILE	ORNAMENT
102490	SHARING OUR CHRISTMAS TOGETHER	FIGURINE

SUSPENDED 1989

ITEM #	NAME	STYLE
E-2346	LET HEAVEN AND NATURE SING	MUSICAL
E-2364	GOAT	FIGURINE
E-2851	KRISTY DOLL	DOLL
E-5213	GOD IS LOVE	FIGURINE
E-5378	JOY TO THE WORLD	FIGURINE
E-5390	MAY GOD BLESS YOU WITH A PERFECT HOLIDAY SEASON	ORNAMENT
E-5391	LOVE IS KIND	ORNAMENT
E-9252	FORGIVING IS FORGETTING	FIGURINE
12149	PART OF ME WANTS TO BE GOOD	FIGURINE
12165	LORD KEEP MY LIFE IN TUNE	MUSICAL
15822	MAY YOUR CHRISTMAS BE HAPPY	ORNAMENT
15830	HAPPINESS IS THE LORD	ORNAMENT
16012	BABY'S FIRST TRIP	FIGURINE
16020	GOD BLESS YOU WITH RAINBOWS	NIGHT LIGHT
100544	BROTHERLY LOVE	FIGURINE
100625	GOD IS LOVE, DEAR VALENTINE	THIMBLE
102415	IT'S A PERFECT BOY	ORNAMENT
102962	IT'S THE BIRTHDAY OF A KING	FIGURINE

SUSPENDED 1990

ITEM #	NAME	STYLE
E-0512	IT'S A PERFECT BOY	FIGURINE
E-0517	THE PERFECT GRANDPA	ORNAMENT
E-9259	WE'RE IN IT TOGETHER	FIGURINE
E-9282A	TO SOME BUNNY SPECIAL	FIGURINE
E-9282B	YOU'RE WORTH YOUR WEIGHT IN GOLD	FIGURINE
E-9282C	ESPECIALLY FOR EWE	FIGURINE
12157	THIS IS THE DAY THE LORD HAS MADE	FIGURINE
12173	THERE'S A SONG IN MY HEART	FIGURINE
12254	LOVE COVERS ALL	THIMBLE
12378	HAPPINESS IS THE LORD	FIGURINE
12386	LORD GIVE ME A SONG	FIGURINE
12394	HE IS MY SONG	FIGURINE
12580	LORD, KEEP MY LIFE IN TUNE	MUSICAL
100145	GOD BLESS THE DAY WE FOUND YOU	FIGURINE
100153	GOD BLESS THE DAY WE FOUND YOU	FIGURINE
100161	SERVING THE LORD	FIGURINE
100293	SERVING THE LORD	FIGURINE
104027	LOVE IS THE GLUE THAT MENDS	FIGURINE
104396	HAPPY DAYS ARE HERE AGAIN	FIGURINE
104825	SITTING PRETTY	FIGURINE
105813	TO TELL THE TOOTH YOU'RE SPECIAL	FIGURINE
106216	LORD HELP ME MAKE THE GRADE	FIGURINE
111120	I'M A POSSIBILITY	ORNAMENT

SUSPENDED 1991

ITEM #	NAME	STYLE
E-2385	OUR FIRST CHRISTMAS TOGETHER	ORNAMENT
E-2834	SHARING OUR JOY TOGETHER	FIGURINE
E-3104	BLESSED ARE THE PURE IN HEART	FIGURINE
E-5397	TIMMY	DOLL
E-9267A	TEDDY BEAR	FIGURINE
E-9267B	DOG WITH SLIPPER	FIGURINE
E-9267C	BUNNY WITH CARROT	FIGURINE
E-9267D	CAT	FIGURINE
E-9267E	LAMB	FIGURINE
E-9267F	PIG	FIGURINE
12009	LOVE COVERS ALL	FIGURINE
100056	SENDING MY LOVE	FIGURINE
100633	THE LORD BLESS YOU AND KEEP YOU	THIMBLE
102474	ROCKING HORSE	ORNAMENT
105635	HAVE I GOT NEWS FOR YOU	FIGURINE
105643	SOMETHING'S MISSING WHEN YOU'RE NOT AROUND	FIGURINE
106151	WE'RE PULLING FOR YOU	FIGURINE
109487	BELIEVE THE IMPOSSIBLE	FIGURINE
111333	O COME LET US ADORE HIM	FIGURINE
113972	GOD SENT YOU JUST IN TIME	ORNAMENT
113999	CHEERS TO THE LEADER	ORNAMENT
114006	MY LOVE WILL NEVER LET YOU GO	ORNAMENT
115290	OUR FIRST CHRISTMAS TOGETHER	FIGURINE
520802	MY DAYS ARE BLUE WITHOUT YOU	FIGURINE
520810	WE NEED A GOOD FRIEND THROUGH THE RUFF TIMES	FIGURINE
520853	I BELONG TO THE LORD	FIGURINE
521868	THE GREATEST OF THESE IS LOVE	FIGURINE

SUSPENDED 1992

ITEM #	NAME	STYLE
12041	GOD'S PRECIOUS GIFT	FRAME
15776	MAY YOU HAVE THE SWEETEST CHRISTMAS	FIGURINE
15784	THE STORY OF GOD'S LOVE	FIGURINE
15792	TELL ME A STORY	FIGURINE
15806	GOD GAVE HIS BEST	FIGURINE
15814	SILENT NIGHT	MUSICAL
102296	SHEEP, BUNNY, TURTLE (3 PC. SET)	FIGURINE
102369	WEDDING ARCH FOR BRIDAL PARTY	ARCH
112372	I'M SENDING YOU A WHITE CHRISTMAS	ORNAMENT
522856	HAVE A BEARY MERRY CHRISTMAS	FIGURINE
524883	FIREPLACE FOR FAMILY CHRISTMAS SCENE	FIGURINE
526568	BLESS THOSE WHO SERVE THEIR COUNTRY (NAVY)	FIGURINE
526576	BLESS THOSE WHO SERVE THEIR COUNTRY (ARMY)	FIGURINE
526584	BLESS THOSE WHO SERVE THEIR COUNTRY (AIR FORCE)	FIGURINE
527289	BLESS THOSE WHO SERVE THEIR COUNTRY (GIRL SOLDIER)	FIGURINE
527297	BLESS THOSE WHO SERVE THEIR COUNTRY (AFRICAN AMERICAN)	FIGURINE
527521	BLESS THOSE WHO SERVE THEIR COUNTRY (MARINE)	FIGURINE

SUSPENDED 1993

ITEM #	NAME	STYLE
E-0511	TUBBY'S FIRST CHRISTMAS	FIGURINE
E-2810	COME LET US ADORE HIM	MUSICAL
E-7166	THE LORD BLESS YOU AND KEEP YOU	FRAME
E-7179	THE LORD BLESS YOU AND KEEP YOU	BELL
E-7184	THE PURR-FECT GRANDMA	MUSICAL
15849	MAY YOUR CHRISTMAS BE DELIGHTFUL	ORNAMENT
15857	HONK IF YOU LOVE JESUS	ORNAMENT
100285	HEAVEN BLESS YOU	MUSICAL
102288	SHEPHERD OF LOVE	ORNAMENT
104418	FRIENDS TO THE END	FIGURINE
105953	BRIGHTEN SOMEONE'S DAY	FIGURINE
106836	HAPPY BIRTHDAY POPPY	FIGURINE
109746	PEACE ON EARTH	MUSICAL
113964	SMILE ALONG THE WAY	ORNAMENT
520357	JESUS THE SAVIOR IS BORN	FIGURINE
520691	LORD, KEEP MY LIFE IN BALANCE	MUSICAL
520756	JESUS IS THE ONLY WAY	FIGURINE
521043	TO MY FAVORITE FAN	FIGURINE
521205	HOPE YOU'RE UP AND ON THE TRAIL AGAIN	FIGURINE
521310	YIELD NOT TO TEMPTATION	FIGURINE
521434	TO A VERY SPECIAL MOM AND DAD	FIGURINE
521949	WISHING YOU A COZY SEASON	FIGURINE
521957	HIGH HOPES	FIGURINE
522031	THANK YOU LORD FOR EVERYTHING	FIGURINE
522252	HE IS THE STAR OF THE MORNING	FIGURINE
522988	ISN'T HE PRECIOUS	FIGURINE
522996	SOME BUNNY'S SLEEPING	FIGURINE
523097	JESUS IS THE SWEETEST NAME I KNOW	FIGURINE
524875	HAPPY BIRTHDAY DEAR JESUS	FIGURINE
527165	THE GOOD LORD ALWAYS DELIVERS	ORNAMENT

SUSPENDED 1994

ITEM #	NAME	STYLE
15482	MAY YOUR CHRISTMAS BE DELIGHTFUL	FIGURINE
109754	WISHING YOU A YUMMY CHRISTMAS	FIGURINE
429570	THE EYES OF THE LORD ARE UPON YOU	MUSICAL
429589	THE EYES OF THE LORD ARE UPON YOU	MUSICAL
520705	BABY'S FIRST PET	FIGURINE
521272	TAKE HEED WHEN YOU STAND	FIGURINE
521280	HAPPY TRIP	FIGURINE
521302	MAY ALL YOUR CHRISTMASES BE WHITE	ORNAMENT
521574	DASHING THROUGH THE SNOW	ORNAMENT
522104	IT'S NO YOLK WHEN I SAY I LOVE YOU	FIGURINE
522244	DO NOT OPEN TIL CHRISTMAS	FIGURINE
522953	I BELIEVE IN THE OLD RUGGED CROSS	ORNAMENT
523224	HAPPY TRAILS IS TRUSTING JESUS	ORNAMENT
523763	I CAN'T SPELL SUCCESS WITHOUT YOU	FIGURINE
524484	NOT A CREATURE WAS STIRRING	FIGURINE
526959	WE HAVE COME FROM AFAR	FIGURINE

SUSPENDED 1995

No pieces were Suspended from The Enesco Precious Moments Collection in 1995.

SUSPENDED 1996

ITEM #	NAME	STYLE
E-2821	YOU HAVE TOUCHED SO MANY HEARTS	FIGURINE
E-2852A	BOY STANDING	FIGURINE
E-2852B	GIRL STANDING	FIGURINE
E-2852C	BOY SITTING	FIGURINE
E-2852D	GIRL CLAPPING HANDS	FIGURINE
E-2852E	BOY CRAWLING	FIGURINE
E-2852F	GIRL LYING DOWN	FIGURINE
E-2855	GOD BLESSED OUR YEARS TOGETHER WITH SO MUCH LOVE AND HAPPINESS – 5TH ANNIVERSARY	FIGURINE
E-2856	GOD BLESSED OUR YEARS TOGETHER WITH SO MUCH LOVE AND HAPPINESS – 10TH ANNIVERSARY	FIGURINE
E-2859	GOD BLESSED OUR YEARS TOGETHER WITH SO MUCH LOVE AND HAPPINESS – 40TH ANNIVERSARY	FIGURINE
12238A	BOY BALANCING BALL	FIGURINE
12238B	GIRL WITH BALLOON	FIGURINE
12238C	BOY HANDING BALL	FIGURINE
12238D	GIRL WITH FLOWER POT	FIGURINE
111163	TIS THE SEASON	FIGURINE
112577	YOU HAVE TOUCHED SO MANY HEARTS	MUSICAL
520535	THE LORD TURNED MY LIFE AROUND	FIGURINE
520543	IN THE SPOTLIGHT OF HIS GRACE	FIGURINE
520551	LORD, TURN MY LIFE AROUND	FIGURINE
520659	WISHING YOU A HAPPY BEAR HUG	FIGURINE
520721	JUST A LINE TO WISH YOU A HAPPY DAY	FIGURINE
521485	THERE'S A LIGHT AT THE END OF THE TUNNEL	FIGURINE
521671	HOPE YOU'RE OVER THE HUMP	FIGURINE
521698	THUMB-BODY LOVES YOU	FIGURINE
521841	LOVE IS FROM ABOVE	FIGURINE
522082	MAY YOUR WORLD BE TRIMMED WITH JOY	FIGURINE
522201	BON VOYAGE	FIGURINE
522287	THINKING OF YOU IS WHAT I REALLY LIKE TO DO	FIGURINE
522910	MAKE A JOYFUL NOISE	ORNAMENT
527343	HAPPY BIRDIE	FIGURINE
527580	TIED UP FOR THE HOLIDAYS	FIGURINE
527661	YOU HAVE TOUCHED SO MANY HEARTS	FIGURINE
528099	MARKIE	FIGURINE
528196	CIRCUS TENT	NIGHT LIGHT
529168	JORDAN	FIGURINE
529176	DUSTY	FIGURINE
529184	KATIE	FIGURINE
529192	TIPPY	FIGURINE
529214	COLLIN	FIGURINE
163708	JENNIFER	FIGURINE

Alphabetical Listing by Description ©

ANNIVERSARY

ASTRONAUT

BABY

Item	Number	Type	Page
Boy by Pot Belly Stove	E-2348	Figurine	10
Boy by Sign Post with Bag	520756	Figurine	106
Boy Caroling	E-0531	Ornament	4
Boy Caroling/Lamp Post	E-2352	Musical	10
Boy Caroling/Lamp Post	E-2353	Musical	10
Boy Carrying Lamb	E-2010	Figurine	8
Boy Carrying Lamb	E-6120	Ornament	35
Boy Carving Tree	E-3116	Figurine	23
Boy Chimney Sweep	150096	Figurine	84
Boy Clown	100455	Doll	60
Boy Clown with Ball	15830	Ornament	54
Boy Clown with Cannon	529176	Figurine	148
Boy Conducting Meeting	E-0103	Figurine	157
Boy Conducting Meeting	E-0303	Figurine	157
Boy Crawling	E-2852E	Figurine	20
Boy Drawing Heart in Sand	129488	Figurine	80
Boy Drawing Valentine	PM873	Figurine	164
Boy Dressed as Scarecrow	183849	Figurine	89
Boy Eating Cake with Fingers	524069	Figurine	123
Boy Feeding Dog	531944	Figurine	145
Boy & Girl on Seesaw	E-1375A	Figurine	6
Boy Giving Flower to Girl	521728	Figurine	111
Boy Giving Girl Ring	104019	Figurine	67
Boy Giving Heart to Baby Jesus	150088	Figurine	84
Boy Giving Teddy to Poor Boy	E-0504	Figurine	1
Boy Giving Toy Lamb to Jesus	E-2802	Figurine	14
Boy Giving Toy Lamb to Jesus	E-2806	Musical	15
Boy Golfer	532096	Figurine	146
Boy Graduate	E-4720	Figurine	24
Boy Graduate	E-7175	Bell	39
Boy Graduate	E-7177	Frame	39
Boy Graduate	106194	Figurine	70
Boy Graduate with Scroll	E-9261	Figurine	42
Boy Handing Ball	12238C	Figurine	48
Boy Hanging Sign	529222	Figurine	148
Boy Helping Friend	E-5201	Figurine	25
Boy Helping Girl at Fountain	520675	Figurine	105
Boy Helping Lamb	E-1377B	Figurine	7
Boy Hitching a Ride with Angel	525979	Figurine	129
Boy Holding a Pearl	521000	Figurine	107
Boy Holding Blue Bird	E-7156R	Figurine	36
Boy Holding Bottle	15903	Ornament	54
Boy Holding Bottle w/ Message	532010	Figurine	145
Boy Holding Cat/Dog	E-3107	Figurine	22
Boy Holding Chick	E-9257	Plate	42
Boy Holding Cross and Lily	532002	Figurine	145
Boy Holding Empty Frame	E-2823	Figurine	16
Boy Holding Heart	E-7153	Figurine	35
Boy Holding Heart	12017	Frame	46
Boy Holding Teddy	E-9278	Mini Figurine	44
Boy Holding Yellow Chick	E-7156	Figurine	36
Boy Ice Skating	E-2350	Figurine	10
Boy Ice Skating	E-2369	Ornament	12
Boy in Airplane	12416	Ornament	50
Boy in Car	PM862	Figurine	164
Boy in Car	PM863	Mugs	164
Boy in Car with Dog and Suitcase	522872	Figurine	116
Boy in Dad's Duds	E-0515	Ornament	2
Boy in Dad's Duds	E-5212	Figurine	27
Boy in Dad's Shoes	532061	Figurine	146
Boy in Nightcap/Candle	E-0502	Figurine	1
Boy in Nightcap/Candle	E-0537	Ornament	5
Boy in Pajamas with Teddy	E-2345	Figurine	9

Item	Number	Type	Page
Boy in Santa Cap/Dog	E-2805	Figurine	15
Boy in Santa Suit	527629	Figurine	134
Boy in Santa Suit	528226	Ornament	136
Boy Jogger	E-3112	Figurine	22
Boy Kneeling at Church Window	102229	Figurine	62
Boy Kneeling at Manger/Crown	E-2803	Figurine	15
Boy Kneeling by Plaque	530700	Figurine	141
Boy Kneeling Manger/Crown	E-2807	Musical	15
Boy Kneeling with Engagement Ring	520845	Figurine	107
Boy Leading Lamb	E-1377A	Figurine	7
Boy Lion Tamer and Kitty Lion	529168	Figurine	148
Boy Looking in Package	522244	Musical	114
Boy Lying on Stomach with Lamb	PM852	Figurine	163
Boy Making Snow Angel	183776	Figurine	89
Boy Marching with Drum	521981	Figurine	113
Boy on Bench/Lollipop	E-3110B	Figurine	22
Boy on Cloud with Bow and Arrow	100056	Figurine	57
Boy on Globe	E-2804	Figurine	15
Boy on Life Preserver	150061	Figurine	84
Boy on Rocking Horse	521272	Figurine	108
Boy on Skis	524905	Figurine	127
Boy on Sled with Turtle	527599	Figurine	134
Boy on Stick Horse	184004	Mini Nativity	90
Boy On Telephone	PM811	Figurine	162
Boy Painting Lamb	E-7161	Figurine	37
Boy Painting Picture with Animals	523038	Figurine	118
Boy Patching World	E-1381	Figurine	8
Boy Patching World	E-1381R	Figurine	8
Boy Pilot Angel	E-9289	Figurine	45
Boy Pointing to Ring on Finger	531006	Figurine	142
Boy Pulling Girl with Lily in Wagon	521892	Figurine	112
Boy Pushing Girl on Sled	E-0501	Figurine	1
Boy Pushing Girl on Sled	E-0519	Musical	3
Boy Selling Newspapers	E-4723	Figurine	25
Boy Singing	529494	Figurine	149
Boy Sitting	E-2852C	Figurine	20
Boy Sitting on Pot with Teddy Bear and Balloons	531022	Figurine	143
Boy Sitting on Star	142727	Ornament	83
Boy Sitting with Teddy	100021	Figurine	57
Boy Standing	E-2852A	Figurine	20
Boy Standing by Chapel	530484	Ornament	150
Boy Standing by Sugar Town Sign	529842	Figurine	150
Boy Standing by Tree Stump/Squirrel	521949	Figurine	113
Boy Tangled in Lights	15482	Figurine	52
Boy Tangled in Lights	15849	Ornament	54
Boy Tennis Player	100293	Figurine	60
Boy Train Conductor with Sign Population	150169	Figurine	152
Boy Trimming Globe	522082	Figurine	114
Boy Watching Seeds	PM872	Figurine	164
Boy Whispering into Girl's Ear	521841	Figurine	112
Boy with Alphabet Blocks	523763	Figurine	122
Boy with Apple and School Book	522015	Figurine	113
Boy with Barbells	109487	Figurine	71
Boy with Basketball	521221	Figurine	108
Boy with Basketball in Wheelchair	192368	Figurine	91
Boy with Basketball in Wheelchair	192384	Ornament	91
Boy with Bear in Sleigh	115282	Ornament	78
Boy with Bell	524468	Figurine	126
Boy with Black Eye	E-1373B	Figurine	5
Boy with Block	E-2372	Ornament	13
Boy with Bowling Ball and Pins	521191	Figurine	108
Boy with Box of Christmas Decorations	529435	Figurine	149
Boy with Box of Valentine Candy	526487	Figurine	130

CHAPEL ONLY FIGURINES

CHAPEL WINDOW

CHILD EVANGELISM FELLOWSHIP

CLOWNS

COLLECTOR'S SETS

DOCTOR

Boy Angel with Doctor's Bag	525286	Mini Nativity	128
Doctor	102415	Ornament	64
Doctor with Bag	529850	Figurine	151
Doctor's Office	529869	Night Light	151
Doctor's Office	530441	Ornament	153
Doctor's Office Collector's Set	529281	Figurine	150

DOG

Angel with Newspaper And Dog	520357	Figurine	103
Angry Boy and Dog on Stairs	E-5203	Figurine	26
Anniversary Couple with Puppy	106798	Figurine	70
Baby Boy with Dog/Stocking	109231	Figurine	71
Baby Girl with Puppies	272477	Figurine	96
Baby/Father, Puppy with Bottle	520705	Figurine	105
Boy and Dog Filling Sandbag	603864	Figurine	147
Boy and Dog Running Away	E-0525	Figurine	3
Boy and Dog with Pizza	521884	Figurine	112
Boy Feeding Dog	531944	Figurine	145
Boy in Car with Dog and Suitcase	522872	Figurine	116
Boy with Dog Ripping Britches	E-9253	Figurine	41
Boy/Gift Box with Dog, Ball and Bat	522120	Figurine	114
Boy/Girl Painting Dog House	E-7164	Figurine	37
Cat and Dog Holding a Paint Brush	BC912	Figurine	173
Christmas Puppy	520470	Ornament	103
Clown with Dog and Hoop	12467	Figurine	51
Couple with Dog and Puppies	114022	Figurine	78
Dalmatian Pup in Gift Box	BC-961	Figurine	174
Dog and Cat on Bench	529540	Figurine	153
Dog and Dog House	533165	Figurine	151
Dog Balancing Ball and Mouse	529192	Figurine	148
Dog in Skate	183903	Ornament	90
Dog on Belly	184063	Figurine	154
Dog on Heart-Shaped Container	E-9283	Container	45
Dog with Hair Covering Eyes	531057	Figurine	143
Dog with Sheep Skin	BC922	Figurine	173
Dog/Gift Box	520462	Ornament	103
Girl Holding Doll with Dog	105643	Figurine	69
Girl in Raincoat Holding Puppy	530158	Figurine	139
Girl in Raincoat with Puppy	529974	Ornament	138
Girl Puppy/Marbles	163759	Figurine	86
Girl Putting Puppy in Box	C-0109	Figurine	159
Girl Putting Puppy in Box	C-0009	Figurine	159
Girl with Box of Puppies	522961	Ornament	117
Girl with Box of Puppies	522961	Figurine	168
Girl with Dog and Sign	260924	Figurine	93
Girl with Dog Holding Alarm Clock	260932	Figurine	93
Girl with Puppies in Cart	E-1378	Figurine	7
Girl with Puppy and Marbles	163759	Figurine	86
Girl with Puppy Holding List	272663	Figurine	97
Girl with Puppy in Basket	110051	Figurine	74
Girl with Puppy in Blanket	527122	Figurine	131
Girls with Puppy	E-5394	Musical	30
Grandpa in Rocking Chair with Dog	E-7160	Figurine	37
Grandpa with Dog	520810	Figurine	107
Puppy in Stocking	520276	Ornament	102
Sharing Season Girl with Box of Puppies	522961	Ornament	117
Three Puppies in Basket with Sign	528064	Figurine	150
Two Dogs Hugging	527270	Figurine	132
Two Puppies	520764	Figurine	106
Two Puppies with Sled	272892	Ornament	98

DOLLS

Baby Boy	12475	Doll	51
Baby Girl	12483	Doll	51
Baby Girl in Sleigh with Doll	523208	Ornament	118
Blue Baby Boy Doll on Pillow	429570	Doll	101
Boy Angel	12424	Doll	50
Boy Clown	100455	Doll	60
Bride	E-7267G	Doll	40
Christmas Girl	417785	Doll	100
Connie	102253	Doll	63
Debbie	E-6214G	Doll	35
Four Seasons Autumn	408808	Doll	100
Four Seasons Spring	408786	Doll	100
Four Seasons Summer	408794	Doll	100
Four Seasons Winter	408816	Doll	100
Girl Angel	12432	Doll	51
Girl at Table with Dolls	E-2826	Figurine	16
Girl by Christmas Tree with Doll	E-2349	Figurine	10
Girl Clown	100463	Doll	60
Girl with Doll	136239	Figurine	81
Girl with Hearts	427527	Doll	101
Girl Holding Doll with Dog	105643	Figurine	69
Girl Pushing Doll/Sleigh	109983	Figurine	73
Girl Reading Book to Doll	E-0533	Ornament	4
Girl with Clown Doll	204889	Figurine	92
Groom	E-7267B	Doll	40
Jogger	E-5397	Doll	30
Katie Lynne	E-0539	Doll	5
Kristy	E-2851	Doll	20
Mikey	E-6214B	Doll	35
Mother with Needlepoint	E-2850	Doll	20
Nurse	12491	Doll	51
Pink Baby Girl Doll on Pillow	429589	Doll	101

Dome with Kids on Cloud Figurine	E-7350	Figurine	41
Donkey	E-5621	Figurine	31
Donkey and Boy	106151	Figurine	69

DRUMMER BOY

Drummer Boy	E-2358	Bell	11
Drummer Boy	E-2359	Ornament	11
Drummer Boy	E-2360	Nativity	11
Drummer Boy at Manger	E-2355	Figurine	10
Drummer Boy at Manger	E-2356	Figurine	11
Drummer Boy at Manger	E-2357	Plate	11
Miniature Drummer Boy	E-5384	Figurine	29

Dunce Boy	E-9268	Figurine	43

EASTER EGG

Girl at Birdbath	529095	Easter Egg	137
Girl Looking at Goose	528617	Easter Egg	136
Girl w/Butterfly	525960	Easter Egg	128
Girl with Cross	523534	Easter Egg	120

EASTER SEALS

See Easter Seals Listing on page 178.

ELEPHANT

Age 4 - Elephant	15970	Figurine	55
Clown on Elephant	102520	Musical	66
Elephant Showering Mouse	105945	Figurine	69

Mother & Daughter	163600	Figurine	86
Mother Goose	15857	Ornament	54
Mother in Chair Sewing	E-0514	Ornament	2
Mother Needlepointing	E-7181	Bell	39
Mother Needlepointing	E-7182	Musical	39
Mother Needlepointing	E-7241	Frame	40
Mother Rocking Baby	523941	Figurine	123
Mother with Cookies	15776	Figurine	53
Mother with Needlepoint	E-2850	Doll	20
Mother with Needlepoint	E-3106	Figurine	21
Mother with Needlepoint	E-5217	Plate	27
Mother with Needlepoint	13293	Thimble	52
Mother Wrapping Bread	E-2848	Plate	20

MOUSE

Cat with Mouse on Cheese (2 pc. set)	524484	Figurine	126
Clown with Mouse Wiping Tears	520632	Figurine	104
Dog Balancing Ball and Mouse	529192	Figurine	148
Elephant Showering Mouse	105945	Figurine	69
Girl Giving Cheese to Mouse	E-5377	Figurine	28
Mouse in Salad Bowl	261122	Figurine	94
Mouse in Sugar Bowl	BC871	Figurine	172
Mouse Sleeping in Matchbox	272590	Figurine	97
Mouse with Cheese	E-2381	Ornament	13
Skunk and Mouse	105953	Figurine	69
Turtle with Mouse on Back	BC941	Figurine	173

MAGNET

Mugs, Boy in Car	PM863	Mugs	164

MUSICALS

Angel with Animals Caroling	E-2346	Musical	9
Angel with Trumpet	E-5645	Musical	34
Angels Making Star (3-pc. set)	12408	Musical	50
Animated Angel Tree Topper	617334	Musical	147
Baby with Toys	100285	Musical	60
Ballerina on Base	520691	Musical	105
Blue Baby Boy Doll on Pillow, straight hair	429570	Musical Doll	101
Boy and Girl in Box	101702	Musical	62
Boy and Girl in School Play	E-2809	Musical	15
Boy and Girl Reading Book	E-2808	Musical	15
Boy Angel on Cloud	E-5205	Musical	26
Boy Caroling/Lamp Post	E-2352	Musical	10
Boy Caroling/Lamp Post	E-2353	Musical	10
Boy Giving Toy Lamb to Jesus	E-2806	Musical	15
Boy Kneeling Manger/Crown	E-2807	Musical	15
Boy Looking in Package	522244	Musical	114
Boy Pushing Girl on Sled	E-0519	Musical	3
Boy/Girl in Tub	E-7186	Musical	40
Boy/Piano (2 pc. set)	12165	Musical	48
Bride and Groom/Cake	E-7180	Musical	39
Choir Boys	E-4726	Musical	25
Clown on Elephant	102520	Musical	66
Girl Angel on Cloud	E-5206	Musical	26
Girl at School Desk	E-7185	Musical	40
Girl by Lamppost	521507	Musical	110
Girl by Wishing Well	526916	Musical	130
Girl Mailing Snowball	112402	Musical	76
Girl with Bible and Cross	523682	Musical	121
Girl with Piano (2 pc. set)	12580	Musical	51
Girl with String of Hearts	112577	Musical	77
Girl/Cradle	E-5204	Musical	26

Girls with Puppy	E-5394	Musical	30
Grandma in Rocker	E-7184	Musical	40
Jack in the Box	15504	Musical	52
Jack-In-Box Girl w/Hearts	422282	Musical	100
Jack-In-The-Box Christmas Girl	417777	Musical	100
Jack-In-The-Box Four Seasons Autumn	408751	Musical	99
Jack-In-The-Box Four Seasons Spring	408735	Musical	99
Jack-In-The-Box Four Seasons Summer	408743	Musical	99
Jack-In-The-Box Four Seasons Winter	408778	Musical	100
Kids Caroling	109746	Musical	72
Mother Needlepointing	E-7182	Musical	39
Nativity	E-2810	Musical	15
Pink Baby Girl Doll on Pillow, curly hair	429589	Musical Doll	101
Sleeping Knight with Angel	E-5642	Musical	34
Sugar Town Train 3-piece set	152595	Musical	153
Three Kings on Base	E-0520	Musical	3
Tree	15814	Musical	53

Mr. Webb Building a Bird House	PM921	Figurine	166

NATIONAL DAY OF PRAYER

Girl Holding Up a Torch	528862	Figurine	137
Girl Kneeling at Altar with Bible	524158	Figurine	124
Uncle Sam Kneeling	527564	Figurine	134

NATIVITY

See listing of regular and miniature Nativity and Additions on page 191.

NEEDLECRAFT

Girl with Lambs	PM853	Needlecraft	164
Race Car Driver	PM843	Needlecraft	163

NIGHT LIGHT

Angel Behind Rainbow	16020	Night Light	56
Boy/Girl Angels Cloud	E-5207	Night Light	26
Chapel	529621	Night Light	149
Circus Tent	528196	Night Light	147
Doctor's Office	529869	Night Light	151
House	529605	Night Light	150
Noah's Ark (3 pc. set)	530042	Night Light	138

NOAH'S ARK

3 pc. set Noah's Ark	530042	Night Light	138
Bunnies – Noah's Ark	530123	Figurine	139
Elephants – Noah's Ark	530131	Figurine	139
Giraffes – Noah's Ark	530115	Figurine	139
Llamas – Noah's Ark	531375	Figurine	144
Noah's Ark	530948	Figurine	142
Pigs – Noah's Ark	530085	Figurine	139
Sheep – Noah's Ark	530077	Figurine	139
Zebras – Noah's Ark	127809	Figurine	79

Nun Figurine	12203	Figurine	48

NURSE

Nurse	12491	Doll	51
Nurse	102407	Ornament	64
Nurse Holding Clipboard	529826	Figurine	151
Nurse with Alarm Clock	523739	Figurine	121
Nurse with Bear	E-7158	Figurine	36
Nurse with Flower	102482	Figurine	65

THANKSGIVING

THIMBLES

VALENTINE

WREATH

See entries on page

Alphabetical Listing by Inspiration

A

Autumn's Praise

B

Baby's First Christmas - Boy

Baby's First Christmas - Girl

M

Summer's Joy

Surrounded With Joy

T

Great – Now Do Behind my ears!

— R.STUBLER —

Collectibles Database™

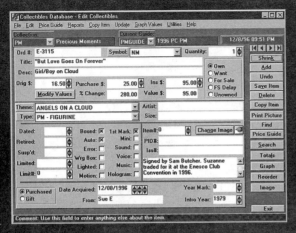

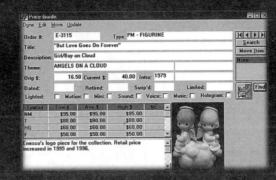

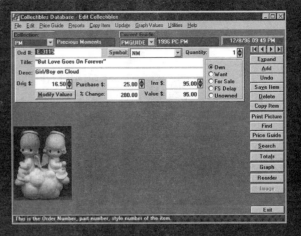

The Best Collecting Software for Collectors

Price Guides available for:
Precious Moments® *(includes color, licensed photos),*
Hallmark Ornaments (includes color photos), Dept. 56 (includes color licensed photos), Radko Ornaments, Swarovski, Cherished Teddies® *(includes color licensed photos), Boyds Collection, Walt Disney Classics, Forma Vitrum (includes color photos), Hallmark Merry Miniatures (includes color photos), Memories Of Yesterday, Shelia's Collectibles, Hallmark Kiddie Car Classics (includes color photos), Harbour Lights,*
Precious Moments® **Applause Dolls** *and Longaberger Baskets!*
Hallmark Tender Touches List available. Call or write for brochure.

Stay organized with Collectibles Database!

Which items do you have for sale? How many items do you have? How much are your collections worth? How much did you spend? How much is it insured for? Which items do you want?

$49.95
plus $5 per photographic collection on CD-Rom only.

$49.95 + $5 Shipping & Handling
(includes 3 price guides - your choice)
Additional guides $9.95 each.
Specify 3.5" floppy or CD.

Easier to install and use – Guaranteed!

Ad design: ©1997 Rosie Wells Enterprises, Inc.

☞ Create insurance reports, inventory lists, want lists. Unlimited reporting capabilities.

☞ Include your own images and long comments. Unlimited searching and sorting capabilities.

☞ Telephone technical support, printed manual and on-screen help.

☞ Integrated price guides, add item, update values.

☞ 30 day money back guarantee.
IBM compatible, 486 or better, 4 MB RAM or better (Mac with SoftWindows).

MSdataBase Solutions, Inc.

614 Warrenton Terrace NE, Leesburg, VA 20176

Phone: **1-800-407-4147**
Fax: 703/777-5440
http://www.collectorsoft.com

Gifts International

SPECIALIZING IN THE SECONDARY MARKET

For Past Years'
Precious Moments® Collectibles & Others

WE BUY TO RESELL!

Send your "For Sale" list with prices!

**22341 EAST WELLS RD.
CANTON, IL 61520**

SERVING THE COLLECTOR
SINCE 1984

- X Cherished Teddies®
- X Boyds Bears
- X Precious Moments® Collectibles
- X Hallmark Ornaments
- X Barbie™ Dolls
- X Beanie Babies™
- X Tender Touches
- X Bradford Collector Plates
- X Disney Classics
- X Swarovski & More!

MONDAY – THURSDAY 8 AM – 8 PM
FRIDAY 8 AM – 5 PM
SATURDAY 9 AM – 3 PM

IL residents add 6.25% Sales Tax

U.S. Funds Only

1-800-445-8745

WANTED	FOR SALE	FOR SALE	WANTED	WANTED	WANTED	FOR SALE
Baby's First Trip	God Loveth A Cheerful Giver	Love Makes The World Go 'Round	Daisy	Beth	Carrie	mallory with patsy & jb...

This Guide Belongs To:

Name _____

Address _____

Phone _____

If you find this lost guide...
please return to Desperate Collector above.

Notes

Notes

Notes

Notes

Notes